THE ENGLISH BAPTISTS

OF THE

NINETEENTH CENTURY

A History of the English Baptists
Volume 3
General Editor: Roger Hayden

THE ENGLISH BAPTISTS OF THE NINETEENTH CENTURY

J. H. Y. Briggs

The Baptist Historical Society

This is the third volume in a new series on the English Baptists originally planned under the editorship of the late Dr E. A. Payne, subsequently under Dr B. R. White, and now edited by Dr Roger Hayden.

Already published

THE ENGLISH BAPTISTS OF THE SEVENTEENTH CENTURY

by B. R. White

THE ENGLISH BAPTISTS OF THE EIGHTEENTH CENTURY

by Raymond Brown

In preparation

THE ENGLISH BAPTISTS OF THE TWENTIETH CENTURY

by W. M. S. West

Cover design by Jo Small

The Baptist Historical Society
Baptist House, 129 Broadway, Didcot, OX11 8RT

ISBN 0 903166 18 6 (paperback)
ISBN 0 903166 19 4 (casebound)

THE ENGLISH BAPTISTS OF THE NINETEENTH CENTURY

CONTENTS

ACKNOWLEDGEMENTS

Three people deserve my special thanks. My former research student, the Revd Geoffrey Breed, a mine of information and resource in Baptist biography and bibliography, has helped me with photocopies of documents and his expert knowledge of Baptist heritage. He has also checked my statistics as only he could do, and I am deeply grateful. The Revd Dr Roger Hayden, the energetic secretary of the Baptist Historical Society and General Editor of this series, has read my draft in proof, has helped to clarify my ideas and has saved me from a number of infelicities. The members of the Baptist Historical Society have been immensely patient in waiting for this much delayed volume. Dr Hayden has been a gracious prompter of the need to advance this text towards publication. I owe him, also, a debt of gratitude. Mrs Faith Bowers, my associate in editing the *Baptist Quarterly*, has not only wrestled with my horrendously untidy manuscript, redeeming it from its many imperfections, but has been generous with advice at every point in the slow development of this text, which without her encouragement might not have emerged. To her especially I am deeply grateful.

The map on page 266 is reproduced by permission of Gerald Duckworth & Co Ltd. The staff of the Angus Library, Regent's Park College, Oxford, the Dr Williams's Library, London, and the University of Keele Library have ever been most helpful and supportive in making available the richness of their collections. This kind of study obviously depends extensively upon the researches of many other scholars whose monographs and articles have been plundered for the benefit of this group biography of the people called Baptists. I have derived great benefit from such work which I hope is duly acknowledged in footnote references. A special debt is due to those postgraduates who have worked with me on aspects of Baptist history and to their successors who are still surprising me with the discoveries of their researches. I am grateful for the education they have given me.

My understanding of these subjects derives from the lives of parents and grandparents who were members of that remarkable Victorian Baptist church, Upton Chapel, Lambeth, where my first understanding of the convictions of Baptist Christians began. In later years these have been enriched both by my experience of Baptist congregations all around the world, from Sweden to Argentina, from Zimbabwe to Korea, as also by the deep faith and dedicated service of Christian brothers and sisters with whom I am happy to share in the life of the ecumenical movement, and within the committees of the World Council of Churches in particular. I like to think that William Carey and Robert Hall would have rejoiced to see their descendants sharing fully in that ecumenical fellowship and evangelical catholicity of which they dreamed, and for which they worked without stint.

JHYB

ABBREVIATIONS USED

BAR	ed. John Rippon, *Baptist Annual Register*, I 1790-93, II 1794-97, III 1798-1800, IV 1801-2.
BH	*Baptist Handbook*
BM	*Baptist Magazine*
BMS	Baptist Missionary Society
BQ	*Baptist Quarterly*
CMS	Church Missionary Society
GBM	*General Baptist Magazine*
GBMS	General Baptist Missionary Society
GBYB	*General Baptist Year Book*
HBB	W. T. Whitley, *A History of British Baptists*, 1923
LMS	London Missionary Society
NBM	*New Baptist Miscellany*
TBHS	*Transactions of the Baptist Historical Society*

1

INTRODUCTION

The two earlier volumes in this series were fortunate to work with an historiography already well-developed and signposted by the classic Baptist historians: Thomas Crosby (1740), Joseph Ivimey (1811-1830), and Adam Taylor of the General Baptists (1818). For the nineteenth century these sources are not available; instead one has the popular story told by J. C. Carlile, W. T. Whitley's account which for all its strengths is not as full as it might be, and A. C. Underwood's rather episodic account. Beyond these syntheses is the wealth of articles written over the last eighty years, appearing in the *Transactions of the Baptist Historical Society* and subsequently the *Baptist Quarterly*.

On the other hand, the historian of the nineteenth century is fortunate in that his account does not have to tell the whole story since the institutional perspective has been reviewed with great wisdom in E. A. Payne, *The Baptist Union: A Short History* (1963), and Brian Stanley, *History of the Baptist Missionary Society* (1992). The existence of these two volumes means that the perspective of the present work can be Baptist life throughout the century not unduly weighted by a London or headquarters perspective on changing patterns of denominational life.

The nineteenth century, it can be argued, is a century of denominational emergence, at least if the technical usage developed by H. R. Niebuhr is applied to the concept of denomination.[1] Baldly stated, Niebuhr's thesis is that in the post-industrial period both sects and churches accommodate themselves to new social realities and to the permanent existence of other church bodies. Thus whilst the Established Church came to accept the durability of dissent, and even by the end of the century the need to work with it, that same dissent shed much of the exclusive sectarianism of its past and was prepared to see its own life as one legitimate variety of Christian obedience

---

1 H. R. Niebuhr, *Social Sources of Denominationalism*, 1957 edition.

rather than the only allowable form. At the same time the concept of denomination suggests an increasing coherence amongst the diverse manifestations of each dissenting body with a willingness to develop and to own a wide variety of denominational agencies, from colleges to periodicals, to an emerging national bureaucracy, though for the Baptists there remained a sense in which the denomination was larger than all that. Narrowly expressed this means that the Baptist denomination cannot simply be equated with churches in membership with the Baptist Union but has to include other groupings and non-groupings as well. Even those churches who did identify with the Baptist Union were not all of one outlook: there were Calvinist Baptists in the tradition of the Particular Baptists and Arminian Baptists from the New Connexion with its origins in the Methodist Revival. Beyond this Baptists differed on the terms of communion, the conditions of church membership, the legitimacy of biblical criticism, their acceptance of the impact of secular culture, and the degree to which association with other Christians was desirable. Outside the Union were the various groupings of Strict Baptists, and new bodies like the Old Baptist Union,[2] not to mention the many Baptist churches that lived in splendid isolation without associating with anybody else. Moreover a number of Baptists were members of united churches which also maintained links with other denominations, especially the Congregational Union, whilst many Baptists were to be found in membership with the wider congregations of Evangelical Dissent - possibly balancing out, according to one calculation, the number of those not baptized as believers in membership of open-membership Baptist churches. When Silvester Horne, the minister of Whitfield's Tabernacle in Tottenham Court Road, set out to write a *Manual of Church Fellowship*, he asked his 'Baptist' deacons for a

2 Founded in 1880 but on the basis of Baptist confessions of 1611 and 1660, the Old Baptist Union is a small group of evangelical Arminian churches. See Inter-Church Process, *Reflections: How twenty-six churches see their life and mission*, 1986. An association comprising most of their churches affiliated to the Baptist Union of Great Britain in 1993.

Baptist view of baptism and was not surprised to get conflicting advice.[3] The outposts of denominational allegiance are not easily defined.

The approach of the present volume is to eschew a discussion framed around successive periods of innovation, stability, progress and decline, and instead to pursue ten analytical focuses which provide the chapter headings of what follows. Within these divisions a number of sub-themes are introduced and developed: for example, the way in which the Christological debates of the previous century, with the consequent loss of both congregations and ministry to Unitarianism, left a legacy of suspicion which was part of the landscape for a century following. Another theme is clearly the interplay between a cherished independency, sometimes pathologically exaggerated, and the constant need to associate with others in the interests of the Kingdom: thus the need to develop flexible regional and national instruments to assist the weak and to promote strategic advance.

The history of Baptists in the nineteenth century is very largely a reactive and responsive one: consciously to the Catholic Revival, which must be held partly responsible for the development of low views of church-manship, ministry and the sacraments; and unconsciously to the many secular pressures which also shaped the pattern of church life, with voluntaryism all too easily construed as *laissez-faire* politico-economics on its knees. There is throughout the period a legitimate debate - even a dialectical discourse - between the congregation as gathered church as systematically set out in Puritan theology and that same congregation as mission agency energized by the expansion of the Evangelical Revival, which clearly represents a major watershed in British Baptist history. Baptists particularly faced difficulties as Christians became more tolerant of one another, because their restrictive baptismal practice, that is their distinction in confining baptism to believers only, necessarily challenged any easy accommodation even to other recognizably evangelical groupings; the

3 Cited in E. A. Payne, *The Fellowship of Believers*, enlarged edition 1952, p.83.

consequences of that are to be seen in the debates about open communion and open membership, and the long-running dispute with the Bible Society on the legitimacy of translating βαπτιζω by words signifying immersion. Freedom was a much trumpeted concept amongst Baptists - freedom of conscience, freedom of confession, freedom of worship, and freedom to develop new patterns of Christian mission and ministry - but such freedoms, lest they became a synonym for footloose liberal licence, had to be set within a context of fidelity to the inherited tradition without being imprisoned by it.

An attempt has been made to garner some representative statistics so that both the progress and the scale of the denomination across the century may be recognized. Any history has to admit the bias of its sources which are clearly weighted towards the strong and the successful, the prosperous and the progressive. Accordingly, there is also recognition here of the part played by small and struggling congregations which were often backward-looking and reluctant to respond to the needs of a changing world. The built-in bias of church history is to stay within the compass of the sanctuary: some endeavour is made here to appreciate the layman's world, to follow the congregation out of church into their everyday experience as far as the sources allow, and to question whether by the end of the century Baptists, with their fellow free churchmen, were not more conformist than non-conformist, exemplars of Victorianism in its most conscientious aspect.

2

CONGREGATIONAL LIFE AND WORSHIP

The particularity of the Baptists has as much to do with their doctrine of the church as with their baptismal practice. Indeed, Horton Davies argues that 'if the Prayer Book is the nexus of Anglicanism', for Baptists it is the covenant relationship with God and each other that makes their churchmanship 'an anvil that will wear out the hammer blows of persecution and that requires them, as God's people, to stand for His rule in the life of the nation.'[1] Whilst other protestant churches follow the thought of the pre-reformation Catholic Church in seeing baptism as the sacrament by which a child is incorporated into the church 'as an ontologically given community', Baptists (and others who restrict baptism to believers) believe that the church is in fact created by the Spirit of God as, working in the lives of individuals, he brings them to faith and commitment.[2] Accordingly, this account of Baptist life starts with their churchmanship both in theory and practice.

CHURCH AND MISSION

A correspondent to a nonconformist periodical at the beginning of 1866 complained that a chapel with over a thousand seats was a denial of basic nonconformist principles.[3] Sir John Betjeman attacks the same point when he compares the chapels of the seventeenth century, domestic in scale, exhibiting the quality of a well-scoured farmhouse kitchen and meeting the needs of their theologically literate congregations, with the great preaching houses built in the late eighteenth and nineteenth centuries to enable the untutored masses of the industrial revolution to congregate under the sound of the gospel.[4]

---

1 Horton Davies, *Worship and Theology in England*, III, 1961, p.128.

2 See W. M. S. West, 'Towards a Consensus on Baptism', *Baptist Quarterly* [hereafter *BQ*] 28, 1980, p.227.

3 *The Patriot*, 11 January 1866.

4 John Betjeman, *First and Last Loves*, 1952, pp.97-105.

The two types of chapel bear witness to an essential tension in Baptist understanding of the nature of the church, a tension ante-dating the Evangelical Revival, but much heightened by it. It is the tension between the church, on the one hand, seen as the constitutional body of the saints in covenant both with God and with one another, and, on the other, the church mandated as some great missionary society, set energetically to the all important task of extending the kingdom. It seemed as if the old view of the locally gathered church, so identified with the manifestation of Christ's body that its acts became his acts, was threatened by the great upheaval in late eighteenth-century religious thought and practice. God's blessing continued to be requested for all that the saints sought to do, but their corporate identity was less certain, as the theological underpinning of church activity became less well focused, less clearly identified.

R. W. Dale took the Evangelical Revival to be largely responsible for the change, for, whilst it

> insisted on the union of the individual saint with Christ . . . the union of the Church - an organized society of saints - with Christ was not familiar to it. It cared little for the Church; its whole solicitude was for the rescue of the individual sinner from perdition and the growth in holiness of the individual Christian. It failed to recognize the great place of the Church both in the rescue of men from irreligion and in the discipline of the Christian perfection.[5]

The impact of new thought and practice on Puritan churchmanship in Baptist circles may not have been quite as theologically careless as Dale suggests. In 1797 John Fawcett, very much a child of the Revival, persuasively restated the case for a gathered church as over against parochial inclusiveness, arguing that the primitive apostolic church grew up in a pluralistic society where some were Jews, some infidels, and only a few Christian: accordingly, 'gospel churches consist of such as make an open profession of their faith in Christ and

---

5 R. W. Dale, *History of English Congregationalism*, 1907, p.590.

of their subjection to the Gospel'.[6] Such a church was a spiritual creation created by the work of grace in the lives of its members, 'the subjects of that divine change which is so often insisted on in the Sacred Scriptures as essential to vital Christianity'.[7]

BAPTIST ECCLESIOLOGY

Deftly John Fawcett defines the church in a way which both reflects the divine intention in establishing it, but also incorporates evangelical experience as determining its limits. Each church then was bound together under Christ by a covenant, either written or implicit: a written covenant, he affirmed, was 'by no means unwarrantable'.[8] Fawcett's articulation of the theology and practice of the church cannot be described as either careless or casual, even if it embraces some peculiar if perennial emphases, which inhibited the growth of positive churchmanship. Thus on baptism he writes, 'Baptism is not properly a church ordinance, since it ought to be observed before a person be admitted into this relation. It is nevertheless the ordinance of Jesus Christ.'[9] In so writing, he spells out an individualistic understanding of baptism that has had a perverse longevity.

The language used of the local church is societal: the local church as 'a free and voluntary society' derives from its head full power for its own government. On this independence no other church nor influential minister dare trespass: 'no synodical assembly or association of ministers or elders has any power of this kind.'[10]

Meanwhile Andrew Fuller warned against any slavish attempt to reconstruct the apostolic norm of churchmanship, arguing that the Scriptures afforded no such model but only general moral principles. Thus,

---

6 John Fawcett, *The Constitution and Order of a Gospel Church considered by John Fawcett*, 1797, p.6.

7 *ibid.*, p.8.

8 *ibid.*, p.12.

9 *ibid.*, p.24.

10 *ibid.*, p.26.

> We learn, from the Acts and the Epistles, that the first churches were congregations of faithful men, voluntarily united together for the stated ministration of the word, the administration of Christian ordinances, and the mutually assisting of each other in promoting the cause of Christ: that they were governed by bishops and deacons of their own choosing; that a bishop was an overseer, not of other ministers, but of the flock of God; that the government and discipline of each church was within itself; that the gifts of the different members were so employed as to conduce to the welfare of the body; and that in cases of disorder every proper means was used to vindicate the honour of Christ and reclaim the party.[11]

Christian believers were not, consequently, to attempt to copy even the Biblical past but rather to use their God-given wisdom to devise procedures appropriate to their own situation. It was not, therefore, a question of order for order's sake but of order appropriate to present 'utility'. In such a fashion Fuller creates space in which both to be faithful to Biblical authority and yet to respond to the new cultural context of the nineteenth century with its new esteem of functional purpose.

Fuller goes on to note that the apostolic church was a missionary and a dynamic church in which the apostles 'were not constituted such by the churches, but received their appointment immediately from Christ' with an authority not limited to any particular church but extending to all, thus distinguishing them from 'ordinary pastors, who are elected by the churches, and whose authority is confined to the churches that elected them'. In the new missionary situation, following on the initiative of the 1790s, a similar distinction had to be noted: 'the first missionaries to a heathen country could not be chosen by those to whom they were sent, but by him or them who sent them'; nor would their influence be confined to a single congregation, but,

---

11 Andrew Fuller, 'Constitution of Apostolic Churches', Letter X in 'Strictures on Sandemanianism', 1810, in ed. A. G. Fuller, *The Complete Works of the Revd Andrew Fuller, with a memoir of his life*, II, 1831, p.429.

by a kind of parental authority 'would extend to all the societies that might be raised by means of their labours'. Thus Fuller distinguishes two types of ministerial authority: in the normal and well-established situation the church appoints its minister, but in a missionary situation the process is reversed: the missionary, under God, creates the church, which in due course, it is hoped, will call its own pastor from amongst those converted to Christ.

The important thing was the extension of the kingdom. 'Let but churches be planted, set in order, and scripturally organized and, whether it be by the missionaries or succeeding native pastors, all is good and acceptable to Christ. And such, I conceive, is the state of things with respect to the apostles and succeeding ministers.'[12] In making such an affirmation, Fuller at once questioned not only all mechanistic theories of apostolic succession but more radically, in terms of the Puritan inheritance of early nineteenth-century Baptists, the model of the self-governing gathered church as the only model of churchmanship heralded in Scripture. If Fuller's perceptions are correct, then Dale's concern for the evangelical dilution of Puritan high churchmanship, though pointing up a particular danger, may not represent the whole story. This would also imply a need to question that whole strand of historical writing about Victorian Nonconformity that emphasized an evangelical dilution of Puritan churchmanship without positive evaluation of its evangelistic energy and achievement.[13]

There were other implications too. Professor Ward observes,

> The Sunday School open to all rather than the covenanted meeting of baptized saints was the sign of the times. Evangelism rather than sanctification was the church's business, and the more the slogan of 'the missionary church'

---

12 *ibid.*, p.433.

13 See not only the writings of Dale himself but J. W. Grant, *Free Churchmanship in England, 1870-1940*, n.d. but c.1951-2, p.87, and Daniel Jenkins, *Congregationalism*, 1954, pp.60-61.

> caught on, the more the kingdom of God seemed delivered over to associational principles.[14]

In other words, the form of church life became much more complex, the local church employing a rich diversity of agencies in its witness within its own community, acknowledging now the need to associate with others to promote gospel obedience nationally and internationally.[15] The actual experience of the missionary revival at home and abroad was radically changing Baptist thinking about the nature of the church: now the argument was that 'doctrinal religion should be founded on experimental religion'.[16] Moreover it was argued (and common practice confirmed it) that 'Christian people needed more intimate opportunities for the mutual analysis of their religious experience than was provided by the traditional covenant relations of church members'. 'The advantages of church communion will be in great measure lost to us if we forsake the assembling of ourselves together as the manner of some is,' counselled Fawcett, following the scriptural injunction, but then he added a contemporary gloss, in defence of his argument that revival of Christian communion precedes the revival of religion, scolding those who 'have no other intercourse than barely seeing one another's faces in the same house on a Lord's Day'.[17]

The concept of the church, then, was perhaps the most important arena in which the tensions between systematic Puritanism and dynamic Evangelicalism were worked out: in the process the definition of the church was in danger of becoming more congregational than covenantal. Consider, for example, Robert Hall's lament for the low view of the church which was gaining all too much support amongst dissenters generally. Hall countered this trend by campaigning for an

---

14 W. R. Ward, 'The Baptists and the Transformation of the Church, 1780-1830', *BQ* 25, 1973, p.172.

15 See, in addition to W. R. Ward's work above, R. H. Martin, *Evangelicals United: Ecumenical Stirrings in Pre-Victorian Britain*, 1963.

16 Ward, *op.cit.*, p.173.

17 Fawcett, *op.cit.*, pp.55-7.

important distinction: 'Congregations are the creatures of circumstances; churches the institution of God'. He regretted that, 'in the economy of modern dissenters, a growing tendency may be perceived to merge the church in the congregation and to commit the arrangement of the most weighty matters (especially ministerial calls) to a body of subscribers in preference to the members; an innovation, should it generally prevail, productive of incalculable evils'. Indeed, in Hall's judgement, lack of respect for the proper distinction between church and congregation was at the root of the difficulties of the Presbyterians in the previous century and their 'most melancholic departure, in a word both in principle and practice, from genuine Christianity.'[18]

Clearly Christians, in such a commitment to some particular form of ecclesiastical polity, had to avoid the dangers of censorious attacks upon fellow Christians. In a Bristol Address of 1820, entitled 'The Signs of the Times', remarkable as being preached by a dissenter in aid of the work of the National Society, which promoted specifically Anglican education with reference to the catechism and the Book of Common Prayer, Hall makes a powerful plea for Christian unity, claiming 'the reason why Christians have been so tardy in arriving at a disposition so much to be desired, is principally to be found in those exaggerated notions of the importance of church government under some particular form, which so long swayed the minds of excellent men.'[19] In Hall, particular commitment and ecumenical charity are held together; the danger was that amongst others, less catholic and comprehensive in their thinking, charity towards other Christian bodies would also become a solvent of all that was distinctive in the inherited tradition of churchmanship between the different Christian bodies.

A new ecumenical spirit was heralded by Robert Hall. He delighted in the fact that 'the most enlightened, the *selectest* Christians

---

18 Robert Hall, 'Memoir of the Rev. Thomas Toller', 1821, in ed. Olinthus Gregory, *The Works of Robert Hall*, 1866, IV, pp.296-8.

19 Robert Hall, 'The Signs of the Times', 1820, *Works* VI, 1866, p.192.

in every denomination, are ready to cultivate an intercourse with kindred spirits, with all who hold the same essential principles, in any other'. More particularly, he noted, 'Even protestants and catholics, influenced by a kindred piety, can now cordially embrace each other; as in the case of that zealous Professor of the Romish Church [elsewhere identified as "the most successful advocate beyond comparison of the Bible Society"] . . . who corresponds in terms of cordial affection with the Protestant secretary of the Bible Society . . . '.[20]

If the Evangelical Revival and the institutions it begat - missionary societies abroad and itinerancy at home - served to challenge an inherited Puritan churchmanship, an alternative threat came from the secular thought of the new century. When a youthful Joseph Angus in 1839 wrote an apology for the voluntary system in reply to Dr Chalmers' defence of established churches, he felt no compunction in integrating his views of ideal church and ideal state: to secure the maintenance of 'the religion of the Bible and of the heart', the supreme end of the voluntary system, 'it adopts the prominent principle of free trade and leaves demand and supply to their own adjustment'.[21] Significantly, he did not call upon any of the great Puritan statements about the nature of the church but rather cited Locke's definition of the church as 'a voluntary society of men, joining themselves together of their own accord, in order to the public worshipping of God, in such a manner as they judge acceptable to him and effectual to the salvation of their souls'.[22] His description of the fundamental rules of a congregation was essentially secular in that no theological imperative was invoked; accordingly, he set out a four-fold pattern of church government:

> First, that each church be kept in union by oneness of faith and feeling; secondly, that each member belong to the society and contribute to it just so long as he continues to approve its

---

20 Hall, *ibid.*, pp.190-191.

21 J. Angus, *The Voluntary System*, 1839, p.22.

22 Cited *ibid.*, p.128.

> objects and procedure. The only law is the law on which all agreed at its formation; the only means of maintaining authority that which the members have sanctioned; and in case of obstinacy, the only penalty unless others have been added by unanimous consent - expulsion.[23]

Quite where the apostolic model makes its impact is not clear, since the principles Angus enunciated could be adopted by any group of people sharing a common commitment; the teaching of scripture hardly determines either shape or content in any particular in this highly secularized ecclesiology.

By the time of his *The Christian Churches* of 1862, a Prize Essay celebrating the 200th anniversary of the Great Ejection, Angus was more inclined to emphasize the spiritual dimension of church life: 'Christian voluntaryism, it cannot be too often repeated, is not the authority of self-will. It is the willing submission of the heart and of the life to Christ, and the after-devotion of will to his cause.'[24] The crucial question to be asked of a church's membership was whether its members were a converted people, seeking, however fallibly, to walk in holiness, for this was essential for the church to be the church:[25] 'The Christian Church is a theocracy administered through the conscience and heart of Christians'.[26] The very need, however, to argue such an emphasis was in itself a testimony to the impact of secular liberalism upon the ecclesiological thought and practice of mid-century Baptists.

Quite obviously, the voluntarist view of the church was not without its critics. Robert Hall, in his debate with Joseph Kinghorn on strict communion, directly attacked such a position: the analogy between voluntary society and voluntary church was fraught with great danger because it played down the crucial fact of divine institution. By contrast, 'the church is a society instituted in Heaven' and is,

---

23 *ibid.*, p.194.

24 J. Angus, *The Christian Churches*, 1862, p.19.

25 *ibid.*, pp.21-2.

26 *ibid.*, p.70.

therefore, subject to divine authority; indeed, it is because 'it is amenable to a higher than human tribunal that it must insist on freedom from external control, but that freedom is not a freedom for private judgement but a freedom the more devotedly to conform to the mandates of revelation'.[27] In like fashion, Charles Stovel in 1835 asserted that, 'In the church, a Christian cannot make laws, his whole business is to understand and obey them'.[28]

This was a perennial emphasis in Baptist ecclesiology. In 1872 Charles Williams denied that Baptist churches were republics in which the membership made laws, rather they were part of a kingdom 'in which the Lord Jesus Christ reigns'.[29] But such lofty emphases were always in dialogue with more mundane approaches to churchmanship. Stovel, though affirming that 'the Church is called a Christian Church because it is redeemed by the blood of Christ, governed by the law of Christ, and formed for his praise', could lapse into the candid admission: 'A voluntary Christian church has thus come to be a little cluster of benevolent societies, more or less closely united with each other, but all deriving their nourishment from the same branch of the spiritual vine'.[30] In J. W. Grant's terse judgement: 'The original desire to spiritualize the nation had tended to secularize the Church'.[31]

JOHN CLIFFORD'S DIMINISHED ECCLESIOLOGY

Nineteenth-century Baptists were never isolated from the wider development of nonconformity: accordingly, concepts of the church were influenced not only by Baptist authors but by other nonconformists, and in particular Congregationalists, who often assumed the role of speaking for nonconformity at large, with more

---

27 Robert Hall, 'A Reply to the Revd Joseph Kinghorn', 1818, in *Works*, III, 1858, pp.325-6.

28 C. Stovel, *Hints on the Regulation of Christian Churches*, 1835, Preface.

29 C. Williams, *Principles and Practices of the Baptists*, 1872, pp.92-3.

30 Stovel, *op.cit.*, pp.17, 164.

31 Grant, *op.cit.*, p.87

(but sometimes less) justification. Not that the Congregational influence was all of one kind; whilst R. W. Dale sought to recall the Free Churches to the Puritan high churchmanship of the seventeenth century, others, influenced by the incarnational theology of F. D. Maurice, emphasized the more immanent dimensions of the life of the church. This was seen especially in the outlook of J. Baldwin Brown of Brixton, and his successor, B. J. Snell. That Maurice was also influencing younger Baptist ministers unhelpfully was one of Spurgeon's concerns as early as 1860.[32]

Rather later, with the impact of an embryonic social gospel, the witness of the church was sometimes in danger of being overshadowed by concern for the kingdom. John Clifford, for example, maintained that the history of Christianity was 'the story of the contest for primacy between the idea of Christ, as to the "Kingdom of God", and the ideas of men as to the Churches.'[33] The churches, he accordingly affirmed, 'are Christ-appointed instruments for establishing the Kingdom of God and his righteousness, and for extending the gracious and redeeming power of God over the world.'[34] In this process there was potentially loss and gain: loss of theological identity for the covenanted fellowship but gain of functional purpose in mission and outreach. As J. W. Grant notes, 'Whereas Nonconformists of an earlier period had been content to enrol small groups of elect Christians, Clifford and his contemporaries aimed at nothing less than taking up the whole world into the Body of Christ.'[35]

Clifford's theological approach is at once socially engaged and beyond the confines of mere words. Earlier in the century theologians spoke 'as if they had fathomed all knowledge and could compress the

---

32 C. H. Spurgeon, *Autobiography* (edited by his wife and his private secretary) II, 1899, p.271.

33 J. Clifford, in 'The Place of Baptists in the Evolution of the Churches', *Religious Systems of the World*, 1892 edition, p.559.

34 J. Clifford, *The Free Churches of London*, 1896, p.13.

35 Grant, *op.cit.*, p.179.

infinite into a phrase', but modern thought was characterized by a true Christian agnosticism: 'such knowledge is too wonderful, we cannot attain unto it.' Writing of the 'philosophy of the Atonement', earlier theologians imagined that they could exhaust its immeasurable meaning, whilst Clifford, more and more conscious that its depth could not be encased in the frailty of human language, still rejoiced in 'the free and full pardon it offers and the hope it creates'. The previous century, with its concern for evidences, undervalued the emotional and mystical elements in human experience; by contrast, Clifford's generation had learnt that 'the heart is the best theologian', believing that the Holy Spirit 'has led us out of our verbal controversies and creed-fights, and helped us to cross the barrier of our ecclesiasticism and stretch out lame hands but earnest hearts of faith and prayer to God, in recognition of the definite laws and conditions of the perfection of the Christian life.'[36] But these were laws of experience not the impositions of theological dogma. Thus he affirms, 'a man's real creed is not a catechism-phrase lodged in his memory, but a living conviction, the growth of his soul experience, making him the man he is . . .'[37] The basis of religious communion was spiritual, not intellectual:

> Christ Jesus built His Church on men not on a book; on living and loving disciples, enthusiastically attached to His Person, and not on philosophical creeds and rubrical regulations . . . The Church of Jesus Christ is not a miscellaneous gathering of professors of theology industriously grinding catechisms, nor a fortuitous concourse of unrelated atoms intelligent enough to sign a dry formula but a company of

36 J. Clifford, *The Religious Life of England during the Reign of Queen Victoria*, reprinted from *The Christian World*, n.d., but ?1887, pp.7-8.

37 J. Clifford in *A New Testament Church in its Relations to the Needs and Tendencies of the Age*, [on the laying of the foundation stone of Westbourne Park Chapel], 1876, p.9.

> brothers breathing the same life, refreshed at the same points of inspiration and fed from the same board.[38]

Baptists, he argued, had treated systematic theology with what some might regard as censurable indifference, being more concerned with the essential experience of making response to the command, 'You must be born again'.[39]

Clifford's view of the church is seen in his evaluation of church buildings, different once more from the Puritan and Evangelical arguments of earlier ages. Of the new Westbourne Park Chapel he said,

> We are not rearing this edifice merely 'for the public worship of Almighty God' during two or three hours a week; or chiefly for the 'administration' of the ordinances of Baptism and the Lord's Supper instituted by our King; but mainly, and in the first instance, as a meeting-place, drill-ground and working centre of a community of men 'whose heart the Lord has touched', and who will be better themselves as Christian men and citizens, and do better work in the world by means of their fellowship in the Gospel of Christ.[40]

The church existed not for itself but for a world of need - an understanding that immediately moved the church from its individualistic origins towards a corporate purpose. Although God saved men and women as individuals, it was so that he might save the whole world through the living and loving and confederate action of Christian people, a judgement well tuned to Clifford's Fabian political evaluation that 'Laissez Faire in government is as dead as Queen Anne'.[41]

---

38 *ibid.*, pp.7-8.

39 J. Clifford, 'Baptist Theology', from *The Contemporary Review*, n.d. but post 1888, p.4.

40 J. Clifford, *A New Testament Church*, p.5.

41 J. Clifford, *The Church of Christ: Its Work, Character and Message* [on the dedication of Westbourne Park Chapel] 1877, p.5, and *The State, the Church, and the Congregation* [delivered at the European Baptist Congress in Berlin] 1908,

The glory of the late nineteenth century, he argued, was the increase in Applied Christianity which contrasted most favourably with the esoteric and sectarian religion at the time of Queen Victoria's succession. Then the established church, unreformed by the activities of Lord Shaftesbury, still taught a class religion, whilst the dissenting conventicle was preoccupied with other-worldly themes which likewise detached religion from real life. The Christian religion then was a religion of the sanctuary, 'not of factory and trade, of politics and social progress'. Clifford identified Arnold of Rugby as 'the herald of religion in common life', an emphasis which Clifford heartily endorsed, affirming that 'to the real man of God there is no secular'. Accordingly, alongside the democratic movement of the century and in no way separate from it, he perceived also the fruit of 'vast cosmopolitan movements, strong in the passion of the Cross, rich in the spirit of self-sacrifice and prophetic and far-reaching issues of good for all men', doing battle with slavery, intemperance, and the tyranny of capital, protecting women and children at work and caring for orphans and the unfortunate: all this was Applied Christianity.[42]

The vision and the vigour with which such views were advocated ensured Clifford's command not only of his own denomination but of the many audiences and congregations he addressed up and down the country. Two things were crucial in maintaining the health of Clifford's undogmatic, experience-based, world-encountering ecclesiology. One was the unrelenting primacy of Christology to Clifford's discipleship: 'Christ is Christianity and the function of the Church is to make Him manifest to men . . . dependence on His guidance is entire; loyalty to his authority is unbroken'.[43] The other was his deep personal commitment to personal evangelism. Without such commitment such a programme would generate a vapid,

---

p.6.

42 J. Clifford, 'The Religious Life of England during the reign of Queen Victoria', reprinted from *Christian World*, n.d. but clearly 1887, pp.5-6.

43 J. Clifford, 'Why I am a Congregationalist', for the *Congregational Review*, 1887, p.10.

humanistic organization, devoid of the particularities of both grace and redemption.

GLOVER, WHITLEY AND THE THEOLOGY OF THE CHURCH

Baptists at the end of the nineteenth century prided themselves on their clear view of the importance of personal responsibility and of the dangers of what they called 'sacramentalism'. This applied even to such moderate spokesmen as Dr Richard Glover of Bristol, himself educated as a Presbyterian, and Dr Whitley, one of the denomination's most distinguished historians. In 1898 Glover wrote, 'The way in which the Saviour individualizes men . . . impresses me greatly . . . There is in Christ's teaching no suggestion of gregarious or corporate salvation'.[44] The whole teaching of the New Testament emphasized personal response and personal responsibility. That was the basis of the church, which thus encountered a major offence in the practice of infant baptism.

'Moses legislated for a State, Christ for persons; and to me it seems discordant with the spirit of the New Testament to provide a place for any who have not the fitness to fill it.'[45] Fitness, with its Darwinian overtones and lack of apostolic modesty, was not perhaps the most appropriate word: by it, of course, he means the development of a reasoned consciousness capable of responding to God's grace in faith. Once more the nature of the church was at stake: 'Whatever permits the membership or quasi-membership of the unconscious [clearly pointing to the baptismal practice of other churches] tends to facilitate the membership of the unconverted'. By contrast, believer's baptism 'tends to restrict the membership of the Church to the converted, and by so doing, to keep the Church pure: to the great advantage of the world outside, and to the great advantage

---

44 R. Glover, 'The Baptist Church', in *Our Churches and why we belong to them*, 1898, p.82.

45 *ibid.*, p.83.

also of those who might have deluded themselves with the thought that they were Christians when they were not'.[46]

Glover emphasized the individual responsibility implicit in baptism by comparing it with the Lord's Supper: 'the latter is a joint rite in which, unitedly, Believers commemorate the death of Christ, the former an individual rite, in which each simply confesses his submission to the Lord.'[47] Late nineteenth-century Baptists were constantly in danger of over-responding to the ritualist movement within the Church of England and to the expansion of the Roman church. Accordingly, their sacramental theology was all too often reactive, responsive to this revived Catholicism, rather than exploratory of their own Puritan and Evangelical origins - though, of course, they themselves did not see it like that.

John Clifford argued that the return of the Christ of the New Testament was delivering the churches from the blinding doctrine of the magical efficacy of sacraments and sapping the inward forces of sacerdotalism.[48] Glover agreed. Thus he argued in favour of reformed sacramental teaching: 'The theory, that the efficacy of the sacraments depends on the faith that accepts them and animates their observance, is a theory which keeps us looking to spiritual forces and spiritual conditions, and prevents our mind dwelling on the external, the official, the imaginary elements of the rite'.[49] This was sure ground for regretting the impact of the Tractarians in the Established Church which 'blurred and weakened' that church's 'movement forward into life', rather taking her 'backward into Romish errors': 'all Priestly pretensions are arrogant invasions of the sole sovereignty of Christ on the one hand and of the freedom and self-respect of His disciples on the other'.[50]

---

46 *ibid.*, pp.91-2.

47 *ibid.*, p.86.

48 J. Clifford, 'The Place of Baptists in the Evolution of British Christianity', in *Religious Systems of the World*, 3rd edition, 1892, p.573.

49 Glover, *op.cit.*, p.88.

50 *ibid.*, pp.105-6.

By contrast with what he regarded as the sectarianism of the ritualists, Glover argued that the free-communion stance of many British Baptists (in this respect more radical than the closed-communionists who were in fact applying the general principles of Christendom to the Baptist denomination) was taking a very practical step in favour of the unity of the church: 'when in every Christian Church the Lord's table is free to every Christian who wishes to bear witness that Christ crucified for him is the Bread of Life and the Wine of Life to his soul, then a basis of broad simple brotherhood is laid which keeps, and manifests, and extends the unity of the Church of God.'[51]

Whitley was every bit as aggressively anti-sacramentalist as Clifford or Glover. Of sacerdotalism and sacramentalism he writes,

> believe one and the other must follow; destroy either and the other must die. Once let the term Priest be applied to a minister specially, or Sacrifice to the bread and wine, or Altar to the communion table, and history has shown after the widening of the breach in true evangelicalism. Once admit that in baptism and the Lord's supper such grace is bestowed as can come in no other way, and soon a minister for these will be sought, and their observance will be exalted above preaching, whereas such mere manual acts were often remitted to inferiors, while our Lord and the apostles would not baptize or serve tables but proclaimed salvation.[52]

Like Clifford's, Whitley's view of the church is essentially functional, relating to the great work the church was commissioned to undertake. Thus he argued, 'Foreign missionaries are the most honoured priests, a convert from heathendom is the grandest sacrifice, for the Church is Christ's agent on earth to win all men to Himself'.[53] By contrast, attacking a venerable evangelical tradition as much as the influence of

51 *ibid.*, p.108.

52 W. T. Whitley, *Church, Ministry and Sacraments in the New Testament*, 1903, p.244.

53 *ibid.*, p.281.

modern ritualists, he argued, 'To ordain ministers with a special mention of their authority to baptize and to administer the Lord's supper is natural for a community that in defining a church specifies that the sacraments are duly administered, but has no word to say about its duty to the outside world. Such a community has lost Paul's sense of proportion.'[54]

Clifford made the same point even more insistently: 'Service to humanity in its higher ranges of life and work is the supreme test of the worth of Churches . . . Each Church must be made manifest according to its utterance of the "word", and offering of the service by which men and nations really live and securely advance towards their true ethical and spiritual goal.'[55] The broadness of the church's mission might seem impossibly and even dangerously amorphous but the essential evangelicalism of these *fin-de-siècle* Baptists was not in doubt. Whitley, using the autograph summary at the end of the Epistle to the Galatians, construed it as an argument against ritualism in any age: 'It will cut the ground from under the man who urges confession to a priest or frequent communion as an indispensable help, or baptism as the condition for the forgiveness of sins. What is vital - a rite or a refusal to adopt it? Neither, the new life from above.'[56] At the end the church remains the church of men and women who have responded to the imperative to be born again, for, in Clifford's words, 'the possession of the regenerate life is the indispensable condition of admission to the privileges of Church membership'.[57]

PULPIT ORATORY

Among other titles assignable to the Victorian period is the undoubted fact that it was the age of the sermon, both heard and read. Some forty volumes of Spurgeon's sermons were printed and Alexander McLaren's expository preaching reached a similarly wide audience

---

54 *ibid.*, p.176.
55 J. Clifford, 'The Place of Baptists . . . ', pp.560-1.
56 Whitley, *op.cit.*, p.208.
57 J. Clifford, 'Baptist Theology', p.4.

both in Britain and throughout the English-speaking world. The great pulpit orators were assured of an attentive immediate audience of members, adherents and sermon-tasters. Printed sermons were avidly read up and down the country and doubtless judiciously re-preached thereafter. Their sale overseas was a small but significant part of cultural imperialism: Spurgeon's sermons, for example, were carried in full by American and Australian dailies.[58]

Whilst the coming together of Dissenting and Methodist traditions had undoubtedly inspired an improvement in the pulpit in the early nineteenth century, there remained an unhelpful tendency to overworked, verbose oratory amply demonstrated by the surviving written evidence, until the late 1820s to 1830s when, with the growth of evening sermons, a more popular style developed.[59] Describing Alexander McLaren's arrival in Manchester in 1858, Ian Sellers argues, 'Baptist sermons to date had generally been either a medley of biblical texts employed to support or controvert a particular theological tenet . . . or else, in the hands of outstanding men like Robert Hall, rolling classical periods directed to the same end but with less obstructive scriptural reference'.[60] For its part the *Eclectic Review* complained in 1860 of 'the dullness and uselessness' of dissenting preaching.[61] That was a serious criticism granted the importance of the sermon within the economy of Baptist liturgy.

From the opening of the Metropolitan Tabernacle in 1861 until his death in 1892, Spurgeon preached to 10,000 people every Sunday. At the heart of his sermons lay a traditional Evangelical Calvinism, but applied topically in compelling and evocative Anglo-Saxon speech directly to the everyday experience of the artisans and lower middle class residents of South London, with ample pathos, sympathy and humour. 'I wish,' he once said, 'to lay the formalities of the pulpit

---

58 Horton Davies, *op.cit.*, IV, p.286.

59 R. Tudur Jones, *Congregationalism in England, 1662-1962*, 1962, pp.218-20.

60 I. Sellers, 'Other Times, Other Ministries: John Fawcett and Alexander McLaren', *BQ* 32, 1987, p.189.

61 *Eclectic Review*, 1860, p.2

aside and talk to you as if you were in your own houses.'[62] His were sermons to be remembered and pondered, a process aided by the deployment of dramatic openings, arresting epigrams, homely illustrations and by 'a structure that imprinted "headings" on the retina of the memory'.[63] In 1858 it is recorded that he preached from the grandstand of Epsom Race Course: his text was 'so run that we may obtain'. A contemporary cartoon contrasted Treacle, the average mollifying cleric from the Established Church, with Spurgeon cast as a robust Brimstone determinedly declaring the doom of sinners: 'If there be no hereafter live as you like; if there be no heaven, if there be no hell, laugh at me. But if these things be true, and you believe them, I charge you as I shall face you at the judgment hour of the Lord Jesus in the day of judgment - I charge you by your own eternal welfare, lay these things to heart'.[64] The *Evening Star* for 1856 carried this description of Spurgeon preaching, 'When he has read his text, he does not fasten his eye on a manuscript and his hands to a cushion. As soon as he begins to speak, he begins to act - and that, not as if declaiming on the stage, but as if conversing with you in the street. He seems to shake hands with all around, and put everyone at their ease'.[65]

Alexander McLaren was as shy and retiring as Spurgeon exuded robust energy. A retiring diffidence, profound scholarship, but more importantly a clear dependence upon a rich spiritual life enabled McLaren, with the expenditure of much nervous energy, to lead his congregation to the very gates of heaven through the lucid and relevant exposition of scripture. Ian Sellers identifies the strength of this Evangelical mystic:

> Once the preliminaries were over and the pastor had brought the whole weight of his philological knowledge of Greek and Hebrew, and of his reading, especially in German, to the

---

62 Sermons IV, p.108.

63 Horton Davies, *op.cit.*, IV, p.337.

64 Sermon IV, p.208, cited by Horton Davies, *op.cit.*, IV, p.292.

65 C. H. Spurgeon, *Autobiography* III, p.157.

> meaning of his text and its context, distinguishing figurative from literal meanings, noting the various usages of the same expression in other parts of Scripture, once, in other words, the force of the text had been established, McLaren would turn to the message. Now the hours of spiritual wrestling and intellectual concentration in the study and the time spent with treasured volumes of Carlyle and Browning bore fruit . . . as exposition turned to application and finally to appeal and the Word was transformed from external authority to a dynamic penetrating the preacher's and his hearers' innermost being.

McLaren himself put it like this: 'when so many brethren are speaking to the times, let one poor brother speak of eternity'.[66] His Christology was the epitome of orthodoxy, his intentions always evangelical, his approach to Scripture reverentially critical. 'Whatever the Higher Criticism has done,' he affirmed, 'it has not touched the main substance of the Gospel which we have to preach, nor do even its most advanced positions seem to me seriously to affect the homiletic worth of Scripture'.[67] The translucency of McLaren's preaching swiftly attracted a substantial congregation, and like Spurgeon he was as much read as listened to.

SCRIPTURE READING, PRAYERS AND CHURCH MEETING

Clearly the offering of the average minister was very much more prosaic than that of those who occupied the denomination's great pulpits. The older practice of the minister also offering a running commentary on the scripture reading had by the second half of the century fallen into disfavour; the one notable exception was Spurgeon whose expository comments were often published.[68] The idolization of the pulpit tended to make worship more passive with less congregational participation. The prayers - the short and the long prayer - that most services contained were nearly always extempore

66 *BQ* 32, 1987, p.188.

67 A. McLaren, cited by H. Jeffs, *The Art of Exposition*, 1910, p.86.

68 H. Jeffs, *The Art of Exposition*, 1910, pp.102-3.

and of some length, more doctrinal than specific - though it was said of the Congregationalist, Pye Smith, that his intercessions were so detailed that the daily news could be extracted from them.[69]

Public prayer was always to be seen as supplementary to family and private prayer. There would also be weekly lectures on Scripture or Bible expositions and weekly participatory Prayer Meetings, which had been a major instrument in the revival of denominational life at the end of the eighteenth century. E. A. Payne observed: 'Never has the whole membership been able or willing to join in such worship. They have waxed and waned in strength from generation to generation', especially as they have faced the competition of the multifarious activities of the institutional church, and as church members have developed 'a greater reserve and inarticulateness in religion'.[70]

A similar process overtook church meetings. Their proper functioning lay at the heart of congregationalism: here the believers met under the authority of scripture to discern the mind of Christ alike in matters of theology, in extending the pastoral call, in electing officers, and in the exercise of church discipline. The vulnerability of the saints was clearly admitted, as much in financial incompetence as in sexual deviance. Here men and women who earnestly resisted the interference of government in their lives submitted themselves to the mutual judgement of their fellow saints. There was, however, a growing self-consciousness. The Loughwood Church Books in Devon are not untypical in that, whereas full details of church discipline cases appear up to the middle of the nineteenth century, thereafter there is a very discernable thinning out of such material, with such descriptions of disciplinary cases as appear given in only the most general language: for example, on 7 February 1883 they record, 'Elizabeth Pavey's name was struck out and our prayer is that she may be led to repentance'. Clearly such delicate matters were increasingly

69 R. Tudur Jones, *op.cit.*, pp.222-3.

70 E. A. Payne, *Fellowship of Believers*, 1952 edition, p.108.

dealt with by deacons and minister rather than the membership at large and without the same kind of documentation as previously.[71]

HYMNODY

Any account of the life of a Baptist congregation and its worship would be incomplete without comment on its hymnody. From the end of the eighteenth century, Baptist history is punctuated by the fairly regular publication of denominational hymnbooks, starting with Rippon's *Selection of Hymns from the Best Authors* in 1787. This was to serve as a Baptist supplement to Watts' *Psalms and Hymns*. Rippon's editorial work, it has been claimed, made him a relatively wealthy man, selling some 20,000 copies by 1791, the year in which he added *A Selection of Psalm and Hymn Tunes*. Rippon was, according to H. S. Skeats, 'the first person to compile, on an extensive scale, a book of tunes with a companion Hymn Book suitable for religious worship'.[72] Rippon's books were widely received by the denomination both in Britain and in North America. They were in use at New Park Street and then the Metropolitan Tabernacle until 1866, when Spurgeon produced his own selection, entitled *Our Own Hymn Book*. Thus Kenneth Manley rightly comments on Rippon's 'profound - and often overlooked - theological influence on his fellow Baptists', with his *Selection* doing what any good hymnbook does, namely interpreting and defining the nature of

71 J. B. Whiteley, 'Church Discipline in the Loughwood Records', *BQ* 31, 1986, pp.293-4.

72 O. A. Mansfield, 'Rippon's Tunes', *BQ* 8, 1936, pp.36-43; W. T. Whitley, *BQ* 10, 1941, pp.434-443; H. S. Skeats and C. S. Miall, *History of the Free Churches of England, 1688-1891*, 1891, p.433; John Bowen to John Rippon, 15 August 1801, 'Letters to Dr Rippon from New York', *Transactions of the Baptist Historical Society*, I, 1909, p.72, gives an indication of the overseas market for Rippon's Hymn and Tune Books and their influence upon New-World liturgy. Benson, the renowned hymnologist, affirms Rippon's reputation as an editor of hymnbooks.

the Christian faith for its own generation.[73] Meanwhile the New Connexion of General Baptists had Samuel Deacon's *Barton Hymns* (1785) from very early in their history.

Amongst the Particular Baptists, Rippon soon had a rival in a *New Selection of Hymns* first published by the printer, John Haddon, in 1828, with revised versions published by his son in 1850 and 1855 to the benefit of the widows and orphans of Baptist ministers and missionaries, for hymnbooks had become successful money-raisers, and for the next hundred years were to feed Baptist charities. In 1858 S. G. Green, representing a group of ministers accustomed to work together in support of the missionary society,[74] brought Watts and other authors together again in a Baptist *Psalms and Hymns* which served alongside the New Connexion *Baptist Hymnal* (1879) for almost half a century until both were replaced by the *Baptist Church Hymnal* of 1900. The new book was a mark of the newly united denomination and significantly served the interests of a developing denominational identity.[75] At the same time, of course, a hymn book serves a catholic purpose in so far as it brings to any one confessional group the riches of other confessions, sometimes far distant from them; were Baptists to be limited to singing only the compositions of their co-religionists, then the diet would be rather mean and limited.

John Wesley's apology for a hymnbook remains an important statement of function: such a collection has to be 'large enough to contain all the important truths of our most holy religion, whether speculative or practical; yea to illustrate them all, and to prove them both by Scripture and reason; and this is done in a regular order, the hymns are not carelessly jumbled together, but carefully arranged under proper heads according to the experience of real Christians. So

73 K. Manley, 'The Making of an Evangelical Baptist Leader: John Rippon's Early Years, 1751-73', *BQ* 26, 1976, p.256.

74 *BQ* 6, 1933, p.380.

75 To bring together the different streams of denominational life, it was set in process by the *Psalms and Hymns Trust* [Particular Baptist], the trustees of the *Baptist Hymnal* [New Connexion], and the Baptist Union.

that this book is, in effect, a little body of practical divinity'.[76] For many it was the only book of divinity with which they were acquainted, which surely heightened its significance.

The debate about hymns in the eighteenth century moved from form to content, from whether or not to sing (the question which had occupied earlier generations), to what to sing. Wesley's hymns defy all restricted views of election, with emphasis on such universal language as 'all', 'whoever', 'every', and 'Saviour of mankind'. The preface to *Gadsby's Hymns* (1838) claims to be a selection, 'free from Arminianism and sound in faith': a modest selection of Wesley's hymns is included but carefully chosen and heavily edited for strict Calvinist use; for example, 'Universal Saviour' in 'Light of those whose dreary dwelling' becomes 'Dear Exalted Saviour'. The all-embracing claims of 'Spirit of Faith come down' are carefully excluded; no prayer here to see 'Who did for every sinner die, Hath surely died for me'. Similarly,

> The grace which all may find,
> The saving power impart,
> And testify to all mankind,
> And speak in every heart.

had to go, as do the references to the 'whosoevers' responding in faith to the witness of the Spirit. 'When shall thy love constrain' bears in *Gadsby* the warning, 'altered', and so it has been, with Wesley's pictures of grace wrestling with the will of the individual until that individual yields to divine persuasion firmly excluded.[77]

---

76 Wesley's Preface of 20 October 1779 to his *Collection of Hymns for the use of the People called Methodists*.

77 *Gadsby's Hymns*, No.1057 compared with Wesley's *Collection of Hymns* No.687; No.1053 with No.385; No.983 with No.85; No.1050 with No.137. The first of these alterations was followed in other Baptist collections, e.g. in John Haddon's *Selection of Hymns*, 1850 edition, No.103. That same collection, however, also contains the most explicit lyrical attack upon the hyper-Calvinism of the eighteenth century in the hymn, 'Lord, didst Thou die, but not for me?', No.240, with its exclamation, 'Presumptuous thought! to fix the bound, To limit mercy's

The editing of Watts' 'How sweet and awful is the place' is singled out for editorial comment from the younger Gadsby. Verse 5 originally read:

> 'Twas the same love that spread the feast
> That sweetly forced us in,
> Else we had still refused to taste,
> And perish'd in our sin.

That might seem determinist enough but there was a problem in the word 'refused', for Gadsby's son logically argued that 'to refuse a thing implies an offer', and this was contrary to the Calvinistic Articles of the Strict Baptists. Accordingly, the third line was altered to the awkward 'Else we had still ne'er had a taste', to expunge the distasteful concepts of offering and refusing. The hymn before in *Gadsby's Hymns* is 'When I survey the wondrous cross', but significantly it is shorn of its final verse with its articulation of human response, 'Were the whole realm of nature mine'.[78] Within such editorial activity is depicted the debate between 'Strict and Particular' and the more optimistic evangelism born of Wesley and domesticated to Baptists through the New Connexion fathers and through the missionary theology of Fuller.

Essentially all these early collections embrace a selection of hymns weighty in their Biblical allusions and expressive of the theologies of the period, firmly Trinitarian, deliberately rejecting all weak Christologies. But other emphases and styles were also needed. The much-condemned chorus hymns of the nineteenth century offer narrative to dogma in much the same way as the event and story-orientated gospels complement the theology of the epistles. The emphasis is not unrelated to the difference in mood between a systematic Puritanism and an Evangelicalism which stressed a common

---

sovereign reign'. Unfortunately on this occasion the author of the hymn is not recorded.

78 *Gadsby's Hymns*, Preface and Nos. 439 and 440.

experience, focused in the distinction between 'real' and 'nominal' Christians.

Many are critical of the compositions of the nineteenth century for being over-sentimental: thus Horton Davies, noting the widening range of the hymnodist's concern, writes, 'an expansion of themes was accompanied by a thinning of theology, and sometimes the objectivity of the mighty acts of God in creation, redemption and sanctification was sacrificed for the sugary subjectivity and introspection of lyrical spiders for ever examining their own insides', whatever that may mean; though significantly he adds, 'Even this was greatly to be preferred to the formalism and sheer dullness of much eighteenth-century praise'.[79] It is not necessary for the objective and the subjective to be as exclusively opposed the one to the other as that might suggest. Nor in the total corpus does the nineteenth century have a monopoly of the subjective. Clearly in usage a balance of outlooks needs to be secured, and a concentration on the human mood to the detriment of the nature of grace is unhelpful.

A study of Baptist hymnbooks, at least until recent times, emphasizes a basic conservatism: only slowly, for example, did Wesley get admitted to collections dominated by Watts and Doddridge, together with eighteenth-century English Baptists like Benjamin Beddome, Samuel Stennett, Samuel Medley and Anne Steele. Equally it took time for the Sankey-type hymn to penetrate British Baptist collections, though hymns of a similar type by British authors were introduced rather earlier, so that the last editions of *Psalms and Hymns* included some by Frances Havergal, Anabella Hankey and Mrs Clephane, as well as the American, Fanny Crosby. Sankey published his *Sacred Songs and Solos*, which embraced 'the folk-song of their piety', in North America in 1872, introducing 'the music of the music hall into the sanctuary'.[80] Here was a serious attempt at popularizing the appeal of religion: 'That the rhythmical

---

79 Horton Davies, *op.cit.*, IV, p.86.

80 E. Routley, *The Music of Christian Hymnody*, 1957, p.132, and Horton Davies, *Music, Sacred and Profane*, 1960, p.129.

hymn-tunes of Sankey, the intense preaching of the devout but unsophisticated Moody, and the military marches played on street corners by Salvation Army bands were the only truly successful attempts to popularize worship among the masses', argues Horton Davies, 'shows that there is a vast difference between the shock-tactics necessary for evangelism and the slower cultural maturation of the Christian within the Church learned through the art (not the craft) of Christian worship'.[81]

The popularizing influences of the music hall can also be seen if the Sankey-type hymn is construed as a sanctified ballad which, in proper Hebraic form, tells a story. Some examples relate to incidents in the life of Jesus,[82] others to the parables Jesus taught.[83] Others focus on very concrete analogies: pilgrims, strangers and wanderers, military and nautical images, storms enough to invoke incipient sea-sickness.[84] Such concreteness of imagery, however, was partly the common currency of the period: consider, for example, the imagery of Joseph Parker's 'God holds the key of all unknown'.[85] At extremes the anecdotage of the hymn is separated from that of scripture and set within the experience of the believer - 'Where is my wandering boy tonight?', to which presumably it was hoped the

---

81 Horton Davies, *Worship and Theology in England*, IV, p.88.

82 Ira D. Sankey, *Sacred Songs and Solos, with Standard Hymns Combined [750 Pieces]*, undated, 'She only touched the hem of his garment', 'Master the tempest is raging', Hymns 293, 395. Various editions were published between 1874 and 1895.

83 *ibid., 750 pieces* No.43, 'There were ninety and nine'; *ibid., 1200 Pieces*, n.d., No.175, 'Behold the bridegroom cometh'.

84 'Will your anchor hold in the storms of life?', 'Only an Armour Bearer firmly I stand', 'O where are the reapers?': *Sacred Songs and Solos: 1200 Pieces*, No.879; *750 Pieces*, Nos.33, 199. 'Ho, my comrades, see the signal', with its better known chorus 'Hold the fort for I am coming': *Sacred Songs and Solos: 750 Pieces*, no.1.

85 Included in *Sacred Songs and Solos: 750 Pieces* at No.592, but Parker's theological pedigree was very different, witness his conflict with Spurgeon, as recorded in my article, 'Charles Haddon Spurgeon and the Baptist Denomination in Nineteenth-Century Britain', *BQ* 21, 1986, p.234.

answer amidst some scepticism would be having 'the courage to say No', the refrain to 'You're starting, my boy, on a journey'.[86] But these hymns were in a second book until the twentieth century dawned, for Baptists seemed to have got their respectable hymns from one book and their Sankey's from another, which was essentially seen as a weekday rather than Sunday book.[87] The two books were symbolic of the two traditions in Baptist life: the doctrinal worship of the gathered church and the evangelistic proclamation at the heart of her urgent mission.

The Sankey type of hymnody was taken up by other evangelical and evangelistic agencies; for example, in the songs of the Salvation Army, with their refusal to let 'the devil have all the best tunes'; by later campaign evangelists influential in the Baptist constituency such as Torrey and Alexander, in anniversary hymns promoted by the Sunday School movement, and in the various editions of *Golden Bells* produced by the Children's Special Service Mission.[88] The two extremes of hymnody - the classic doctrinal hymns and the new popular hymn-ballads - found Baptist congregations stretched between the theological literacy of their inherited past and the popular culture

---

86 *ibid. 750 Pieces*, Nos.303, 579.

87 See Faith Bowers, 'The Benhams of Bloomsbury', *BQ* 29, 1981, p.69, where she notes that James Benham suggested to the Deacons' Meeting at Bloomsbury in 1883 that the increasingly popular Sankey collection might be used at the Monday evening prayer meeting.

88 *Golden Bells*, replacing the earlier *Songs of the Better Land* (1870), and *Songs of Love and Mercy*, was first published in 1890, with a more influential and improved edition published ,in 1926, and became an important vehicle for disseminating post-Sankey gospel hymns. In slum areas, village work and other mission activities, it was soon found that the choruses of these hymns were more useful than the hymns themselves, but that sometimes these incomplete choruses were deficient in meaning. As early as 1897 George Goodman produced a small collection of purpose-written choruses, or 'potted hymns', as they were called at the time, for use in beach missions. For twenty years these were circulated in leaflet form until the CSSM produced two enduring collections in 1921 and 1929. J. C. Pollock, *The Good Seed: the story of the CSSM and the Scripture Union*, 1959, pp.82-3.

of the modern world only able to appreciate narrative lyrics with little theological thinking behind them.[89]

Sankey's hymns, less burdened perhaps with dogmatic theology than those which went before, tended to continue in the liturgical diet of some institutional churches, Pleasant Sunday Afternoons, and Brotherhoods long after those organizations had moved away from the conversion theology out of which the hymns were born, and so exercised a mediating role between the old evangelical and broader understandings of the gospel. A specialized form of this process can be traced in the history of the temperance movement, which was perhaps the most significant way in which late nineteenth-century nonconformity moved out from the concerns of the sanctuary to consider those of society. *Hoyle's Hymns and Songs for Temperance Societies and Bands of Hope* presents a representative sample '175 Gems of Song', which move all too easily from conversionist songs to the a-theological and merely moral, earnest in purpose but theologically trivializing.

The pattern seen in Baptist hymnody mirrors the tensions present in congregational life more widely. Inherited was the theological tradition of Watts and Doddridge, reflecting the classical reformed doctrine of the English separatists, but supplemented now by the evangelical Arminianism of the Wesleys. During the nineteenth century that tradition faced the opposing strains of the spiritualizing emphases of the revivalist and conversionist tradition of Baptist missionary engagement, and at the same time secularizing influences of the institutional church - temperance societies, youth work, and urban missions. In the context of a Calvinism whose expression seemed not to be meeting modern needs, voluntaryism and activism were in danger of being sanctified as the new religion of the Free Churches to such an extent that the high ideals of the gathered church were sometimes put at risk.

---

89 For the more doctrinal hymns that nineteenth-century Baptists used for baptismal services see pp.54-55, and for communion see M. Walker, *Baptists at the Table*, 1992, pp.17-30.

3

BAPTISM AND COMMUNION

In his Hulsean Lectures, David Thompson notes that books, pamphlets and tracts on baptism were being produced in large numbers in the first three decades of the nineteenth century, in contrast to a lack of interest in the issue thirty years earlier. Such a debate, he argues, was, in part at least, fathered by the Evangelical Revival, and threw up three main areas of concern. First, who should be baptized? Secondly, was baptism as a believer a precondition to communion? And thirdly, how was baptism related to regeneration?[1]

The posing of the first question had its locale in Scotland, where in 1808 Robert Haldane, a wealthy Calvinist revivalist, who advocated a closed sectarian evangelicalism, came to the conclusion that he could no longer in conscience baptize infants, and that he himself should seek baptism as a believer. The ensuing split in his Edinburgh church not only brought a new source of recruits into Baptist life in Scotland, but also provided arguments on baptism that secured notice south of the border, particularly from the pen of F. A. Cox of Hackney, a former Bristol student who completed his education at Edinburgh. In response to arguments of covenant theology, Cox grounded his defence of the Baptist position on, as he saw it, the essential gospel understanding, 'that man is individually responsible to God for his actions'; 'No one can profess faith, no one can put on Christ, no one can obey God, no one can perform a duty which is enjoined as a public expression and avowal of any Christian principle, for another.' In this as in other respects the preconditions for the two sacraments should be the same. How likely was it then that the practice of baptism would have been allowed to breach the fundamental principle

---

1 D. Thompson, 'Baptism, Church and Society in Britain since 1800', unpublished Hulsean Lectures 1983-4, p.4.

that, in making a response to the gospel, no-one could act for another?[2]

The debate here seems at times to evoke the Enlightenment concept of rational man as defining candidacy for baptism. John Ryland, Senior, in a tract revised by his son and often reprinted in the nineteenth century, speaks of candidates being 'capable of exercising reason and conscience'.[3] Isaiah Birt, minister successively in Plymouth and Cannon Street, Birmingham, and one of those Baptist preachers who early welcomed the onset of the French Revolution 'as the day-break of liberty for continental Europe', refers to 'rational and intelligent creatures'. The appeal of the gospel was to a degree cerebral: 'it is the ministry of divine truth and addresses itself to the mental and moral capacities, and through them to the sinful condition of men.' Accordingly Birt conceived of baptism as 'an act of intelligence and volition on the part of the person baptized'.[4]

'WATER BAPTISM NO BAR TO COMMUNION'

Bunyan's convictions as to 'Water Baptism no Bar to Communion' have frequently been rehearsed, and the growth of churches in Bedfordshire and neighbouring counties that held together Baptists and paedobaptists in one fellowship remained a tribute to the strength of that view-point. E. A. Payne, whilst noting that churches such as College Street, Northampton, Chipping Norton (in a covenant drawn up by Benjamin Beddome), and New Road, Oxford, made the form of baptism no bar to membership, records a tendency amongst Particular Baptists to move to stricter patterns of church membership at the end of the eighteenth century. For its part, the last of the Articles of Religion of the New Connexion was quite specific on the

---

2 F. A. Cox, *On Baptism* [in reply to the writings of Greville Ewing, Timothy Dwight and Ralph Wardlaw]; Thompson, *op.cit.*, pp.5-8.

3 J. Ryland, *Six Views of Believer's Baptism*, 1821 (an expansion of his father's tract of 1744).

4 I. Birt, *Personal Religion Vindicated in Relation to Christian Baptism*, 1833, pp.23, 248.

issue: 'Baptism by immersion was required of believers to enable them to be initiated into a church state; and that no person ought to be received into the church without submission to that ordinance.'[5]

Robert Hall and Joseph Kinghorn were entirely agreed both as to who should be baptized and the mode of that baptism. Hall, however, prompted by the shared experience of the Evangelical Revival, concerned for the unity of the Church as the Body of Christ, and persuaded that schism was 'by far the greatest calamity that has befallen the christian interest', argued that it was remarkable that 'the rite, which, of all others, is most adapted to cement mutual attachment, and which is in a great measure appointed for that purpose, should be fixed upon as the line of demarcation, the impassable barrier, to separate and disjoin the followers of Christ.' Objecting to the Lord's Supper becoming the focus for a religious test, he perplexedly confessed, it 'is no longer a symbol of our common christianity, it is the badge and criterion of a party'. In other areas of Christian witness and service it was clear that Baptists regarded paedobaptists as fellow believers, even sharing in one another's ordination services. Having this common communion in day-to-day activities, there could be no logic for separation at the table which celebrated the death of their common Lord, who alone could set the terms for communion, which related to the one issue of salvation, and no other. Only Baptists, asserted Hall, rejected at the table those whom Christ had received, arguing that Strict Communion thereby became a sure recipe for making Baptist principles unpopular.[6]

BAPTISM AND SALVATION

If the precondition for communion was a salvation secured by a faith-response to the grace of God, Baptists argued that it was that same faith that was a pre-condition to baptism, and that, therefore, there could be no equation between baptism and regeneration. Dissenting

---

5 E. A. Payne, *The Fellowship of Believers*, 1952 edition, pp.77-80; A. Taylor, *History of the English General Baptists*, 2 vols., 1818, p.476.

6 R. Hall, *On Terms of Communion*, 1815, in *Works*, III [1858], pp.7-11.

paedobaptists, whilst challenging the precedence of faith, agreed that baptism did not secure regeneration, and in this were joined by many evangelical clergy of the Church of England, prayer-book formulae notwithstanding. The context for the debate soon became that heightened sacramentalism within the established church which mid-Victorian Baptists perceived to be the fruit of the Oxford Movement, with its accompanying secessions to Rome. In such a dangerous context in 1842, twenty years before Spurgeon's intervention, Charles Stovel asked evangelical paedobaptists to ponder whether their practices did not belie the gospel they preached.

Reaction to changes in the Church of England made dissenters at once both assertive and hesitant about their own articulation of sacramental theology. In *The Baptismal Regeneration Controversy Considered* (1843), Stovel boldly asserted of baptism: 'its *prerequisites* were conversion and peace in Christ. The *act* was a voluntary, open and sacramental self-consecration to God. The result was a recognition of the person baptized, as a new character, as an inheritor of new privileges, and the subject of new responsibilities, both in the church and the world.' Later such boldness was moderated by an anti-sacramental conscience: 'the idea of a spiritual gift in baptism, together with the whole doctrine of sacramental grace, was derived from heathen philosophy by heretics'.[7]

BAPTIST NOEL AND THE BAPTISM OF BELIEVERS

The language of baptismal regeneration, and the debate associated with it caused the Revd Baptist W. Noel, a celebrated and aristocratic Evangelical Anglican preacher, to vacate the pulpit of his proprietary chapel in Bedford Row in the summer of 1849 and seek believer's baptism from the local Baptist minister. Five years earlier, in *Protestant Thoughts*, he had challenged the exclusiveness of the dogmatic claims of the new Anglicanism. Of Carey, Robert Hall and others he wrote,

---

7 C. Stovel, *The Baptismal Regeneration Controversy Considered*, 1843, pp.51, and 141.

All these your bigotry outcasts make
Not for their sins, but for your dogma's sake.[8]

At least 24,000 copies of the sermon he preached on the occasion of his baptism were published. In this he tells how he had come to a position where he could no longer reconcile infant sprinkling with New Testament teaching as a valid form of baptism, but was perplexed as to how he, who had professed faith at the Lord's Table so many times, could so late come to what he saw as an initiatory rite. Further reflection led him to the conclusion that to refuse immersion would be an act of disobedience, noting at the same time that in the New Testament record he could find no instance of the unbaptized coming to the Lord's Table. He was also influenced by his understanding that Jesus' baptism followed years of devotion to God, and by the evangelistic impact on others he believed that the witness given in baptism provided. Baptists, he concluded, were loyal to a principle common to all Christendom in not offering communion to the unbaptized, and that accordingly logic was with them in requiring valid baptism as a prerequisite to communion.

He did not, in fact, long remain a strict-communionist, but he did retain a sacramental understanding of the necessity for baptism. On Acts 2.38 he commented, 'Since then baptism is thus necessary to remission of sins and is so closely connected with it . . . Repentance and baptism are declared in the text to secure the gift of the Holy Ghost.' Further, there was the definitive assertion, 'Baptism is the profession of faith, the public confession of Christ, without which there is no true faith and no salvation . . . As the confession of Christ is necessary to salvation, so is baptism to those who know that this is the appointed method of confessing him.'[9] Here Noel presented something more than the moral obligation of other Baptists: he viewed baptism not as an option but as a necessity.

---

8 B. W. Noel, *Protestant Thoughts*, 1844, p.44.

9 B. W. Noel, *Essay on Christian Baptism*, 1849, pp.94-5, 99.

SPURGEON AND BAPTISMAL REGENERATION

Spurgeon's first entry into the baptismal controversy was in 1861 when he preached on 'Infant Salvation' and in passing made comments on Puseyite practices.[10] Three years later he returned to the theme in a sermon which he firmly believed would put an end to the popularity of his published sermons. In fact, nearly a quarter of a million copies of this particularly sensational example of pulpit oratory were sold. Encompassed within the sermon was a forthright attack on Anglican Evangelicals, which gave plenty of ammunition to the high-church party and, therefore, offence to those who thought that the Gorham Case had established the legitimacy of an Evangelical reading of the Book of Common Prayer. The attack was the more hurtful for being offered in the context of respect for those actually committed to the doctrine which the language of the Prayer Book seemed to spell out: 'God forbid that we should censure those who believe that baptism saves the soul, because they adhere to a Church which teaches the same doctrine. So far they are honest men, and in England, wherever else, let them never lack full toleration . . . I hate their doctrine but I love their honesty.'[11]

This did not prevent Spurgeon from jeering at the doctrine by making reference to prisons filled with baptized burglars, forgers, harlots and murderers.[12] He also took the opportunity to spell out what he saw as the relationship between baptism and conversion: by conversion a man becomes a soldier of Jesus Christ, and in baptism he dons his regimentals. Turning to the Evangelicals, he impassionately declared, 'I impeach before the bar of universal Christendom, these men, who, knowing that baptism does not regenerate, yet declare in public that it does.' The credibility of the clergy was at stake: 'when worldly men hear ministers denouncing the very things which their own Prayer Book teaches, they imagine that

---

10 C. H. Spurgeon, 'Infant Salvation', *Metropolitan Tabernacle Pulpit*, VII [for 1861], p.505.

11 C. H. Spurgeon, *Metropolitan Tabernacle Pulpit*, X [for 1864], p.317.

12 *ibid.*, p.318.

words have no meaning among ecclesiastics' (a grievance which seems to have much in common with that which Charles Kingsley perceived in J. H. Newman).[13]

Spurgeon was saying that the Church of England could not keep its Prayer Book and its Catechism and still claim to be reformed: 'I am not aware that any Protestant church in England teaches the doctrine of baptismal regeneration except one, and that happens to be the corporation which, with none too much humility, calls itself *the* Church of England.'[14] Furthermore, Spurgeon made the issue one of fellowship: 'Where union and friendship are not cemented by truth, they are an unhallowed confederacy. It is time that there should be put an end to the flirtations of honest men with those who believe one way and swear another.'[15] Such a judgement was not made any easier by the imputation that the Evangelicals subscribed to these forms to hold on to their livings, and such rhetoric as 'Out of any system which teaches salvation by baptism must spring infidelity, an infidelity which the false church already seems willing to nourish and foster beneath her wing. God save this favoured land from the brood of her own established religion.'[16]

Three further sermons followed, advancing his case, including a specific plea to Evangelical clergy to leave the established church under the text, 'Let us go forth'. The controversial literature thus provoked came to fill more than three large octavo volumes.[17]

This controversy not only called forth from Lord Shaftesbury the riposte that Spurgeon was 'a very saucy fellow', who must not think himself at all representative of the mainstream of English Nonconformity, but also a published letter from Baptist Noel, reminding Spurgeon that the fourth resolution of the Evangelical Alliance specifically outlawed such sectarian attacks on fellow

---

13 *ibid.*, p.317.
14 *ibid.*, p.313.
15 *ibid.*, p.317.
16 *ibid.*, p.328.
17 C. H. Spurgeon, *Autobiography*, III, pp.83-4.

members, and objecting to certain expressions used in the sermon.[18] Spurgeon took that letter to express the mind of the leadership of the Evangelical Alliance, whose secretary, James Davies, actually laid before Spurgeon the alternatives of retraction or withdrawal from the Alliance. It is hardly surprising that, in such circumstances, Spurgeon chose the latter, at least for a period of years; he later returned to membership and to a position on the Alliance's Council and adopted its basis of belief for the Pastor's College Evangelical Association. Once again Baptists in the nineteenth century were forced to choose between wider evangelical and ecumenical relationships and particularities of conscience, for Spurgeon was far from being alone in this controversy. Among many who gave him support in London were Dr Brock, Dr Landels, and Daniel Katterns of Hackney, together with Dr N. Haycroft (of Broadmead, Bristol), T. W. Medhurst (then of Glasgow), and Arthur Mursell (Manchester).

FAITH, BAPTISM AND CHURCH

It is not surprising that many Baptists in their attitudes towards the sacraments tended to employ negative slogans. Thus J. H. Hinton argued that those scriptures that seemed to teach that baptism does confer some blessing always referred to the faith that preceded baptism: 'I affirm, in the most unqualified terms that baptism is not the means of conferring any spiritual blessings whatsoever.'[19] Charles Williams was hardly more positive in affirming that grace did accompany baptism, for he added the qualification: 'I say that blessing was not present in the baptism, it was not communicated by the baptism. Those baptismal waters were not either the cause or the means, though they may have been the occasion of these blessings.'[20]

---

18 B. W. Noel, Letter to C. H. Spurgeon respecting his attack on the Evangelical Ministry of the Church of England, 1864.

19 J. H. Hinton, *The Ultimatum*, 1854, in *Collected Works*, V, 1864, pp.466ff.

20 C. Williams in H. Pitman, *A Discussion of Infant Baptism*, 1858. Pitman, a reporter for the *Manchester Courier*, here reports a debate between Charles Williams of Accrington and the Revd Dr Joseph Baylee, Principal of St Aidan's College, Birkenhead.

Twenty years later Williams remained as emphatic that the critical changes in a person's life had always to occur prior to baptism: 'Professedly regenerated and redeemed, converted and made disciples before baptism, it is impossible that candidates should fall into the error that baptism regenerates or redeems, converts or disciples, or even assists in or perfects the process by which "a child of wrath" is made an "heir of glory".' What was at stake, then, was not grace, which was a precondition in the conversion experience, but obedience. Little wonder that Victorian Baptists were sometimes chastised by other Christians for being frightened of giving any import to baptism at all. Indeed stronger statements on the effectiveness of believer's baptism will be found penned by Plymouth Brethren and those who later formed the Churches of Christ than by the great weight of Baptist apologists.[21]

Not all Baptists, however, were unhappy with sacramental language. William Hawkins, a pupil of Joseph Kinghorn's who completed his education at Edinburgh and served a number of churches on supply before he was ordained at Portsea in 1816, argued that baptism was, in the truest sense of the word, a sacrament, 'a sovereign oath which we take to our Sovereign Prince, in which we swear allegiance to him as our rightful king, renouncing all other Lords who may have dominion over us, and declaring that henceforth we will be called by his name.' Hawkins then picked up Calvin's definition of a sacrament as 'the outward and visible sign of an inward and spiritual grace' as a 'beautiful and accurate definition', adding with due caution, 'But the sign ought never to be separated from the thing signified, which must necessarily be the case when it is applied in the period of unconscious infancy. . . While we are careful, on the one hand, not to confound the sign with the thing signified, we are

---

21 This is a phenomenon unfortunately not appreciated by J. R. C. Perkin in his Oxford DPhil (1955), 'Baptism in Nonconformist Theology, 1820-1920, with special reference to the Baptists', where he fails to identify either B. W. Newton or R. Govett of Norwich as Plymouth Brethren.

equally solicitous, on the other, not to produce an entire separation between them.'[22]

A rather similar position was advocated by J. E. Roberts, minister of Union Chapel, Manchester, at the beginning of the twentieth century. Whilst vehemently arguing that no Evangelical Christian could defend infant baptism since it represented 'a denial of the concept of the church as the community of regenerate believers', he sought to interrelate outward forms and inward meanings; accordingly he argued that 'baptism is the rite which marks the believer's initiation into the new covenant, that baptism and faith are but the outside and the inside of the same thing. . . Baptism represents forgiveness of sins, regeneration, union with Christ, crucified and risen, the baptism of the Holy Spirit; and because it represents these spiritual experiences, it is the rite of admission into the Christian Church.'[23]

This same view was articulated by Wheeler Robinson in his *Baptist Principles*, the first edition of which was published in 1911: 'Believers' Baptism . . . carries with it an unmistakable definition of the *Church*, to which it is the door of entrance. The Church is a spiritual society composed of converted men who acknowledge the supreme Lordship of Christ.' At the same time he was quite clear that the New Testament, confining water baptism, itself representative of baptism in the Spirit, to believers, knew nothing of unbaptized believers.[24]

All too many Baptist apologists were at once too protestant, too rational, too didactic and too individualistic. Sacraments smacked of magic; by contrast, post-Enlightenment Baptists saw believer's baptism as the mental response to the revelation of truth, undertaken with free volition by rational men and women. Writing at the end of the century, W. T. Whitley, in his grand survey of *The Witness of History to Baptist Principles*, included one chapter on the 'great twin errors' of 'sacerdotalism and sacramentalism', followed by a complementary

22 W. Hawkins, *A Sermon on Baptism*, 1827, pp.22-5.

23 J. E. Roberts, *Christian Baptism* (n.d., but 1905 by deduction), pp.107-110; 22.

24 H. Wheeler Robinson, *Baptist Principles*, 1911 (extended edition 1925), p.25.

chapter on 'Private Judgment', which is seen as closely allied to the separation of church and state. Sacramentalism was the earlier perversion and was derived from Jewish and heathen sources, whereas sacerdotalism came a little later, creating a separated priestly caste. The chapter on 'Private Judgment' is significant in being twice as long as that on 'the Authority of Scripture'.[25]

At the same time nineteenth-century Baptists, unlike their predecessors, seemed anxious not to impute corporate ecclesiastical significance to the rite, placing it wholly in the realm of personal responsibility, where the witness of one individual was seen as having a powerful influence on another in a church fellowship where signs and symbols were few. As early as 1833, Isaiah Birt saw baptism in terms of a personal contract - 'an affair wholly between God and the individual' - reflecting the personal nature of the spiritual conversion which thus became the prime focus of attention.[26] Such personalist attitudes long controlled much Baptist thinking. John Clifford's Westbourne Park church opened its membership to all who professed faith in Christ and sought to obey him. Baptism, it taught, was the privilege of the believer: 'Every applicant for membership is urged to consider the Lord's will on this subject, but the rule followed is "Let every man be fully persuaded in his own mind" and act according to his judgement of the Master's teaching. The whole question is left to the individual conscience', but then illogically, or so it seems, the Church Constitution continues, 'The obligation to be baptized springs out of the relation of the believer to the Church'. Was the old individualism, for which in many ways Clifford had little time, already breaking down by 1877? Clifford himself represented a curious marriage between secular corporate socialism and ecclesiastical individualism.

25 W. T. Whitley, *The Witness of History to Baptist Principles*, 1897, ch.V.

26 Birt, *op.cit.*, pp.13-14.

BAPTISMAL HYMNODY

Nineteenth-century Baptists came to prefer the language of ordinance rather than sacrament, emphasizing obedience to a Christ-given instruction as a principal motivation:

> Hear the voice that speaks from heaven,
> 'This is my appointed way.'
> You, whose sins He has forgiven,
> Follow Him without delay.[27]

For a believer to refuse baptism was both to slight an institution established by Christ and to despise his example. From this relational argument on required obedience, Baptists perpetrated a highly personalized view of baptism.

In contrast to this J. R. C. Perkin interestingly draws attention to the fact that, whilst references to the gift of the Spirit in Baptist apologetics are only sparingly recorded, no such inhibition engaged Baptist hymn-writers.[28] Maria Saffery writes:

> Blest Spirit! with intense desire,
> Solicitous we bow;
> Baptize us in renewing fire,
> And ratify the vow.[29]

It is difficult to find a baptismal hymn by Baptist Noel that does not evoke the Spirit:

> Lord, Thou hast promised to baptize
> Those in the Holy Ghost,
> Whose faith on Thee alone relies,
> Thy cross their only boast.
>
> Baptize us in Thy Spirit, Lord,
> And in that promised fire,

---

27 Joseph Swain, 1792, *Psalms and Hymns* 702.

28 J. R. C. Perkin, *op.cit.*, p.240.

29 M. Saffery, 1818, *Psalms and Hymns* 707.

Which may to us all zeal afford,
All gratitude inspire.[30]

In like measure the hymns spell out fairly fully the death-resurrection imagery of baptism, thus John Fawcett's invitation:

View the rite with understanding:
Jesus' grave before you lies!
Be interred at his commanding -
After His example rise.[31]

Essentially for Baptists, George Rawson, himself a Congregationalist, wrote:

Immersed beneath the closing wave,
We're into death baptized;
And enter thus our Saviour's grave,
Buried with him that died.

With Christ we die! That, freed from sin,
With Christ we may arise;
New thoughts, new hopes, new lives, to win
To fit us for the skies.[32]

Rawson's verses indicate that many Baptist congregations at this time sang baptismal hymns by paedobaptist, particularly Congregationalist, authors, whose words and theology seem more completely reflected in Baptist principles and practice.

ΒΑΠΤΙΖΩ AND SCRIPTURE TRANSLATION

Debate focused as much on the mode of baptism as its subject. Long dissertations on the appropriate translation of the Greek verb, *βαπτιζω*, were penned by Baptist scholars and their adversaries. The most famous of the Baptist treatises was that published in 1841 by

30 Baptist Noel, 1853, *Psalms and Hymns* 713.
31 John Fawcett, 1782, *Psalms and Hymns* 703.
32 George Rawson, 1857, *Psalms and Hymns* 716.

F. W. Gotch, later President of Bristol College.[33] The issue had become a critical one, not only because of theological debate at home, but because of the success of overseas missions and the need to translate the scriptures into other languages. To immerse or not to immerse was the vital question, an equation normally being drawn in the nineteenth century between immersion and a believing candidate, and sprinkling and infancy.

Up to 1827 the Bible Society gave frequent help to the Serampore missionaries, supporting about fifteen versions employing immersionist language, work which played an important part in establishing the early reputation of the Bible Society. Then a complaint emerged from paedobaptist members of the Calcutta auxiliary, which already supported versions employing the terms *sprinkle* or *pour*. In 1833 the Bible Society replied to a request from BMS missionaries for help with a Bengali New Testament: 'That this committee would cheerfully afford assistance to the missionaries connected with the Baptist Missionary Society in their translation of the Bengalee New Testament provided the Greek terms related to baptism be rendered either according to the principle adopted by the translators of the English Authorized Version by a word derived from the original, or by such terms as may be considered unobjectionable by other denominations of Christians comprising the Bible Society.'[34]

Because of the inability of the BMS missionaries to comply with this requirement, help was not forthcoming, to the disgust of many Baptists, especially since aid was continued, inconsistently, to some agencies which produced versions which did not transcribe but used the language of pouring or sprinkling. How many Greek words needed to be transcribed rather than translated to keep peace among Christians, Hinton wondered. According to Dr Wenger, the rules of translation which were used against the Baptists had originally been drawn up to combat the danger of the Bible Society patronising so-

33 F. W. Gotch, *A Critical Examination of the reading of the word Baptizo*, 1841.

34 Cited by Perkin, *op.cit.*, p.126, from J. H. Hinton, *Collected Works*, 7 vols. 1864-7, III, p.490.

called critical versions, 'believed to be tinged with neology' - that is, German reductionist theology.[35] In the event, salt was rubbed into the wound because the Calcutta Auxiliary accepted a translation into Portuguese, 'full of the gravest doctrinal error because it was acceptable to the Romish clergy'. Joseph Hughes, a fellow Baptist and Secretary of the Bible Society in London, leant on Carey to no avail. John Dyer of the BMS wrote to Joseph Kinghorn that he would rather forfeit Bible Society aid than accede: for 'it is selling the truth for the sake of gold'. The Bible Society, of course, could not win: it was bound to lose either the services of skilled translators in India or influential paedobaptists not only in Calcutta, but more importantly in London, and especially upon the Bishops' bench. So far as the Bible Society was concerned, and the American Bible Society followed suit, the Serampore translations as such fell under an interdict, though with permission they were circulated by the Bible Society in an amended version with baptism transcribed rather than translated.

By now the issue had ceased to be one of linguistic scholarship, having become effectively and practically a serious breach in the unity of both mission and translation work. Repeated Baptist attempts to seek a compromise were all refused, notwithstanding the fact that the vast majority of independent lexicons rendered βαπτιζω by 'immerse'. This lead to the formation of a separate (Baptist) Bible Translation Society to aid the Indian mission. For much of the nineteenth century this schism was perpetuated, with ongoing hurt being expressed in Baptist circles, especially since Roman Catholic versions were still circulated, and others containing doubtful translations, such as that used in Mongolia which used a word for God which denoted 'Buddha and no one else'.[36] The problem was for the most part confined to India, for in China the translators left a number of critical words blank, allowing each agency to insert therein 'translations most

35 ed. E. B. Underhill, *Baptists and the Bible Society: Sermons preached to the BFBS in relation to the Versions of Scripture prepared by Baptist missionaries*, 1868, p.iii.

36 *ibid.*, p.ix.

comfortable to its conscience'.[37] In Europe, by contrast, the Bible Society sponsored a number of immersionist versions.

Not all Baptists were happy with this schism in Bible promotion, especially as a younger generation grew up, unaware of its history but very aware of the lack of unity manifested, in what some called 'exaggerated sectarianism'.[38] This provoked jibes from other Christians, as that from Dr John Eadie, a United Presbyterian much interested in the revising of the English version of the New Testament, that the Baptists were the only Christians who insisted on having a denominational Bible. T. V. Tymms, later Principal of Rawdon, defended the denomination against such charges of 'unparalleled selfishness' by arguing that in this respect the Baptist conscience was supported by 'many ancient versions not to mention the originals': 'Happy is the denomination which can insist on having its own Bible when it can do so by insisting that the ancient oracles of God shall be given in their integrity, and without being tampered with in the least degree.'[39] Tymms argued that not to translate βαπτιζω was an affront to the population of India, for that was to fail to provide them with a written standard as an external authority by which they could judge the spoken teaching of the missionaries; not to translate produced an alien word which necessarily drove the reader to seek advice from a missionary, in which case the two authorities became one. Against charges of sectarianism, he pleaded that a 'Christian union based on a conspiracy to hide a word of our Master's instructions' was not a union worth upholding.[40]

As late as the late 1870s an appeal was made to the Earl of Shaftesbury to secure a change in Bible Society rules to allow whole-

37 *ibid.*, p.x.

38 T. V. Tymms, Baptist Translation Society Occasional Paper No.II, 1877, p.2; cf. T. G. Rooke, *Doctrine and Theology of Christian Baptism*, 1894, p.2: 'Nor can I quite understand why so many Baptists persist still in their quarrel with the British and Foreign Bible Society on account of this untranslated word'. Rather he saw it as provoking questions inviting explanation.

39 Tymms, *op.cit.*, p.2.

40 *ibid*, p.5.

hearted Baptist participation. The Bible Society did help with Old Testament circulation, and made a gift of paper for Alfred Saker to use in the Cameroons. This hardly mollified Baptist sensibilities: H. C. Leonard of Bournemouth wrote: 'I cannot but think that the spectacle thus exhibited of the Bible Society presenting blank paper to Africa and Old Testaments to Asia is not worthy of the history and catholic claims of the Society. At the same time it is not easy to see the justice of giving to Romanists the aid refused, with small exception, to Baptists, especially when the corruption of the Romanish, and the purity of the Baptist version are generally admitted.'[41] Some movement was made by the Bible Society when in 1883 it allowed a marginal note to accompany *βαπτιζω*, indicating that some had translated this immerse, but this proved insufficient to reconcile the Baptist interest. Faithfulness to principle, with deep regret, caused many Baptists to separate from other Christians in joint action to distribute the scriptures.

When the linguistic arguments were deemed to be lost to the immersionists, then other arguments were employed against Baptist practice. Apostolic practice should not determine the practice of nineteenth-century Christians living in temperate climates, who had also to take cognizance of arguments of seemliness, the strength of officiants, and the availability of replacement clothing.

As immersion was identified with believer's baptism, so generally sprinkling was identified with infant baptism. In attacking this Baptists often espoused a higher theology of baptism than in their defences of their own position. Thus the claim that infant baptism 'corrupts the gospel by destroying the spiritual condition of the church', and that by contrast 'believer's baptism was originally the borderline of the church',[42] clearly assigned to baptism an initiatory function. Dismissing the claims of the children of believing parents to baptism, Washington Wilks counterclaims, 'Christian baptism is the

41 Baptist Translation Society Occasional Paper No.III, n.d. (?1878), p.5.

42 T. B. Crowest, *Sprinkling the Giant Error of the Professing Church of Christ*, 1845, p.21.

external initiatory ordinance into the visible church of Christ; so most conclusively I argue that none are scripture subjects for this initiatory ordinance, but such as are right subjects for the visible church into which baptism initiates.'[43] Wilks thus articulated high claims, even if the controlling category remained that of ordinance.

THE BURIAL OF THE UNBAPTIZED

What were the practical consequences for those whose baptismal doctrine opposed that upheld by the incumbent of the local parish church? Some clergy argued that they could not legally provide prayer-book burial for anyone who had not been baptized. This only served to sustain much sub-Christian folk prejudice as to the ultimate destination of the unbaptized. T. G. Rooke, Principal of Rawdon, gave testimony, as late as 1887, to the superstition that the unbaptized dead 'are supposed to wander disconsolately around the gloomy confines of the unseen world, or to be shut up in a dreary place of inaction and fruitless longing, called a "limbo", or even to be cast into the place of torment by reason of the sin and condemnation of our first parent, Adam.' 'I have, myself,' he continued, 'met with clear proofs of this lasting, astonishing and melancholy ignorance of the first principles of the Gospel of God's grace among the dwellers in some rural parts of England. The damp and nettle-grown corner of the churchyard in which such unbaptized infants are buried is often popularly known as "Hell's Corner", being the portion not supposedly made holy by episcopal consecration.'[44]

Isaiah Birt also testified to the superstitious regard for infant baptism that led to the denial of consecrated ground for the burial of unbaptized infants. Indeed it was this kind of hostility that first provoked him to write on baptism, when he discovered that a rector who denied him use of the churchyard was in the habit of breaking the

---

43 W. Wilks, *Jazer, by Mr Joseph Irons, in Defence of Infant Sprinkling, Dissected and Disproved*, 1826, p.19.

44 T. G. Rooke, *op.cit.*, pp.48-9.

basin that held the baptismal water after each ceremony, lest it subsequently be profaned by common use.[45]

It is, therefore, not difficult to comprehend why Baptists suffered more from churchyard controversies with the established church than other dissenters. The cases spanned the century: some of the more famous were those at Shrewsbury in 1814, Eatington (Warwickshire) in 1829, and much later at Akenham in Suffolk in 1878, and at Ruthin in North Wales in 1884.[46] Sir Morton Peto, a Baptist MP, took up this issue from the late 1860s, introducing a series of bills to open churchyards to dissenters and to allow them use of their own burial services there. Legislation was not secured until 1880. The first funeral under the new Act was conducted by the minister of Penge Baptist Church in the churchyard at Beckenham.[47]

Early in the century, baptism was also seen by many clergymen as a precondition to marriage, which many still sought in the parish church. Perhaps the most celebrated case of discrimination here was when J. H. Newman refused to marry Miss Jubber, the unbaptized daughter of one of his Baptist parishioners.[48]

BAPTISTS AT THE TABLE[49]

The critical years of civic uncertainty that took British society from the ending of the Napoleonic Wars in 1815 to the Reform Crisis of the 1830s saw the Baptists critically engaged in the communion controversy, yet another series of debates showing how their traditional puritanism accommodated itself to the ongoing vital forces of the Evangelical Revival. The debate was not about the nature of sacrifice or the real presence or the mode of consecration of the bread

---

45 *Baptist Magazine* (hereafter *BM*), 1838, p.198.

46 B. L. Manning, *The Protestant Dissenting Deputies*, 1952, pp.286-288, 301, 325.

47 P. T. Marsh, *The Victorian Church in Decline*, 1969, pp.243, 251-63; Owen Chadwick, *The Victorian Church*, II, 1970, pp.206-7.

48 Owen Chadwick, *The Victorian Church*, I, 1966, pp.63, 116-7.

49 Under this title, Michael Walker, *Baptists at the Table* (Baptist Historical Society, 1992) gives fuller coverage to the area of the following section; to Dr Walker's study indebtedness is acknowledged.

and the wine, but about the terms of communion, language which foreshadows a far more radical debate amongst the Congregationalists in the 1870s. For them the question turned upon the necessary agreement in doctrinal essentials for Christian communion in the most general terms to be established. For Baptists, at the beginning of the century, the question was whether baptism as a believer was a necessary pre-condition for fellowship at the Lord's Table. The dispute referred back to Abraham Booth's *Apology for Baptists* of 1778, which was the starting point for Robert Hall's *On Terms of Communion* (1815), advocating an open table; this duly provoked Joseph Kinghorn of Norwich to reply with *Baptism a Term of Communion at the Lord's Supper* (1816). There was a further round of argumentation with Robert Hall replying with *A Reply to the Revd Joseph Kinghorn, being a Further Vindication of Free Communion* (1818), and Kinghorn responding with *A Defence of Baptism a Term of Communion in Answer to the Revd Robert Hall's Reply* (1840).

The arguments hardly met. Robert Hall, in advocating open communion, was seeking from a mission situation to express the unity of experience that had come out of the Evangelical Revival. Kinghorn, by contrast, was concerned to protect correctness of church order. Thus Hall argued:

> The right of rejecting those whom Christ has received; of refusing the communion of eminently holy men, on account of unessential differences of opinion is not the avowed tenet of any sect or community in Christendom, with the exception of the majority of the Baptists.[50]

Exclusion from the table Hall reckoned to be tantamount to excommunication, and for one part of the church to excommunicate another part which was recognized to contain true followers of Christ was to favour schism over against unity. For Hall the problem was that he quite clearly repudiated all forms of infant baptism:[51]

50 Robert Hall, 'On terms of communion', 1815, *Works*, III, 1858, p.57.
51 *ibid.*, p.77.

therefore, those of other confessions had to be welcomed at Baptist communion tables as if they had not been baptized. They were to be welcomed on the basis first and foremost of their 'union to Christ . . . formed by faith',[52] secondly as those who had manifested the gifts of the Spirit in their Christian living, and thirdly because of the magnanimous toleration embraced by the invitation offered by open-communion Baptist churches.

This clearly reflected the ongoing Baptist emphasis that the thing signified was necessarily more important than the sign which manifested it, a position believed to be in the tradition of prophetic preference for mercy rather than sacrifice. This meant that so far as baptism was concerned saving faith always had the logical priority. Hence the deduction, in Hall's mind, that faith, and faith alone, was the essential prerequisite for table fellowship. This effectively set aside the traditional order in the church that baptism should precede communion, for which Hall argued there was no scriptural requirement. Thus Hall, in his eagerness to secure unity at the communion table, was in danger of downgrading the importance of the sacraments within Baptist life, for the only way discerned of opening the table to all in union with Christ was to downgrade the significance of baptism. Hall moved all too quickly, according to Walker, 'from the perfectly proper observation that baptism was not a condition of salvation to the far more dubious argument that baptism was not essential to church order'.[53] Hall made his position quite clear: 'While we acknowledge baptism to be a duty, we do not invariably demand it as a preliminary to church fellowship'.[54] Hall's devaluation of baptism was at variance with his own understanding of communion:

> To consider the Lord's supper . . . as a mere commemoration of [our Lord's death and passion] is to entertain a very

52 *ibid.*

53 Walker, *op.cit.*, p.98.

54 Robert Hall, 'A reply to the Revd Joseph Kinghorn, being a further vindication of the practice of free communion', 1818, *Works*, III, p.236.

> inadequate view of it. If we credit St Paul, it is also a *federal rite* in which, in token of our reconciliation with God, we eat and drink in his presence; it is a feast upon a sacrifice, by which we become partakers at the altar, not less really, though in a manner more elevated and spiritual, than those who under the ancient economy presented their offerings in the temple. In this ordinance the cup is a spiritual participation of the Word, the bread of the body, of the crucified Saviour.[55]

Hall's reductionist view of the symbolism of baptism was clearly challenged by Kinghorn.

Kinghorn and those who supported him, like Joseph Ivimey, William Button, William Norton, William Newman and George Pritchard, believed that they were defending truth: open the table to all regardless of the baptism they had experienced and how would the distinctive Baptist insight into the need for believing faith to precede baptism be preserved? The purity of such views faced the closed-communionists with the difficulty 'of excluding the greater part of Christendom from communion on the grounds that it was unbaptized'.[56] In refusing communion to others, the closed communionists, Robert Hall argued, were like the Roman Catholics setting themselves up as the only true church. It was clearly difficult for the closed communionists to acknowledge that the members of other denominations had every right to expect eternal communion with God but could not find that fellowship at a Baptist communion table. So Kinghorn questioned:

> Is baptism to be thrown into the shade as a mere ceremonial, to make way for another institution which is equally ceremonial? The direct effect of mixed communion, as far as I can discover, justifies this expostulation. The Lord thought fit to appoint a ritual observance, as the declaration of our trust in him, and subjection to him; and thus obedience to one rite, opens the way for attention to another. Nor can any object,

55 Hall, 'On Terms of Communion', 1815, *Works* III, pp.45ff.

56 Walker, *op.cit.*, p.49.

> that men are debarred from communion on account of a rite, when communion itself is supported by ritual observances.[57]

The close communionists defended a higher view of the sacraments than that to which Hall by default was driven. As relations across denominational boundaries opened up, so the pressures for open communion - and later open membership - developed. In such a context it was all too easy for the low view of the sacraments Hall had come to support to become widely pervasive, especially as it accorded with evangelical antipathy to a revived catholicism, which made Baptists far too negative and reactive in their thinking about the sacraments, now more frequently referred to as ordinances, although all too often conceived in such minimalist terms as even Zwingli would not own.

A correspondent to the closed-communionist *Primitive Church Magazine* for April 1844 rightly perceived that neither side had logic wholly with them:

> Each brother is compelled by the stern necessity of the case to depart from the practice of the primitive churches. The Strict Baptist refuses to receive those whom he knows are christians indeed. This the primitive churches did not. The Open Baptist receives those whom he knows are unbaptized. This the primitive churches did not. Therefore neither can plead exact conformity to apostolic example; both are driven away from the primitive practice - one sacrifices visible unity, the other ritual uniformity.[58]

---

57 Kinghorn, *Baptism a Term of Communion at the Lord's Supper*, 1811, p.165; see also William Newman, *Baptism an Indispensable Pre-Requisite to Communion at the Lord's Table*, 1805, p.10.

58 *Primitive Church Magazine*, April 1844, p.187.

CONTINUING CONTROVERSY

Some churches adopted open communion without controversy (e.g. Queen's Road, Coventry[59]). That C. H. Spurgeon came to advocate open communion in combination with closed membership helped many churches to move in that direction.[60] Elsewhere there was great controversy, notably at St Mary's, Norwich, Kinghorn's church, which after his death appointed two successive open-communionists, William Brock and George Gould. Their preaching not unexpectedly attracted a wider group of adherents who did not subscribe to the older, restrictive views. Three times during Brock's pastorate the issue came to the church meeting: in 1845, whilst retaining the existing closed celebration of communion, he introduced an open celebration once a month on a Sunday afternoon. Under his successor, George Gould, those who wished the terms of communion to remain closed took the case before Chancery where the Master of the Rolls gave judgment in favour of Gould, noting that no necessary equation could be drawn between Particular Baptist doctrine and the practice of strict communion, indeed historical precedent arguably supported an open table. He noted that in any case Gould continued a closed celebration so that those who conscientiously dissented from open communion were not deprived of the sacrament. He also understood the Particular Baptist denomination as affirming the jurisdictional discretion of each local congregation, whilst arguing that opening communion did not constitute any fundamental change of practice and did not, therefore, involve any breach of trust.

The first minister of the Avenue Church at Southend-on-Sea, John Wilson, announced in March 1881 his desire of inviting to communion 'all those who love the Lord Jesus Christ', including those who had never been baptized, even in infancy. A leading deacon took the view that the limits of the invitation should be to baptized believers, even

---

59 Irene Morris, *Three Hundred Years of Baptist Life in Coventry*, 1925, p.25, cited Walker, *op.cit.*, p.35.

60 B. R. White, 'Open and Closed Membership among English and Welsh Baptists', *BQ* 24, 1972, pp.330-34.

though he did not wish to exclude those baptized in infancy. A split took place and the minister with twenty-six members left to establish a new church.[61]

Other matters of concern included the legitimacy of lay presidency, some churches early in the century denying themselves communion in the absence of an ordained minister.[62] Because the Lord's Supper was seen as a sacrament of the church, there was objection to communion being celebrated for any group less than the whole church, or for large bodies such as associations or union assemblies. Such fears notwithstanding, communion was first celebrated at a Baptist Union Assembly in 1867. Should communion, increasingly celebrated with non-alcoholic wine,[63] be held irregularly, monthly, or weekly, as was generally the practice amongst Baptists in Scotland? In the 1840s several associations called for a consideration of weekly communion as apostolic practice.[64] Weekly communion was certainly Spurgeon's personal practice but in this he seems to have been less influential on his fellow Baptists than in other areas.

Exclusion from the table was a principal device for disciplining miscreant church members. The theology of such a restriction is arguably as open to objection as the exclusion of divorced persons from receiving the elements in the eucharist in the Roman Catholic Church today, namely a denial of the means of grace to those most in

---

61 D. J. Jeremy, J. Barfield and K. S. Newman, *A Century of Grace: the history of Avenue Baptist Church, Southend-on-Sea, 1876-1976*, 1982, pp.10-16.

62 As, for example, at Fuller's Kettering church, where communion was not celebrated during and after Fuller's absence during his final illness; his assistant J. K. Hall was not ordained until the November following Fuller's death in May, and only then was communion recommenced. Walker, *op.cit.*, pp.131-2, on the evidence of the Diary of George Wallis.

63 Temperance enthusiasts succeeding in persuading their churches to convert from alcoholic to unfermented wine from the second half of the 1830s onwards, but the process was slow. The *Freeman* carried an advertisement for Irish Whiskey into the 1870s, and in the late 1880s the debate was still in process. Walker, *op.cit.*, pp.149-55.

64 Walker, *op.cit.*, pp.145-6.

need of such succour. On the other hand, if communion was not to be seen as a means of grace the need for exclusion is even more puzzling. Be that as it may, Walker notes that, whereas suspension from communion had been used as a means of discipline in the early nineteenth century, by the end of the century absence from communion had become a principal occasion for discipline.

SPURGEON AND CLIFFORD

Whereas Clifford to the end of his life lived very much within the councils of the Baptist Union and Spurgeon was wholly estranged from it at his death, it was Spurgeon who upheld the traditional teaching and practice of the denomination, and Clifford who promoted dangerously minimalist views of church and sacraments. Both men were concerned at the revival of catholicism in both its Roman and Anglo-Catholic variants, but 'whereas Spurgeon had renounced Catholicism without conceding what was of theological importance to his own beliefs, Clifford here left himself with an emasculated notion of the church', with the sacraments conceived of as mere symbols.[65] By contrast, Spurgeon is very much more positive:

> Here, at the communion table, we are at the centre of truth, and at the well-head of consolation. Now we enter the holy of holies, and come to the most sacred meeting-place between our souls and God.[66]

He even explores a Baptist understanding of real presence:

> The priest who celebrates mass tells us that he believes in the real presence, but we reply, 'Nay, you believe in knowing Christ after the flesh, and in that sense the only real presence is in heaven; but we firmly believe in the real presence of Christ which is spiritual, and yet certain'. By spiritual we do not mean unreal; in fact, the spiritual takes the lead in real-ness to spiritual men. I believe in the true and real presence of

---

65 Walker, *op.cit.*, p.185.

66 C. H. Spurgeon, *Till He Come*, 1894, p.148.

> Jesus with His people, such presence has been real to my spirit. Lord Jesus, Thou Thyself has visited me. As surely as the Lord Jesus came really as to His flesh to Bethlehem and Calvary, so surely does He come really by His Spirit to His people in the hours of their communion with Him.[67]

Spurgeon's exploration of the union that takes place between believer and church in the taking of bread and wine in communion is again expressed in language which is daringly concrete:

> No power upon earth can henceforth take from me the piece of bread which I have just now eaten, it has gone where it will be made up into blood, and nerve, and muscle, and bone. That drop of wine has coursed through my veins, and is part and parcel of my being. So he that takes Jesus by faith to be his Saviour has chosen the good part which shall not be taken away from him.[68]

Whereas in many matters Spurgeon was massively influential, in the theology of communion Clifford seems to have both reflected the theology of the denomination and sealed its thinking for several generations to come.

---

67 *ibid.*, p.17.
68 *ibid.*, p.319.

4

MINISTRY AND MINISTERIAL TRAINING

Early in its work the Faith and Order Movement sought agreement to six marks of an authentic church: 'the possession and acknowledgement of the Word of God as given in Holy Scripture and interpreted by the Holy Spirit to the Church and to the individual; the profession of faith in God as He is incarnate and revealed in Christ; the acceptance of Christ's commission to preach the Gospel to every creature; the observance of the Sacraments; a ministry for the pastoral office, the preaching of the Word, and administration of the Sacraments; a fellowship in prayer, in worship, in all the means of grace, in the pursuit of holiness, and in the service of man'.[1] With the exception of the fifth point, the Baptist Union Council was prepared to endorse this statement, but of the fifth it said: 'We cannot agree that the ministry, as commonly understood, is essential to the existence of a true Christian Church, though we believe a ministry is necessary for its highest effectiveness. We think of the function of ministry in terms of leadership rather than of government and discipline'.[2] Such an aberrant position, Payne argues, was not the fruit of the whole Baptist heritage, which until the beginning of the nineteenth century retained a high view of ministry, but of certain developments within that century, particularly a reaction to a renewed Catholicism which led Baptists to see sacerdotalism as much as sacramentalism as one of the great evils of the age.[3] There were even churches which dispensed with a separated ministry - the most famous example was the People's Chapel in Birmingham[4] - but they were exceptional.

---

1 E. A. Payne, *Fellowship of Believers*, 1952 edition, pp.38-9, citing H. N. Bate, *Faith and Order*, 1927, p.464.

2 *Report of the Baptist Union Council*, 1930, pp.38-9.

3 W. T. Whitley, *Church, Ministry and Sacraments in the New Testament*, 1903, p.244.

4 A S. Langley, *Birmingham Baptists*, n.d. but 1939, pp.107ff.

At the end of the eighteenth century and well into the nineteenth, because of the poverty of their congregations, many ministers had to supplement their stipends by other employment. A number opened schools; more famously Carey combined the pastoral office with shoemaking.[5] In Newcastle-under-Lyme Thomas Thompson ran a cotton factory, the place where the congregation was first gathered for worship (1821).[6] In neighbouring Hanley L. J. Abington, a product of the Northamptonshire Association, was a ceramic designer and a partner in a pottery manufactory with the Ridgways, pillars of the Methodist New Connexion.[7] Payne pays tribute to the ministerial achievements of such men, denying that this was an attempt to secure 'ministry on the cheap', or that it was the fruit of the ministerial office being 'carelessly regarded'.[8]

THE CALL TO MINISTRY

Christian ministry as exercised amongst the Baptists may be seen to embrace a series of partnerships, not least because ministry is perceived first as that of the whole church rather than the separated ministry alone. In establishing a call to ministry, a balance needed to be struck between congregational perception and individual conviction. At the beginning of the nineteenth century the former played a rather larger part than in the denomination of recent years - it was deemed to be the responsibility of the congregation to survey all its members and to explore which of them had gifts that might be developed for ministry. The prime requirement for Baptist ministers was to have a personal experience of conversion. K. D. Brown notes that Baptist candidates for ministry offered very much clearer personal testimony (by a factor of 4 or 5) to such an experience than either their

---

5 Whitley, *History of the British Baptists* (hereafter *HBB*), 1923, p.152.

6 J. H. Y. Briggs, *A Hundred Years and More: Baptists in Newcastle-under-Lyme*, 1972, p.8.

7 Anon, *Personal Recollections of the Late Leonard James Abington of Hanley, Staffordshire*, Hanley, 1888.

8 Payne, *Fellowship of Believers*, p.51.

Wesleyan or Congregational peers.[9] Perhaps the difference is not surprising, given the nature of believer's baptism. Thereafter the call to ministry was to be tested by the local congregation. Samuel Ruston of Hamsterley in County Durham was first called by the congregation 'to exercise his talents before the church alone on the Lord's day evenings'. That accomplished, 'the whole church unanimously agreed to call him to the work of the ministry'. There followed a special service at which 'the church's call of him to the ministry, to preach the word and baptize those who were proper subjects, under the direction of the church, and as eligible to the pastoral office, when called to it, was announced'.[10]

Seymour Price's history of Upton Chapel contains further examples. John Rance, who confessed to swearing and cursing during a reckless youth, was reluctant to undertake ministry because he was the proprietor of a successful business in Newgate Street, an argument which did not convince his fellow members, who voted that he should preach before them on three Monday evenings 'after strangers are withdrawn'. Rance was still not convinced but his fellow members were persistent and eventually he undertook the trial preaching. Seven months after the matter was first raised, on 17 July 1797, the members resolved:'That we as a Church are so satisfied that Mr Rance has received gifts from the Lord which through a divine blessing may be useful to immortal souls, that we request him to exercise those talents publicly wherever the Lord in the course of his providence may give him opportunity'. Fifteen months later he was called by the infant church at Shore Place, Hackney, to be its pastor, having previously sold his business. Thomas King, a china retailer, persisted longer in maintaining his business interests: it was seven

9 K. D. Brown, *A Social History of the Nonconformist Ministry in England and Wales, 1800-1930*, Oxford 1988, Table 1.11, pp.51-2: 1860-1909: Congregationalist cases 17, Wesleyan 20, Baptist 79.

10 Payne, *op.cit.*, p.46, citing *Baptist Annual Register* (hereafter *BAR*), II, 1794-7, p.483.

years after the members had first perceived ministerial gifts that he accepted the pastorate of Mill Street, Bedford, in 1816.

Others were ordained to more adventurous ministries. C. H. Hosken went to Clonmel with the Baptist Irish Society, riding over 4,000 miles a year in discharge of his duties. Subsequently he preached in Holland before being sent in 1841 by the BMS to work in Honduras. Thereafter he had pastorates in the USA before returning to England, and in his Crayford pastorate provided oversight of the first student Spurgeon accepted for ministerial training.

Not all investigations of gifts at Upton Chapel were positive. In the summer of 1815 this minute is recorded:

> That it does not appear to us that Br. R. Upton is distinguished with such talents as make it our duty to encourage him to devote himself to the Christian Ministry; nevertheless as we believe that many godly men, whose talents are not equal to the full discharge of ministerial duties, frequently speak in suitable situations to the edification of their hearers, we advice Br Upton for the present to follow their example.

Notwithstanding this unpromising beginning, three years later he was inducted to the pastorate of the Kensington Gravel Pits Church (later Westbourne Grove).

The initiative in these cases was with the church rather than the individual. Some thought the church's role exaggerated, believing it 'a manifest infringement of Christian liberty'. The church expressed a very clear contrary view in its Circular Letter of 1806, 'On the duty of Churches to encourage the exercise of Spiritual Gifts':

> It is not sufficient that individual Members press after those things which may enable them to do good to others; the Churches must become nurseries to their gifts. Bold ignorant and conceited characters may be found, it is true, who need something very different from encouragement, but men of modesty and worth will not push themselves forward; they must be sought after, and brought forth, or you may expect them to pass their valuable lives in obscurity. Every man that hath received a gift is commanded to minister the same as a

> good steward of the manifold grace of God, but no man is a competent judge of his own gifts . . . Hence it becomes the duty of Churches, whilst they show a proper disregard to those who aspire after things to which they are incompetent, to watch the growth of Talents in worthy characters, and encourage them.[11]

THE EVANGELICAL REVIVAL AND THE NEW ACADEMIES

Critical as was the call to the pastoral ministry, to supplement calling with training became increasingly necessary in the new industrial world of the nineteenth century. Yet nineteenth-century Baptists could never wholly forget the story of Arian and Socinian decline in the eighteenth century, and that memory served to foster a suspicion of the intellectual world. In fact, the history of Baptist colleges during the century was relatively peaceful: in so far as the denomination was troubled by religious controversy, the controversy was for the most part in the churches, not the colleges, where such matters were handled with the utmost discretion.

It is tempting to say that the colleges were essentially the fruit of the Evangelical Revival and that would be broadly true, save that those who have studied the Bristol situation increasingly emphasize the evangelical continuity of the West Country Particular Baptists in contrast with the prevailing heavy scholarship of high Calvinism in the capital. Even in Bristol, 1770 marked something of a new beginning, with the launching of the Bristol Education Society. The General Baptists had founded what was to become their Midland College a few years earlier in 1787. These were followed a generation later in 1804 by the Baptist Education Society that fathered Stepney, and the Northern Education Society, the parent of Horton-Rawdon.

These new institutions of the Particular Baptists were the fruit of a changed theology. The moderate Calvinism of Andrew Fuller was an important intellectual restatement of the tradition, symbolic of the

---

11 S. J. Price, *Upton: The Story of One Hundred and Fifty Years, 1785-1935*, 1935, pp.70-82.

new thinking which reflected a changed attitude amongst Baptists and made them look again at their doctrines of ministry, the church and Christian mission.

The French historian, Elie Halévy, draws attention to the decay of the older academies in the latter decades of the eighteenth century and the emergence 'of new schools of another type, orthodox and pietist'.[12] Deryck Lovegrove writes of 'A new generation of evangelical academies . . . theologically grounded in moderate, evangelical Calvinism and in consequence displaying a strongly practical bias, the new seminaries (the term itself indicates their divergence from the earlier pattern) afforded regular opportunities for practice in evangelical preaching and encouraged the growth of personal devotion'.[13] The model was the Countess of Huntingdon's foundation at Trevecca: 'the interest in itinerancy shown by the long-established Baptist academy at Bristol, and by the new foundations at Bradford and Stepney, owed as much to the demonstrable success of Whitefieldite theological education exemplified in Trevecca as it did to any personal insight of Baptist leaders such as Andrew Fuller, Hugh and Caleb Evans, and Robert Hall senior'.[14] These Baptist institutions, however, did not generally reflect the anti-intellectualism that at times seemed to threaten Trevecca. Even at Bristol though, as sympathetic a commentator as Joseph Hughes, first secretary of the Bible Society, reckoned that, as a theological college, the institution was deficient both 'in system and in stimulants'.[15] Part of the problem was constituency demand, still suspicious of the intellectualism of the old academies and its associated heterodoxy, and still opposed to the concept of 'man-made' ministers.[16]

---

12 E. Halévy, *England in 1815*, revised edition 1949, pp.418-9.

13 D. Lovegrove, *Established Church, Sectarian People: Itinerancy and the Transformation of English Dissent 1780-1830*, 1988, pp.67-8.

14 Lovegrove, *op.cit.*, p.69.

15 J. Liefchild, *Memoir of the late Revd Joseph Hughes*, 1835, p.39, as cited by Lovegrove, *op.cit.*, p.76.

16 Lovegrove, *op.cit.*, p.67.

Students at the new academies were put to work as evangelists and church planters, making the college not just a place of training but an immediate ministerial resource effective in the life of the churches. As early as 1773 the Bristol Education Society organized a Gospel Mission into Cornwall with Benjamin Francis as its itinerant, following the injunction of Caleb Evans 'that the society's work was not only to offer basic theological education but to encourage missionaries to preach the gospel wherever providence opens a door for it'.[17] In the north, the work had been pioneered by John Fawcett at Hebden Bridge, who educated a series of ministerial candidates in his own home, ran a distinguished private academy, and in 1773 sought, with the encouragement of Hugh Evans, to establish a northern college but to no avail. It was to be more than thirty years before the Northern Education Society (1804) got off the ground with William Steadman as principal, whose ideal a punster has said was always for 'evangelism *steadied* by education'.[18]

Steadman, sound in his Calvinism but warm and energetic as a Christian evangelist, was more concerned with training preachers than educating scholars, and was little worried when itinerancy and student pastorates interfered with disciplined study. The Northern Education Society was not only training ministers for the church, but provided the northern counties with stormtroopers to engage in the immediate task of itinerancy. When Benjamin Godwin became Steadman's coadjutor, Godwin was frustrated by student absences at weekends to allow them to travel to distant preaching stations, as also by their studies being interrupted by invitations to distant congregations for four to six weeks at a time. Steadman for his part was loath to reject any such invitations. Nothing daunted, Godwin set about repairing

17 Raymond Brown, *The English Baptists of the Eighteenth Century*, 1987, p.115; N. Moon, *Education for Ministry: Bristol Baptist College 1679-1979*, Bristol 1979, p.20; Lovegrove, *op.cit.*, pp.3, 70, 79.

18 A. C. Underwood, *A History of the English Baptists*, 1947, p.176.

their general education. 'The age', he confessed, 'was advancing and the ministry to meet its wants must not be stationary.'[19]

Holding the balance between education and evangelism was to prove very difficult. At first indifferent to intellectual attainment, the new evangelical academies moved fairly swiftly to a more traditional academic outlook, shedding on the way something of their concern for aggressive evangelism. This happened partly to meet the needs of a better educated society, partly because prosperous urban and suburban churches demanded well-educated and respectable ministers able to communicate the eternal message in language and concept meaningful to the new industrial world - to the employers, managers and skilled artisans rather than the serried ranks of the poor, the unskilled and those only partially employed. The demands of the new world were constantly underlined. Speaking at Stepney College in 1812, John Ryland was sure that 'an illiterate though pious ministry must be exposed to needless contempt'. Isaac Mann made the same point in 1829: ministers who failed to keep up with their reading would lose their congregations to those who exercised 'a more enlightened ministry'. At the Rawdon Jubilee celebrations in 1854 Benjamin Godwin warned that, whilst spiritual qualifications must remain the vital qualifications for entry into the Christian ministry, in the enlightened age in which they lived these were not on their own sufficient, - 'qualifications of an intellectual character are needed, the power of both acquiring and imparting knowledge'.[20]

Robert Hall, in canvassing support for 'A new seminary intended to be established near London', thought it unnecessary to argue in defence of such a project, 'since whatever prejudices unfavourable to learning may have formerly prevailed in serious minds they appear to have subsided and christians in general admit the propriety of enlisting

---

19 Benjamin Godwin, Letter to his son, 8 December 1849, concerning the period 1822-5, in the Angus Library, Regent's Park College, Oxford.

20 Moon, *op.cit.*, p.28; D. Himbury, 'Training Baptist Ministers', *BQ* 21, 1966, p.343; J. O. Barrett, *Rawdon College: A Short History*, 1954, p.48; K. D. Brown, *A Social History . . .*, p.65.

literature in the service of religion', adding 'while we assert the absolute sufficiency of the Scriptures for every saving purpose it is impossible to deny the usefulness of the knowledge derived from books' in establishing its meaning. The 'light of revelation' was not opposed to the 'light of reason': 'the discoveries of the Bible, however supernatural, are addressed to the understanding', the only instrument available to appreciate divine revelation. Such advocacy was not intended to denigrate the sincerity of those who had effectively taught themselves to be able Christian ministers, nor was it intended to idolize education. 'An unconverted ministry we look upon as the greatest calamity that can befall the church; nor would we be supposed to insinuate . . . that education can ever be a proper substitute for native talent, much less for real piety'. The theology to be taught in the seminary was that of the Reformation, more precisely defined in terms of 'the privileges which distinguish the body of Christians denominated Particular or Calvinistic Baptists'. The new institution would disclaim 'all pretensions to that vaunted liberality which masks an indifference to revealed truth', but would extend 'cordial esteem to all who love the Lord Jesus Christ in sincerity'. The intention of the education provided was to produce pastors who could exercise an effective ministry amongst the higher classes whose salvation was no less important that that of the lower orders, and whose influence in society urgently needed to be christianized.[21]

THE DENOMINATIONAL COLLEGES IN THE LATER NINETEENTH CENTURY

Whereas the history of Congregational colleges in the nineteenth century is full of crises and controversies, the record in the Baptist colleges is far less troubled, though not without some minor disturbances. The open or closed table was an area of disagreement. William Newman, the first president of Stepney, like many Baptist leaders in the first half of the century, had been a closed

21 Robert Hall, 'Address on behalf of the Baptist Academic Institution at Stepney', *Works*, IV, 1866, pp.361-6.

communionist, pressing that view on the Stepney students till some rebelled against his leadership in something like a fully-blown academic strike![22] At Bristol in 1837 three students were dismissed and others censured in the conviction that 'no greater injury can be inflicted on the churches of Christ than to send among them ministers of unsettled principles and doubtful piety'. Eight years later the college parted company with the services of Edgar Huxtable, sometime a scholar of St John's College, Cambridge, who no longer held Baptist views of baptism and the church. He therefore resigned his tutorship to join the Church of England, subsequently becoming a canon of Salisbury Cathedral. Four students resigned with him. In 1872 there was concern at the views of a particular tutor (the layman, E. W. Catchpole), and the college committee resolved that 'the tutors be in general agreement with the vital doctrines entertained by the Baptist denomination'.[23] In the Report of Regent's Park College for 1871 the old spectre of Socinianism reasserted itself in the committee's 'dissatisfaction with the views of four of the students on some vital truths'. Two of the four resigned, whilst the courses of the other two were discontinued.[24]

The 'Down Grade Controversy', with all its potential peril, was not directed specifically at the colleges, even if those whose names were most often mentioned as suspect - J. G. Greenhough and James Thew - had both been trained at Rawdon under the principalship of S. G. Green. Some had hoped that the strict communionist, Henry Dowson, minister of Westgate, Bradford, and the college secretary, would have become Rawdon's principal on the retirement of James Acworth, but Green was chosen instead. Before long conservative

22 R. E. Cooper, *From Stepney to St Giles: The Story of Regent's Park College, 1810-1960*, 1960, pp.40-41.

23 Moon, *op.cit.*, pp.43, 46-7; L. G. Champion, 'The Contribution of Bristol College from 1770-1970', in L. G. Champion, et al., *The Bristol Education Society 1770-1970*, Bristol, n.d. but 1970, p.15.

24 Cooper, *op.cit.*, pp.63-4.

spirits were objecting to his 'latitudinarianism' and offering their support elsewhere.[25]

This led to the founding of what was to become the Manchester College on closed-communion principles. Its origins were in the separation of the North Western Association from the Lancashire and Cheshire Association in 1860. Six years later the new Association founded a college at Bury to train candidates of a strict-communionist persuasion.[26] Dowson was the first principal. The new institution sought to embrace distinctive principles: it was not to be resident (for that 'had some of the disadvantages of the Monkish system'), it eschewed 'classical, mathematical and secular studies', which all too often interfered with the study of theology, and the study of the ancient languages was not to be insisted upon. Language study was seen as unrealistic for the talents of many candidates: 'to take them from the loom, the plough, the shop or the counting house, unaccustomed to habits of study and only imperfectly acquainted with their own language' and expect them to master Latin, Greek and Hebrew was in a majority of cases 'simply an absurdity'. Such skills were not now necessary in view of the tools available for biblical exposition, though of course 'the principal book for the ministerial student is the English Bible'.

The syllabus still included English Literature and the written and spoken use of the English Language, General History, Geography, Natural Philosophy, Logic and Mental Science, as well as Theology, Church History, and Pastoral Studies. There was also a voluntary Latin class but no teaching in Greek or Hebrew. Beyond the academic course, practical work in city missions was presented as an essential part of the Bury training. In the event languages and

---

25 E. A. Payne, *The Baptist Union: A Short History*, 1958, p.130; A. C. Underwood, *op.cit.*, p.209.

26 Charles Rignal, *Manchester Baptist College, 1866-1916*, 1916, pp.36-7. The wastage rate of students who graduated from Manchester during the period of Rignal's study was 7.5%: of 200 alumni, 11 joined the Church of England, 2 the Wesleyans, and 1 each the Presbyterians and the Congregationalists.

classical literature could not be kept out and despite all the early protestations came to occupy a central place in the curriculum within a decade.[27]

The college moved to Manchester in 1873, and to a residential suite of buildings, which took the students out of the community once more. Spurgeon preached at the stone-laying, although he necessarily distanced himself from the total viewpoint of the college (for the principal of his own college was a paedobaptist), pointing to his own open communion views. He addressed himself to the accusation that the colleges were producing more men than pastoral vacancies required, but was not at all daunted by this for he believed they were training men to take charge of churches yet to be founded. The college developed strongly there not least because of its location and the development of healthy relationships first with Owen's College and then with the Victoria University in Manchester.[28]

Baptist colleges in England, whilst retaining their independence, generally developed university relationships. Beyond Oxford, Cambridge and Durham, the University of London[29] with its federal structure sponsored new institutions of higher education. When in 1884 the new Victoria University was established in the north, it too was a federal institution with a presence in Liverpool, Manchester and Leeds. The University of Wales, established in 1893, similarly embraced several separate University Colleges. Such structures made it easy for Baptist colleges both to retain their independent status and to affiliate to a university discipline. Accordingly, aided by the advocacy of the Unitarian, James Martineau, both Stepney and Bristol affiliated to London University in 1841, followed by Horton (Rawdon) in 1852.[30]

---

27 Rignal, *op.cit.*, pp.34, 48-51.

28 *ibid.*, pp.63-5, 150ff.

29 For the part played by Baptists in the founding of London University see chapter 10, Baptists and Education.

30 When Bristol became a separate university in 1909, the Baptist College affiliated to it, eventually helping to establish a faculty of theology. Similarly Rawdon affiliated to Leeds in 1915. Manchester College became active in the Theology

It was hoped that this might bring some relief to the small over-stretched staffs of the Baptist colleges as ministerial candidates would be able to attend the local university or university colleges for that contextual education in arts and sciences which was still considered very important, allowing the college staffs to concentrate exclusively on biblical work, theology, and pastoral studies. This never fully occurred, perhaps because too few candidates were able to matriculate (as required from 1858) to take advantage of the university courses, though some Baptist leaders acquired London BAs and MAs. Economies and improvements in teaching were, however, secured by co-operation with other Free Church colleges in the same location. Even so the tutorial resource remained pitifully slender so that the denomination's best academic talents were exhausted in teaching, and were not able to contribute as much as they might otherwise have done with their pens to wider debates. The pastorate as much as the college, therefore, became the likely location for Baptist contributions to scholarship: thus neither John Foster nor Andrew Fuller, John Howard Hinton nor Samuel Cox, J. H. Shakespeare nor John Clifford held college office, rather were they publishing pastors who wrote from the manse.

Relations with London University were not altogether easy because of that institution's exclusion of theology from its curriculum at the time of its foundation, the only exception being the 'First Scriptural Examination', available to BAs from 1839, and a 'Further Scripture Examination' available from 1840. The syllabus covered the Hebrew and Greek Scriptures, Butler's *Analogy* and Paley's *Evidences* and *Biblical History*. No questions were allowed on topics disputed by Christians and no answer provided by a student was to be objected to for 'peculiarity of doctrinal views'. From 1847, King's College London offered an associateship in theological studies (AKC) to those of its graduates who were successful in a special series of theological

---

Faculty of Manchester University, having first negotiated the inclusion of Hebrew, Greek Testament and Philosophy as subjects within its arts degrees; it was also involved in the teaching of a separate BD established in 1904.

papers, but for theological degrees as such students still had to go to Oxford, Cambridge, Durham or Scotland. S. W. Green argued that the University of London gave great benefits to the various theological colleges in general but not direct stimulation to theological studies in particular.[31]

This difficulty led to the Congregational colleges establishing a Senatus Academicus in 1879, which was swiftly subscribed to by many other theological institutions. Its function was to set an annual examination, both internally and externally examined, of approximately degree standard. After two years of study an ATS could be obtained, with a Fellowship (FTS) at the equivalent of Honours standard available after four years.[32] To all intents and purposes London University students were thereby taking the equivalent of theological examinations and many Baptist ministers boasted of such qualifications after their names. The ATS and FTS prepared the way for the establishment of the London Theological Faculty and of the Bachelor of Divinity degree in 1901, once more to be available 'without the imposition of any test or disqualification whatsoever'. The BD was available not only to internal students but also through the Council for External Students to those studying part-time. The same Council also made available a Certificate in Religious Knowledge for those not able to matriculate, a provision which was to prove most helpful to many Baptist students without formal secondary education.[33]

Candidates offering themselves for training for the Baptist ministry came from a very wide range of backgrounds and abilities. The absence of a decent standard of secondary education, not publicly available in England until 1903, was a major reason for the inability

---

31 E. A. Payne, 'The Development of Nonconformist Theological Education in the Nineteenth Century, with special reference to Regent's Park College', in ed. E. A. Payne, *Studies in History and Religion*, 1942, pp.229-53; W. T. Whitley, 'Our Theological Colleges', *BQ* 1, 1922, p.16.

32 ATS and FTS indicate respectively Associate and Fellow of the Theological Senate, i.e. the Senatus Academicus. *Baptist Handbook*, 1965, p.232.

33 ed. S.W. Green, *London Theological Studies*, 1911.

of the colleges to confine themselves to theology and pastoral training. Regent's Park College, London, academically the most prestigious of the Baptist colleges by the end of the century, had set itself the task of 'showing that between nonconformity and mental incapacity there is no inseparable relation as is sometimes taken for granted', but proved unable or unwilling to confine its entrants to those able to matriculate.

There were still many Baptist questions regarding the interrelatedness of academic achievement and potential for ministry in a society of many diverse educational, not to say spiritual, needs. This is clearly stated in a report on the work of the colleges presented to the Baptist Union Council in 1896: whilst not wanting to 'discourage any man who has received from the Lord the gifts and call which qualify for the work of a pastor and teacher', it did want to exclude 'unworthy men', with the significant rider that non-graduates were to be encouraged to go to college, with the Baptist Union assisting financially where this was necessary. Perhaps at a slower speed than other Free Churches, Baptists were developing a denominational consciousness, and the colleges were among the agencies of that change.

As late as 1870, less than half of the ministers in charge of English Baptist churches had been trained in denominational colleges, but by 1901 the proportion had risen to some 64%. The colleges, however, were seriously under-providing for the denomination's needs at this time, for whereas 1165 ministers left churches between 1890 and 1901, the college output was only 605, falling far short of the Spurgeonic ideal of providing for causes yet to be planted.[34]

Diversity of work, it was argued from the mid-century onwards, called for some rationalisation of resources. The rightness of such proposals as were forthcoming foundered on the independency of the separate colleges, backed by differences of theological outlook, regional sentiment, and functional focus: proposals to amalgamate the New Connexion Midland College, Rawdon and Manchester foundered

---

34 K. D. Brown, *A Social History . . .* , esp. chapters 2 and 3.

as much on Trans-Pennine mutual suspicion as on the number of close-communionist tutorships to be guaranteed in the new institution, whatever the vital significance of that to Baptist life on the eve of the twentieth century.

The most distinctive of all the colleges was Spurgeon's (originally Pastors') College. It was founded in 1856, the same year that Dr Angus moved his institution from a Stepney that was becoming socially problematical to the salubrious environment of Regent's Park. Spurgeon's was well placed to become an arm of Baptist advance in the Second Evangelical Awakening in Britain when, it has been calculated, there was something like a 40% growth in Baptist church membership. Behind the new college lay Spurgeon's judgement on the existing theological scene. After referring to costs and social class, he concluded: 'I may have been uncharitable in my judgment but I thought the Calvinism of the theology usually taught to be very doubtful and the fervour of the generality of the students to be far behind their literary attainments'. Spurgeon believed that the academies had a history of warning to give Baptists, citing the decline of Doddridge's in particular, which 'sought to make ministers rather than to aid them' and therein imperilled its success.

In his own college Spurgeon set himself the task of producing preachers of the gospel: not scholars or cultural adornments but those who could 'get to the hearts of the masses, to evangelize the poor - this is the College ambition, this and nothing else', and if for this purpose it was necessary to allow a 'lowering of the average of scholarship', so be it. The curriculum of the college embraced classic Puritan theology set within a broad context of scientific, philosophical and historical knowledge, with appropriate instruction in biblical language and contemporary church work.

The principal problem was not the syllabus but the length of a student's course. Initially set at two years, with only short vacations, it was increased to three in 1880, the college arguing that the third year was 'more useful than the other two', but all too often students shortened their courses as deacons of vacant churches seduced them into early service. Spurgeon was thought a 'harsh jailor' if he detained men in college when there was urgent work to be done in the churches. Like all institutions, even Spurgeon's was growing into conformity with its sister colleges, increasing its interest in academic education, and eventually preparing many of its students for London University examinations.[35]

ORDINATION

Ordination practice within the denomination was very varied. It was common, for example, early in the century for both Particular and New Connexion ministers to participate in one another's ordinations, along with other dissenting clergy, most often the local Congregationalist. Few can have achieved the ecumenical authentication secured by the Revd J. Statham, previously a missionary in Bengal, who boasted the presence of thirty ministers of different denominations at his ordination at the Lower Meeting, Amersham, in 1828.[36] The involvement of ministers of other denominations clearly indicated that ordination was not to a separate Baptist ministry but to the Christian ministry: for Robert Hall this represented a helpful ecumenism that made closed communion negatively isolationist.

The common elements within ordination services were reflections on the nature of a gospel church (often accompanied by an enunciation of the principles of dissent), a statement by a deacon as to how the church concerned was led to issue a call, and testimony from the new minister as to his religious experience, accompanied by 'the usual questions' as to confession of faith and call. A 'charge' was given to the new pastor and the people were 'addressed'. The language of ordination and 'public recognition as pastor' seem to have been interchangeable, with the distinction between ordination to a first pastorate and induction to a new sphere of influence less clear than it subsequently became. An ordination prayer was universally present,

---

35 M. Nicholls, 'Charles Haddon Spurgeon, Educationalist', *BQ* 31, 1986, pp.384ff, continued in *BQ* 32, 1987, pp.73ff.

36 *BM* 1828, p.622.

sometimes 'with imposition of hands'.[37] Andrew Fuller believed the practice of ordination to be wise rather than essential - wise because it enabled the ministers of the locality to exercise some control over the admission of undesirable persons to the ministry in their area.[38]

In 1828 a correspondent complained that ministers trained in denominational colleges were settling in churches without ordination, though the novelty of such practice was challenged.[39] The argument was that the verb 'ordain' in Scripture merely meant to appoint and that no ceremony was necessary for the labourer to start upon his labours; ordination ceremonies suggested a church authority present in those ordaining which was foreign to Baptist understandings of the Church. Eschewing anything that smacked of Catholicism, the argument was that commissioning came with the church's call, not through any subsequent ceremony. Occasional omission of a service of setting apart was a helpful demonstration that such services were far from essential.[40] The eighteenth-century distinction between the 'ministerial office' and the 'pastoral office', the former signifying the general exercise of ministerial gifts, particularly that of preaching, and the latter the appointment as pastor of a stated congregation, complicated the argument in the first half of the nineteenth century.[41]

The *Baptist Magazine* for 1838 even presents the interesting spectacle of John Howard Hinton publishing the ordination sermon he preached at the setting apart of Joseph Angus because he believed ordination 'has of late been all but abandoned, as by common consent, to an almost hopeless obscurity' so that it was 'ready to vanish away',[42] only to have Angus reply, 'I cannot but wish that the solemn assumptions of a modern ordination service were exchanged

---

37 Early issues of the *Baptist Magazine*.

38 *BM* 1815, p.455.

39 *BM* 1828, p.63 and p.150.

40 *BM* 1828, pp.151-2.

41 *BM* 1828, p.494.

42 *BM* 1838, p.100.

for the "affectionate greetings of a public recognition"'.[43] William Newman, President of Stepney, had admitted a similar position a quarter of a century earlier. Alongside accounts of formal ordinations in the later 1830s there appear simple notices that 'a pastor had commenced upon his labours' in a given location. Spurgeon himself deliberately rejected ordination and his example was nationally very influential.

A SOCIOLOGY OF MINISTRY

Baptist ministry in the first half of the century had a rather fustian social image as a ministry of 'very obscure men'.[44] Kenneth Brown offers as evidence for this judgement the isolation of the Baptist minister in Mark Rutherford's description of the quasi-fictional Cowfold, 'half village, half town'. The Baptist minister was 'a poor man and poor persons sat under him . . . His ministrations were confined to about fifty sullen, half stupid, wholly ignorant people', but it should be noted that the description of this congregation was 'strict Baptist, ultra Calvinistic, Antinomian', and that the minister was not in any way a characteristic Calvinist: 'the Calvinistic creed was stuck in him as a lump of fat, and had no organizing influence upon him whatever'.[45] Zoar, Cowfold, and its poor minister, it is submitted, tell us little about the ministry at large.

Kenneth Brown qualifies the image: a high number of sons of the manse entered the ministry, and from the eighteenth century up to 1910 around 5% of Baptist ministers came from the professional classes.[46] Small craftsmen, however, represented the most likely

---

43 *BM* 1838, pp.147-8.

44 A. Armstrong, *The Church of England, the Methodists, and Society, 1750-1850*, 1973, p.175, and Mark Rutherford (W. Hale White), *The Revolution in Tanner's Lane*, 1893, p.197.

45 BM 1838, pp.235-238.

46 L. G. Champion, 'The Social Status of Some Eighteenth-Century Baptist Ministers', *BQ*, 25, 1973, pp.10-14; K. D. Brown, *A Social History . . .* , 1988; K. D. Brown, 'The Baptist Ministry of Victorian England and Wales: A Social Profile', *BQ* 32, 1987, pp.105-20. I readily acknowledge my debt to Professor

social origin for Baptist ministers in the first half of the nineteenth century. From 1860 onward white-collar workers, including teachers, were increasingly significant, outnumbering artisans after 1880.[47] Brown also notes that Wales and more especially Scotland were net exporters of ministers. Until the latter decades of the nineteenth century ministers were likely to have a rural or small town background, but from 1880 urban and suburban backgrounds began to increase.[48]

The number of Baptist ministers who were formally trained for ministry in contrast to the older pattern of 'learning on the job' rose markedly from 1850: as late as 1871 only 58% had training at academy or college, but by 1911 that figure had risen to 84.5%, including some who entered the ministry direct from education and without prior secular employment. Within that increase, however, Pastors' (later Spurgeon's) College played a major role. Brown offers the following percentages of total ministry deriving from the college: 1871 c.10%, 1891 c.20%, 1911 24%. These percentage increases were important for Baptist success in increasing the proportion of its ministry coming from a genuinely working-class background, for Spurgeon's vision was of an institution which would make pastors out of ordinary working-class men. 'What was wanted', Spurgeon argued, 'was an institution where these rough and ready men could be drilled in the simple rudiments of education and so fitted for the work of preaching and the discharge of plain pastoral duties . . . I shall not, in order to increase our prestige, refuse poor men, or zealous young Christians whose early education has been neglected'.[49] No fees were levied on students where real promise was detected (but this was not unique to Pastors' College). Nevertheless, Brown believes it

---

Brown for the analysis which appears in this section.

47 K. D. Brown, *A Social History . . .*, pp.30-35, Table 1.5 in this work offers a full occupational analysis of Baptist ministers and their fathers for the period 1810-1929.

48 See Table 1.10 in K. D. Brown, *ibid.*, pp.47-9.

49 K. D. Brown, *ibid.*, p.33, citing A. Dallimore, *Spurgeon*, Chicago 1964, p.102.

likely that at Spurgeon's a break-through was made in securing more recruits from the lower classes.[50]

A considerable proportion of Spurgeon's students were to exercise their ministry overseas: between 1856-1880 the number was 511 men or 13% of those trained, rising to 23% for the sixty years 1856-1916. Brown inclines to the view that this was a function of Spurgeon's international reputation and concern rather than any failure of his graduates to settle satisfactorily in this country, though some may have found emigration a happy release from causes of marginal viability to which many went for first pastorates.[51]

The denomination exhibited a very wide range of salaries. Bloomsbury paid William Brock £700 p.a. in 1861, whilst Stowell Brown at Myrtle Street, Liverpool, achieved £900 p.a. Others cited by Brown earned between £200 and £300 in the second half of the century. Much more typical, he believes, was John Cragg of rural Norfolk in the 1860s who had a rent-free manse, income from church property of £25 a year, and a hope of raising another £10 or so from subscriptions, giving a total of some £65 per year, slightly less than the £75 p.a. taken by the Baptist Union as the average received by men in English churches.[52] Spurgeon asked deacons to reflect on the unfortunate truth that 'ministers of the Gospel were not able to live on much less than other people. They cannot make a shilling go as far as other people make a sovereign. Some of them try very hard, but they do not succeed'.[53]

Thus financial worries were added to the other strains of congregational life where harmony between pastor and people was essential. There is some evidence that responsibility for constant evangelistic enterprise amongst the ungodly, who unless they responded to the evangelist's pleading, it was certainly believed, faced

50 K. D. Brown, *A Social History . . .* , pp.33-4.

51 *ibid.*, pp.131-2.

52 *ibid.*, pp.156-7, citing *Baptist Handbook*, 1873, p.59.

53 Quoted in *The Congregationalist*, 1874, and cited by K. D. Brown, *A Social History . . .* , p.157.

a Christless eternity, may have led some ministers to nervous breakdowns and even to premature death.[54] The young William Best faced different problems. He was perplexed as to whether to respond to a particular call: 'My preaching perhaps would not suit them. It might be too simple or too elaborate; too intellectual or not sufficiently so; too highly Calvinistic or not doctrinal enough; the tie of my cravat might not suit their taste, or the fashion of my whiskers. I might not be tall enough. Churches are very funny sometimes'.[55] In fact they were very loving for most of the time, if the frequent pain expressed in the accounts of parting with a beloved minister be any kind of guide. There is also the evidence of length of pastorates, shown in Table 1.[56]

From these figures it will be seen that Baptists had fewer short pastorates than the Congregationalists, though still a very substantial proportion, until the 1880s from which time approximately a half of Baptist pastorates for whatever reason were of five or less years' duration. The pastorates of six to ten years remained pretty constant throughout the period but very long pastorates tended to decline. The most likely explanation of the large number of very short pastorates seems to be a not very responsible issuing of calls by marginal congregations where full-time ministry could only continue if the pastor collected, by forthright preaching, evangelism and pastoral care, a sufficient number of members and adherents of sufficient affluence to sustain the cause. Another aspect of the same phenomenon was the reluctance of once well-supported causes in downtown areas or in the countryside to react to a changed social situation.

Shorter pastorates also entailed more labour in securing satisfactory settlements. James Owen, from the presidential chair of the Union in

54 K. D. Brown, *A Social History . . .* , p.190.

55 'Selections from the Letters of the Late Rev. William Best, BA', *BM*, 1877, pp.208-9, cited K. D. Brown, *A Social History . . .* , p.163.

56 Extracted and simplified from Table 4.5 in K. D. Brown, *A Social History . . .*, p.166, where a ten point scale of length of pastorate is used.

Table 1: Length of Congregational and Baptist Pastorates

Length of pastorate	Year of entry					
	1841-1861		1851-1871		1861-1881	
	B%	C%	B%	C%	B%	C%
0-5 years	43.5	51.8	44.8	50.2	44.1	47.5
6-10	26.9	23.9	27.0	24.8	29.0	26.1
11-20	18.4	14.7	17.6	14.3	17.5	12.4
21+	10.8	9.3	9.0	10.2	8.8	13.3
	1871-1891		1881-1901		1891-1911	
0-5	46.0	47.2	49.6	46.9	51.2	45.7
6-10	30.0	27.6	29.1	28.5	30.4	30.3
11-20	13.9	12.6	13.6	15.4	13.2	18.6
21+	9.5	11.2	7.7	7.2	5.6	4.3

1891, admitted to a surplus of ministerial supply over demand, partly because the denomination was fairly generous to those who offered experience, perhaps as an evangelist, colporteur or lay pastor, rather than a college training, and partly because of the large numbers trained at Spurgeon's, many of whom it was claimed featured amongst the unemployed.[57] This invited increased initiatives at a national level. The Spring Assembly of the Baptist Union in 1887 had set up a Board of Introduction and Consultation which embraced more

57 K. D. Brown, *A Social History* . . ., p.167, citing *Baptist Handbook*, 1891, p.37; *British Weekly*, 28 March 1891, and *The Baptist*, 4, 11, 18, 25 January 1895.

comprehensive procedures for the recognition of ministers as appropriate to appear in the Union's accredited list. The independency of the local church survived but with the assistance of national institutions: a new partnership was being forged between the local church exercising its freedom in calling a pastor and the Baptist Union offering recognition of that pastor's ministerial status, and ever more often providing part of the salary, together with security for the pastor in retirement.

The situation in Wales was worse than in England. Few Baptist ministers in the principality achieved £100 a year and the average was nearer £50. In 1862 the average for some 77 serving small Baptist churches was as low as £25 p.a.[58] Clearly there was a relationship between ministerial salary and size of congregation: in 1884 it was argued that a church with a membership of under 100 members (and many rural congregations had less than 50) needed a subsidy of £20-£30 p.a. to sustain full-time ministry. As late as 1911 it was suggested that only a half of English Baptist ministers and under a third of Baptist ministers in Wales secured £100 p.a.[59] In particular the increasing cost, and the perceived cost, of ministry put 'village nonconformity in a perilous position'.[60]

The problem was exacerbated by the fact that the minister was perceived as a professional man, a status that congregations wished for their pastor but for which they failed, for the most part, to make adequate provision. The real heroes were in many cases the women of the manse who managed a decent appearance out of very inadequate means: well might a correspondent to *The Baptist* in 1873 argue the difficulty of discharging pastoral responsibility on £60 p.a.[61] Another Baptist minister on the eve of the First World War, receiving £50 p.a. plus a small Association allowance for rent, compared his lot

---

58 K. D. Brown, *A Social History . . .*, pp.157-8.

59 *ibid.*, pp.158-9, citing *Baptist Handbook*, 1884, p.24, and *Christian World*, 27 April 1911.

60 A. McLaren, 1876, cited K. D. Brown, *A Social History . . .*, p.159.

61 *The Baptist*, 14 February 1873, cited K. D. Brown, *A Social History . . .*, p.160.

unfavourably with the Wesleyan minister on £150 p.a. with free manse: 'I am expected to dress as well as he, to move in the same society, to be able to put my hand in my pocket just as he does, to send my children to the same school, and what applies to me applies also to my wife'.[62] All argued for some amendment of independency, with the Baptist Union providing some relief for inadequately remunerated pastors. By 1914 Shakespeare's robust energies had raised £250,000 to secure a ministerial salary of between £100 and £150 a year for all co-operating churches and pastors.[63]

Quite apart from low incomes, hardly improved by modest parting or retirement gifts,[64] there was the temptation of inertia of ministers hanging on to the pastoral office long after they had the ability to discharge its duties. Thus in the 1830s Isaac Mann wrote to James Upton of those facing 'too great an anxiety to retain the emoluments arising from the discharge of pastoral duties, and have found there a temptation sufficiently powerful to prevent their quitting the pulpit'.[65] The argument was set for the provision of retirement annuities first on an association basis and from 1875 on a national basis, though the consolidation of the national scheme awaited a princely endowment in 1911 from one of the denomination's few merchant princes, the Lancashire coal-master and brick manufacturer, Sir George Macalpine of Accrington, a year after he had held the presidency of the Union.[66]

A proper theology of ministry had to embrace the complexities of call, ordination, training, and ministry itself. Beyond these, there was increasing concern for retired ministers who had given themselves faithfully to the churches, as also for their families for whom few ministers had sufficient opportunity themselves to provide. A rightly

---

62 *Baptist Times and Freeman*, 4 April 1914.

63 K. D. Brown, *A Social History* . . ., p.161.

64 *ibid.*, p.195.

65 I. Mann to J. Upton, 30 October 1830, cited in 'J. Upton: Remembered Problems, 1830', *BQ* 10, 1940-41, pp.178-9.

66 D. J. Jeremy, *Capitalists and Christians: Business Leaders and the Church in Britain, 1900-1960*, 1990, pp.364-5.

perceived call, duly recognized, both by sponsoring church and that in which ministry was to be exercised, presumed gifts for the edification of the saints and for the presentation of the gospel in the world. Programmes of ministerial formation which combined academic training with pastoral studies and evangelistic opportunities could both develop ministerial personalities and ground them in an understanding of mission and ministry that would sustain them in the cultural crossfire that was the necessary context of their professional service. Increasingly this put as much emphasis upon success as faithfulness. Maintaining ministerial focus when the pulpit could at different times be both idolized and discounted, and when the local manifestation of the people of God could all too easily be confused with a giant battery of philanthropic and educational activities, was not easy, especially when powerful lay leaders had a determined vision of programmatic priorities. The minister was at one and the same time to be energetic in developing means of dealing with the most basic needs of a motley humanity, caught up in the traumatic changes of urbanization and industrialization, to be the interpreter of new thought in science and criticism to cautious congregations suspicious of all novelty, and in a world of increasing diversions to encourage his flock to nurture a relevant spirituality. In such a world it was not difficult for the minister to be oppressed by the weight of all the problems of a changing mission, pressing hard upon his all too often lonely shoulders. That said, relationships between pulpit and pew were most often cordial and the ministerial task for most Baptist ministers one that yielded abundant satisfaction.

5

GENERAL AND PARTICULAR

Whereas elections split the nation, election, in the singular, for some three centuries split the common life of the Baptists. The growing together of the New Connexion and the Particular Baptists, after a courtship that lasted some sixty years, is one of the happier stories of denominational life in a century in which congregational splits appeared a major methodology for church planting. This growing together was, in large part, the legacy of the Evangelical Revival, as strength in mission was the most often announced goal of such an amalgamation. It was the Evangelical Revival which both gave birth to the New Connexion and occasioned the theological revision of the inherited Calvinism amongst the Particulars.

Such developments offered a new potential to ancient hopes of unbroken accord within the Baptist family, for as long ago as 1678, Thomas Grantham had made his plea 'for the fellowship of all churches confessing one baptism for the remission of sins', arguing that what churches agreed was of greater significance than that on which they differed.[1]

The amalgamation of the two branches of the family can conveniently be allocated three phases, focusing respectively in the 'thirties, 'sixties and 'eighties of the nineteenth century. Significantly the first and the last phases, which were both prompted by missionary concern, bore conspicuous fruit, in the restructuring of the Baptist Union to be more inclusive as well as more functional, and in the movement in the 'eighties leading into amalgamation. By contrast, the debates of the 'sixties, which were more a function of General Baptist despondency and loss of nerve, produced no conspicuous fruit, unless it was the determination of a youthful John Clifford to restore to his denomination its self-respect so that any amalgamation would be out of strength rather than weakness.

---

1 W. Underwood, *The General Baptist Denomination: its past history, distinctive peculiarities and present condition* (hereafter *Past History*), 1864, p.24.

ORIGINS OF THE NEW CONNEXION

The story of how a small group of Christians in Leicestershire, born of the Evangelical Revival and focusing initially on the village of Barton, came to Baptist beliefs in 1755, and the similar story of the pilgrimage of Dan Taylor, a West Riding Methodist dissident, to Baptist convictions in 1763, is the necessary starting point. Both groups, with immediate experience of the warm fires of revival, found themselves occupying an uncomfortable middle ground between high Calvinist Particular Baptists who refused fellowship with Arminians, and General Baptists who were open enough, but problematically also open to those whose Christology had become heterodox.

Whilst Dan Taylor initially sought to work with existing General Baptists, the conscience of the Leicester group did not allow that. Their resistance confirmed Dan Taylor's disquiet with the tone of the churches of the General Assembly of General Baptists and on 6 June 1770 a separate New Connexion of General Baptists was formed.[2] Its early strength, apart from the Yorkshire churches, was clearly located in the East Midlands. The records of the General Assembly usually referred to it as the 'Leicestershire Association'. Initially its members called themselves Free-Grace General Baptists and soon claimed kinship with the Free-Will Baptists of the USA and Canada (founded in New Hampshire in 1780 and grown to a denomination some 60,000 strong by 1860); such kinship fortified their sense of distinctiveness.[3]

Their basic doctrinal standard, the six articles on Free Grace, 'were such as many Calvinists might conscientiously subscribe, as well as pious Arminians, since they include little more than an

---

2 The description 'General Baptist' in this volume must be understood to apply to the members of the New Connexion unless the context clearly indicates to the contrary, since in common usage they most generally referred to themselves thus.

3 A. C. Underwood, *The History of the English Baptists*, 1947, pp.149-157. 'The Free Will Baptists correspond by letter and delegations with the General Baptists of England with whom they agree in doctrine'. *General Baptist Magazine* (hereafter *GBM*), March 1860, pp.89f., and November 1860, p.424.

acknowledgment of those first principles of the gospel on which all who rely on Christ's atoning work are of one accord'.[4]

The existing General Baptist Messengers or superintending ministers managed to win back to the Assembly those old General Baptists initially inclined to throw in their lot with the New Connexion, with the exception of Boston, but the new Yorkshire and Leicestershire Churches proved adamant in their attachment to the New Connexion. Later, a considerable number of old General Baptist churches, some of great age, that had remained orthodox in theology transferred their affections to the New Connexion.[5] Elsewhere, both churches and ministers, in not inconsiderable numbers, took the more radical action of transferring their allegiance to the Particular Baptists.

FULLERISM AND THE PARTICULAR BAPTISTS

The impact of Fullerism represents the other side of the coin of Baptist theological accommodation to the experience of the Evangelical Revival. Older notions as to the universal dominance of the theology of Brine and Gill, with what Ivimey called their 'non-application, non-invitation scheme' of High-Calvinist theology, now need to be corrected in terms of a greater continuity of Evangelical Calvinism in provincial churches, especially those influenced by the Bristol Academy.[6] Nevertheless, a remarkable re-assessment of theology and mission took place amongst Particular Baptists in the last quarter of the eighteenth century. Ivimey goes so far as to speak of 'the commencement of a new era in the history of our denomination',

---

4 W. Groser, cited in W. Underwood, *The General Baptist Denomination: A Centennial Survey*, 1870 (hereafter *Centennial Survey*), pp.4-5, attached *General Baptist Year Book* (hereafter *GBYB*), 1870.

5 Examples include Berkhamsted, Bourne, Chesham, Downton, Great Yarmouth, Leake and Wymswold, Leicester (Friars Lane), Lincoln, London (Commercial Road), March, Peterborough, Ramsgate, Sittingbourne, Southwark (Borough Road), Spalding, Tarporley, Wendover, West Retford, Wisbech.

6 Joseph Ivimey, *The History of the English Baptists*, III, 1823, p.272. See also Roger Hayden, 'Evangelical Calvinism and English Baptists', unpublished PhD thesis, University of Keele, 1992.

referring first to the elder Robert Hall's address in 1779 to the Northamptonshire Association on the removal of stumbling blocks to Christian commitment, published in 1781 as *Help to Zion's Travellers*.

In 1784 came that same association's Call to Prayer for the revival of religion, and in 1785 Fuller's *The Gospel Worthy of All Acceptation*, prepared four years earlier, with its affirmation 'that faith in Christ is the duty of all who hear or have the opportunity to hear the gospel'. The goodness of God, properly presented, virtually entailed within itself a moral demand for a 'return of gratitude'. The censures in scripture on those who fail to respond to the invitation to receive Christ were so severe that they had to be taken as a judgment upon those wilfully spurning the gospel opportunity: 'if the inability of sinners to believe in Christ were of the same nature as that of a dead body in a grave to rise up and walk, it were absurd to suppose that they would on this account fall under divine censure.' Fuller further argued that every preacher ought, therefore, to govern his preaching by the understanding that every sinner, whatever his character, was 'completely warranted to trust in the Lord Jesus Christ for the salvation of his soul'.[7]

Andrew Fuller and his friends, by calling Baptists back from the extremes of hyper-Calvinism, created the potential for the unification of a divided denomination. The same period witnessed the rise of that evangelical catholicism, to whose existence W. R. Ward has drawn attention, which called for maximum inter-denominational co-operation.[8] By the same token there needed to be unity of purpose within denominations.

Mission overseas as much as evangelism at home drew Baptists together. Those Baptists who boasted the universal availability of the gospel could not lag behind the particularizers in the task of world mission. The problem was not one of will but of capacity: what could a denomination of only 10,000 members do on its own? When

7 E. F. Clipsham, 'Andrew Fuller and Fullerism: A Study in Evangelical Calvinism', *BQ* 20, 1963-4, pp.99-114, 146-154, 214-225, 268-276, esp. 215-8.

8 W. R. Ward, *Religion and Society in England, 1790-1850*, 1972, pp.2-6.

Anglicans and Wesleyans gave support to the new Baptist Missionary Society, it was hard to refuse it from General Baptists, who in fact already supported the society.

After the Serampore fire of 1812, the General Baptists reactivated an earlier concern about participation in overseas missions. John Gregory Pike, the long-serving secretary of the General Baptist Missionary Society, and appropriately the first General Baptist to be elected to the chair of the Baptist Union in 1842, recorded a note on the society's origins:

> About 1812. the present secretary of the society [himself] applied to Mr Fuller, the venerable secretary of the Baptist Missionary Society to know if that society would employ as a missionary a person who might be a member of a church belonging to the General Baptists. His answer amounted to a negative. About 1814 or 1815 the Independents formed a society for the counties of Derbyshire, Nottinghamshire and Leicestershire, auxiliary to the London Missionary Society. The same person again applied to Mr Fuller suggesting the formation of an auxiliary Baptist Missionary Society which should include both the bodies of Baptists, denominated General and Particular. It was thought this might be supported by churches of the former description and yet it was observed to Mr Fuller as such a society would be a mere auxiliary it would not interfere with the management of the Baptist Mission. This would have continued on the same footing as before. His answer to this proposition was most decidedly unfavourable. It now remained for the friends of the heathen among the G. Baptists to see a little done among themselves for the support of a missionary cause as carried on by others or to make a fresh attempt at the foundation of a missionary society in their own connection.[9]

9 In the manuscript 'Minutes of Transactions at the Meetings of the Committee of the General Baptist Missionary Society', Angus Library, Regent's Park College, Oxford.

That conclusion was unfortunate but perhaps understandable in the context of the times. Fuller was near the end of his life and already well aware of the difficulties of managing the affairs of the mission, not to mention the difficulties his own restatement of Evangelical Calvinism had caused. He may well have judged it unwise to add further complications, such as relations with the General Baptists would have generated. Accordingly, the General Baptist Society was founded in June 1816 at the Association at Boston, though it was to be five years before the first missionaries arrived in Orissa.

There was soon vital co-operation between the two bodies, with William Ward much involved with the preparation of the first General missionaries who were directed to Orissa by the Serampore leadership. Dyer also offered assistance to the new society, now safely independent. However, Fuller's two refusals clearly entered into the folk memory of the General Baptists, to be rehearsed before Particular Baptist ears and eyes whenever talk of union at home was subsequently proposed.[10]

FIRST STEPS TOWARDS BAPTIST UNITY

The first modern proposal for a union of the two branches of the Baptist family appeared in the *New Baptist Miscellany*, a Particular Baptist journal, for December 1830. Two months earlier a young correspondent[11] drew attention 'to the undue estimation in which the denominational difference between us and the non-essentials of religion are held', arguing that Christians spent too much time perpetuating separation rather than giving their energies to unite in communion and fellowship, citing in particular 'the difference between congregational churches on the subject of baptism'.

He argued, in terms that John Clifford was later to adopt, that there was a difference between the two scriptural ordinances: churches 'are authorized as collective bodies to celebrate and take cognizance

---

10 John Clifford in *GBM*, March 1887, p.103, and the *Missionary Observer*, June 1891, pp.237-40.

11 J. A. of Perth.

of one rite only, viz., the commemoration of Our Lord's death', whereas 'baptism is simply a personal obligation, over which they ought to have no control, and as especially distinguished from the other by St Paul', for while no command was given concerning baptism to any church Paul was explicit with regard to the Lord's Supper. Similarly the apostles were commissioned not to baptize but to preach, and thus there was no necessity for the act of baptism to be undertaken by the minister. This was an important clarification, for if the act of baptizing were separated from the ministerial office then it would make it easier for churches containing both paedobaptist and baptist Congregationalists to exist in the way that they had developed in Huntingdonshire. In such a way the issue of baptism could be prevented from becoming a barrier to unity, and somebody convinced of the appropriateness of baptismal obedience did not need to change denominations.[12]

The leading article in the December issue, entitled 'Scriptural Thoughts on the Doctrine of Election', also concerned itself with the issue of unity from a Particular Baptist perspective:

> The divided condition of the church has greatly increased the obstacles which impede the diffusion of truth. There is something so artificial and sectarian in the lines by which the various sections of the church are separated from each other, that they cannot in the nature of things but exert an injurious

---

12 *New Baptist Miscellany* (hereafter *NBM*), October 1830, pp.415f. The *New Baptist Miscellany* was a Particular Baptist magazine whose editors at this time were Edward Steane, Thomas Price and John Haddon: Rosemary Taylor, 'English Baptist Periodicals 1790-1865', *BQ* 27, 1977, pp.61-2. The location 'Perth' appears next to the same initials at the end of a letter in the next issue. 'J. A.', a new correspondent, also refers to an earlier letter on the same subject from 'A.B.' to the editor of the *Baptist Magazine*. 'A Lover of Good Men', who feared that the editor would not print his letter as it was a few years ahead of opinion, made a similar plea in April 1831 (pp.144-5) for the union of Baptists and extending it to all Independents, arguing not the methodology of the growth of mixed communion churches but a conference of ministers from each side to examine the baptism issue.

> influence. We look at the creed of our own sect, not through the pure light of evidence but through the prejudiced medium of our partiality . . . Our party zeal blinds our judgments to the perception of truth and frequently induces some of the excellent of the earth to pursue a course from which the principle of common honesty should be sufficient to preserve all men.

This was especially the case with regard to the doctrine of election, the exposition of which had proved a stumbling block to many serious enquirers.[13]

A further correspondent - 'a lover of Christian unity' - provided details of the scale of the New Connexion in the 1830s. It embraced about 11,000 members in 109 churches with 82 full-time ministers, of whom Isaac Mann had said that no body of ministers was 'more distinguished for their holy zeal, self-denial and universal labours in the cause of Christ', a judgement which challenged the coldness of some Particular Baptist patterns of ministry.

Two major obstacles to denominational fusion were anticipated. The first was the traditional divergence of doctrine. However, sectarianism in the nineteenth century was impeding the expansion of the church. Therefore, the convergence of understanding between Particular and General Baptists ought to be translated into united institutions. Dan Taylor's article on election was not expressed in the exact words a Particular Baptist would choose to use, but

> What have our brethren done, that we must not hail them as partakers of the same grace, that we must refuse their counsel and their labours in carrying on the cause of our redeemer? . . . We refuse Christian fellowship and co-operation with these zealots of Immanuel while we actually tolerate differences of opinion among ourselves of very far greater importance.

If the maintenance of fellowship with hyper-Calvinistic brethren could be useful in moderating their opinions, why should the same argument

13 *NBM* December 1830, pp.489ff.

not obtain with regard to General Baptists, who could thus be persuaded of the moderate Calvinist position, 'if it be correct, or if otherwise, to obtain a clearer view of truth from him'?

The second, organizational, point was more difficult to counter.

> Here, it must be acknowledged, the General Baptists have the advantage on us. Decidedly favourable as I am to the scriptural independence of our churches, I am yet assured that more union might exist in our body than does at present, and that an association of the churches, which should annually meet to promote the good of the whole in the week of our Missionary Meetings would be highly advantageous.

In this respect the paedobaptist Congregationalists with their proposed union should have set Baptists an example.

Meanwhile more immediate action could be taken by inviting General Baptists to participate in Associations and in the work of those institutions 'whose committees exert a powerful influence over the denomination at large'. Particular Baptist resources should be made available to General Baptists, by exchanges of pulpits, General Baptist activities being reported in Particular journals, and consideration being given to the amalgamation of missionary societies and periodicals. Because the denomination in the past had proved slow to move on a wide front it was better to start with specific initiatives.

All this was crucial to the mission of the church:

> When we indulge a spirit of party we are encouraging the sarcastic sneer of the infidel and allowing stumbling blocks to remain in the way of those who would walk to heaven . . . deferring to a distant period the fulfilment of the Redeemer's prayer that his servants ought to be all one, that the world might believe in the divine organization and heavenly character of his mission.[14]

This plea secured several sympathetic responses. 'A Calvinistic Baptist' from Leicester argued that in the midland counties practical

14 *NBM* December 1830, pp.500-2.

co-operation was already well advanced, so that he entertained hopes that prejudice would soon be eradicated and suspicion abandoned 'until the intervening ground silently and imperceptibly gives way and the appellation General or Particular is merged and gone for ever.' Nevertheless he still wondered if the moment was ripe for formal union, though convinced it would be a very great good. A principal difficulty that he, like many others, identified was that of systems of church government, since the partial presbyterianism of the New Connexion challenged the boasted independency of the Particulars. This last comment was challenged by 'A General Baptist', also from Leicester, who believed 'partial presbyterianism' was an exaggeration: General Baptist churches defended their independency as fiercely as Particular Baptists, and the authority of their national association did not greatly differ from that of Particular Baptist county associations.[15]

Similar questions were also raised on the General Baptist side. Rather earlier a correspondent to the *General Baptist Repository* said that he had been asked by an Independent 'why the Orthodox General Baptists, as a late editor was accustomed to designate us, and the Moderate Calvinistic Baptists did not unite as one denomination, since their creeds appeared to be rapidly approximating'. Such a development would be of mutual advantage to both bodies, especially since the doctrines on which they agreed greatly outnumbered those on which they differed. The writer knew of no good reason, and accordingly reprinted Thomas Grantham's plea of 1678 which had yet to receive an adequate answer.[16]

The specific plea in the *New Baptist Miscellany* called forth a refutation in the *General Baptist Repository* of the following year, which although initially cordial, especially as to local co-operation, concluded 'But such a oneness of the two denominations as would merge all distinction between them, is in the present state of things, both unattainable and by no means to be desired'. The writer

15 *NBM* January 1831, p.12; and February 1831.

16 *General Baptist Repository*, January 1830, pp.5f.

questioned the general moderation of Particular Baptist views and their lack of denominational identity and organization. Their diversity in fact occasioned a practical disunity, and the relative size of the two bodies threatened that amalgamation would lead to the total submerging of the distinctive witness of the New Connexion. In addition, union with the Particular Baptists would mean joining a body in a state of confusion over the issue of mixed communion, the practice of which was doing anything but promote unity. The issue was especially acute because those nearest in faith to the General Baptists were generally those most energetic in opening the communion table.[17]

The proposal was doubtless well-intended but General Baptists had to be wary of betraying their tradition: 'If we love our denomination, if we love what we believe important truth . . . we must not be hasty in contemplating any such plan'. The unnatural unions to be found within the Church of Rome and the Church of England should stand as an eternal warning. Having piled up the negatives, the writer concluded, 'at the same time, every well-wisher to christianity, every one influenced by the Spirit of Christ, will desire that increasing fellowship and union should prevail between the two denominations, as well as among Christians in general'.[18] At this stage only 'friendly intercourse' was advised, not any attempt at formal union.

All this provides the background to the reconstruction of the Baptist Union in 1832 whose revised constitution clearly opened the way for closer association between the New Connexion and Particular Baptists on a more formal basis. The doctrinal clauses of 1813 were dropped in favour of seeking union amongst Baptist ministers and churches 'who agree in the sentiments usually denominated evangelical'. Thus was the breach between free-will and pre-ordained election boldly

---

17 *General Baptist Repository* 1831, p.95.

18 W. Underwood, *Past History*, fn.1, pp.22f. He identifies the writer as the Revd Joseph Jarrom of Wisbech, but the initials at the foot of the letter are J.W. not J.J., suggesting rather J. Wallis, minister at Commercial Road, London, but one hesitates to correct Underwood on such an issue.

spanned and a first step taken to enable Baptists to walk in harmony.

The churches in the reconstructed Baptist Union were now organized partly in geographical associations, and partly, as far as the New Connexion was concerned, on a confessional basis. As General Baptists were fully involved in the life of the Union, paying their subscriptions with other member churches, it was not unnatural that ministers from their ranks should occupy the presidential chair, thus J. G. Pike was president in 1842, Jabez Burns in 1850, and John Clifford in 1888.[19]

Evangelicalism, with its powerful missionary concern, was parent to the desire for greater unity. John Foster, in his *Observations on Mr Hall's Character as a Preacher*, says of Robert Hall 'that he was exempt from all those restrictions, in respect of the mode of presenting and urging the overtures of redemption which have been imposed on some good men of the Calvinist faith . . . He took the utmost liberty in this strain of inculcation; exhorting, inviting, entreating, expostulating, remonstrating; in language of nearly the same tenor as that which might be deployed by an Arminian preacher'.[20] It was the same evangelistic impulse that made Hall the champion of open communion: partnership in mission necessarily demanded partnership at other levels of experience.

Engagement in home and overseas missions necessarily challenged the inherited theology of the Particular Baptists. Even Fullerism was, in Underwood's words, 'only a half-way house' in their theological development. The further they moved, the closer they came to the New Connexion, whose very existence purged the General Baptist tradition of its Socinian associations.[21]

Some within the Particular Baptist tradition also questioned whether Fullerism was a satisfactory resolution of the relationship of Calvinist theology to gospel preaching. Hinton's writings raised the issue anew,

---

19 E. A. Payne, *The Baptist Union: A Short History*, 1959, pp.60f.

20 J. Foster, 'Observations on Mr Hall's character as a preacher', in ed. O Gregory, *Works*, I, 1858, pp.201-55, esp.230-2.

21 W. Underwood, *Centennial Survey*, p.202.

and one Baptist deacon writing to the *Baptist Magazine* in June 1858, raised the question 'Where is the foundation of a sinner's hope unless he can be assured that Christ died for him personally and individually, and where is the attraction of the cross?' Particular Baptists had abandoned the hyper-Calvinism of earlier years and in that process got rid of many of the distinguishing marks that separated them from the New Connexion. Andrew Fuller's theology still left them with the difficulty of 'the necessity of an almighty and invincible power to renew the heart', which clearly did not operate in the lives of all men, leaving others incapable of responding to the gospel. Whilst the editor and other correspondents argued with him, this deacon persisted in making effective evangelism pose questions of received theology.[22]

Much later, Spurgeon, whose invitation preaching was to come under the fire of the new Strict Baptists, indicated a difference of approach from his high Calvinist precursor, John Gill.

> My venerated predecessor, Dr Gill, has left a body of divinity, admirable and excellent in its way, but the body of divinity to which I would pin and bind myself for ever, God helping me, is not his system of divinity or any other human treatise, but Jesus Christ, Who is the sum and substance of the Gospel, Who is Himself all theology, the Incarnation of every precious truth, the all-glorious embodiment of the way, the truth and the life.[23]

In a Baptist Union sermon preached in a Methodist Chapel in Leeds he noted the 'whosoever' in Romans 10 as a 'Methodist word', especially significant as coming after Romans 9, where Paul speaks in Calvinistic tones. 'The fact is,' he argued, 'that the whole of truth is neither here nor there, neither in this system nor in that, neither with this man nor that. Be it ours to know what is Scriptural in all systems and to receive it.'[24]

---

22 *Baptist Magazine* (hereafter *BM*), June 1858, pp.379f; see also *GBM*, January 1859, p.27.

23 C. H. Spurgeon, *Autobiography*, III, 1899, p.1.

24 W. Y. Fullerton, *C. H. Spurgeon*, 1920, p.121.

Some judged such theological latitude dangerous in the extreme. 'What is Spurgeonism but Fullerism?' posed the *Earthen Vessel*; 'What is Fullerism but moderate Arminianism, and what is Arminianism but free-will and free-grace mixed with the traditions of carnal men, dished up by a depraved, inventive genius, and instructed by the Devil to overthrow the grand old cardinal doctrines of the Bible, and rob Jesus Christ of his crown?' Spurgeon himself, it was argued, was the source of his own 'Down Grade' by offering hospitality at an open table.[25]

THEOLOGICAL CONVERGENCE, POSED AND QUESTIONED

E. A. Payne was of the opinion that the Baptist Union meetings in Nottingham in 1857 did much to assist closer relationships, leading on to the advocacy of a more complete fusion of the two strands of denominational life in the 1860s.[26] Certainly the invitation in 1857 was issued by the General Baptist Association, 'with the avowed desire of cultivating an enlarged fraternal fellowship'. In Nottingham the delegates acknowledged in resolution, 'the vital unity which prevails among them' and rejoiced 'in this opportunity of cultivating and expressing their sincere mutual love'.[27]

The principal argument for integration was the theological convergence which had already taken place. The *General Baptist Magazine* for February 1859, reflecting on the growing unity of those who in England advocate Evangelical Religion, welcomed the good work being undertaken by the Evangelical Alliance. Among the Wesleyans, 'from the Conference to the Primitive', contentions had subsided. Amongst the Baptists the situation was of the same order:

> Is it not true that throughout this body there is broader catholicity of feeling, and a greater measure of free evangelical preaching than formerly? The two great sections, Particular and General, are so blended as scarcely to maintain the old line

25 Cited *BM* March 1888, pp.129-31.

26 Payne, *Baptist Union*, p.146.

27 A. C. Underwood, *op.cit.*, p.214.

> of demarcation . . . There may be less of denominational bigotry, but there is not, we opine, less of enlightened zeal in advocating the truth, or in vindicating the ordinances of Christ.[28]

'A Business Man' in 1860 argued that a union of General and Particular Baptists would in his view be 'a nearer approximation on our part to the model of the apostolic church, the model and the only model which we as Baptists are bound to recognize', arguing that denominationalism was unknown to the apostles who were swift to condemn sectarianism as in I Corinthians 1. It was tradition rather than principle that lay behind present separation, especially when the breadth of opinion allowed within each section of the Baptist family was taken into account. Union would strengthen the influence of Baptist principles within the church, and such a catholicity of spirit, which knew 'less of dogmatism, more of truth', would make its contribution to the outcome. Allowing individuals full freedom of judgement could only serve to commend such polity: 'let us become more catholic, and we shall be more influential'. For the two branches of Baptists to compete in any given locality only served to confuse and to weaken the witness: in unity lay the route to strong gospel witness.[29]

Not improperly, Richard Hardy of Queenshead (Yorkshire) argued that the logic of this case could not rest just with the unification of Particular and General Baptists but ought to be pursued on a larger Congregational, Protestant, or even pan-Christian basis, for some might argue that 'one Lord, one faith, one baptism' would embrace each of these categories. The contrary argument demanded more rigour in talking about oneness of faith, baptism, and of Christ's Lordship, namely that there should be real agreement in doctrine, and of that he remained to be persuaded. In fact the foundation of the North Western Baptist Association, limited to churches practising strict communion, might, he argued, suggest the contrary: 'if the

---

28 *GBM* February 1859, pp.46-9.

29 Letter from 'A Business Man' to *GBM*, October 1860, pp.383ff.

[Particular Baptists] are not united among themselves, by what power is a cordial union to be formed between them and us?' But such principled arguments were also tied up with the practicalities of a concern for property, as well as the demands of trust deeds.

> Any attempt to force the union before the churches are ripe for it, by a formal vote of the Association, would be most disastrous in its consequences . . . the best, in fact the only thing that can be done at present is for the two bodies to act together when necessary on public questions, exchange kind sentiments and manifest a Christian spirit.[30]

So grudging was such a statement that the reader would be pardoned if he failed to understand that the New Connexion had for almost thirty years been formally accepted as an association of the Baptist Union. The language indicates just how fragile the authority of the Baptist Union still was as late as 1860, with only about one third of General Baptist congregations in membership with the larger body.

In September 1859 a special meeting had been convened to consider the extension of the work of the New Connexion which described its present position as 'humiliating and affecting', citing the number of counties where the Connexion had no churches or only a nominal presence - some twenty-eight of the forty counties of England. Though the previous quarter of a century had seen some progress, almost a third of the churches had failed during the last year to report any increase through baptisms. It was determined to give greater support to home missions, to unite small local causes overcoming an unhealthy independence, and to foster the use of lay agency. In the months following this gathering, the magazine reported further on the modesty of progress and the various solutions suggested, which as yet fell short of a whole-hearted seeking of amalgamation with the Particulars.[31]

---

30 *GBM* November 1860, pp.421f.

31 Appendix to *GBM* for 1859, pp.441-64.

NEW INVITATIONS

The Times, commenting in 1860 on the Norwich Chapel case, wrote:

> The denominations of 'General' and 'Particular' as applied to the communities of Baptists do not denote any diversity whatever on the fundamental points of their creed . . . The distinction of title between the two communities of which we are speaking is based on differences entirely independent of their peculiar creed, and which are found in fact, in all Christian congregations, including the Church of Rome itself.[32]

At the end of the previous month, Benjamin Evans of Scarborough, Baptist minister and historian, himself significantly a strict-communionist, had, through the pages of the *Freeman*, also taken up the cause of advocating amalgamation: 'on all the verities of the Gospel there is a oneness, and those points on which they differ are not vital'.[33] Evans's letter evoked half a dozen letters of support and no opposition, but the matter had only the seriousness of a correspondence column debate in a denominational journal. One corespondent wrote: 'Could not the Baptist Union be made a most valuable agency for such a purpose? I am already aware that it already professes to seek some of these objects. Perhaps in a good measure it meets our politico-ecclesiastical needs but it does not adequately meet our religious ones.' The fault lay not with the officers of the Baptist Union but with its members, who needed to inject more warmth into their commitment to its activities.[34]

Samuel Green, reflecting that the subject was 'an old one, often mooted before', but none the less important, drew attention to J. G.

---

32 Cited, *Freeman*, 6 June 1860, p.360.

33 *Freeman* 30 May 1860, pp.345.

34 *Freeman* 6 June 1860, p.362; 20 June, p.395; 27 June, p.411; 11 July, p.441. Evans' own church at Scarborough was split over the issue of open/closed communion: if such differences could be coped with amongst the Particulars, why was union with the Generals not a practical possibility?

Pike as a reconciling theologian.[35] Pike was later to be identified as 'the General Baptists' Andrew Fuller'. In letters to his son, a student at Stepney College, made available in his recently published *Recollections*, Pike discussed the issues of free-will and election in terms which Green found acceptable to moderate Calvinists.[36]

Another contributor put the issue more forcefully: 'General and Particular Baptists have to consider not whether they should unite; but whether they are at liberty to continue their long and disastrous compromise of a union which the Lord, into whom they have been baptized, has ordained.'[37]

The General Baptist Association responded cautiously, deferring the matter to the agenda of the Association meetings for the following year.[38] It then secured rather bland support, with the passing of a resolution which simply rejoiced 'in the constant exhibition of the union that already exists, and also in extending this union as far as is practicable, for the honour of our one Lord and the greater efficiency of combined operations.'[39]

John Baxter Pike, though a graduate of Stepney College, was decidedly lukewarm in his crucial Halifax Association Letter of 1862. Nominally upholding the goal of closer co-operation, J. B. Pike veered away from any possible exploration of the creative potential of the resolution and immediately focused on the word 'difficulties' - which meant, in language almost exactly repetitive of that used thirty years earlier, that 'a full discussion . . . would be neither desirable nor expedient.' Partly this was a consequence of what he deemed to be the inadequate response of the Particulars: 'We have extended the right hand of fellowship but it has not been very cordially grasped'.

---

35 See the testimony of Dr Trestrail in *BM*, March 1889, pp.106f.

36 *Freeman*, 13 June 1860.

37 *Freeman*, 18 July, pp.457f.; 25 July, p.473. *GBM* July 1860, p.271.

38 *Minutes of the Ninety-First Annual Association of the New Connexion of General Baptists*, 1860, p.37.

39 *Minutes of the Ninety-Second Annual Association of the New Connexion of General Baptists*, 1861, p.32.

Thus further consideration was deemed 'premature and unnecessary', for most seemed content with the measure of unity already attained without any apparent desire to deepen it.

A major part of the difficulty was, in J. B. Pike's judgement, that the independence of Particular Baptists inhibited them from establishing a denominational mind on the subject; 'They are not as we are, an organized denomination . . . To speak of them as a body is a misnomer. They are a multitude of independent churches - in many instances isolated churches'. He claimed that the meetings of the Baptist Union did not possess ecclesiological authority, rather were they a series of subscribers' meetings for the different Particular Baptist institutions and agencies than 'a representative assembly of all the associated churches', which was his description of the Annual Association of the New Connexion churches.[40]

John Clifford was of a similar mind: the Particular Baptists were

> not one 'connexion' but a series of 'connexions' under one denomination, not a 'body' with a well-defined or easily discovered head, speaking with one voice, but three or four 'bodies', separated by prodigious differences though agreeing on baptism.

Clifford argued that Particular Baptists came in three varieties: 'Strict', 'Spurgeonic' and 'Miscellaneous', the latter group finding 'their visible centre in the Colleges of Regent's Park, Bristol and Rawdon, and the Baptist Missionary Society'.[41]

---

40 John Baxter Pike, 'What practical measures can be proposed for effecting a closer union between the two evangelical sections of the Baptist body?' *Minutes of the Ninety-Third Annual Association of the New Connexion of General Baptists*, 1862, pp.44f.

41 *GBM* January 1877, p.2. The point about Particular Baptist lack of organizational coherence was persistently made from the time of the first overtures to the final amalgamation debate, when Dawson Burns opposed the proposal by arguing that outside the General Baptists, 'There are High-Calvinistic Baptists, Spurgeonic Baptists, Scotch Baptists, and Plymouth Brethren Baptists who would not join in any common organization'. *GBM* January 1891, pp.44f.

But the Particular Baptists were not without instruments for expressing their common mind: it saddened Pike that scrutinizing the reports of association meetings, 'in no one instance, so far as the writer has been able to ascertain, has there been any reference to a "closer union" or any resolution adopted concerning it'. Thus for General Baptists to press the notion of a United Baptist Denomination, even when they saw no insurmountable difficulties to such a development and much good in terms of influence and effectiveness, would seem to be presumptuous, until more tangible response was forthcoming from Particular Baptists.[42]

J. P. Mursell, an unashamed political dissenter, one of the more liberal minds amongst the Particulars, and significantly of Leicester where there were close relationships with the New Connexion, undaunted tried again. Using the opportunity provided by the Baptist Union's experimental provincial assembly in Birmingham in October 1864, Mursell devoted his address to the concept of 'Union'. Moving from the political to the religious sphere, he identified 'the supercession on practicable, sound and safe principles of the distinction between General and Particular Baptists' as a worthy object for the Union, which he congratulated on 'its revival, its widening influence, and augmenting strength'. Formal follow-up to such a proposal, which was only one of a number of concerns listed, was scant though briefly noticed by the magazines. However, there had been a further growing together which could be built on, if the Baptist Union would take the initiative in increasing the number of places for General Baptists on the Union Committee, understanding that, in the explorations of further union, the representatives of the New

42 *Minutes of the Ninety-Third Annual Association of the New Connexion of General Baptists*, 1862, pp.4f. T. W. Mathews of Boston in 1865 was more optimistic and spoke of unity coming about 'by a process as silent yet as sure as chemical affinity' which was 'gradually fulfilling itself', arguing that full participation in the work of the Baptist Union and its assemblies was a way to achieving that end. *Minutes of the Ninety-Sixth Annual Association of the New Connexion of General Baptists*, 1865, p.5.

Connexion had necessarily to occupy 'new and difficult positions'.[43]

Throughout the 'sixties the debate rumbled on. The *General Baptist Magazine* for April 1868 argued,

> There is no need now that we should be distinct from the other section of the Baptist body. The extravagant Calvinism of years gone by in Particular Baptist churches has been discarded or moderated and rendered agreeable. Our existence has been necessary as a protest. Our existence now is necessary as a friend and an ally. Our views of the atonement are held in so-called Particular Baptist churches, and a moderate Calvinism exists even among our own. Now we are really one with the other body. General and Particular are words which might be disused. Our greater brother has become wiser; we need not now protest but may walk and prosper with him.[44]

THE PERSISTENCE OF THE DEBATE ABOUT ELECTION

William Underwood, disclaiming the title Arminian for the New Connexion, preferred to argue that the General Baptists were second to none as Evangelical Christians. Indeed, it was his belief that a denomination could perfectly well defend its orthodoxy without subscribing to either Calvinism or Arminianism.[45] Ironically, in 1870, J. C. Pike argued of the New Connexion position: 'We believe that it was ordered by Divine Providence that we should be General Baptists. We were predestinated to be such.'[46]

There remained a lingering suspicion of the Particular Baptist position from the New Connexion point of view. 'As a body we have a latent disaffection to Calvinism, even when it is modified and

---

43 J. P. Mursell, Inaugural Address, 1864, pp.3-11; W. Underwood, *Centennial Survey*, 1870, p.15; *Freeman*, 19 October 1864, p.668; A. C. Underwood, *op.cit.*, p.214.

44 *GBM* April 1868, p.101.

45 W. Underwood, *Past History*, '. . . knowing little of Arminius beyond his name, and not liking all the little which we know, we never call ourselves his followers', pp.18f, p.15. *GBM* January 1877, p.3.

46 J. C. Pike, *Our Future: the Association Letter for 1870*, p.6.

mitigated by some of its modern abettors,' confessed Underwood; 'but it is seldom that this dislike draws any of us into declared antagonism to it.' Though the agility of thought of the moderate Calvinist might be admired, his use of word and concept seemed too contrived. There remained at the end of the 'fifties a continuing fear that the doctrine of particular redemption cut away 'the foundation of a sinner's hope and faith', and that of itself was 'condemnation' enough.[47]

The election issue still bred a rancorous spirit. The Revd James Salisbury of Hugglescote wrote:

> The spirit of fierce theological partizanship is not dead . . . There are yet little popedoms in our midst, and from many 'infallible' chairs proceed bulls, fulminating decrees, and excommunications which only give rise to counter denunciations . . . the aggressive agency of the church is injured in its exercise; . . . and the church of Christ, instead of commending itself to men as the great instrumentality of God, established for their conversion and salvation . . . may be fitly compared to a poor invalid, whose system is tainted with poison . . . We hope, therefore, that the members of our denomination, though they may differ somewhat in their opinion respecting the inspired teaching upon the subjects of election and predestination, will never so far involve themselves in controversies respecting these deep things of God as to forget that a wide field of christian labour lies before them, and that God commands us 'to enter in and possess the land'.[48]

John Clifford, however, was bold in defence of what he called his 'scriptural, broad, and anti-Calvinistic creed', whilst Matthew

---

47 W. Underwood, *Past History*, pp.15-17; *GBM* January 1859, p.27. The *GBM* review of Hinton's Lectures on Redemption is instructive in both rejecting Hinton's synthesis, and in indicating the resolute way in which the reviewer holds to his own views on an atonement offered to all. February 1860, pp.52-62.

48 See James Salisbury's Association Letter on 'Scriptural Election and Predestination', *Minutes of the Ninety-First Annual Association of the New Connexion of General Baptists*, 1860, pp.38-47.

Arnold's reference to the impact of that system as 'the iron grasp of the heavy handed Protestant Philistine of Geneva' appealed sufficiently to General Baptist minds to have been quoted on a number of occasions. John Clifford believed that by the 1880s the hand of Calvin had become an extinct force in living theology.[49] At the same time, General Baptists had to defend their belief in universal redemption: this did not, claimed Dawson Burns, imply any form of universalism, but rather that the redemption secured on the cross could be universally accepted - the important idea was that of 'potentiality' rather than 'actuality'.[50]

In the *General Baptist Year Book* for 1870, the editorial pen of Clifford offers this ambiguous explanation of a want of General Baptist success in growth, and the unwisdom of pursuing unity schemes:

> The pervasion of the body of Particular Baptists with our distinguishing sentiments, and their adoption of the method of giving 'universal invitations' to sinners to accept the gospel even when they do not allow of a universal provision for the salvation of men, has probably tended to diminish our interest in denominational work and institutions, and so hindered our progress. The necessity for our separate existence, it has been said, is gone by, and we have been talking of union and absorption, and neglecting our own immediate work of preaching the gospel of the grace of God to all men . . . But we may add that if we rightly understood what we have and hold as General Baptists, and knew the theological sentiment still avowed and taught in many quarters on the other side, we

---

49 *GBM* January 1877, p.3; Thomas Goadby, *ibid.*, November 1880, p.407; January 1881, p.11; March 1881, p.107.

50 *GBM* August 1891, pp.299f. Fuller's writings did not, in his judgement, help: for the sum of their teaching was that 'the barrier was not put at Christ's work but at the Spirit's operation'. Indeed, Dawson Burns found the older Calvinism, much as he disagreed with it, more logical and consistent than the moderate version.

> should not breathe another word about 'absorption' for the next twenty-five years at least.[51]

Clifford still maybe represented the enthusiasms of youth, for in that same year, Underwood, ever consistent in his search for denominational harmony, argued:

> *The union of Baptists is especially to be sought.* I mean a much closer one than now exists. For our present semi-separate state is neither satisfactory nor seemly . . . For all practical ends what might be called the Calvinism of one party is exactly the same as the Arminianism of the other. What doctrinal sentiments have been expressed from the chair of the Baptist Union Meetings (which has nearly always been filled by a Particular Baptist) which might not have been uttered with equal approval from the Chair of the General Baptist Association?

Indeed he argued that the two bodies were united in their religious aims and in the language and content of their pulpit utterances.[52]

From the other side of the divide, there is the witness of Spurgeon himself, who was quite willing to give donations towards New Connexion church-planting and to commend their appeals for chapel

51 *General Baptist Year Book* (hereafter *GBYB*), 1870, p.56. This was the second edition of the Year Book which replaced the published Minutes of earlier years. The title 'Year Book' was first used in 1869 but the subsidiary description of Minutes was perpetuated whilst the Chairman's address and the Association Letter were separately paginated. In the letter for 1870 on 'Our Future', J. C. Pike, whilst believing that time had changed from the situation existing a hundred years earlier which had dictated the need for the New Connexion's separate existence, and that there was now 'a much closer approximation of sentiment in reference to the leading truths of the gospel', still cautioned against too swift a move to union, hankering after the familiarity and friendship of the smaller association, pp.6f.

52 W. Underwood, *Centennial Survey*, 1870, pp.14f.

building.[53] Though on occasions he had not been slow to condemn what he took to be dangerous trends in New Connexion teaching, he marked its centenary by confessing: 'We belong to another school of thought, but our General Baptist brethren are so thoroughly evangelical that our differences are lost in our unities.'[54] But future union schemes were undermined by the report that he had said that 'towards his General Baptist friends he had friendly and loving feelings, but he recognized the District Union brethren [the London Strict Baptists] as being even closer akin'. John Clifford riposted for the New Connexion: 'we should recognize Mr Spurgeon as being in nine-tenths of his sermons and nearly all his works much closer akin'.[55]

The New Connexion membership was, however, becoming increasingly generalized. Jabez Burns in 1870 confessed that New Connexion congregations were largely composed of persons who had never heard of the General Baptists, and, therefore, knew nothing of the differences of 'Old' and 'New', of 'General' and 'Particular': this was especially true of new churches in London whose membership contained few convinced Baptists of any kind. Better then to concentrate on nurturing Baptist identity than fragmenting it with sectional titles.[56]

WIDER ASSOCIATIONS

The issue of merging the two parts of the Baptist family must always be set within the larger prospect of an amalgamation of the two parts of the Congregational family, Baptist and paedobaptist. At one time a separate union of General Baptists and Independents was even suggested by W. G. Soper when Chairman of the Surrey

---

53 Witness his support in word and donation for the new church at Hucknall, Notts. He also made a contribution to the building fund for John Clifford's Westbourne Park. *GBM* June 1875, p.229; November, p.430.

54 *GBM* February 1871, p.46; but cf. December 1870, p.353.

55 *GBM* January 1877, p.2.

56 *GBM* March 1870, p.67.

Congregational Union. 'Who', he asked, 'in faith, purpose and life are so like ourselves as the General Baptists? Is an alliance utopian? . . . in our opinion a serious attempt at union should be made.' It was noted by the *General Baptist Magazine* on the authority of no less a person than R. W. Dale that 'Calvinism is almost an obsolete theory amongst Independents'; and that 'the doctrine of "general redemption" which is one of our main distinguishing tenets, is generally accepted and preached' amongst them.[57]

Thus two potential merger schemes - of General and Particular Baptists, and of paedobaptist and non-paedobaptist Congregationalists - were intertwined in the discussions that spanned the century. J. P. Mursell's son, Arthur, in 1877 wrote to the *Christian World* proposing the larger merger of all congregational Christians: Baptists and Congregationalists holding parallel but separate 'union' meetings represented not unity but divergence which ought by the 1860s to have become an anachronism. 'From any but a purely technical point of view, these two denominations differ in scarcely anything. Socially, evangelically, and in their church polity they are at one.' To achieve unity he suggested the rather curious methodology of the Baptists conceding the mode as immaterial while the Congregationalists should 'concede the question of the subjects and administer the initiatory rite only to responsible and voluntary applicants.'[58]

A number of correspondents supported the intention but few the methodology. C. Stovel of Lincoln suggested instead that each Union should continue with joint Spring Meetings in London and separate autumnal meetings in the provinces. At the same time. H. W. Earp, a leading General Baptist layman, argued 'The union of Baptists and Independents is rapidly becoming, in country districts especially, a pressing question'. Others looked to the day when the millennial dream of all Free Churches combining in witness and ceasing from the mistaken multiplication of competitive chapels in rural areas would become a reality, though the boundary between chapel and church still

57 *GBM* February 1876, p.66.

58 *Christian World*, 26 October 1877, p.766.

needed to be fiercely guarded. For his part Clifford, with his unecclesial view of baptism, addressed Baptists and paedobaptists alike: 'we anticipate a time when the Congregationalist churches of the land shall so completely understand baptism that it shall cease to be a divisive element.'[59]

The proposals for Baptist union had always to be set within this larger context, and were often interwoven, as in the Chairman's address delivered by Watson Dyson of Halifax to the General Baptists in 1886. Contemplating Methodist amalgamation he bore witness that many Baptists and Congregationalists were asking why one controversial point was sufficient to divide brethren with similar interests and aims, noting that presidents of the Baptist Union saw no reasons for 'Generals' and 'Particulars' continuing apart. The disposition of the times was towards union, and that surely was a Christ-like end.[60]

The very same issues of the *Christian World* that were commenting on Mursell's initiative were also reporting on the Leicester Conference on 'the Terms of Religious Communion', which was seen to challenge the theological orthodoxy of the Congregational body. The handling of this perhaps provides one marker, Down Grade notwithstanding, that the two parts of the congregational family were developing in different directions in their relationship to historic evangelicalism. Thus, despite much talk, the union of the two parts of the congregational family did not follow on the union of the Baptists.[61]

---

59 *ibid.*, 2 November, p.784; 9 November, p.812; 30 November, p.863. *GBM* January 1877, p.2; February 1878, pp.57-9. Chairman's Address, in *GBYB*, p.5. *GBYB* 1886, p.8.

60 *GBYB* 1886, p.11; see also, 1889, p.5, 'Union was in the air, and the goal to which it pointed was not union amongst Baptists simply but a general amalgamation of all churches of the congregational order'.

61 For the Leicester Conference, see M. D. Johnson, *The Dissolution of Dissent 1850-1918*, 1987, esp. chapter II, and on Baptist-Congregational divergence, J. H. Y. Briggs, 'Charles Haddon Spurgeon and the Baptist Denomination in Nineteenth-Century Britain', *BQ* 31, 1986, pp.218-40.

THE ROLE OF THE BAPTIST UNION

Notwithstanding the discussions concerning unity, an ambivalence of relationship between New Connexion churches and the Baptist Union clearly existed. Certain unfortunate actions by the Baptist Union did not help. For example, a statement appeared in the *Baptist Handbook* for 1873 that the General Baptists had seceded from the Particular Baptists a hundred years previously! To make matters worse the judgement was repeated by the Union's lawyer-treasurer, S. R. Pattison, and reported in the *Freeman* in the middle of the final discussions on amalgamation.[62] New Connexion numbers and organization did not entitle them to extensive representation on the Baptist Union Committee, where for many years only Clifford, the Secretary of the General Baptist Missionary Society, and the Principal of the College served, with Dr Underwood an honorary member from 1874. In the 1880s the numbers of General Baptists serving on the council gradually increased though never reaching double figures. Scrutiny of those who spoke at the annual meetings of the Baptist Union indicated the leadership afforded by a number of New Connexion ministers: Dr Underwood, Mr Stevenson, various members of the Goadby, Burns and Pike families, and, above all others, John Clifford, whose ubiquitous presence greatly increased the General Baptist participation in Union affairs.

'The main reason for retaining the "General",' its advocates agreed, 'is that we have no intention of dropping our organization'. For this the General Baptists exhibited a not unwarranted pride. No other pattern was as effective, not county associations because restricted in area, nor the Baptist Union which 'has hardly reached, as yet, the condition of a living organism' - a surprising argument since in 1873 it had been argued by General Baptists that the Baptist Union was getting too big for deliberative purposes.[63] By 1883 it was argued:

---

62 *GBM* March 1873, p.108; *Freeman*, 15 February 1889.

63 John Clifford in *GBM* July 1878, p.265; June 1873, p.230.

> we General Baptists are a portion of the Union. We were in at the beginning, and have been all along the whole course. Of late, as everybody knows, the Union has changed its front, and is rapidly becoming a Baptist Home Mission Organization. From that part of its work 'Generals' are shut out; but we feel we ought to do our utmost for the 'Annuity', 'Augmentation', and 'Education' Funds, and therefore we have, at our recent Assembly . . . created a Baptist Union Department, of which the Rev. W. Avery is Secretary . . . Since we have no reason for belonging to the Union except to aid in its work, we ought to do that as far as we possibly can.[64]

But it was uphill work. Indeed, W. J. Avery, one-time coadjutor of Clifford in Paddington, proved to be one of the unsung heroes of amalgamation, engaging in much patient lobbying and encouragement to secure greater General Baptist participation in the work of the Baptist Union of which he became Assistant Secretary from 1884-99.

THE FULL SPECTRUM OF BAPTIST ORGANIZATIONS

From the very beginning, members moved from churches of one connexion to those of the other. They were so fully accepted that, if possessing the appropriate gifts, they soon secured appointment to the diaconate within churches of the other communion. There was little restriction on pulpit access - the same sermons, it was claimed, were equally acceptable in both parts of the family. Thus there soon developed an interchange of ministry. Study of the magazines and handbooks swiftly reveals examples of men trained in one of the Particular Colleges serving in New Connexion pastorates and conversely men from the New Connexion College serving Particular Baptist charges. One sixth of New Connexion pastors serving in 1870 came direct from Particular Baptist Colleges or from Particular Baptist churches. 'If this extensive co-mingling of ministers who were trained outside of us, and who were once otherwise associated, has occurred

64 *GBM* October 1883, p.387.

without any harm, and with some positive benefit, may not a much wider comprehension be wished and welcomed?'[65]

But that 'wider comprehension' had to take account of the total context, for the modified Calvinism of post-Fuller Particular Baptists and the revival faith of the New Connexion still represented median positions, between the remaining High Calvinists and those General Baptists who adopted a unitarian Christology. Those positions, and more particularly the suspicions that they bred, continued to exercise an influence on those who trod the middle ground.

Whilst the Gadsbyites and the new Strict Baptists of the 1830s, who left the Church of England at a time when an innovative form of high-churchmanship was beginning to stir,[66] had little to do with the reformulated Baptist Union, other Strict Baptists holding the doctrine of particular redemption were prepared both to join and participate fully in its life. These included those who promoted the activities of the Baptist Tract Society, founded in 1841, which later became the Strict Baptist Society and then the Baptist Evangelical Society.[67] The northern branch of this society was active, leading in 1860 to the withdrawal of strict-communionist churches from the Lancashire and Cheshire Association to form the North Western Association. After sixteen years of separate existence, however, this reunited with the older association in 1875, bringing Manchester College with it.[68] Whilst it lasted, the North Western Association represented within the Baptist Union a second confessionally, rather than geographically, defined association.

The New Connexion, notwithstanding Dan Taylor's withdrawal from the assembly of the Old Connexion in 1803, and the declaration by New Connexion ministers ten years later condemning the 'baneful

---

65 W. Underwood, *Past History*, p.23; *Centennial Survey*, pp.14,16.

66 See J. H. Philpot, *The Seceders, 1829-69*, 2 vols, 1931-2.

67 Geoffrey Breed, *The Baptist Evangelical Society - An Early Victorian Episode*, 1989, and the same author's 'Strict-Communion Organizations amongst the Baptists in Victorian England', University of Keele, MA thesis 1991.

68 John Lea, 'The North Western Association of Baptist Churches, 1860-76', *BQ* 23, 1969, pp.77-90.

poison of Socinianism', continued in some kind of conversation with the older body. Within the counsels of the latter, J. C. Means, minister of their leading London congregation, Messenger, Secretary of the Assembly, and editor of the *General Baptist Advocate* from 1831 to 1836, attacked the unitarianism of many General Baptists and sought to steer the original body away from such tenets into closer fellowship with the New Connexion. Means's energies over many years secured an exchange of delegations in 1868: two messengers from the Old Connexion were received at the assembly of the New Connexion in Derby, and the New Connexion sent two delegates to the Worship Street Assembly in London, an exchange that was repeated and consolidated in 1869 and 1870. An ageing Means, as a last act before resigning the Secretaryship of the General Baptist Assembly, proposed what amounted to the absorption of the few remaining old General Baptist Chapels by the New Connexion, which had so signally demonstrated its more effective evangelistic fervour.

Not surprisingly, such proposals were opposed by the more rationalist of the old General Baptist congregations, their ministers and their Unitarian friends. At the same time, some in the New Connexion were concerned at this amount of fellowship with those whose orthodoxy remained suspect. In 1868 the *General Baptist Magazine*, commenting on the proceedings of the General Assembly, wrote, 'When we are informed that to be designated Unitarian and to hold the Unitarian doctrine "is neither a qualification nor a disqualification of communion" with it, our approval ends and our judgment begins to discern the secret of diminished numbers and decreasing influence'.[69] In 1875 at the New Connexion Assembly at Wisbech, there was a hostile demonstration against the visiting delegates.

In 1878, however, Means, through personal friendship, secured John Clifford as preacher of the annual sermon at a rather more optimistic assembly of the older body. By then a number of New Connexion ministers had accepted pastoral charges in Old Connexion

---

69 *GBM* October 1868, p.289.

churches and were bringing more vigorous evangelistic leadership to their outreach. Thus the improved relationship continued through the early 'eighties, with Clifford again addressing the assembly in both 1887 and 1888 when the ageing radical reformer, Henry Solly, on behalf of the more conservative elements in the Old Connexion, made a bold plea for reunion. But 1888 was to prove the end of a process rather than a new beginning. Arguably the early rumblings of Down Grade and the delicate negotiations between the New Connexion and the Particular Baptists within the Baptist Union made the New Connexion chary of going further down the road of reunion with the Old Connexion, which seemed to offer little for the future of the churches. However, four Old Connexion churches - Headcorn, Winchmore Hill, Long Sutton and Saffron Walden - were subsequently recognized as members of the Baptist Union.[70]

MID CENTURY BLUES

New Connexion minds were most disposed to consider total integration into the life of the Baptist Union when the progress of their own connexion was brought into question. This seems to have been particularly true of the late 1860s.[71] In a paper to the autumnal session of the Baptist Union in 1864, Dr Underwood, then Principal of Chilwell College, provided interesting statistical data for the Connexion which had just over 21,000 members in about 150 churches served by some hundred ordained clergy, about three-quarters of whom had academic training. Although ministerial salaries had improved over the past twenty years they were still lower than for other denominations. About 20% of the ministers came from other traditions, principally the Particular Baptists.[72]

---

70 See I. Sellers, 'The Old General Baptists, 1811-1915', *BQ* 24, 1971, pp.30-41, 74-88. Dr Sellers is not wholly correct in suggesting that 1888 was the last year in which delegates were exchanged. In 1889 accident prevented the Old Connexion representatives from coming to Walsall, but in 1890 two fraternal delegates were once more present. *GBM* January 1890, p.21.

71 *GBM* January 1858, pp.18-19; April 1868, pp.97-100; June 1868, p.178.

72 W. Underwood, *Past History*, pp.8-9.

In the late 'sixties there was a great consciousness that baptisms had been on the decline in the Connexion from 1862, and that membership too had declined from 1865 to 1867. Thomas Goadby of Derby, writing in 1868, thought the watershed came earlier: denominational expansion up to 1846 had been steady, doubling every twenty years, but in 1846 such progress suddenly halted and the growth over 1847-1867 was only 13%, equally spread between town and country. The towns of the East Midlands, the heartland of the Connexion, actually showed a decline in membership during these twenty years. All this, he reluctantly concluded, presented a fearful testimony to a decline in evangelistic zeal. In London, although there had been some increase, there was not the bold expansion secured by the London Baptist Association with its target of at least one new church each year. The Connexion's centenary found it in a grave crisis of 'comparative languor and inefficiency', which certainly did not make it an attractive option to any body seeking amalgamation.[73]

Yet for all his pessimism concerning the last twenty years of the Connexion's history, Goadby was ambiguous about further integration with the Particular Baptists. In an interesting analysis, he affirmed,

> Not as yet has denominationalism completed its work in the world . . . Not as a loose and heterogeneous mass would we best wage the warfare of the time . . . Nothing is gained by laxity of principle or looseness of fellowship or motley or disjointed agglomerations of unorganized and undisciplined units. In relation to other Baptist churches our duty is plain and clear. So far as they can unite and coalesce with us, we are anxious to unite and coalesce with them. Already we are blended with the larger body of Baptists in the Baptist Union, and take rank as a recognized and distinct community. For there is a main body of Baptists, and there are a right wing and a left wing: the brave-hearted Spurgeon commands the one, and we are remanded to the other. We cannot alter this if we

73 *Minutes of the Ninety-Ninth Annual Association of the New Connexion of General Baptists*, 1868, pp.45-8.

> would, and it is scarcely possible for us except by gradual steps to effect any closer amalgamation. We must grow into union; resolutions and plans can only open and clear the way. It is, I believe, the desire of our churches to preserve their autonomy as a Connexion. Great and insuperable, or well-nigh insuperable, difficulties stand in the way of any immediate or important change, and the difficulties as we have at length discovered are not only or mainly upon our side. Union not absorption; brotherly love not denominational disintegration; catholicity of spirit not dissolution of the body - these are our truest maxims and our wisest watchwords.[74]

Goadby argued that it was best not to over-press the issue but to remain with the fraternal relationship that already existed. He was fearful of the various societies becoming over-centralized and controlled by 'irresponsible officialism'. The distinction between *General* and *Particular* - 'the relics of scholastic speculation' - were of less than major importance to the theological and social strivings of the day. The contemporary challenge came in the form of rationalism, Romanism, and their associates, raising large issues as to 'the inspiration and authority of the Word of God and the character and claims of Our Lord Jesus Christ.' At the same time there were possibilities of wider coalitions of Evangelical Christians and Free Churchmen which were most encouraging. Thus, somewhat changing his earlier emphasis, he argued,

> The principle of denominationalism must not be, as I sometimes fear it has been of late, too prominent and conspicuous among us . . . Brethren, what is our distinctive creed but an idle speculation, what are our churches but purposeless institutions, what is our denomination but a blunder and a mistake, if we are not bringing sinners to repentance and saving souls from death?[75]

---

74 *ibid.*, p.49.
75 *ibid.*, pp.51-3.

In July 1868 came the baldest statement of the situation: 'There seems to be an impression abroad that General Baptists have done their work, and that nothing remains for them but either absorption into some other body, or else perpetual decline and ultimate extinction'.[76] When, however, the statistical reports improved in the 'seventies, then talk of unification tended to disappear from the agenda. Reviewing the mid-century melancholy, John Clifford mused that anybody reading the magazine for the late 'fifties and 'sixties could not but deduce that here was the record of a Connexion that 'had lived too long' and was 'asking for somebody in sheer pity' to bury it. So desperate was the situation that 'if the leaders of that incoherent denomination [the Particular Baptists] had only given us the faintest encouragement, we should have performed the Japanese Trick with inimitable dexterity'. So by 1877, Clifford maintained, 'compelled to go our own way . . . now the subject of the union is not so much as named amongst the possibilities of our near future'.[77] As editor of the denominational magazine, Clifford himself had played a considerable part in raising denominational morale and saving it from overmuch navel-gazing. In part there was better news to report and, when it was not particularly encouraging, Clifford could still produce an inspiring vision of the future.

NON-THEOLOGICAL FACTORS

One of the features that brought the two parts of the family together was joint participation in a number of Baptist societies and funds. In addition to the Baptist Union itself, both supported the Bible Translation Society, the Baptist Total Abstinence Association, and the Hanserd Knollys Society, together with the Augmentation Fund, the National Association for Aged and Infirm Baptist Ministers, and the Board of Education. Support for ministers of both sections of the family increasingly involved some kind of subsidy of General Baptist work by Particular Baptists. When John Clifford was ordained at

---

76 *GBM* July 1868, p.198.

77 *GBM* January 1877, pp.1-2.

Paddington on Good Friday 1859, Dr Underwood of the New Connexion College at Nottingham preached in the afternoon and Dr Angus of Regent's Park College in the evening.[78]

Common interests and common needs played their part. The distribution of the funds collected by the Baptist Lancashire Relief Committee during the cotton famine of the 1860s to General Baptist churches without distinction was warmly appreciated. A resolution from the New Connexion expressed warmest thanks 'for this timely help, while it hails the spirit in which that help was given as an expression of true brotherly love, and as a means of drawing the two sections of the Baptist body into closer and more practical union'.[79]

In 1864, a proposal to establish a General Baptist Building Fund[80] had interesting results. The committee appointed to investigate this, composed of Leicester ministers and laymen, soon discovered that the older Baptist Building Fund was restricted to assisting Particular Baptist churches; considerable legal difficulties would be entailed in dispensing with this restriction. Thwarted in their attempt to join the older body, their preferred mode of operation, their response was to widen their brief and set up what they called, 'The Union Baptist Building Fund', in the interests of avoiding anything that would 'in the least degree tend to fetter or hinder united action on the part of the whole Baptist body at any future time'. The new fund was to 'be exclusively a loan fund for Baptists without distinction.' Regrettably the fund did not secure the anticipated scale of support and this seriously circumscribed its usefulness in its early years. By 1877, the Fund Treasurer was asking benefactors not to use the title Union

78 *GBM* June 1859, p.232.

79 *Minutes of the Ninety-Fourth Annual Association of the New Connexion of General Baptists*, 1863, p.43.

80 *Minutes of the Ninety-Fifth Annual Association of the New Connexion of General Baptists*, 1864, p.37.

Baptist Building Fund in their wills as this had changed to the General Baptist Building Fund.[81]

In 1865 the New Connexion established a Board of Reference, consisting of four senior ministers serving for three years, 'to facilitate the removal of ministers and the supply of churches'.[82] It was to be almost twenty years before the Baptist Union considered a similar proposal and even longer before it took action.[83] In 1884 the Association became incorporated, thereby providing the precedent for the creation of the Baptist Union Corporation, which, as an instrument of the Baptist Union, helped to make amalgamation effective.[84]

As New Connexion members became more mobile so they tended to move to areas with either no New Connexion chapel or only a struggling one. Whereas the earlier tendency would have been to establish a New Connexion cause, later in the century it became more acceptable to join the nearest Particular Baptist or Independent church, especially where that offered lively fellowship and good opportunities for Christian service. Underwood believed that it was 'no uncommon thing for our members, when they rise in worldly position, or when their comfort is disturbed, to retire from our communion to that of the other section, which is considered to be more respectable, or which has, perchance, a more able ministry or more attractive sanctuaries'.[85]

---

81 *Minutes of the Ninety-Sixth Annual Association of the New Connexion of General Baptists*, 1865, pp.34-7. E. A. Payne is thus accurate in talking of the assets of the General Baptist Building Fund being fused with the older body in 1891, though in the debate on amalgamation many speakers used the older, deliberately irenic title. Payne, *Baptist Union*, p.147; *GBM* 1876, cf. pp.182, 217, 311, 440; March 1877, p.104.

82 *Minutes of the Ninety-Sixth Annual Association of the New Connexion of General Baptists*, 1865, p.37.

83 Payne, *Baptist Union*, p.123.

84 Sir John Marchant, *Dr John Clifford, CH,* 1924, pp.220-1, where a number of organizational features are listed and their New Connexion precedents recorded.

85 W. Underwood, *Centennial Survey*, p.6.

There had also been too much unhealthy independence among the churches: there was a failure to realize that 'when the individual unites with a church or the church with an association of churches, a portion of individual liberty is necessarily surrendered'. Too many churches had been founded by domineering figures who, not being able to get their own way in larger bodies, seceded to found congregations that they could dominate, and which were thus doomed to weakness by the very way in which they had been brought to birth. Such churches, schismatically founded, were in their debility a living testimony to the antithesis of the strength of unity.[86]

Proposals for amalgamations within other denominations also affected Baptist minds, as did secular celebrations. For example, J. Perry of Hitchin argued that 'a union of PBs and GBs' would be an excellent way of celebrating the Queen's Jubilee in 1887, especially since 'the union of various sections of the Wesleyan body is in the air'; this would represent a 'needful husbanding of our resources' and would help 'in the spread of the gospel in the villages'.[87]

LOCAL INITIATIVES

Growing together also began at the local level.[88] In 1861, the London Baptist ministers, accustomed to meet in 'The Particular Baptist Board', 'after much prayer' agreed to strike through the word 'Particular' and admit John Clifford to their fellowship. Other forms of co-operation developed. One was for associations to embrace members of both parts of the family. When the London Baptist Association was refounded in 1865, with Spurgeon presiding over the planning group, the *Freeman* recorded that those present represented 'well-nigh every shade of opinion amongst us, whilst if any party predominated, we should say it was that of our Strict-Communion brethren'. There was thankfulness 'that the basis of this new association is so broad. It does not rest in a creed, but simply with

86 *GBM* 1868, pp.165ff.

87 *GBM* February 1887, p.63, and March 1887.

88 W. Underwood, *Past History*, p.23.

[a] wide basis of evangelical sentiment.'[89] John Clifford referred to London General Baptist churches 'entering therein on perfectly equal terms without any question being raised as to theology, and expressly for the prosecution of chapel-building work'.[90] Granted such unity of concern about church extension, and the participation of both bodies in promoting new causes, the question was how distinctive in loyalty such newly founded churches would be. Haven Green, Ealing, for example, was a New Connexion venture but Particular Baptists including Spurgeon were involved with its establishment.[91] Ferme Park, Hornsey, opened in 1889, was another late New Connexion planting, but Charles Brown, its first minister, trained at Bristol. It would be right to question whether within such churches any adjective could properly be put in front of Baptist.

Buckinghamshire provided another example of widened association life. The General Baptists, with a disused chapel in Aylesbury, first deferred reopening it as a preaching station because the Particulars had successfully inaugurated services in the Corn Exchange. Then in November 1868, they decided 'that as the Buckinghamshire Association now gives the opportunity of membership to all evangelical Baptist churches in the district irrespective of the distinctions of "Particular" and "General".' the chapel should be made available to the new congregation at a nominal rent.[92]

In 1870 a Midlands Baptist Union brought churches of the two traditions together in joint evangelistic activity, including the employment of an evangelist to work with churches of both families.[93] The founding of the Cheshire Baptist Union in 1879 experimented with uniting the Cheshire churches of both sections of the denomination, 'whilst retaining existing denominational ties', in

89 *Freeman*, cited in W. Y. Fullerton, *op.cit.*, p.309.

90 *GBM*, August 1881, p.284.

91 *GBM* July 1880, p.242; September, p.326.

92 *GBM* November 1868, p.340.

93 See *GBM* October 1868, p.306; August 1877, p.315; July 1879, p.291; September 1879, pp.413-4 for references to this. The Midland Baptist Union 'departed this life at Burton, 12 September 1881', October 1881, p.389.

order to promote evangelistic services. In North Staffordshire a similar body seems to have operated, with T. G. Head, funded by the British and Irish Home Missionary Society, serving a joint pastorate between the Particular church at Fenton and the General congregation at Eastwood Vale, Hanley.[94] Another local strategy was for General Baptist District Conferences to affiliate with the Baptist Union on the same terms as other associations: the Northern Conference did this in 1885 and commended the procedure to the other conferences. In like manner the Connexion determined to make sure it always took up its allotted place on the Baptist Union Council, and urged churches not in membership with the Council to join.[95]

BAPTISM, COMMUNION AND MEMBERSHIP

Both sections of the denomination moved on from the open-communion debate of the Hall-Kinghorn era to the issue of open membership. Whereas the General Baptists of the 1830s had been suspicious of the open table of an increasing number of Particular churches, by 1877 John Clifford could declare that over the last fifty years their tables had become universally open.[96] John Clifford's view of baptism, constantly stated and soon taken up by others, was very clear. Baptism

> is associated in the closest way with man's spiritual welfare, with the remission of sins through repentance and faith; and with the gifts of the Holy Ghost. But in no part of the Gospels, Acts, or Epistles, is it described as a condition of admission to the church. Uniformly and exclusively it is prescribed as a solemn transaction between the soul and the Saviour - nowhere as a portion of church government, or as indispensable in order to entrance upon a church state.

94 *GBM* November 1879, p.454; October 1881, p.388.

95 *GBYB* 1885, p.36; 1888, p.33.

96 *GBM* December 1877, p.448.

Thus the church was not involved in approving candidates for baptism: 'No church is asked to approve the person as fit: the church is not taken into the question at all'. This was not simply Clifford's view but, he believed, that of the 'growing part of the denomination'. Westbourne Park was established as an open-membership church, and a small number of General Baptists adopted Clifford's position and practice. When baptism was so viewed, and when Congregational churches welcomed people into membership on the basis of a confession of faith, the argument for denominational unification was compelling.[97]

Advocating the establishment of open-membership churches in the General Baptist Association Letter for 1882, W. L. Jones of Spalding called for a

> union not of perfect uniformity in creed, not of absolute agreement in outward forms, not of mechanical attachment to a vast ecclesiastical confederation, whose members are held together by the iron hand of law; but rather the union of common life, the union of true affection, binding all in the silken cords of love to a Common Lord, the union of a common aim, the union of a common experience, a union so clearly visible, so striking and impressive, that an unbelieving world, allured and won by its fascinating and attractive power, will say, 'We will go with you, for we perceive that God is with you'.[98]

The implication of the letter provoked the calling of a special conference on Conditions of Church Membership. Such romantic revisionism was strenuously opposed by Joseph Fletcher. Article Six of the New Connexion was clear enough in requiring 'all who repent and believe the gospel, to be baptized by immersion in water, in order to be initiated into a church state: and that no person ought to be

---

97 *GBM* December 1877, pp.448-9; April 1881, p.122; March 1883, p.89. Clifford's teaching lay behind W. L. Jones' controversial Association Letter of 1882 on 'Conditions of Church Membership', p.9.

98 W. L. Jones, 'Conditions of Church Membership' p.13, in *GBYB*, 1882.

received into the church without submission to that ordinance'. Modern practice, Fletcher contended, stood that teaching on its head: baptism, no longer a duty, was but a privilege, and 'if it be deemed a privilege not worth having, he who so deems it is to be received into the church all the same and is to be accounted quite as good a Christian as one who hails it with unquestioning loyalty, and observes it with unfaltering fidelity'.[99] Clearly the real target of Fletcher's attack was Clifford rather than Jones, and it is significant that Fletcher and Clifford were to serve as two of the last presidents of the General Baptist Association, the one doing all he could to obstruct, the other all he could to aid, the process of integration. In their persons they illustrate the inner tensions within the body, between the credal semi-presbyterianism of Fletcher and the functional congregationalism of Clifford.

For his part, Clifford pointed to the increase of open membership among Particular Baptists, naming Bloomsbury, Regent's Park, Hampstead, Clapton, and Camden Road, London; Broadmead and Tyndale, Bristol; and St Mary's, Norwich, together with the information that all the Birmingham churches, except the New Connexion congregation, were open membership, and all but one of the new churches founded by the London Baptist Association were founded on that basis. His enquiries indicated that two out of every three of 'the leading churches of the Particular Baptist type' were open membership.[100] The toleration of differences on the terms of communion within both sides of the family raised questions as to why they should allow their historic differences over election to perpetuate separate identities.

99 *GBM* February 1883, p.49. Clifford added that from 1870 he had appended a note each year in the *GBYB* that not all New Connexion churches believed the Sixth Article and this had gone unchallenged until 1882. *ibid.*, p.54.

100 *GBM* February 1883, pp.53-4.

NEW LEADERS AND NEW INITIATIVES

John Clifford's conversion to denominational amalgamation was crucial to the success of the whole operation, and added significantly to the patient advocacy of older leaders like Underwood. But the contribution of less charismatic figures must not be ignored. W. J. Avery was appointed to head up the Baptist Union Department of the General Baptist Association, when an increasing conscience developed as to the very low level of support being given. Avery subsequently became assistant to Booth as secretary of the Baptist Union (1884-99), thus providing a General Baptist presence within the secretariat. The other architect of amalgamation was the last secretary of the General Baptist Association, Mr Foulkes Griffiths, QC, of Hornsey, barrister at the Temple, whose clear legal mind helped iron out the details of procedure, decision-making and institutional mergers in the final acts of amalgamation.

After the frustrated attempts to amalgamate General and Particular Baptists in the 1860s, the matter seems to have been removed from the agenda for the best part of fifteen years, during which the New Connexion recovered something of its self-confidence. When in 1884 Richard Glover, as President of the Union, visited the annual assembly of the New Connexion, he exhorted his hearers with the message that 'the more perfect denomination of the future will be when "PB" and "GB" are moulded into some other "B" nobler and larger'.[101] At the same time, there was renewed awareness of the slowness of growth within the churches of the New Connexion. The number of baptisms per annum was actually declining (1882:1542; 1883:1344; 1884:1291), whether because of under-stress in open-membership churches or over-stress in closed-membership churches, the analyst was uncertain.

The issue of amalgamation was put back on the agenda once more by Charles Williams in his presidential address to the Baptist Union Assembly on 10 May 1886. The focus for that assembly was rural

---

101 *GBM* August 1884, p.292.

evangelism and within that context Williams made two significant points. First was the argument that today's mission must not be fettered by yesterday's caution. Secondly, he emphasized that for true union to exist, faith and freedom must be harnessed together. The faith once delivered to the saints, and the freedom for the disciple to develop his own pattern of fidelity in active discipleship in the contemporary world, were not hostile to one another if both flowed from a fundamental allegiance to Christ. In this way liberty served to conserve truth: liberty and loyalty belonged together when the object of the exercise was not a union of coercion or cold logic but of spiritual reality.[102]

Arguing from John 17, he posed the questions: 'Can we justify the division of our denomination into two sections? . . . We preach the same gospel . . . What hinders?' Whilst some might too quickly answer, 'Trust Deeds', W. H. Tetley of Derby, President of the General Baptist Association in 1888, was convinced it was not a universal want of inclination, nor an indistinguishable passion for maintaining the distinction between Particulars and Generals, now recognized as a difference without a distinction. It certainly was not any want of General Baptist ministers serving in Particular Baptist churches, or Particular Baptists pastoring General Baptist churches, nor could it be attributed to any superfluity of resource and support for the denomination's institutions. Thus the answer to the question, 'What hinders?' remained an enigma.[103]

The resolution consequent upon Charles Williams's address to the Baptist Union was proposed by Alexander McLaren, seconded by Colonel Griffin, then Treasurer of the Home Mission Fund, and spoken to by Edward White, as Chairman of the Congregational Union. It read:

> That this Assembly, deeply impressed both with the importance of the evangelisation of our country and with the special needs

---

102 *Baptist Union Handbook* (hereafter *BH*) 1887, Presidential Address, 'A Plea for Union among Baptists', pp.21-9.

103 *GBYB* 1888, 'Church Rest', Presidential Address by W. H. Tetley, pp.15ff.

> of our village churches, earnestly commends to the denomination the appeal made this morning from the Presidential Chair on behalf of the Home Mission of the Baptist Union.[104]

The strategic concerns of a president from Lancashire, intent upon improving the denomination's capacity for bold missionary endeavour at home and overseas, needed the determination of the Yorkshire Association Secretary, John Haslam, to give shape and form at the autumnal meetings of the Baptist Union in Huddersfield in 1888, for even presidential pleas do not become denominational policy unless they are provided with effective institutional teeth.[105] In this instance, of course, there was the added complication that the affairs of the Baptist Union in the years 1887-88 were overshadowed by the threats inherent in the Down Grade Controversy, though Spurgeon made it quite clear that as far as he was concerned the free-will/destination issue was to be respected as an open question. Votes in councils had to be backed up by the education of affections. 'The union cannot be accomplished', affirmed J. C. Jones, 'by passing resolutions at meetings and recording such resolutions with pen and ink'.[106]

THE GENERAL BAPTISTS RESPOND: THE WALSALL ASSOCIATION OF 1889

With the authority of that Huddersfield resolution, S. H. Booth, the Baptist Union Secretary, wrote to the General Baptist Association as did the Secretary of the Leicestershire Association. Foulkes Griffiths persuaded the executive to set up an investigative committee, which brought unanimously supported resolutions to the Association Meetings in Walsall in 1889, where the vital decision was taken in

---

104 *BH* 1887, pp.28-9.

105 Payne, *Baptist Union*, p.146, refers to Haslam's resolution without referring to Williams' presidential initiative two years earlier.

106 *BM* March 1889, pp.105-7.

principle to proceed towards amalgamation.[107] This it only did after rehearsing its earlier pro-union decisions from its initial approach to Andrew Fuller about participating in the work of the Baptist Missionary Society. Most recently, when the New Connexion College had moved from Chilwell to Nottingham, the opportunity had been taken to revise the trust to open it to all evangelical Baptists. This historical consciousness was very important to the General Baptists. Thereafter, the delegates expressed 'a hearty desire for complete and thorough-going union - union not of fragments of one body but of all and the whole, and as far as may be, with all and the whole of the Particular Baptists.' Fifty-one delegates voted for the resolution with twelve voting against. The Baptist Union was assured that if it would take the necessary action to promote such a union it could count on their support. The prospects seemed good, since, following Williams's initiative, some twenty General Baptist churches had joined the Union, whilst the giving to Union funds had shown a significant increase. What was involved was not, of course, an amalgamation with the Baptist Union, for the New Connexion had been a full member of that body from its commencement, and thus all its institutions were jointly owned. The union was with Particular Baptist brethren and their institutions, though again the difficulty was underlined that the Particular Baptists were without corporate identity.

The decision was not, however, without dissent. The Revd Joseph Fletcher of Commercial Road, East London, and one of the editors of the denominational journal, was President of the Association that year. Soon revealing himself as one of the major opponents of the scheme, he used his address to express his disquiet. The issue was, he contended, 'a question which primarily concerns the Foreign Mission'. He was not convinced that the Particular Baptists were really committed to the proposal: even Charles Williams's plea occasioned

---

107 This analysis of the Walsall Association has been reconstructed principally from the *GBYB*, 1889, pp.21-31, and the President's Address, 'Your Denominational Organization', supplemented by additional references from the *GBM* for that year.

'no practical step . . . until the amalgamation question went forth from our own Foreign Mission Committee', and even then, when the Secretary of the BMS was pressed to take a seat on the General Baptist Missionary Society Committee investigating the implications, he 'found reasons for not doing so'. Indeed, when the Report of the Council first came before the Baptist Union, the first proposal was that it should lay on the table, which Fletcher judged 'the same thing as throwing it into the waste paper basket', and there it would have lain, had not a General Baptist ex-president [John Clifford] intervened to rescue it. The leadership of the Baptist Union, which itself was still but a lodger in the Mission House, was guilty of being supine in passing a resolution on union and then naively asking others to implement it. Further allegations were that the Baptist Union Council had judged that it was impractical to amalgamate the organization of the Colleges whilst the fusion of the Building Funds was beyond contemplation.

The problem was in attempting amalgamation at a national level: locally, Fletcher was happy to be a full member of the London Baptist Association and to work harmoniously with Pastors' College men in East London. He was also happy to serve loyally on the Baptist Union Council. Spiritual union was what mattered, not a paper union: if there had been theological convergence well and good but, if not, let not the divisions be papered over. He was not convinced that the Particular Baptists really wanted amalgamation. Reflecting on their failure to take up the initiative earlier, he confessed, 'I am too independent to knock a second time at any door where I have been repulsed once'. Whether amalgamation took place or not, the union most to be desired was the strengthening of existing organization. This, could be done 'by combining with it something of the essence of Methodism or Presbyterianism, or a judicious blend of both', in order to counter the ultra-congregationalism of the present day. Even General Baptists were suffering from 'independency run mad': city churches which did not work together, denominational institutions which secured only whimsical support, church schisms leading to rival congregations, ministerial invitations to men of no standing or approbation with disastrous consequences for the churches, and denominational authorities which were either powerless or ignored.

What Fletcher sought for the good of the churches was a new standard of faith and practice to replace Dan Taylor's 'Six Articles', which no longer met the needs of the late nineteenth century. A new statement was needed, based perhaps on John Clifford's three universals: the universality of the love of God to man, the universality of the redeeming work of the Son, the universality of the convincing work of the Spirit.[108] Coupled with these should be a statement on Baptist convictions on polity, freedom and the ordinances. The over-vague non-credalism of earlier years required qualification. 'J. A.' (whom Fletcher took to be Joseph Angus) had indicated that Baptist objections were to creeds as human statements going beyond the limits of scriptural teaching, but Baptists had always required certain beliefs of those seeking their fellowship. 'We must have beliefs or we are not Christians. We must have beliefs - great principles of truth and life - or we cannot have Christian churches; and we must avow and proclaim them or we are useless Christians, if we be Christians at all'.[109] Such sentiments Fletcher endorsed with all his heart. In the context of Down Grade, it was not only Spurgeon who sought some confession of faith: a committed General Baptist was of the same mind.

Where Fletcher parted company with Spurgeon was in his desire for a tighter denominational organization: a Model Trust Deed to protect the denomination's interests at a time when there was suspicion of trust deeds as inhibiting the development of new strategies; a Board of Reference to act like a Methodist Stationing Committee to examine candidates for training and to help place ministers, noting that in the pioneer years of the New Connexion the mind of the whole association was from time to time sought on critical placements; and finally a Sustentation Fund to prevent churches creating ministerial penury, and to secure proper respect for the ministry. Such was the programme

---

108 Joseph Fletcher, President's Address, *GBYB*, 1889.

109 *Freeman*, 13 April 1888.

he offered as an alternative to amalgamation.[110] In fact, when amalgamation took place, one of the major contributions of the General Baptists to the enrichment of the whole denomination was this well-developed sense of denominational cohesion and the development of appropriate instruments to secure it.

BAPTIST UNION AND BAPTIST MISSIONARY SOCIETY PROCEEDINGS

For its part the Baptist Union Assembly, meeting in Birmingham in October 1889, received from the Council a resolution in favour of amalgamation, proposed by John Clifford, and unanimously agreed. This would require the integration of the various societies and institutions of both bodies and a reconstruction of association life on a geographical principle only. The Union was fortified in its decision by reports that the proposal was practical and did not encounter any major legal difficulties, and also by securing a return from all but two of the thirty-four Associations. The non-respondents were Monmouthshire Welsh, and the Bedfordshire Union of Christians, who may well have abstained deliberately, as the Huntingdonshire Association did, recording that it could not discuss the question since it comprised Independents as well as Baptists. Three other Associations had deferred consideration, including the important Yorkshire Association which had arranged to meet with representatives of the Northern Conference first,[111] whilst the Spurgeonic Surrey and Middlesex Association voted 'that no opinion on this subject be expressed by this Association'. This left twenty-seven associations supporting the proposed action and none dissenting.[112]

---

110 Fletcher, President's Address, *GBYB 1889.*

111 The other two were Wiltshire and East Somerset, and Worcestershire.

112 *BH* 1890, pp.46, 70-2. Clifford called the Birmingham resolution 'the first business transaction in connection with the question of fusion', *GBYB* 1890, p.25.

The Council affirmed that the designations 'General' and 'Particular' should be discontinued as a means of identifying different Baptist churches, societies and institutions: all institutions denominationally promoted should be designated by the term 'Baptist' only, with the obvious requirement that all Baptists should be free to participate in their management and, as appropriate, their benefits. It was necessary for those societies, and critically the two missionary societies, to take independent action, since a resolution of the Baptist Union Council could in no way initiate or determine action in these independent bodies, though the General Baptist Missionary Society was by this time constitutionally integrated into their Association.

Joint meetings of the two missionary societies took up the task as early as September 1888, with a number of joint meetings following. A special meeting of the BMS, held on 29 April 1890, to secure necessary action, devised the form of words which adopted the popular name of the society as its formal title. with the explanation that the society embraced the 'Particular Baptist Missionary Society for Propagating the Gospel among the Heathen' founded in 1792, and the 'General Baptist Missionary Society' formed in 1816. The proposal was unanimously and heartily adopted and six General Baptists were immediately elected as Honorary Members of the Baptist Missionary Society to guarantee that denomination's Orissa interest. Herbert Cozens-Hardy, QC, MP, had given legal advice without charge on the feasibility of amalgamation. In due time the General Baptist Association and the subscribers' meeting of the General Baptist Missionary Society took reciprocal action.[113]

---

113 *Missionary Observer* June 1891, pp.237-40. Charles Williams, who was to have proposed the motion, was late, arriving only in time to second it. Thus the motion was proposed by Dr Underhill, who referred to his joy at seeing amalgamation taking place in his lifetime and in time for the centenary of Carey's initiative. William Hill, the Secretary of the GBMS, became 'Secretary at the Bible Translation Society', dividing his time between that task and undertaking deputation work for the joint society.

THE GENERAL BAPTISTS RESPOND: THE NOTTINGHAM ASSOCIATION OF 1890

The 1890 Association of General Baptists meeting in Nottingham began to engage with the issue in greater detail.[114] Three documents were tabled and at last the General Baptists were convinced that the Particular Baptists meant business. The passing of the resolution last October in Birmingham, recorded the *General Baptist Year Book*, 'had completely changed the position of the question.'

The first report of the Baptist Union Joint Committee was generally optimistic. As yet there was no resolution concerning the amalgamation of the two Building Funds because of the strong opposition of the Secretary of the General Baptist Building Fund, who considered the Particular Baptist Building Fund remained too much a private enterprise and lacked sufficient denominational security. This issue needed prior resolution. On Home Missions, the General Baptist Association had yet to decide, but the Baptist Union was prepared to take on existing liabilities if the previously sponsoring churches would commit their future donations to the Baptist Union.

The second report, on the realignment of associational loyalties, noted the Northern Conference churches were to divide between the Yorkshire Association, and the Lancashire and Cheshire Association which would also receive the churches of the old Cheshire and North Staffordshire Conference. The Midlands Conference, in the General Baptist heartlands of Lincolnshire, Nottinghamshire, Derbyshire and Leicestershire, was to join with the Particular Baptists in those counties to form a strong new East Midlands Baptist Association. The Warwickshire churches were advised to join the Midlands Association, renamed the West Midlands Association. Churches of the Southern Conference, and of other Conferences not mentioned, were free to realign as seemed best to them. That the boundary issue was so easily resolved confirms John Clifford's judgement that the churches were

---

114 The account of the Nottingham meeting is principally taken from the *GBYB* for 1890, pp.22-47, supplemented by references to the *GBM* for that year.

ahead of the leadership in their desire for unity - though Joseph Fletcher argued that it represented an abdication of responsibility by the leadership in permitting such undesirable 'drifting'.

With 1892 and the centenary of Carey's great initiative in view, there was a growing desire that that celebration 'should find all Baptists united in proclaiming through one brotherly organization, the fact that there was an "atonement given" and "hope" for "all" the heathen', and that differences of declaring doctrines should not impair the enthusiasm of this long awaited centenary, 'as Carey belongs to us all'. Alfred Baynes, the Secretary of the BMS, had recently visited Orissa and was able to bear ready testimony to the splendid work undertaken by the Orissa missionaries 'of whom any society might feel proud'.

The third report from the Joint Committee of the two missionary societies unanimously recommended complete amalgamation, but with proper provision for continuing the services of the missionaries and the present Secretary of the General Society. Any unforeseen legal difficulties were to be resolved by referees, with the requirement that the proposed amalgamation be completed by June 1891.

Foulkes Griffiths proposed that, whilst discussion might freely range over all three reports, the first focus should be a general vote on the desirability of amalgamating the missionary societies. Executive action on this would be taken by the society itself, acting as a department of the Association. The amalgamation of the missions, he argued, was really the 'pith' of the matter, without which the other proposals would be robbed of significance.

Dr Underwood proposed the adoption of the report. At the end of a long life, he recalled that the first proposal for joint missionary activity had been made four years after his birth - a proposal that the two strands of the family 'though separated in England . . . should be united in India'. He had lived with that possibility ever since, encouraged by the support that the Orissa missionaries had constantly received from their Particular brethren in India. He categorically denied that the union was motivated by the poverty of the General Society. It would in fact inject significant capital into the combined society, which at last could properly be called by the popular title already in use - the Baptist Missionary Society. The financial situation was maybe a little more complicated than Underwood admitted. R. P. Cook, of Edgware Road, admitted that the work of the mission had been adversely affected by the chronic depression which had unduly affected those parts of the nation where the General Baptists had their greatest strength. This had inhibited developments on the mission field, and led to calls for retrenchment. It had also affected the raising of funds for student support at the College, and the resourcing of home mission, which under amalgamation would benefit from being able to appeal to 'a much wider and wealthy constituency'.[115]

Objections ranged around organization, theology and sentiment. Joseph Fletcher made the familiar point that whereas the General Baptist Missionary Society was a department of the Association, the Particular Baptist Missionary Society was an entirely independent body without denominational control. Foulkes Griffiths simply countered that by subscription to the new society General Baptists would earn the right to full participation. Whilst one speaker indicated that he was so confident of the present leadership that he was happy to forego his part in management to such capable direction, a former chairman of the association's Foreign Mission Committee confessed that the management of the General Society had been far from perfect, suffering from infrequent meetings and lack of continuity of membership, faults which would be easily overcome within the larger body.

Theologically, the supposed convergence to which many paid testimony was questioned by others. In particular, it was argued that Calvinism remained dogmatically strong in Yorkshire, with Calvinist articles printed each year within that association's yearbook. Clifford interposed that he had it on the authority of two Yorkshire Particular Baptist leaders that in fact two-thirds of their members were not in full accord with every clause there provided, which offered an historic

115 *BM*, March 1889, pp.103-5.

manifesto rather than 'an expression of the living faith of the churches'. In fact, when the representatives of the two sides met, they swiftly agreed to union in denominational work in Yorkshire, 'without reference to the declarations of faith set forth by either body'.[116]

J. D. Godfrey, from the Barton church, expressed the significance of long-established sentiment, underlining the very well-developed ties between the churches and the Orissa field through generations of missionary service and support. More aggressively, Mr Weightman, an ex-Mayor of Boston, recalled that the GBMS had been founded in Boston and that the local congregation was unprepared for amalgamation. 'They objected,' he said, 'to subscribe to hyper-Calvinistic doctrine'. This intervention was neutralized by Weightman's minister indicating that neither Mr Weightman nor he were mandated by the deacons; some members of the congregation were in favour of amalgamation but the general sentiment was to trust the missionary committee of the association.

The debate was long. John Clifford threw his weight behind the new initiative: 'the attitude he had already taken had been, never to have resting upon his shoulders the responsibility for separation, when union could be secured on terms honourable alike to members of the union and to the Christ who was their supreme Master and Lord'. He confessed that earlier he had devoted his energies to perfecting General Baptist organization but he believed that Charles Williams's invitation had created a new situation, 'and that the man who was loyal to Christ must not only understand the past but must be ready to face the new future'. The exchange ranged widely, some voices were combatant or suspicious, others reconciliatory, speaking of an

---

116 John Clifford suggested that this obstacle could simply be overcome by appending a note that these doctrinal statements were historical expressions of belief, a device he had used with regard to the reprinting of Dan Taylor's Six Articles in the *GBYB* when he was editor, and may suggest who was the author of a similar footnote appended to the final clause of the Union's Declaratory Statement of 1888 (see Payne, *Baptist Union*, p.140 for the text).

honourable union. Many still wanted to speak when the vote was called. An amendment advanced by Fletcher, to receive rather than adopt the report, was lost and the resolution carried.

After a well-earned break the delegates returned to vote through a series of resolutions on the various aspects of the scheme, with minorities on each of less than 12 out of some 200 present: votes which the *Freeman* characterised as embracing just sufficient dissent to indicate that the consideration had been exhaustive and that the conclusions were well-considered and intelligent. Dr S. H. Booth, who was present to speak on home missions, argued that whereas in time past dogmatic groupings may have been helpful, the climate of the late nineteenth century invited the cultivation of the gentler graces and characteristics of Christian life. Some in the debate had perhaps exaggerated differences, but with good faith, kind feeling and Christian affection, he believed that amalgamation was an effective strategy and that 'improbable difficulties' ought not to be put in its way.

The Nottingham meetings still left powerful voices campaigning against amalgamation, principally those of Joseph Fletcher, who had sole charge of the magazine after W. R. Stevenson's death in July 1889, and Dawson Burns, to whom ready access to the paper was given. Some nine major articles attacked the amalgamation proposals, between February 1890 and July 1891, with titles such as 'The Proposed Extinction of the General Baptist Connexion', 'Shall the General Baptist Connexion be sacrificed to an Illusion?', 'The Coming Association: will it save the Connexion?' Burns made personal insinuations against Clifford, 'so much the main mover and the mainstay of the attempt to bring the Connexion to nothing'. Clifford retorted that Burns's record of attendance at association meetings was such that, if all had behaved like him, the association would have died years ago. The arguments were mostly the old ones of sentiment, theological differences and disparity in organization. Ironically, Dawson Burns had already written in the *Baptist Magazine* in favour of 'the closest possible union between General and other Baptists', but the General Baptists were 'a denomination in a sense not applicable to the Baptists who were formerly called Particular but who are now in the main as "General" in their doctrine as the General Baptists themselves'. This he judged was true of five-sixths of such churches and their ministers. The designation 'Particular' was now only used by those Baptists who would not join with anybody.[117] There was also an economic dimension: Dawson Burns asserted that Dr Clifford 'knows that the comparative facility with which those resolutions [at Walsall and Nottingham] were adopted, arose more from financial considerations than any other'.[118]

As author of the leading article in the *General Baptist Magazine* for September 1890, Burns argued,

> I freely avow that I attach greater importance to the truths implied in the word 'General' than to those indicated by the designation 'Baptist'. I am a Baptist because I believe that a personal profession of faith in baptism, is according to the will of Christ; but I am a General Baptist because I believe that the heart of Christ yearns for the salvation of all mankind.

Significantly, he concluded his article by inviting those interested in opposing amalgamation or at least in securing a continuing General Baptist Association, to write to him.[119] Clifford, responding, suggested that Burns's temperance work had kept him in recent years from close involvement in the work of the association, so he was out of touch with the enthusiasm of the churches for amalgamation.[120] This was evidently a correct judgement for less than ten churches voted against the Burnley resolution.

---

117 *BM* March 1889, pp.102-3.

118 There seems to be some evidence that economic restraint existed amongst the General Baptists, e.g. in *GBM*, August 1890, pp.284-7. R. P. Cook, in 'The Limit of Our Supplies', his address to the Home Mission Meeting at Nottingham, passionately appealed to the General Baptists not to take their debts into amalgamation, *GBM* 1890, p.287. Elsewhere it was suggested that the profits on the hymnal might be used to pay off debts.

119 *GBM* September 1890, pp325-7.

120 *GBM* October 1890, p.367.

THE GENERAL BAPTISTS RESPOND: THE BURNLEY ASSOCIATION OF 1891

As the date for the final association meetings drew near, there was a change of tactic. The opposition accepted amalgamation as unstoppable, and campaigned instead for the maintenance of the name, General Baptist, and for the continuity of the Association in addition to the new geographical alignments. Thus before the delegates met at Burnley, the minority had already moved their ground. Fletcher argued that the *via media*, for which he began crusading in 1891, was the only amalgamation sanctioned by the earlier votes. Others countered, firstly that the speeches of those opposing the Walsall resolution had clearly reflected the mind of those reluctant to disband the association, and if they were not speaking appropriately, they should have been told so by Fletcher who chaired the association that year. G. Howard James, a Regent's Park graduate and minister of Woodborough Road, Nottingham, came to the defence of amalgamation. 'An interpretation,' reasoned James, 'which is not heard of until twenty months after the resolution has been passed, can only be regarded as an untrustworthy gloss.'[121] Secondly, the Association in the earlier stages had clearly set itself against piecemeal amalgamation in favour of more total action. Thirdly, the Nottingham resolutions had also involved the dismantling of several Particular Baptist Associations, so it would be exceptionally difficult to concede that only the General Baptist Association should be exempt.

The forthcoming vote, Fletcher contended, should not be on amalgamation or not: the choice was now 'amalgamation or annihilation' - 'cannot we have a marriage without a funeral?' The issue was whether the churches wanted 'to mutilate their banners by voluntarily picking out the golden letters G-E-N-E-R-A-L, the letters we care for most, so that our title shall henceforth be ______ Baptist, and whether they want the ancient and beloved Association of General

---

121 *GBM* April 1891, pp.125-9.

Baptists to dig its own grave and go to its own funeral', thus destroying 'the most united body of Baptists in the kingdom'.[122]

Clifford suggested that the annual meeting of the Midland College could be the focus for the continuation of old sympathies, using language which subsequently proved unwise. Later focus on the Midland College meetings seems to have been unhelpfully transposed to the meetings of the East Midland Baptist Association, as if they represented a continuation of the General Baptist Association.

The final decision came during the Association Meeting at Burnley in June 1891 under the presidency of John Clifford.[123] One of its first acts was to set up a special committee to confer with representatives of those churches which were encountering special difficulties with the Walsall resolutions. This committee interestingly included most of those who themselves were leaders of the unhappy minority. When the reports from the churches were received only a few recorded *contra* votes: three from Yorkshire, four from the East Midlands, two from the Southern Conference. One church in the West Midlands was initially hostile, but, seeing the weight of the majority, swiftly realigned its vote so that the Warwickshire Conference, like the Cheshire Conference, offered unanimous support. In the Eastern Conference some individuals were opposed but no churches. Opposition was thus very limited but significant in representing many of the most historic churches within the connexion. By votes in church meetings and conferences, and letters to the magazine they had made their position quite clear.

A resolution recorded thanks to God for a tradition which embraced the names of John Smyth and Dan Taylor, expressed gratitude for increasing unity, whilst recognizing some reluctance to

---

122 *GBM* March 1891, pp.95, 102.

123 This reconstruction of the Burnley Association of 1891 mainly derives from the *GBYB*, 1891, pp.55-68, with the support of appropriate issues of *GBM*. *GBM*, June 1891, p.229, refers to Dr Booth's account of the process leading to amalgamation in his *History on the movement for the fusion of the two sections of our body*, but unfortunately no copy of this publication has been traced.

break association with a religious past, and accepted the invitation to unify with the Particular Baptists. Attention was drawn to the plea from the chair of the Baptist Union in 1886, the hearty and unanimous vote from the Associations, and the 'courteous and grace-filled endeavours of the officers of the BMS and the BU to facilitate such a fusion'. Delegates were asked to take cognizance of the practical view of the unity of the Baptist family endorsed by the churches in their elections to the pastoral office over the last thirty years; the reported unanimity of the churches in favour of the proposals; the degree of sharing in association life already accomplished; the previous actions of the General Baptist Association in favour of union; and most of all the promise of greater efficiency in home and foreign missions, and other advantages of real Christian unity. It was Clifford's conviction 'that the unity of Christians should be an evangelizing ministry to the world'.[124]

The *General Baptist Magazine* recorded that the debate was conducted in the most admirable spirit with the fullest liberty of speech. At this late stage, Dawson Burns proposed, and J. R. Godfrey seconded, an amendment to the main resolution, suggesting that the amalgamation proposals did not require as either necessary or desirable the dissolution of the General Baptist Association. John Clifford temporarily vacated the chair to participate in the cut and thrust of the ensuing four-hour debate. Burns was resolute in not withdrawing his amendment. It secured thirty-nine votes, with the support of four Yorkshire churches - Heptonstall Slack, Birchcliffe, Lydgate and Halifax - and Commercial Road, London, with the Barton and Chesham churches splitting their votes. There was some difficulty in counting the opposition to the amendment, because of the numbers involved: tallies varied from 150 to 170.[125] After an attempted second amendment failed, the original resolution was passed overwhelmingly. Dawson Burns was not done. He rose to his feet, waving in his hand a number of protests that he

124 *GBM* January 1891, p.5.

125 Joseph Fletcher in *GBM*, August 1891, p.286, gave the voting as 39 to 155.

had received, each duly signed by two deacons, requiring that they be recorded in the minutes. After a fierce dispute, a compromise was reached whereby the protests were read out by the chairman.

Protests or no protests, amalgamation had been secured, after five years of careful negotiations and consultations, against a background of some sixty years of consideration. Fletcher now turned to reconciliation, recording

> To some I know the grief at the loss of the old Association is so fresh and keen that for the time they refuse to be comforted. It is useless to talk to them of finding new happiness in new relationships. At present the sense of bereavement shuts out all thoughts and feelings. Still in time they may not love the Baptist Union less because they loved the General Baptist Association more.[126]

The amalgamation of General and Particular Baptists still left the larger possibility of a Baptist-Congregational Union on the table in the last decade of the nineteenth century, recognized by the denominational journal as 'one of the pressing questions upon which the Baptist denomination should make up its mind without delay'. In the event it was to prove too difficult, and the Congregationalists were to find union with the Presbyterians on the basis of a common confession of faith rather than with Baptists on the basis of a common polity.[127]

Entwined within this process have been many themes. Changed theological priorities made old divisions obsolete - it was no time to debate general or particular atonement, claimed Alexander McLaren, when 'the whole world was asking is there any atonement at all'.[128] Nostalgic sentiment lived in tension with simple economic incapacity, and all that flowed from it. Concern to balance reckless congregational independence with respect for denominational authority

---

126 *GBM* August 1891, p.313.

127 *BM* November 1892, p.505.

128 *Missionary Observer*, August 1891, p.505.

was needed to develop a strategy for sustaining and developing Baptist witness, which itself required a more specific nurturing of Baptist identity. Increasingly it was realized that talk about spiritual unity could all too easily become an argument for taking no action, and that spiritual aspirations needed to be realized in concrete institutional machinery for prosecuting the interests of the kingdom, for unity was essentially a means to mission, both overseas and at home. Where there was consent about the urgency of that task, broad agreement on evangelical doctrine,[129] and the experience of a common life had established unity already, so to perpetuate division became intolerable.

Where that unity of outlook and experience was lacking, to attempt union might represent a dangerous betrayal, and so, whilst merging the two bodies of Baptists proved possible, Baptists were wary of wider initiatives. The Baptist Union, though grateful for the initative which itself betokened a change in outlook, was not able to respond positively to Archbishop Benson's invitation in 1888 to share in a conference to discuss a possible basis on which corporate reunion or intercommunion amongst the English Churches might take place.

On the other hand, a working relationship with other Free Churches in common outreach was beginning to emerge with the convening of the first National Free Church Congress in Manchester in November 1892, where some 30 of the 370 gathered together were Baptists, and both John Clifford and Alexander McLaren, General and Particular Baptists until the previous year, took leading parts. Again

---

129 I would therefore question Leon McBeth's glosses upon the events of 1891 when he falls to the temptation of the summary judgement that 'the 1891 merger left the Baptist Union with a Particular Baptist organization infused with a General Baptist theology', and adds, 'With the merger of particular and New Connection Baptists in 1891, the exchange of ministers and members spread General Baptist Christology throughout the denomination', using this to lead into his discussion of the Christological debate of 1971. First, the exchange of members and ministers long predated 1891; secondly, New Connexion organization contributed much to the life of the Union post 1891; thirdly, there was no New Connexion Christology as such. H. L. McBeth, *The Baptist Heritage*, Nashville TN, 1987, pp.510, 517.

the prognosis was good, for the work was to be developed upon the basis of shared experience and commitment to mission, which proved to be the essential fundamentals for operational ecumenism.[130]

130 Payne, *Baptist Union*, pp.145-6, and Appendix VII, pp.272-4; E. K. H. Jordan, *Free Church Unity*, 1956, pp.25-34.

6

FAITH AND THOUGHT

The intellectual challenges of the nineteenth century could not be avoided by any group of Christians, and Baptists here were no exception. In successive phases, the challenges to Christian belief were philosophical and theological, critical and scientific, historical and comparative. The inherited debates of the late eighteenth century were largely philosophical and concerned with the moral character of God in relation to his revealed actions. Increasingly the older expressions of Calvinist systematic theology failed to satisfy and were challenged both by new thinking and new action. The corrosive forces were not only moral doubts about predestination and free will but also the success of missionary activity at home and abroad challenging an older theology of church and salvation. Only slowly did higher criticism make its impact on Baptist thinking and even then only became a source of alarm when associated with a radical liberalization in theological outlook. The reaction to new theories of evolution was again cautious, though clearly that same idea when applied to historical studies presented a major challenge as, at the end of the century, did the emergence of comparative religious studies and the many alternative, non-providential explanations both of events in human history and also of human motivation.

The Baptist community in the nineteenth century, though second to none in the power of its pulpit orators, was not greatly gifted with either thinkers of original intelligence or with major theological scholars. Scrutinize most of the standard accounts of the development of theology in the century and it is hard to find a Baptist name. Similarly, Baptist theologians in the twentieth century were at a loss to find nineteenth-century antecedents to cite. Vernon Storr, writing in 1913, perhaps rather too strongly dismissed the Baptists, whom he described as 'conservative and tenacious of their inherited theological beliefs': 'I cannot', he confessed, 'find that the Baptists made any important contribution to theological thought in this period.'[1] The progress of their theological thought has, therefore, on the whole to be charted in terms of reactions to thinkers of other denominations rather than to innovators who were themselves Baptists.

FULLER, HALL AND FOSTER

However, at the end of the eighteenth and the beginning of the nineteenth centuries, the names of Andrew Fuller (1754-1815), Robert Hall, Junior (1764-1831), and John Foster (1770-1843) represent a trio of able Baptist thinkers, whose oratory and writings did much to enhance the intellectual reputation of the denomination. Fuller, without formal education as such, was, in Carlile's words, the theologian who provided Baptists with 'a reasonable way of escape from ultra-Calvinism'.[2] He 'became the emancipator of the Baptist denomination', delivering 'the Churches from that terrible fatalism which resulted from ultra-Calvinism'.[3] He greatly benefited from the work of Jonathan Edwards, who afforded him 'a philosophical basis for his doctrine of a gospel worthy of all acceptation'.[4] Deftly Fuller articulated an evangelical Calvinism which, whilst demonstrating its faithfulness to Calvin's teachings, at once did battle with the desiccating influences of hyper-Calvinists on the one hand, and universalists and unitarians on the other. Fuller independently came to a rejection of what Ivimey called 'the non-invitation, non-application scheme' of the London hyper-Calvinists, those who followed Gill and Brine.[5] Such teaching, however, had never been

1 Vernon Storr, *The Development of English Theology in the Nineteenth Century, 1800-1900*, 1913, p.182.

2 J. C. Carlile, *The History of the English Baptists*, 1905, p.193.

3 E. F. Clipsham, 'Andrew Fuller and Fullerism: A Study in Evangelical Calvinism', *BQ* 20, 1963-4, pp.99ff; 146ff; 214ff; 268ff.

4 *ibid.*, p.110.

5 Cited *ibid.*, p.101.

accepted by those trained at Bristol College who maintained an older tradition of Evangelical Calvinism.[6]

Foster and Hall, together with the Revd Joseph Hughes (1769-1833), founder and secretary of the British and Foreign Bible Society, were highly regarded in literary society. Foster wrote extensively for the *Eclectic Review* and the *Morning Chronicle*, lamenting what he perceived to be Evangelical anti-intellectualism. Thus in his essays *On some of the Reasons by which Evangelical Religion has been rendered less acceptable to Persons of Cultivated Taste* (1805) and *The Evils of Popular Ignorance* (1820), he attacked the way in which some evangelicals claimed 'a kind of merit to their indifference to knowledge, as if it were the proof or the result of a higher regard for religion'.[7] Rather he believed some intellectual alertness was needed to appreciate, for example, the nature of the atonement, the importance of eternal welfare of the soul, and the practice of self-examination. Evangelicalism as a doctrinal faith necessarily made its demands upon the mind, whose cultivation was, therefore, to be encouraged, even if in the end that self-same human mind had to recognise the limits of its own competence. At the same time Foster encouraged his co-religionists to become more widely acquainted with secular culture and to relate their preaching to it.

Foster, Hall and Hughes all extended their influence beyond the dissenting ghetto, becoming the confidants of leading intellectuals and literary men at a crucial period of intellectual crisis. Coleridge, whose own theological awareness and influence was profound, once wrote to Joseph Hughes, whom he called 'that worthy and enlightened man': 'Having no one in the circle of my acquaintance who is at once competent and interested in religion *theologically*, I had additional pleasure in the opportunity of conversing with you'. The High-Church journal, *The British Critic*, eulogised Robert Hall: 'His published specimens of Pulpit Oratory were some of them at least, of

6 R. Hayden, 'Evangelical Calvinism and English Baptists', unpublished PhD thesis, University of Keele, 1992.

7 D. M. Rosman, *Evangelicalism and Culture*, 1984, pp.204, 209.

such surpassing splendour and power, that they took at once an elevated station in our standard theological literature, and placed their author beyond all dispute among the great and commanding spirits of the age'; a judgement confirmed by *The Quarterly Review* which declared that Hall, an 'absolute master of English', was a thinker whose talents were 'surpassed by those of few men in his time'.[8]

Much of Hall's energy was consumed by writings on the polity and sacramental practices of Baptist churches. Beyond that his significance lies in bringing theological principles to bear upon political changes and in defending a Christian understanding of freedom when the ferment of the times induced many clerical minds, especially within the established church, to retreat into justifications of coercion or simple pietism. Educated at the Bristol Academy and as a prize-student at Aberdeen University, he had a voracious appetite for knowledge and was exceptionally well-read in both classical and modern thought. In theology he denied that he was either Arminian or Calvinist, 'but I believe', he confessed, 'I recede further from Arminianism than Calvinism', distinctions which he thought more metaphysical than religious.[9] Nevertheless, it was still necessary for him to defend the evangelical faith from both Socinian error with its reduced Christology on the one hand and hyper-Calvinist and antinomian emphases on the other.

Within the bounds of orthodoxy, Hall was catholic in his outlook. In the aftermath of the French Revolution, he appealed for Christian unity: 'The momentous contest at issue betwixt the christian church and infidels may instruct us how trivial, for the most part, are the controversies of its members with each other.'[10] His gift for apologetics became widely recognised by Christians of all persuasions:

---

8 *ibid.*, p.205, and n.10, pp.235-6.

9 O. Gregory, 'A Brief Memoir of the Revd Robert Hall', in Hall, *Works*, ed. O. Gregory, Vol.I, 1858, p.60.

10 R. Hall, Preface to 'Modern Infidelity Considered with Respect to Its Influence on Society . . . Sermon . . . , Cambridge, November 1799', *Works*, Vol.II, 1866, p.6.

for example, he enjoyed the unique privilege, as a dissenter, of preaching for the National Schools in Bristol in November 1820. The publication of his extended sermon on 'Modern Infidelity' provoked a gift of books from Bishop Porteous of London, bearing the inscription, 'These volumes are presented as an appropriate intimation of that applause, veneration and gratitude that are due to the acute detector, perspicacious impugner and victorious antagonist of the sceptical, infidel and anti-christian sophists of the present times'. Such praise was echoed in the reviews of the day, as also by leading divines, literary figures, academics and politicians.[11]

The impact on the size of Hall's Cambridge congregation was so considerable that some Cambridge Heads of Houses argued for prohibition upon members of the university attending, but this was squashed by the intervention of Dr Mansel, Master of Trinity and later Bishop of Bristol, who refused to be party to such action, arguing that but for his office he would wish to benefit from Hall's ministry; indeed, he went so far as to endeavour to persuade Hall to take a preferment within the established church. Sir James Mackintosh, the great Whig historian and jurist, a friend of Hall from Aberdeen days, was only one amongst many who thought that the dissenting interest would be wise to place Hall in the most conspicuous place available so that he might act as their representative before the nation: 'You will never do all the good which it is in your power to do, unless you assert your own importance, and call to mind that as the Dissenters have no man comparable to you, it is your province to guide them, and not to be guided by their ignorance and bigotry'.[12]

The nature of 'Modern Infidelity' was further elaborated in a sermon preached in 1802 on *The Present Crisis* on the occasion of the calling of a national fast in the context of a threatened Napoleonic invasion. A national fast, argued Hall, required some evaluation of national sins, which he identified with the prevalence of reductionist ethics which reduced 'every moral question to a calculation of

11 Cited Gregory, 'Brief Memoir', pp.76-80.

12 *ibid.*, p.78.

expedience'. Society was not so much prey to the profligate as to the new sophistry which was producing leaders who, argued Hall, advocated such a specious philosophy that, like Caesar, 'they have come with sobriety to the ruin of the country'. Such a temperament in the national character was specifically seen as the consequence of the 'pretended morality' and 'unholy speculations' of William Godwin in his *Political Justice* (1793), which Hall saw as dissolving all distinctions between right and wrong. Such thinking alarmed Hall, not on account of its levelling egalitarianism, but essentially because of its secularism: 'this desecration of virtue, this incessant domination of physical over moral ideas, of ideas of expedience over those of right, having already dethroned religion, and displaced virtue from her ancient basis, will, if it is suffered to proceed, ere long shake the foundation of states, and endanger the existence of the civilised world'.[13]

JOHN HOWARD HINTON[14]

The Baptist denomination embraced those who adhered to both Calvinist and Arminian theologies. Some, like John Howard Hinton, persuaded themselves that they had found a new synthesis between the two systems, though the latest commentator suggests that Hinton's new synthesis was in fact no more than a capitulation to the Arminian position, a position betrayed by his confession that, were predestination and election to be abandoned and Arminianism to triumph, 'I confess it would not be to me the heavy calamity which some people seem to perceive in it'.[15] This was the confession of the minister of the historic Particular Baptist church in Devonshire Square, who also served as a Secretary of the Baptist Union for a quarter of a century.

---

13 'The Sentiments Proper to the Present Crisis . . . Sermon . . . , Bristol . . . October 19 1802 . . . the day appointed for a General Fast', Hall, *Works*, pp.124-6; cf. p.248.

14 See I. Sellers, 'John Howard Hinton, Theologian', *BQ* 33, 1989, pp.19-32.

15 *ibid.*, p.123, citing J. H. Hinton, *Works*, 7 vols., 1864-67, I, p.477; IV, p.288.

The declining functionalism of an inherited Calvinism within the changed world of the mid-nineteenth century is further illustrated by Hinton's denial that mankind shared in Adam's sin, beyond his mortality. Man had a disposition or bias towards sin but his moral being was unfettered. Thus in the post-Adamic dispensation of 'evangelical mercy', in which man lives in 'benignant probation', 'the possession of the means of repentance constitutes the power of repentance. Therefore the sinner has power to repent without the Spirit'. As Sellers remarks, Hinton's theological outlook at this point seems to owe more to the Scottish enlightenment education of his Edinburgh years than to biblical reflection, and was seriously defective in minimizing the work of the Holy Spirit. Such a subordination of the work of the Holy Spirit and such confidence in human responsibility from the pen of its secretary limited the usefulness of the Baptist Union at this time and thus contributed to the formation of the London and East Anglian Associations of Strict Baptist Churches.

Before the forces of theological suspicion run abroad, it should be noted that this same Hinton was also an eager supporter of the Evangelical Alliance.[16] Like Clifford later, he was an ardent advocate of the priority of personal evangelism. Hinton was distinctive in seeking a philosophical mean between the Calvinist and Arminian positions. Many others faced the pressure of no longer being able to affirm the traditional Calvinist received doctrine in practice and in the sermons they preached without formally setting down a revised theology.

HEAVEN AND HELL

Hinton's conservatism is also seen in his concern over the growth of ideas of conditional immortality, available only to a believing elect. His *Athanasia or The Natural Immortality of Man*, published in 1849, traced the idea of conditional immortality back to John Foster, who as early as 1799 expressed his dissent from the orthodox position on

16 E. A. Payne, *The Baptist Union: A Short History*, 1959, p.84.

Future Punishment, in contrast to Robert Hall, who upheld the traditional doctrine.[17]

Also within the Bristol circle was Joseph Cottle, bookseller, friend and patron of Coleridge and Southey, member of Broadmead and of the committee of Bristol College.[18] In his *Essays on Socinianism*, he accused the Unitarians of extinguishing 'hell with a Trope' and of 'confuting Heaven with a Syllogism'.[19] Future Retribution, he argued, was an effective check upon outrageous behaviour: 'what an appalling image would society present if all the salutary checks founded on *Satan* and *hell* were wholly removed, and men believed, as Socinians tell them, that, in the eternal world there is no place found for "the Devil and his Angels"; that, whatever their rebellions against God may be, it will not obstruct their future happiness for the "mansion of the blessed" will be the *ultimate* portion of *one* and *all*.'[20]

Some forty years later Foster entered into correspondence with Edward White who was much exercised by this issue. Foster, negatively, took orthodox theologians to task for giving insufficient thought to the concept of Eternity and for his own part argued for the importance of the idea of the Divine Goodness, questioning whether it could really be good to apply eternal torment for temporal sin - the importance of which he did not wish to diminish - especially when

---

17 *Foster's Life and Correspondence*, ed. J. E. Ryland, 1846, Vol.I, p.86; Hall, 'Letter to Gentleman at Trinity College, Cambridge, April 30 1821', *Works*, Vol.I, 1858, pp.352-3.

18 S. A. Swaine, *Faithful Men, or Memorials of Bristol College*, 1884, pp.136-7. DNB.

19 Andrew Fuller's orthodox view of Final Judgment was also reinforced by the association of revisionist ideas with Unitarianism and their defective view of the seriousness of sin - see his *Calvinist and Socinian Systems, examined and compared*, 1793; G. Rowell, *Hell and the Victorians: a study of nineteenth-century theological controversies covering eternal punishment and the future life*, 1974, pp.39, 46.

20 Rowell, *op.cit.*, p.43.

most men had lived their lives without any 'authentic message from Heaven'.[21]

Hinton found such deviations from orthodox teaching to be growing in the mid-century. H. H. Dobney, Baptist minister in Maidstone, published in 1844 his *Notes of Lectures on Future Punishment*, in which he came to argue a variety of conditional immortality whilst still upholding the reality of divine punishment.[22] Hinton also referred to a series of anonymous lectures delivered in Broadmead Chapel in 1843 on this theme and to Edward White's *Life in Christ* of 1846.[23] White was a Congregational minister in Hereford from 1842 to 1851, but whilst there developed not only his conditionalist views, but also came to reject infant baptism, and was himself rebaptized by Dr Gotch at Broadmead. These two issues together led him to resign his Hereford pastorate and establish a new congregation in a former Countess of Huntingdon chapel in Hawley Road, Camden Town. At that time he came to be regarded as a Baptist[24], at least by Spurgeon, though he later returned to Congregationalism, occupying the Chair of that Union in 1887, by which date conditional immortality, the view that only the righteous enjoy immortality and that the existence of all others simply terminates at death, was no longer threatening to the Congregationalists.

As respected a leader as R. W. Dale had adopted such a position, whilst others had travelled much further in the direction of a more complete universalism. When *The Christian World* ran a series on The Future Life,[25] White canvassed the conditional immortality position, whilst orthodox belief was defended by Joseph Angus. The advocate of the universalist position in this series was Andrew Jukes,

---

21 ed. J. E. Ryland, *Foster's Life and Correspondence*, 1846, Vol.II, pp.232-44.

22 Dobney spent his whole ministry in Maidstone. His views were, on the whole, rejected by his fellow Baptists, whilst his church drifted from a Baptist position towards a more open Congregationalism. J. C. Carlile, *The Story of the English Baptists*, 1905, p.273.

23 See chapter 7, p.238.

24 C. H. Spurgeon, *Autobiography* III, 1899, p.283 note.

25 Tudur Jones, *Congregationalism in England 1662-1962*, 1962, p.265.

who in 1867 published his *The Second Death and The Restitution of All Things*. Like White and Dobney, Jukes also passed in and out of the Baptist ministry. Educated at Harrow and Cambridge, he owed his conversion to reading Thomas Scott. Almost immediately after his ordination to St John's, Hull, in 1842, Jukes began to have doubts about baptismal regeneration and sought rebaptism of a local Baptist minister. He gathered around himself a Baptist congregation to which he ministered for the next twenty-five years, until the publication of his universalist ideas led to conflict with them.[26]

More centrally Baptist than Dobney, White or Jukes, was Samuel Cox, a Stepney graduate who served as minister of Mansfield Road, Nottingham, from 1863-88. From 1875-84 he was founding editor of *The Expositor* which was very influential in introducing English minds to German textual criticism.[27] Beyond that, much of Cox's prolific writings, always sensitive, were sermonic or expository. His most important work was that entitled *Salvator Mundi: or is Christ the Saviour of All Men?* (1877). A rather less formidable text than its title might suggest, it is, in fact, the substance of a series of lectures given to his highly literate Bible Class at Mansfield Road.

In *Salvator Mundi*, Cox confessed to seeking to encourage those who entertained a 'larger hope' of a wider salvation by seeking to show scriptural warrant for such belief, which he had held for more than twenty years. The title of Cox's work derived from I Timothy 4.10. It is significant that Cox expressed his indebtedness to 'my friend, Mr Dobney of Maidstone', and to Andrew Jukes's *The Second Death and the Restitution of All Things*, as also to Dr Dewes's linguistic studies, and later to S. A. Tipple, the extraordinary minister of Central Hill Baptist Church, Upper Norwood. Beyond these references, however, Cox's debt was most obviously to Tennyson,

---

26 Jukes left Hull in 1868 for London and rejoined the Church of England and was drawn into the circle both of the Broadlands Conferences, held at the home of Lord and Lady Mount Temple, and of Anglo-Catholicism. Rowell, *op.cit.*, p.129.

27 *DNB*.

with whom he was in correspondence. Cox had dedicated Volume III of *The Expositor* to the poet, who wrote expressing particular appreciation of Cox's writings on Job.[28] It is Tennyson's words that Cox cites in introducing *Salvator Mundi*: 'and faintly trust the larger hope'.[29] Tennyson's son, Hallam Tennyson, says of this, 'When he speaks of "faintly trusting the larger hope", he means by the larger hope that the whole human race would through, perhaps, ages of suffering be at length purified and saved, even those who "better not with time"'.[30]

What follows is a reverent study of certain aspects of biblical language, namely those terms which express the ideas of hell, the eternal, judgment, damnation and condemnation, whose meaning Cox argues has been distorted by a continuation of the legacy of medieval Catholicism. In this sense his work, like so much else in nineteenth-century Baptist writing, was part of the reaction against a threatening Catholicism. It was a continuation of the task that Cox tried to discharge through his editorship of *The Expositor*, where he was concerned to allow the Scriptures to explain themselves, 'neither thrusting upon them miracles they do not claim nor dogma to which they lend no support, not venturing to question the doctrines they obviously teach and the miracles they plainly affirm.'[31] An extended review of the work in the *Baptist Magazine*[32] was generally critical and in particular challenged the notion that many ministers privately held a doctrine of final restoration but failed to preach it. Others, like Arthur Mursell, who retained the confidence of Spurgeon, were conditional immortality supporters, believing that the doctrine of eternal punishment was a great stumbling block to working men's belief in a God of love.[33] Contradicting the view that 'Neither the

---

28 *The Freeman*, 7 April 1893, p.212.

29 *In Memoriam, LV*, written 'some years before' 1844.

30 C. Ricks, *Tennyson*, 1972, pp.218, 398.

31 *Baptist Handbook*, 1894, pp.149-51.

32 *BM* 1877, pp.157-65.

33 Rowell, *op.cit.*, p.204; J. C. Carlile, *C. H. Spurgeon*, 1933, pp.178-9.

Lord Jesus Christ nor His apostles had any such word as 'Hell' in their vocabulary, or any conception answering it in their thoughts', the *Baptist Magazine* reviewer affirmed that Jesus used the word "hell" in much the way that current usage did to describe 'an indescribable hopeless realm, the abode of lost souls'. Referring both to Jukes and to Tennyson, the article counselled 'we dare not substitute feeling for faith': the search should rather be for the truest not the largest hope: 'In the truest and largest faith we have the truest and largest hope and the truest and largest charity'.[34]

Baptists were not the only critics of Cox's views: Bishop Wordsworth of Lincoln, for example, felt constrained to preach two sermons combating Cox's ideas, and as late as 1884 the publishers of *The Expositor* sought an undertaking from Cox that he exclude from the journal 'all allusions to the larger hope' and even to 'the general tone of thought which it carried with it', which in the event provoked Cox's resignation. Mansfield Road, however, stood firm behind its minister, and when an affectionate address was presented to Cox in that same year, it specifically referred to his 'vindication of the infinite love of God and of its final triumph over all men through Jesus Christ'. Cox, for his part, sought to put the new theology in context as far as his own orthodoxy was concerned:

> We still believe in the sinfulness of man, especially our own sinfulness, but we believe that evil will finally be overcome by good. We still believe in the Atonement, that the forgiving and redeeming love of God is revealed in the life, death and passion of Our Lord Jesus Christ, but we also believe in an Atonement of wider scope, that Christ will see of the travail of his soul and be satisfied in a larger and diviner way than some of our theologians have supposed.[35]

Significantly it has been said of Cox that he was 'conspicuously the helper of men who sought his sympathy and counsel in their struggle

---

34 *BM* 1877, pp.157-65.

35 Rowell, *op.cit.*, p.133, citing Cox MSS in University of Nottingham Library.

with theological difficulties'. It was also affirmed that 'As a theologian Dr Cox was Evangelical. His belief in the Incarnation, the Atonement and the Resurrection of Jesus Christ and in essentially related truths was deep and abiding'.[36]

On the one hand, Cox's work would seem to give grounds for Spurgeon's Down Grade fears, in that Cox confessed he hardly knew any preacher who now held 'the dogma of everlasting torment', though a general silence pervaded the pulpit on this issue for fear of giving offence. Yet on the other hand enigmatically Cox and Spurgeon were apparently good friends,[37] even though Cox advocated the notion of universal restoration so forthrightly condemned by Spurgeon. For its part, *The Sword and the Trowel* contemptuously referred to all such thinking as a species of 'post-mortem salvation'.[38] Cox's views were confirmed in his later volume, *The Larger Hope* of 1883, which was bound together with later editions of *Salvator Mundi*. In it he confessed that if he were starting again in this area of writing he would expound the theme as an aspect of atonement rather than of the nature of eternity, claiming that those who believed in the Larger Hope believed more not less concerning the scope of the atonement.[39]

Sensitivity to the pressures of society and the insights of its poets led Cox into innovative speculation, the value of which was acknowledged by Dean Farrar, who also paid tribute to Jukes's and White's work, in his study of the *Eternal Hope*.[40] By contrast, Spurgeon, innovative in both method and institutions, retained more of the substance of the inherited theological tradition of the Particular Baptists. But men like Dobney, Jukes, White and Cox were not alone

36 *Baptist Handbook* 1894, pp.149-51.

37 R. E. Cooper, *From Stepney to St Giles: The Story of Regent's Park College*, 1960, p.59; *Baptist Handbook*, 1894, pp.149-51.

38 A. C. Underwood, *A History of the English Baptists*, 1947, p.230, footnote.

39 Preface and p.225 of 1890 combined edition of *Salvator Mundi* and *The Larger Hope*.

40 F. W. Farrar, *The Eternal Hope*, 1877, pp.xi, 36.

in their concern about judgment and the after life: eternal punishment seems particularly to have concerned Victorian Evangelicals. T. R. Birks, Edward Bickersteth's son-in-law, sometime vicar of Holy Trinity, Cambridge, and later Professor of Moral Philosophy in the university, in *The Victory of Divine Goodness* (1867) championed the notion of eventual universal atonement after a period of punishment. Challenged as to his orthodoxy, he was forced to resign as Secretary of the Evangelical Alliance in 1868, though making it abundantly clear that he had no intention of resigning his membership. Instead sixteen hard-liners resigned. Evangelicalism, as defined by the Alliance, had at that time a certain breadth and tolerance that later generations have not always admitted.

For its part, in the wake of Down Grade, the Baptist Union in the Declaratory Statement of 1888 affirmed 'the Judgment at the Last Day according to Matthew xxv 46', but appended to that declaration the famous historical note, which, whilst anathematizing both Purgatory and Universalism, noted that 'there have been brethren in the Union working cordially with it, who whilst reverently bowing to the authority of Holy Scripture . . . have not held the common interpretation of these words of Our Lord'.[41]

NON-CREDALISM

On the last judgment and kindred issues, Baptist gave more consistent support to traditional beliefs than did the Congregationalists. Emerging theological trends were, however, beginning to challenge the wisdom of the widespread non-credalism of nineteenth-century Baptists. It has been argued that 'freedom of Baptists from credal and confessional documents' aided the peaceful transition from the old to the new, but it is not clear that this was wholly so.[42] Certainly the Baptist Union at the eve of the Down Grade controversy, unlike seventeenth, eighteenth and even early nineteenth-century Baptists with their confessions and covenants, was the weaker for not having any

41 Payne, *Baptist Union,* 1959, p.271.

42 E. A. Payne, *Studies in History and Religion*, 1942, p.248.

well-defined canons of reference. When the Baptist Union was given a new basis in 1832, the desire to involve both New Connexion General and Particular Baptists led to the briefest of references to the body drawing together 'ministers and churches who agree in the sentiments usually denominated evangelical'. By 1873 such were the fears of centralizing authority that even these words were dropped in favour of a statement indicating the freedom of each local church to interpret and administer the laws of Christ, only particularizing that 'the immersion of believers is the only Christian baptism'.[43]

Even as the Baptist Union was moving towards the declaratory statement of April 1888, H. R. Murray offered this defence of the anti-credal position, in the context, be it noted, of the challenges to the Bible then occurring:

> Now it appears to be of the utmost importance, in the face of the present dilemmas and future probabilities, that we should hold fast to this great principle - that God's word, and God's word alone, is our lamp and guide, and that we are to be judged by its light alone. As a Protestant and a Free Churchman, I am willing to have my orthodoxy tested by the Bible, but by it alone; no man-made creed or humanly-prepared confession of faith is to be that by which my faith shall be tested and tried. Our Creed and Basis of Union should be the New Testament, and we need and should have *none other*. Man-made creeds have always been a source of division and bitterness; the purest age of the church was when it had no formulated creeds; nothing but the sacred writings, which each Christian, as he could obtain them, studied for himself, seeking the illumination of God's Spirit . . .
>
> For we must either assert the infallibility of the men who have drawn up our creeds, or admit that they are liable to err; and if they are liable to err, then we must admit the possibility of their systems being imperfect, partial, containing meagre and one-sided statements of things, or even containing some

43 Payne, *Baptist Union*, p.109. Constitution of the Baptist Union, ¶ III, Declaration of Principle, *Baptist Handbook*, 1878, p.16.

> things that are not true at all. And if *all* human creeds are possibly and probably imperfect, and possibly contain things that are not true, then I do not see how we dare make any of them the basis of Christian union, or the test of a man's Christianity, while we have in the Bible a complete and perfect system of infallible truth . . .
>
> And as this is the right attitude for every Christian man to assume, so is it the right attitude for our churches to take. Each church claiming *liberty* (as the constitution of the Baptist Union declares) to *interpret* and to administer the laws of Christ, we stand responsible to no council and to no creed, but to God and His Word. I glory in this liberty. It is a principle that is of the very essence of Christianity. As a Body we should rejoice in our freedom; for it is peculiar to us as a denomination that we have no human creed or confession of faith to which we are compelled to subscribe upon pain of penalty or expulsion. We are under the dominion, in matters of faith and doctrine, of no Synod, Conference, or Board. The only court of appeal we recognize is the Bible; the only creed we know, the words of Christ and His apostles.[44]

Even a young Spurgeon is on record as showing some suspicion of credal forms,[45] but Spurgeon was sensitive to the changing demands of the times in which he lived, as his letter to Dr Culross in November 1887 makes clear:

> Do I need to say that with you and such brethren as Dr McLaren, Mr Aldis, and Dr Angus I have no sort of disagreement, except that you stay in the Union and I am out of it? . . . So long as an Association without a creed has no aliens in it, nobody can wish for a creed *formally* for the spirit is there; but at a time when 'strange children' have entered,

---

44 H. R. Murray, 'Our Creed; or the Baptist Rule of Faith', *General Baptist Magazine*, March 1888, pp.81-5. The General Baptists had, of course, a well-defined confession of faith drawn up by Dan Taylor in 1785. See A. Taylor, *The History of English General Baptists*, 2 vols., 1818, II, pp.470-77.

45 *Autobiography*, III, 1899, p.1; see chapter 5 of the present work.

> what is to be done? Whatever may *theoretically* be in your power, you *practically* have no power whatever. You will go on as you are; and unless God's grace calls back the wanderers, their numbers will increase, and their courage will call them to speak out more plainly, to the sorrow of the faithful ones who shielded them in patient hope of better things . . .
>
> Your very clear declaration, that the Union could not have a creed, or as I read it, could not declare its doctrinal views other than by practising baptism and the Lord's Supper, closes the door finally against me. Neither do I knock at that door, nor wish for another door to be made. The good men who formed the Union, I fancy, had no idea that it would become what it now is, or they would have fashioned it otherwise. It has, by its centralization and absorption of various Societies, become far other than at the first. This is a good thing, but it involves a strain on the frail fabric which it is ill adapted to bear. So I think; but time will be the best proof of *that*. I wish I could have worked with you in that particular way; but as I cannot, we are not therefore deprived of a thousand other ways of fellowship. You feel union of heart with men who publicly preach Universal Restitution: *I do not*. I mean, you feel enough fellowship to remain in the Union with them: *I do not*. It is the same with other errors. Still, I am in fellowship with *you*, - Union or no Union.[46]

Not only had the older Spurgeon come to see that there could be good purpose in the formulation of credal statements, but the context is such that he seems to be arguing not only in favour of such an exhibition of orthodoxy, but also that such formulations could be used to exclude 'strange children'. Thus Spurgeon's hope that the Baptist Union would adopt a basis similar to that of the Evangelical Alliance had a clear practical purpose in view. That was well understood. In a letter to William Cuff of Shoreditch Tabernacle, John Clifford wrote, 'It is

---

46 *ibid.*, IV, 1900, pp.262-3.

not creeds as creeds; it is *coercion* through and by creeds I object to.'[47] For Baptists to balance the often contradictory demands of freedom of enquiry and fidelity to apostolic faith was no easy task.

ON THE DOWN GRADE?

The mission of the church in the expanding world of the nineteenth century demanded more and more of denominational machinery if any coherent response to the situation was to be made. Spurgeon recognized the need for centralization but was clearly suspicious of it: earlier he had written questioning the whole *raison d'être* of the Union:

> The expedient is not needed among Churches which are each one self-governing and self-determining, such churches can find their own affinities without difficulty, and can keep their own coasts clear of invaders. Since each vessel is sea worthy in herself, let the hampering ropes be cut clean away and no more lines of communication be thrown out until we know that we are alongside a friend who sails under the same glorious flag. In the isolation of independency, tempered by the love of the Spirit which binds us to all the faithful in Jesus Christ, we think the lovers of the gospel will for the present find their immediate safety.[48]

But whereas the autonomy of the Metropolitan Tabernacle with its vast array of agencies was a possibility, the isolation of the average Baptist church was not, without grave danger both to its survival and its mission. The Union was of fundamental necessity in enabling the strong to help the weak in a nationwide missionary fellowship.

The context of the Down Grade dispute was the desire to further the integration of General and Particular Baptist work, which Charles Williams made one of the aims of his presidential year, even though there were fears on both sides. In commending the proposal to the

---

47 Cited E. A. Payne, 'The Down Grade Controversy: A Postscript', *BQ* 28, 1979, p.156.

48 *The Sword and the Trowel*, 1887, p.360 (cited by Payne, *Baptist Union*, p.142).

General Baptists, John Clifford went further, albeit with a highly individualistic view of baptism:

> Will it be long before Baptists and Independents are able to unite in the New Testament principle that 'the obligation to be baptized springs out of the relationship of the soul to the Saviour, and not from the relationship of the believer to the church', and that therefore 'the whole question of baptism must be left to the individual conscience' (Constitution of Westbourne Park Church).[49]

Spurgeon's quarrel was not with Dr Clifford or with the evangelical Arminian tradition as upheld by the various Methodist churches. Spurgeon's position was well expressed in a Leeds Assembly sermon, 'Be it ours to know what is Scriptural in all systems and to receive it'.[50] Scripture was to be placed above systems, in a way which did not diverge in essence from H. R. Murray's non-credalism.

Though brought up in a Congregational manse, Spurgeon's confidence in the Independents was less certain than that placed in his own denomination. With his fellow Baptists, Spurgeon had good relationships with, and a high regard for, a number of leading Congregational ministers: Dr Allon of Islington, Guiness Rogers of Clapham, and Alexander Raleigh in particular received his approbation. But he had already expressed his concern about theological developments among the Congregationalists, as early as 1856, when he had rather mildly joined in the censures on T. T. Lynch's new hymn book, though even so he called Lynch 'a good man, who I think is very much misunderstood'.[51]

Four years later, Spurgeon took on his more formidable neighbour, Baldwin Brown, of Brixton Independent Church, who in 1859 published *Divine Life in Man*. J. Howard Hinton, writing in 1860 'when so many tokens of revival enkindle our hopes', was appalled by

---

49 *General Baptist Magazine*, March 1887, p.103.

50 W. Y. Fullerton, *C. H. Spurgeon*, 1920, p.121.

51 C. H. Spurgeon, *Autobiography* II, pp.262-9; Fullerton, *op.cit.*, pp.291-2.

its contents and published strictures on passages from it in March and April 1860 in *The Baptist Magazine*, afterwards reprinted as *Strictures on Some Passages in Revd J. B. Brown's 'Divine Life in Man'*, characterizing Brown's thinking as 'the first inroad into English Nonconformist churches of a theology totally deficient in the truth and power of the gospel'. This pamphlet was so meanly reviewed by *The Freeman* that seven London ministers (Edward Steane of Camberwell, Daniel Katterns of Hackney, Charles Stanford of Camberwell, W. G. Lewis of Westbourne Grove, C. H. Spurgeon, William Brock and Joseph Angus) wrote a letter of protest which focused not only on the heterodoxy of Brown but on the position of *The Freeman*, as 'the organ of the Baptist denomination', in so dealing with the matter and the 'pernicious error' it promoted.[52]

Between them, Hinton and the seven correspondents represented central denominational leadership, including two secretaries and four presidents of the Union, as well as a college principal and other leading London pastors. The seven correspondents earnestly hoped that Baptist pulpits would be preserved from Brown's teaching, whilst denying that there were any signs that heterodoxy was 'beginning to be rampant in our churches'. They counselled young pastors against affecting an intellectual style and not to be 'ashamed of the old and vulgar doctrines of man's guilt, as well as of his total depravity, of Christ's atonement and satisfaction for sin, of justification by the imputation of righteousness through faith, of the new birth by the agency of the Holy Spirit, and, in a word, of that scheme of dogmatic Christian truth which is popularly known under the designation of "the doctrines of grace".'[53]

Spurgeon subsequently spoke and wrote on the issue on his own account and it became clear that, whilst the main target of his concern lay beyond denominational boundaries, he also feared that the Baptist denomination might be contaminated and was clearly hurt by what he

---

52 Sellers, *BQ* 33, p.129; C. H. Spurgeon, *Autobiography* II, 1899, pp.269ff.

53 *ibid.*, p.271.

regarded as the trivially inappropriate response of *The Freeman*; personal hurt counted considerably with Spurgeon.[54]

In November 1877 Spurgeon gave a foreshadowing of what was to come in his reaction to the Leicester Conference of Congregationalists concerned to extend the bounds of Religious Communion to all men of goodwill.[55] The Conference, organized by the Revd J. Allanson Picton, led to some men questioning the continued orthodoxy of the Congregational Union. Baldwin Brown, then its chairman, made a bold plea for freedom in the Spirit, but despite his eloquence the majority of the Union chose to reaffirm the Declaration of Faith and Order of 1833. In a letter to Henry Allon of November 1877 Spurgeon wrote:

> The delightful liberality of some of your truly good men is abused into a covenant with death and hell. The Arianism of the Doddridge time is upon us again. I thank God that the men are mostly beneath contempt but I am sorry that some of your really solid brethren are the screen behind which they skulk.[56]

He followed this up after the 1878 May Meetings, which reaffirmed traditional doctrines, with congratulations to Allon:

> Many fears are removed and hopes confirmed, God bless the Congregational Union is my hearty prayer. Your loose fish swam so near the top of the water that they were always visible, but now I trust they will seek deeper waters.
>
> I fear I shall never see your brethren up to my standard, but it is a joy to me to feel that at least the great facts of our religion are heartily believed . . . Could we not as

54 C. H. Spurgeon, *Autobiography* II, pp.269-81.

55 The Leicester Conference was convoked during the autumn meetings of the Congregational Union in 1877 by an invitation to all 'who value spiritual religion, and who are in sympathy with the principle that religious communion is not dependent on agreement in theological, critical, or historical opinion'. A. Peel, *These Hundred Years: a History of the Congregational Union of England and Wales, 1831-1931*, 1931, pp.266-72.

56 A. Peel, *Letters to a Victorian Editor*, 1929, p.344.

> Independents and Baptists have some *public* fraternization one of these days?[57]

At that date there was cause for concern, but not sufficient to prevent Spurgeon from desiring joint public action with the Congregationalists.

Spurgeon responded well to generous feelings and the celebration of his jubilee in 1884 was such an occasion, when the demonstration of Christian fraternity led him to confess:

> We are supposed as a Christian Church to be a sort of menagerie needing great skill on the part of our Keeper to prevent our devouring one another - but the supposition is slanderous as the last few days have proved. We do not need to have our teeth drawn and our claws cut out, we have the affection after all. God send us more of it combined with fidelity.[58]

The antagonist in the last external controversy was Joseph Parker of the City Temple and the subject matter has often been represented simply as theatre-going, but that was only part of the issue. At the beginning of the Down Grade controversy in February 1887, Spurgeon had received a letter from Parker, inviting him to participate in a conference concerning the vindication of 'the old Evangelical Faith' - 'the occasion should be devoted to clear and simple testimony to our faithfulness to Evangelical doctrine'.[59] The courteous invitation was equally courteously but emphatically refused.[60] Parker pressed the issue and Spurgeon was forced to be explicit: frankness required him to say that he did not detect in Parker's ministry consistency of support as a champion of the faith: 'The Evangelical faith in which you and Mr Beecher agree', affirmed Spurgeon, 'is not

---

57 *ibid.*, p.345.

58 *ibid.*, p.351.

59 Fullerton, *op.cit.*, p.297. Spurgeon last appeared on the platform of the Baptist Union in 1882, and in February 1886 wrote to Samuel Booth with regard to the work of the Union, 'I am anxious not to be *asked*, that I may not be obliged to decline'. E. A. Payne, *BQ* 28, 1979, p.151.

60 Fullerton, *op.cit.*, p.298.

the faith which I hold', and then he went on to criticise Parker's theatre-going, ending with the hope that the differences could be treated as private to the two parties concerned.[61] The matter did not end there, however, for in April 1890 the *British Weekly* published an open letter, without known provocation, from Parker to Spurgeon, advising him 'to widen the circle of which you are the centre . . . My dear Spurgeon, you are too big a man for this. . . Scatter your ecclesiastical harem. I do not say destroy your circle. I simply say enlarge it!'[62] A year and a half later a somewhat chastened Parker again addressed Spurgeon through the *British Weekly*, paying tribute to Spurgeon's stoic battle with suffering, concluding, 'What if, after all, you should prove to be the broadest-minded man among us?'[63]

That reference to broad-mindedness easily relates to the evaluation of the pastor of the Metropolitan Tabernacle provided by Robertson Nicoll, the Presbyterian journalist, who was exceptionally well-read in Spurgeon's sermons. Indeed, he reckoned Spurgeon one of the greatest English mystics in history. 'There are', argued Nicoll, 'a great many things in these sermons which show that he was not at all the narrow and illiterate bigot that many people think him. On the contrary he had great breadth of mind. He made serious concessions to the new spirit and was far better read and far more able and powerful intellectually than most people think.'[64]

Spurgeon was never the disengaged pietist but rather a political dissenter; not just a generous philanthropist but one who lived out a well-developed social conscience. As early as 1886 Nicoll had argued, 'We cannot overlook facts - and the fact is that the Spurgeonic

---

61 *ibid.*, pp.299-300. Henry Ward Beecher was America's leading pulpiteer and an advocate of 'modern' preaching, though in 1863 he gave an address at James Spurgeon's recognition service as pastor of Bayswater. Beecher visited Britain a second time in 1886, when he occupied Parker's pulpit at the City Temple. This in particular seems to have offended Spurgeon.

62 *ibid.*, pp.300-301.

63 *ibid.*, p.301.

64 T. H. Darlow, *William Robertson Nicoll: Life and Letters*, 1925, pp.402-3.

type of preaching is the only kind that moves the democracy.'[65] Soon after Spurgeon's death, Nicoll chided Marcus Dods on his critical note on Spurgeon, protesting that he had never heard any one speak of the great preacher in such a way. Nicoll affirmed:

> I never knew any character that impressed itself so deeply on the whole English people - and he was regarded with a most unaffected respect and trust by people of all creeds and of none . . . As to his bigotry - yes, and I had my share of his abuse. But think how slowly the critical light has broken - think what most of us did say in the days of our darker ignorance - think how incomprehensible it necessarily was to him. As to weightier matters, he was wiser than the rest - that is if the New Testament has any serious meaning . . . Every Sunday night I spend at least an hour reading him and there is no devotional writing pleases me so well. He was such a great mystic that I doubt if we have had his like since Behmen.[66]

The narrative of the developing Down Grade crisis does not belong here but rather to the Union, in the writing of whose history the story has been carefully told.[67] Here the task is to estimate the correctness of Spurgeon's evaluation of the Baptist denomination in the mid-1880s - were the Baptists on the slippery slope of losing hold of the historic faith of the church?

WHO WERE THE LIBERALS?

Sometimes when Spurgeon is writing, he combines Baptists and Congregationalists as one category,[68] making no distinction between

---

65 *ibid.*, p.73.

66 *ibid.*, pp.103-4.

67 See Payne, *Baptist Union* and 'The Down Grade Controversy: A Postscript', *BQ* 28, 1979, pp.146-58. M. Nicholls, 'The Down Grade Controversy: A Neglected Protagonist', *BQ* 32, 1988, pp.260-73. M. Hopkins, 'Spurgeon's opponents in the Down Grade Controversy', *BQ* 32, 1988, pp.274-94, and 'The Down Grade Controversy: New Evidence', *BQ* 35, 1994, pp.262-78.

68 M. D. Johnson, *The Dissolution of Dissent*, 1987, pp.249-51.

them, failing to make clear that advanced views separated from a commitment to evangelism and a converting ministry had more purchase amongst Congregationalists than Baptists. This was presumably the vital distinction which enabled him to exclude men like John Clifford, Charles Williams and Arthur Mursell from the list of dangerous and treacherous teachers. Whilst Baptists and Congregationalists were convinced that they shared a common congregational polity in the nineteenth century, it has been argued that the practice of believer's and infant baptism of themselves pose different ecclesiologies: on the one hand a pre-existing church into which the child is incorporated, on the other a church which is constituted, created, and brought into being as believers respond in faith to the grace of God at work within them and confess that faith in baptism. On that basis, evangelism was to remain high on the agenda of every Baptist church with the conversion experience remaining a desideratum within the ministry of all its pastors, even though they might in other respects adopt aspects of liberal theology. Indeed, the Declaratory Statement adopted by the Baptist Union in April 1888 makes just that point: the Union 'is an association of churches and ministers professing to believe not only the facts and doctrines of the Gospel, but to have undergone the spiritual change expressed and implied in them. This change is the fundamental principle of our church life.'[69] The evangelicalism of the Baptist people was both doctrinal and experimental.

The difficult issue remaining is to discern how far Spurgeon correctly perceived the loosening of evangelical commitment amongst Baptist members, how far the growth of denominational agencies was necessary to be effective in mission at the end of the nineteenth century, and how much latitude the Baptist Union could with integrity allow to its colleges, churches and ministers, within the fellowship of faith.

Undoubtedly there were some who were foot-loose as to evangelical assurances who inhabited the fringes of the denomination.

---

69 Payne, *Baptist Union*, Appendix VI, ¶ a, p.271.

Dobney and White have already been mentioned in the earlier discussion of heaven and hell. George Dawson, whose broad affections led him to leave the denomination at the end of 1845 for the undenominational Church of the Saviour in Birmingham which soon came to look like a Unitarian church, had had Baptist pastorates at Rickmansworth and Mount Zion, Birmingham, prior to that move. Of similar ilk was W. Carey Walters, one of the organizers of the Leicester Conference on the terms of Religious Communion in 1877. He may have trained at Regent's Park College, but was very much under the influence of Baldwin Brown. He left the Baptists in 1877 and established a non-credal Free Church in Whitchurch, in part modelled on Dawson's Birmingham church, at the inauguration of which Baldwin Brown preached.[70] Associated with him was another liberal Baptist named William Miall, who interestingly brought his formerly Strict Baptist church at Dalston into the Baptist Union during a long pastorate stretching from 1839 to 1890.[71] In Upper Norwood, where Spurgeon had his home, the Baptist minister was S. A. Tipple, variously and perhaps too readily described as 'a Wordsworthian pantheist' who 'emphasized the Immanence of God long before it got into current theology', and a 'forerunner of the New Theology'.[72] Certainly Tipple was hostile to 'the ungodlike and terrible Hell of orthodox Christianity',[73] but there is more of traditional spirituality in his sermons than the above categorization might suggest. He and his church were hardly typical Baptist and his influence seems to have been felt more outside than within the denomination. It is significant that Clifford felt it worth noting very specifically that Tipple's name was not mentioned in the Down Grade discussion.

---

70 *Baptist Handbooks* showed him as having trained at Rawdon and Regent's Park, though he does not appear in the standard listings of those institutions. Johnson, *op.cit.*, pp.71-4, 88, 113.

71 *ibid.*, p.73; and *Baptist Handbooks*.

72 Grant, *Free Churchmanship*, pp.143-4; A. Porritt, *The Best I Remember*, 1922, pp.4-6.

73 Tipple, *Echoes of Spoken Words*, p.146.

One of the most advanced thinkers of the denomination was Charles Aked, advocate of the social gospel, who filled Pembroke Chapel, Liverpool, during his sixteen-year ministry from 1890-1906 and provoked controversy wherever he went. Sellers is devastating in his criticism of Aked's religious outlook: 'his Christology was as impossible as the rest of his beliefs were full of half-truths and glaring contradictions; he coquetted with Unitarianism most of the time and then wondered why the less theologically advanced treated him as a heretic. By 1892 he had enough of such mangling. Quietly he abandoned polemical theology for the more profitable task of enthusing his hearers with a passion for the good life . . . The Cross, as Evangelical critics were quick to note, was conveniently forgotten'.[74] As chaplain to the Liverpool Fabians he advocated collectivism in the government of both city and nation, and gave support to the strikers in the coal and docks disputes of 1893-95. His following was essentially personal and all but evaporated overnight when he left Liverpool for the pastorate of Fifth Avenue Baptist Church, New York.

The three names, however, most immediately associated with Spurgeon's 'Down Grade' fears were those of three Rawdon men - W. E. Blomfield, J. G. Greenhough and James Thew, all of whom stayed in the Baptist family and achieved some stature within it.

James Thew was minister of Belvoir Street, Leicester, from 1872 to 1904, first as assistant to J. P. Mursell and from 1875 on his own. Apart from a brief retirement pastorate at West Bridgford, this was his only charge. The inspiration of his ministry was not traditional: W. E. Blomfield indicates that F. W. Robertson was one who peculiarly affected his style of thought. J. H. Shakespeare testifies that his was a converting ministry, confessing, 'I do not think Mr Thew entered deeply or widely into the controversies of his time'; his preaching exhibited a profound and deep mystical spirituality.[75] The

74 I. Sellers, 'Liverpool Nonconformity', University of Keele PhD thesis, 1969, pp.139-40.

75 J. Thew, *Radiant Hopes*, Leicester 1927.

same mystical quality is attributed to him as was attributed to Spurgeon. Certainly his sermons read as deeply and sensitively reverent compositions, fully aware of the limitations of a merely ethical Christianity. However, questions were aired: 'What is the meaning of creeds which have calmly contemplated infants in hell: which have tried to affix an infinite punishment to the sins of a finite creation?'[76] If the old doctrines of hell were to be amended, did the old missionary mandate still stand?[77] This was the question he sought to answer in a sermon preached on behalf of the BMS at the Swansea Assembly in October 1885:

> Popular Christianity makes much of saving men from death and hell. I am not insensible to the solemnities of such words; but is not ignorance death, and crime and darkness and superstition very authentic Hell? Men are anxious to secure for their fellows a heaven beyond the grave; and any man who has ever known what a grave means will not be indifferent to the pathetic hopes which centre in the Father's home. But the Master's kingdom of heaven was a kingdom of heaven to be established among the sins and sorrows of earth. 'Thy kingdom come, Thy will be done, on earth as it is in heaven.' Men do not sufficiently think of Christianity as a present good, as a present necessity for the individual life, and for the regeneration of society everywhere; as the Father's response to the aching heart of His child; as the Divine idea and law for man and for man's life here below. Why, if there were no future, and all heart were not taken out of us, this Christian life would still be man's proper life - the life of love and sacrifice, the life of God. Men seem to think that if they have any hope of acceptance with God, with a little accompanying philanthropy, Christianity has done her work. But if even personal acceptance be not everything; if even the favour of God be a better thing when it is not a mere benignant condescension, but goes along with knowledge, and trust, and

76 *ibid.*, p.60.
77 *ibid.*, pp.86-9.

> love, and service; if the moral aims and power of Christianity count for something; if a redeemed humanity - redeemed from ignorance and brutality, from war and crime, from all that sets man against man, and fills earth sometimes as with fumes from hell - if this be not a dream, a man's relations to God are more than personal, and 'acceptance' is only right of service.[78]

This drew a sharp response from Spurgeon. Alfred Baynes, the secretary of the BMS, assured him that Thew would not receive further invitations to participate in BMS events. That same month Spurgeon wrote to Booth, accusing the Baptist Union of attempting 'to drive out the orthodox', entering his 'earnest protest against the dubious notes which are continually put forth at its gatherings'.[79]

J. G. Greenhough, although born in Germany in 1843, was brought up in Yorkshire and went out to work as a saddler at the early age of eleven. In 1864 he entered Rawdon College, working for the London University degrees of BA (1866) and MA (1867). Following on early pastorates at Coseley and Cotham Grove, Bristol, he succeeded F. B. Meyer at Victoria Road, Leicester, in 1879, accordingly becoming a near neighbour of Thew's. The testimony of his quarter-of-a-century ministry at Victoria Road was that he 'never preached a bad sermon'.[80] Spurgeon would not have agreed. David Bebbington points out that in one of his scrapbooks Spurgeon had drawn attention to two offending sentences in one of Greenhough's sermons: 'Our preaching of hell wins none but the base and cowardly . . . Hopes are much larger than creeds.'[81] Keenly interested in the work of the BMS, Greenhough was part of a delegation to the Caribbean stations in the early 1890s. Of him L. H. Marshall said, 'Intensely Evangelical', he 'kept to the great eternal verities of the Christian faith which he sought to expound in such a way as to commend them to the

---

78 *ibid.*, p.90.

79 E. A. Payne, 'The Down Grade Controversy', p.151.

80 F. M. W. Harrison, *It all began here: the story of the East Midlands Baptist Association*, 1986, pp.59-60.

81 D. W. Bebbington, *Evangelicals in Modern Britain*, 1989, p.146.

intelligence, as well as to the heart.' Down Grade notwithstanding, he was elected to the Presidency of the Baptist Union in 1895 and the Chairmanship of the Free Church Council in 1901.[82]

W. E. Blomfield, the third of this trio and one of Angus's students at Regent's Park College, undertook further study at the University of St Andrew's. During his first pastoral position as assistant to Dr S. H. Booth, the then Secretary of the Baptist Union, at Elm Road, Beckenham, he had already provoked questions, though it has been suggested that these were ill-judged.[83] Booth was of the opinion that Blomfield was insufficiently affirmative in preaching 'the gospel of Cross, the Atonement and the work of the Spirit in the old way.' The difference may have had more to do with style than substance and may well have been more of a testimony to the heightened sensitivities of the pre-Downgrade years, especially in Booth's mind, since he was already in correspondence with Spurgeon on the issue.

Booth also disliked the constant 'appeal by name to such writers as Maurice, Robertson, George Eliot, Kingsley and other opponents of Evangelical doctrine'. All this led to Blomfield's summary dismissal by Booth in August 1885, on the argument that Blomfield was *his* assistant, because of 'the conviction in his [Booth's] own mind that he [Blomfield] was not sound in doctrine.' The Church protested against Booth's action, both as authoritarian and because 'they differed from Mr Booth as to his estimate of Mr Blomfield's teaching on doctrinal grounds'. Blomfield's supporters agreed that some of the authors whose names offended Booth 'ought not to be quoted in a Christian pulpit with approval', but Blomfield was not so doing but rather using them to illustrate 'some passing thought . . . in attractive language and style'. A committee of inquiry was set up which scrutinized fifty of Blomfield's sermons and decided there was no cause for alarm. The

---

82 *BH* 1935, p.320.

83 Clifford also recalled Booth's testimony in 1888: 'In justice to W. Blomfield I am bound to say I have recently seen in a printed sermon of his a categorical affirmation of the doctrine I had said he did not *teach* (NB not *hold*) when he was at Beckenham.' Payne, 'The Down Grade Controversy', pp.144-5.

resignation forthcoming at Beckenham was Booth's, not Blomfield's.[84]

From a later perspective, Blomfield has been judged 'a model of mainstream soundness', of whom A. C. Underwood later bore testimony: 'he accepts the body of sober, critical investigation . . . though I judge that the conservative bent of his nature did not make it easy for him to do so at first.' Subsequently Blomfield had two eminently successful pastorates at Turret Green, Ipswich, and Queen's Road, Coventry, before more than two decades in the Principalship at Rawdon, including the presidency of the Baptist Union in 1923. To be fair, it is significant that Booth personally commended Blomfield to the church and diaconate at Queen's Road, whilst Booth personally was reconciled to the fellowship at Elm Road, Beckenham, through the successful mediation of Charles Williams.[85]

Of these three potential liberals, two became Presidents of the Baptist Union, two held exceptionally long and succesful pastorates in Leicester, while the third added nearly twenty-five years of College principalship to twenty years' pastoral service. That might indicate that Spurgeon's worst fears were justified in that these men were influential in the life of the denomination, but it could equally be that in a world of turmoil and change he, like his compatriot S. H. Booth, failed to see in the men concerned the essential fidelity that in the maturity of their ministry became much clearer.

THE BIBLE AND CRITICISM

To the Stepney student entering the college for ministerial training and inquiring of the principal what books he would need, William Newman replied, 'You will not want many books. If you have a Hebrew Bible and a Greek Testament, bring them. A Grammar and a Lexicon, a commonplace book and a Concordance - these, I

84 *ibid.*, pp.149-50.

85 See C. Binfield, *Pastors and People: The Biography of a Baptist Church: Queen's Road, Coventry*, 1984, pp.112-7.

conceive, are the books for students.'[86] Clearly the principal wanted his students to think for themselves. Text books were used, however, at Stepney. In Murch's day the students read Whately's *Rhetoric* (1828), James Mill's *Analysis of the Phenomena of the Human Mind* (1829), and Herbert Marsh's *Lectures on the Criticism and Interpretation of the Bible* (1828). Whately was one of the early Oxford liberal theologians attached to Oriel College, known as the 'Noetics'. Reaction to their liberalism was one starting point for John Henry Newman's Tractarianism. James Mill represented the orthodoxy of the older utilitarians, whilst Herbert Marsh was a virulent opponent of the Cambridge Bible Society and sworn enemy of evangelicals. Lady Margaret Professor at Cambridge and Bishop of Peterborough, he is significant for having studied at Göttingen under Michaelis, whose critical works he translated into English, provoking the wrath of the Bishop of Oxford for 'fostering a spirit of scepticism'.[87] Stepney men under Murch were not denied access to modern thinking: Samuel Davidson's *Lectures on Biblical Criticism* were on the reading list within two years of publication in 1839. In 1875 the vacation list included Lightfoot on *Philippians* (1868), and the following year the theist Henry Sidgwick's *Method of Ethics* (1874). In 1877 Lightfoot's *Colossians* (1875) was studied alongside Dale on *The Atonement* (1875).[88]

E. A. Payne comments on Joseph Angus's patterns of training at Regent's Park: 'without any overt breach or crisis men came to appreciate the newer ways of thought and interpretation'. Payne argues that the transition in the college came more gradually than amongst some of its peers, thanks to the lack of Baptist confessional documents, the interest in science and history which characterized the dissenting educational tradition, and thanks, probably most of all, to

86 E. A. Payne, 'The development of nonconformist theological education in the nineteenth century, with special reference to Regent's Park College', *Studies in History and Religion*, 1942, p.246.

87 S. Neill, *The Interpretation of the New Testament 1861-1961*, 1964, pp.5-6.

88 Payne, 'The development of nonconformist theological education . . . ', p.248.

having men of the stamp of Angus and Benjamin Davies in charge of the teaching for nearly half a century.[89] Certainly Baptists such as Gotch and Gould gloried in the non-credalism of their denomination in the nineteenth century.

The development of the times can in part be traced through the several editions of Angus's *Bible Handbook*, first published in 1853, which initially only timidly relates to critical issues. By the posthumous edition at the beginning of the twentieth century, the result of a thorough revision by S. G. Green after Angus's death in 1902, the existence of the Graff-Wellhausen thesis is acknowledged and laid out, though countered by an abundance of conservative criticism. Angus's criticism as early as 1854 of the inaccuracy in the Authorized Version of the Bible, together with the respect secured for his conservative scholarship, led to his being appointed to the company of revisers who worked for some ten years to produce the Revised Version of the New Testament in 1881.

Angus was not alone in challenging the accuracy and usefulness of the King James Version. Spurgeon himself waxed lyrical on the subject in his 'Introduction' to Mrs H. C. Conant's *The English Bible*, published in 1859, a volume which was grateful for 'two hundred years of the most profound and brilliant scholarship the world has ever known', yet 'not one ray of this has yet been allowed to shine through an English Bible', because no new translation had been made available to the British public. By contrast, the scholar of 1859, because of the new understanding of both language and context, 'finds clearness, force and beauty in the original text where the vernacular Bible is dark and confused.' Spurgeon was fully aware that his stance would scandalize some, but he did not mince his words: 'The cant and fudge which cries out against the least alteration to the old version of our forefathers, as if it were positive profanity, are nothing to me. I love God's Word better than I love King James' pedantic wisdom and his foolish kingcraft . . . There is a kind of Popery in our midst which makes men cling fast to their errors and hinders the growth of

89 *ibid.*

thorough reformation, otherwise the church would just ask the question, Is this King James' Bible the nearest approach to the original?' The answer would be, 'No, it is exceedingly good but it has many glaring faults'. Spurgeon concluded, 'I ask, from my love of the best of translations that its obsolete words, its manifest mistranslations and glaring indecencies shall be removed. . . The Book of God is not responsible for the imperfections which are allowed to lie upon its page.'[90]

Benjamin Davies, as Principal of Stepney 1843-6, attracted suspicion because he had studied for his PhD at Leipzig and knew personally a number of the German critics, such as Tholuck and Ewald. The shortness of his tenure of office was more obviously caused by his lack of gifts of discipline and administration. For family reasons he went back to Canada where he had already taught for five years, but after a further ten years he returned to Regent's Park to work with Angus, proving a popular and faith-affirming tutor. He served on the panel of scholars working on the revision of the translation of the Old Testament, as did F. W. Gotch, who in 1868 became at one and the same time President of Bristol College and of the Baptist Union, succeeding the conservative and Calvinistic T. S. Crisp, a good linguist who had held the principalship for more than forty years.

In 1851 Gotch addressed the Bristol Association on *The Inspiration of Holy Scripture*, warning against the demands made by theories of inspiration, and suggesting instead: 'We have a revelation from God - an inspiring word given to us by inspired men. Is that not enough? Ought we to desire more?' In his second presidential address to the Baptist Union, which was entitled 'Christ at the Centre', he argued for a Christocentrism which if properly guarded gave scope for reverent criticism. Once this was secured, he asked,

> Will our faith be in vain if it is proved that the first book of the Bible is compiled from several records or if it is shown that the

90 H. C. Conant, *The English Bible*, 1859, pp.viii-xiii.

> prophecy we attribute to Isaiah or Zechariah have either or both of them four authors instead of one? Only let us see God in the world's history and especially in this history, and we shall not fear critical investigations, even the most adverse.[91]

Whilst allowing for critical investigation of the Bible, Gotch stressed theological orthodoxy in 'Christ at the Centre', which led him to the affirmation that 'the power of Christianity resides not in the example of Christ but in his work of reconciling us to God, His life and His death, a Mediation between God and man'.[92] At the same time Gotch, like so many others, reinforced the advantages of Baptist non-credalism: if it were argued that creeds were more clear and compact than Scripture, Gotch replied that this was secured at the expense of a loss of the fullness and richness of Biblical diversity; moreover, all the early creeds became over-cerebral statements of belief rather than professions of faith. The earliest credal statements, he argued, were simple word-of-mouth baptismal affirmations and commitments, not a rehearsal of the terms of orthodoxy in which task history had shown them to be remarkably ineffective.[93]

S. G. Green at Rawdon also sought to combine scholarly interests with broad evangelical sympathies and for his pains secured an unjust reputation of latitudinarianism amongst the more Calvinistic ministers in Yorkshire. He left Rawdon in 1876 to work for the Religious Tract Society where he encouraged publications which used the critical method for constructive purposes, He himself was the reviser of Angus's *Bible Handbook* and the author of a *Handbook of the Grammar of the Greek Testament*. In his *Psalms of David and Modern Criticism* (1894), he wisely pointed out that the critics themselves had come to Christian faith through the influence of the old Bible, not the new.

Addressing the Baptist Union Assembly in 1864 on 'Romanism and Ritualism', George Gould of Norwich, who was by no means an

---

91 *BH* 1869, p.178.
92 *BH* 1890, obituary.
93 *BH* 1869, pp.181-2.

obscurantist, was much less friendly to Germany's 'higher criticism' or, nearer at home, to either Colenso or the authors of *Essays and Reviews*:

> Their purpose was, and is, to explode all belief in a Divine Redeemer, who by the grace of God tasted death for every man; and to leave us our Bibles as a compilation of myths and poems, of incredible histories and bewildering prophecies, in the midst of which philosophic souls might haply discover a scheme of morals and religion fitted to make a Deist glad.[94]

Even the liberal J. P. Mursell, in his presidential address of the same year, was prepared to identify 'the disciples of Emerson, of Carlyle, of Newman, and of Theodore Parker' with 'the enemies of our faith', planning 'infidel aggression'[95] linking together the sacramentalism of the Catholic with the reductionism of the unitarian and the universalist, a formidable coalition of those agencies most offensive to the Baptist mind.

Much of the best critical work by Baptists was done in the pastorate rather than in the colleges. Of the scholar pastors of the denomination, James Martin (1821-77) played a major part in disseminating German scholarship through some twenty translations he undertook for the Edinburgh firm of T. & T. Clark, with whom he became acquainted during his pastorate of Charlotte Chapel (1856-8). A Stepney College student, taught by Benjamin Davies and F. W. Gotch, he established a lifelong friendship with Alexander McLaren. After Stepney, Martin spent several sessions at the University of Bonn as a Ward Scholar in the late 1840s, settling to his first pastorate in Lymington in 1848. Whilst appreciated by the more intelligent part of the membership, he incurred some suspicion there simply because he had studied in Germany. The authors he translated included German scholars of a more conservative frame of mind than radicals

---

94 George Gould, *Romanism and Rationalism in relationship to Baptist Principles* [Association Address, 9 October 1864], p.22.

95 J. P. Mursell, *Inaugural Address, Baptist Union, 1864*, pp.4ff.

of the ilk of Baur and Wellhausen. Much of the work involved respectful Old Testament commentaries on the Pentateuch, the later histories and the prophets.

There were also works on the Covenant, Christology, and some New Testament principles. The first of several editions of his *Origin and History of the New Testament* was published in 1871. S. G. Green summarized his literary work by indicating that all was the product of 'a mind liberalized by German criticism and philosophy yet steadfastly true to Evangelical Truth'. A notable ministry at Derby Road, Nottingham, 1858-69, during which time he sat on the Committee of the BMS, was followed by creative work in Australia as minister of Collins Street, Melbourne, in which city he died in 1877. Not an enthusiastic preacher, his honesty was transparent, and so he did not shun the polemical. He made a distinction characteristic of many Baptists of his age when he argued, 'The mistake of Roman Catholics is placing the crucifix in lieu of the Cross; the error of the Protestant is substituting a creed for Christ'.[96]

Samuel Cox's literary endeavours were partly the consequence of an illness of the throat which made preaching peculiarly difficult at one period in his life. Exercising his ministry instead through the printed page, he became the paid editor of *The Expositor*, the parent of the present-day *Expository Times*, of which it has been said, 'The influence of the magazine upon religious thought in England can hardly be over-estimated'.[97] His health recovered sufficiently for him to undertake a remarkable twenty-five year long pastorate at Mansfield Road, Nottingham, whilst continuing his editing work. It was said of him that he was 'conspicuously the helper of men who sought his sympathy and counsel in their struggle with theological difficulties'. 'As a theologian', his obituarist wrote, 'Dr Cox was Evangelical, his belief in the Incarnation and the Atonement and the Resurrection of Jesus Christ and in essentially related truths was deep and abiding.' Nevertheless, his work as a scholar was not without

---

96 *BH* 1878, p.348.
97 *DNB*.

difficulty; in 1884 he was parted from the editorship of *The Expositor* by Hodder & Stoughton for not being willing to exclude Robertson Smith and those who shared his 'loose view of inspiration' from the pages of that journal, as also references to Cox's own interest in 'the larger hope'. Cox himself wrote some twelve volumes of exposition. in addition to his editing activity and more general theological works.[98]

John Clifford was at once open to new knowledge and its constructive insights, which he welcomed as liberating the Christian mind from more partial understanding. This he saw as part of the reformed inheritance:

> Therefore we assert the Reformation doctrine that the seat of authority in Christian ethics and teaching is not the letter of the Scriptures alone but is Christ Jesus, dwelling and ruling in the conscience and reason of the Christian man by and through the Scriptures. We cannot suffer the Redeemer to be deposed from His throne in favour of the late and post-Reformation dogma which lifts the letter of Scripture into the position of inerrancy claimed for the Pope.[99]

This is characteristic of Clifford's position, with his focus firmly established on the person of Christ, quite deliberately affirmed as Redeemer, as over against all theories of inspiration of verbal forms which are seen as derivative of a misplaced credalism. Clifford counterposes the protestant doctrine of the Authority of the Bible freely interpreted by each individual over against the Catholic teaching of the authority of the Church, dependent upon Tradition and mediated by a priest. Such a doctrine is quite different from the later developed doctrine of Verbal Inerrancy which he demonstrates was not taught by the reformers or by Christian teachers as late as Richard Baxter,

98 *BH* 1894, obituary.

99 J. Clifford, *The Inspiration and Authority of the Bible*, second revised and enlarged edition of 1895, p.137. 10,000 copies had been published within three years.

arguing that the challenging of the theory of inerrancy leaves those earlier doctrines of Biblical authority intact.

Worried about the life-styles of some of the stoutest defenders of orthodoxy, Clifford believed that the more one made of the letter, the less they found of the Spirit. 'Inspiration', he argued, 'is not and cannot be external or mechanical - a matter of parchment and pages, of letters and type.' Any insistence on the acceptability of a *theory* of the 'how' of inspiration he termed 'anti-apostolic', 'a post Reformation invention', and 'a heresy of measureless mischief'. For the lack of Scriptural warrant for a 'purely organic (that is mechanical) theory of Inspiration', he invoked the authority of Bishop Westcott.[100] By contrast with all formal and literal theories, Clifford, echoing Coleridge's understanding about a hundred years earlier, argued that once the Spirit of God had produced his own evidence in the hearts and lives of men and women, they would existentially know a reality more compelling than that of any theory of Inspiration.[101]

All this led him to welcome the work of the critics:

> Criticism is not, then, the sign of barrenness and decadence. The dead do not criticize. It is one of the proofs of the arrival of an exuberant vitality, of fuller and truer life, yea a sign that God Himself is at work among us, patiently gathering up and re-energizing the purpose men have temporarily frustrated, and generously recalling us from the misuse of his gifts to Himself, the real fount and source of all true religion.[102]

Jesus' use of the Scriptures as he found them was, Clifford argued, of first significance for the Jews had perverted the intent of Scripture by making the Biblical text the warrant for national exclusiveness. By contrast

---

100 *ibid.*, p.162 fn.
101 *ibid.*, p.166.
102 *ibid.*, pp.120-1.

> Christ lifted the Hebrew writing into the light of the Fatherhood of God and showed that as God is not partial and exclusive so His Book is not. The Revelation, in its distinctive elements, its conception of God, righteousness, redemption, and of the Eternal Kingdom came through the Hebrew people. It was their gift to the world, and, as such, stands by itself . . . It began with Adam not Abraham . . . Nothing is common or unclean. The 'Inspiration of Selection' does not shrink from quoting and incorporating the literature of the peoples of the earth. It cites their traditions, gives their genealogies, adds chapters from the annals of Egypt and reports 'the burden of the Lord' concerning Moab and Babylon, Damascus and Assyria, Egypt and Arabia. We speak of 'foreign elements' in our Bible. There are none. It is God's Bible and nothing belonging to His child is or can be foreign. Truth is universal . . . Hear, therefore, and heed the Word of the Lord Jesus, as by His use of the Old Testament He declares that it has immense and inexhaustible stores for the spiritual quickening and guidance of the whole human race. We are only just beginning to know its wealth . . . The Renaissance of the Old Testament is the harbinger of a Spiritual Reformation.[103]

Clifford's view of revelation was unapologetically 'evolutionary',[104] from the crude perception of the early patriarchs through to the incarnate life of Christ, 'the final test of morality, and also of the doctrinal teaching of the New Testament'. Thus imperfection and error are to be expected: 'The Old Testament is the record of the life of Israel, that is, of the activities of God in a frail, erring, and sinful people; and whilst full of God and His inspiration, it bears traces of the weakness, confusion of thought, imperfections and faults of that elect people.'[105]

---

103 *ibid.*, pp.124-5.

104 *ibid.*, p.135 fn.

105 *ibid.*, pp.136-7.

Clifford is, however, realistic about what critical method can offer and what it cannot achieve. It can establish the text, clarify meanings, and denote contexts. But it never supplants the Scriptures and their message as the source of revelation. Thus a call 'Back to the Bible' remains appropriate, understanding that since 'speech is the soul made vocal', 'the soul of the Scriptures, Old and New alike, is Jesus.'[106]

Until Clifford's bold endorsement of the critical method, many ministers exercised discretion in relating their critical understanding to their preaching. Nowhere is this better seen than in the work of a figure like Alexander McLaren, credited by W. H. Bennett, the Congregational scholar, as accepting the value of critical scholarship. Such caution, it has been argued, better served the interests of the churches than a more aggressive handling of changes in thought which were of the same gravity as those which divided the church at the time of the Reformation.[107] Accordingly, 'reverent criticism' in England, associated with a warm affirmation of evangelical doctrine, secured for the most part peaceful change. Baptists, with certain exceptions were, in David Bebbington's judgement, 'less inclined to critical innovations than other Nonconformists'.[108]

---

106 *ibid.*, p.177.

107 Willis B. Glover jun., *Evangelical Nonconformists and Higher Criticism in the Nineteenth Century*, 1954, pp.190, 152.

108 D. W. Bebbington, *op.cit.*, p.186.

7

ASSOCIATIONS, ALLIANCES AND THE WIDER CHURCH

Very early in Baptist life the need to complement the congregational principle by a pattern of association had been readily perceived. In practice, during the eighteenth century, the agencies of association - especially in London - had been weak and intermittent. At the beginning of the nineteenth century all too many congregations lived in total isolation from each other, or at best only related to external agencies informally as the need to secure external funding for ministry or sanctuary became apparent. The Evangelical Revival made its impact on Baptist life at this point as at so many others. In the first place, the Baptist Missionary Society was a child of that revival and underlined the need for denominational cohesion if the work abroad was to be adequately supported. Home mission and efficient itinerancy made similar demands, and even succeeded in some places in providing a practical cause uniting both strands within the congregational family, Baptist and Paedobaptist. As Geoffrey Nuttall has demonstrated, the new associations that date from this period also had an urgent missionary purpose;[1] in Bedfordshire and adjacent counties these were also formulated on a pan-congregational basis.

DENOMINATIONAL AND INTER-DENOMINATIONAL

By the time the Evangelical Revival was making its greatest impact upon the Baptist community, the turbulent years of reaction to the French Revolution and its challenge to the old order throughout Europe were also throwing up a religious response to the social insecurity thus engendered. The reaction was twofold. First, it provided the context in which a battery of organizations that drew evangelical Christians closer together in programmes of inter-denominational action was called into being. The same context also

1 G. F. Nuttall, 'Assemblies and Association in Dissent', in *Studies in Church History*, 7, 1971, pp.304-5.

gave birth to that denominationalism which shaped the divided Christendom of nineteenth-century Britain. On the one hand, joint endeavours in Bible translation, tract production and distribution, the nurturing of Sunday Schools, and a host of philanthropic concerns brought the different strands of evangelical Dissent together, and even bridged the larger gap between them and evangelical Churchmen. The search for unity in mission was under way, but was not without its difficulties. The inter-relatedness of the process is instructive: first the founding of the Baptist Missionary Society, initially with significant support from non-Baptists, then the founding of the *London* Missionary Society, grandly known as *The* Missionary Society in its early years, with aristocratic Baptist support in the person of the Revd Sir Egerton Leigh (Bart.), Baptist minister in Rugby.[2] However, with the forming of separate Anglican and Wesleyan societies, increasingly the London society became *de facto* the instrument of Congregationalists. In similar fashion the development of denominational magazines left the *Evangelical Magazine* increasingly the property of the Congregationalists; the *Baptist Magazine*, for example, published its first issue in 1809.

Accordingly there is a duality of influence at the beginning of the nineteenth century - both proto-ecumenical and denominational. Thus Ruth Rouse argues that the voluntary societies and movements that arose out of the late eighteenth and early nineteenth-century passion for evangelism 'were pioneers, albeit unconscious pioneers, of the movement of Christian unity which was to come'.[3] Similarly, Alan Gilbert has called the age of itinerancy amongst evangelical nonconformists 'the age of popular ecumenism'.[4] W. R. Ward is of similar opinion: 'As men cheerfully shouldered the great missionary

---

2 L. G. Champion, 'The Preaching Baronet', *Baptist Quarterly* (hereafter *BQ*) 10, 1941, pp.429-33.

3 R. Rouse, 'Voluntary Movements and the Changing Ecumenical Climate', in R. Rouse and S. C. Neill (eds.), *A History of the Ecumenical Movement, 1517-1948*, 1954, p.319.

4 A. D. Gilbert, *Religion and Society in Industrial England*, 1976, p.58.

burden, denominational divisions seemed to crumble . . . There was general euphoria at the end of bigotry and the triumph of Catholic Christianity'.[5] All this is evidenced by David Bogue's memorable words in his missionary sermon preached at the founding of the LMS in 1795, when he spoke of those gathered being 'assembled with one accord to attend the funeral of bigotry'.[6] That was the mood of the last decade of the eighteenth century: in similar language, an association letter of the Yorkshire and Lancashire Particular Baptist Association, composed by Thomas Langdon of Leeds, advised in 1791 that nothing was more injurious to the Christian interest than *'Religious Bigotry'*.[7]

Times were changing: that brief era of co-operative Christianity did not last. The Church of England, in the context of social turmoil and charismatic innovation, increasingly laid stress on loyalty to the liturgy of the Prayer Book and obedience to its bishops; in the Wesleyan Connexion the itinerants emphasized their authority over against the laity. In 1811 Lord Sidmouth introduced into parliament his bill against itinerancy, and Ward is compelled to note, 'Conflict was forcing new denominational organizations into being'.[8] Thereafter there was increasing ambiguity of relationship between evangelical churchmen and evangelical dissenters. Sometimes the argument was that the dimensions of the missionary task at home demanded a pan-ecumenical approach, but equally it was sometimes argued that the establishment principle inhibited revival. The more violent the nonconformist advocacy of voluntaryism, the more conservative evangelicals in the Church of England dug themselves in behind the establishment principle.[9]

---

5 W. R. Ward, *Religion and Society in England, 1740-1830*, 1972, p.45.

6 J. Bennett, *Memoirs of the Life of the Revd David Bogue, DD*, 1827, p.184.

7 Yorkshire and Lancashire Lecture, 'On Christian Benevolence', in J. Rippon, *Baptist Annual Register* (*BAR*) II, 1792, p.274.

8 Ward, *op.cit.*, p.53.

9 Donald M. Lewis, *Lighten Their Darkness: The Evangelical Mission to Working Class London, 1828-1860*, Westport, Conn., 1986; see especially chapters 4, 8, 10, 11.

THE GROWTH OF ASSOCIATIONS

Bound into Rippon's *Baptist Annual Register* for 1793[10] is a long poem by Benjamin Francis on 'The Association', a poem most respectfully addressed to the 'Members of Each Baptist Association'. Francis salutes the associations as the 'guardians of the churches' weal', distinguishing them from the 'grave synods' of other churches where 'lords of conscience' convene together and where 'superstition sanctifies old creeds and priestcraft triumphs in oppressive deeds'. By contrast, he applauds the altruism of the association amidst all the seductions of an alluring world:

> No worldly motive and no base design
> But love of truth and purity divine
> With pious zeal for the Redeemer's cause
> That first conven'd thee and ordain'd thy laws.

Associations, meeting under the authority of scripture, properly distinguished between matters of significance and things of indifference. Skilfully deploying spiritual weaponry against the forces of evil, they promoted 'graceful order walking hand in hand with cheerful freedom.'

> So yearly meet, from parts remote, in Thee . . .
> Th'associate brethren, pastors, deacons, friends,
> And the full crowd that in thy train attends

to encourage one another in 'endearing fellowship' with accounts of the progress of the churches, sharing where necessary with one another in distress. Thus Francis admits of many difficulties: 'names disown'd or love and concord fled', disorders to be healed, and the discipline needed to secure 'harmonious order', whilst disclaiming 'all human force to rule the human mind, improve opinion and the conscience bind' - in all a proper blend of fidelity to the gospel and freedom to explore its many truths.

10 *BAR* I 1790-93; bound between pp.384-5.

Conven'd to fan the flames of zeal divine,
And the soft bows of sacred love intwine,
Long hast thou strove, nor hast thou strove in vain,
To strengthen Zion, and her peace maintain.

Notwithstanding such a eulogy, the maintenance and development of Association life had not been without difficulty, largely because of the conflicting forces of Arianism and Antinomianism as the eighteenth century ran its course. Lovegrove describes the inheritance of the Associations as 'limited, faltering and invariably inward-looking'. [11] Although certain associations dated back to the seventeenth century, they had to be re-created, or at least re-invigorated in the second half of the eighteenth century under the impulse of the energies of the Evangelical Revival, especially as influenced by the new theology of Jonathan Edwards and the Great Awakening in North America. Up to that point, 'the churches, as distinct from the ministers, were unsocial'.[12] In 1752 the venerable Western Association restored the practice of printing an annual circular letter, and was soon followed by the Northern Association and the Yorkshire and Lancashire Association.

In 1764 a new Association of great importance was organized, taking the name of the Northamptonshire Association, although many of its churches lay outside the county borders, its influence extending from Nottinghamshire to Hertfordshire. This important marker for future developments was the archetype of the new Associations, born out of the Evangelical Revival. At its head was a remarkable set of leaders - the two Rylands, two Halls, Fuller, Sutcliffe and Carey, with Abraham Booth briefly a member between his leaving the General Baptists and transferring to London. With a renewed spirituality and impelled by the new Evangelical Calvinism, otherwise known as Fullerism, it was one hundred and one per cent committed to mission both at home and overseas, and soon became a model of what

11 D. Lovegrove, *Established Church, Sectarian People: Itinerancy and the Transformation of English Dissent, 1780-1830*, 1988, p.31.

12 W. T. Whitley, *A History of British Baptists* (hereafter *HBB*), 1923, p.204.

associations might become.[13] In 1769 the Norfolk and Suffolk Association came into being and in 1779 the Kent and Sussex. Several of the older associations began to revive, with London conspicuous in its slowness to adapt to the new associational pattern of co-operation.[14]

Reflecting even more closely the connexional organization of the Methodists, the New Connexion of General Baptists was founded under the leadership of Dan Taylor. This was significant in cultivating a more clearly focused denominational identity amongst its adherents. Other new foundations were to follow: Essex in 1796, Oxfordshire and East Gloucestershire in 1802, Shropshire and Cheshire in 1806, Buckinghamshire and Hertfordshire in 1811, Cornwall in 1812. Thus Lovegrove deduces that, despite 'contemporary emphasis upon the resilience and vitality of the congregational principle, it is impossible to ignore the real movement towards association, interdependence and the growth of external authority: a process not capable of reversal, arising as it did from the confluent pressures of permanent social change and the practicalities of concerted evangelism'.[15]

James Hinton of Oxford, in the 1821 Circular Letter to the Oxfordshire Association (which like the Northamptonshire Association was broader in its membership than the geographical county), compared the health of the churches in the early 1820s with that thirty or forty years previously, when, he maintained, 'they suffered death to desolate their assemblies and contented themselves with following good men to their graves'. He argued that the greater health of the churches in the latter period was in no small measure due to the 'rise and support' of the 'Association, which by its annual and other

13 E. A. Payne, *Prayer Call of 1784*, 1941; *The Baptist Union: a short history*, 1959, pp.36-8. But note Lovegrove's point that in terms of chronology the Western Association was actually ahead of Northamptonshire in its advocacy of evangelism and itinerancy (Lovegrove, *op.cit.*, p.32).

14 Nuttall, *op.cit.*, pp.304-5; W. T. Whitley, 'Association Life till 1815', *TBHS* 5, 1916, pp.30-1.

15 Lovegrove, *op.cit.*, p.29.

assemblies, has dispersed more widely a spirit of Christian love and called into more frequent exercise a spirit of zeal for public good.' It had encouraged every 'means of instruction', and made some provision for members' widows and orphans, 'while the churches, otherwise unable to sustain a stated ministry, have been preserved in the enjoyment of this most important privilege; and many remote villages have, by the same aid, been favoured with the blessing of the preached gospel'. 'To this Association', continues Hinton, 'we also owe that very important institution, the Auxiliary Missionary Society', which, in many instances, by its vigorous reaction had produced a revival at home: 'The invaluable institutions of Bible Associations and Sunday Schools, have been greatly promoted by the mutual examples of the churches.' He therefore encouraged church members to be more diligent in attending Association meetings and in supporting their work.[16]

Year by year the *Baptist Magazine* bears testimony to the work of the Associations with its many reports upon their meetings and activities. These can be further checked by consulting their several histories. For example, in Yorkshire and Lancashire the turn of the century saw remarkable changes: 'The newer evangelism, associated with men like Fawcett and Medley in Liverpool, clashed with the "walled garden" mentality of the older eighteenth-century Dissent.'[17] This new spirit was soon manifest in the founding of the Northern Education Society (1804), in the appointment of William Steadman as first principal, and in the establishment of an associated Itinerant Society which took the students of the academy out into the districts in effective evangelistic endeavour. Churches were planted and ailing causes revived, with, from 1827, an Association Fund to help needy pastors. In these industrializing counties, the Association, with Steadman as its secretary from 1805 to 1839, was an essential vehicle for enabling the churches to minister to people on the move from the

---

16 *BM* November 1821, pp.465-9, December 1821, pp.511-516.

17 I. Sellers, *Our Heritage: Baptists of Yorkshire, Lancashire and Cheshire, 1647-1987*, 1987, p.21.

countryside into new rootless, industrial towns and villages. Between 1835 and 1845 both Particular and New Connexion Baptists doubled their membership.[18]

Not all were convinced of the effectiveness of Associations. A correspondent to the *Baptist Magazine* in December 1833 claimed that less than a half of Baptist churches were in associations, a view confirmed by Joseph Belcher, secretary of the Baptist Union 1832-40.[19] Two years later a 'Baptist of the Old School', writing under the heading 'Unity is Strength', drew attention to large parts of the country lacking in Baptist witness, lamenting the isolationist reputation of Baptists: the Independents and Methodists were much more united than they were. Such a lament was a recurring theme in the first half of the century, and occasioned a plea for a greater prayerfulness and a greater willingness for rich and poor to co-operate to the advantage of the extension of a gospel ministry.[20]

In 1840 Mr Tilly of Forton, Hampshire, secretary of the Southern Association, underlined the increased importance of Associations in promoting the welfare of their member churches, with 'the strong and much-favoured churches sustaining the infirmities of the weak', and with ministers encouraged to undertake itinerancy in the villages of their area. 'Union is strength and much is easily effected by collective and organized bodies which could not be effected by individual effort.' 'The history of our Bible societies, our missionary and tract societies, confirms the same fact, and proves the utility of combination'. Associations were also able to promulgate strategic plans for denominational extension work, not in any sectarian spirit but because the nation was grossly under-churched. Finally, 'important questions of a civil nature' were properly addressed by associations who were able to offer 'concentrated wisdom and influence'. All these objects accounted for the increasing importance of Associations which were thus to command the respect of the

---

18 *ibid.*, Chapter 2.

19 *BM* December 1833, pp.595-6; January 1834, pp.11-12; March 1834, pp.103-4.

20 *BM* May 1835, pp.223-4.

churches and their members: at the same time, they called for efficient administration, with the proper preparation of business by an Association committee.[21]

In 1857 Samuel Manning, the editor of the *Baptist Magazine*, surveyed the work of the Associations and strongly defended their usefulness, both in terms of their formal actions and the informal opportunities they afforded for securing advice and sympathy. He also argued their importance in promoting occasions of celebration, especially for those from rural situations for whom the regular dimensions of worship were often small and local.[22] Association meetings, when held in rural areas, also served to enhance the respect for the local congregation within that local community. Annual circular letters represented an attempt at contextualization, speaking as they did to the needs of the particular group of churches. Association resolutions offered a vehicle whereby the mind of the churches could be articulated on public issues to good effect: over the years the Yorkshire Association supported resolutions on nonconformist grievances, negro slavery, Catholic emancipation, the emancipation of the Jews, Free Trade, education, and the evils of gambling and drink.[23]

Home Mission was powerfully promoted by the work of the Associations. The care of the churches was uppermost, with the appointment of visitors to meet with congregations in a distressed condition. Church planting (or extension) was strategically considered, alongside a more broadcast sponsorship of village preaching. Without infringing the independence of local churches, the Associations helped them to monitor their progress: 'each church is led to review its labours, its failures, its successes during the previous year', and increasingly to provide those statistics that enabled a general picture of the state of the denomination to be determined. Associations, it was argued, were vital to the life of the denomination,

21 *BM* December 1840, pp.669-70.

22 *BM* September 1857, pp.533-4.

23 Sellers, *op.cit.*, pp.34-5.

even though there was much scope for further improving their usefulness.[24]

Associations increasingly took on new functions. Already many were raising money for chapel building, to replace the old system of pastors travelling the country to solicit funds. A consequence of the development of Association funds for building churches was that they also became trust bodies. In British law there is a need for a 'legal personality' to hold property, and a changing church membership cannot easily meet that need. Hence the practice has been for a select group of trustees to act in trust for any given chapel building. The trusts upon which church properties have been held represent an important series of documents, specifying the doctrine to be upheld, the ministry to be undertaken, and the conditions of membership. By theological definitions they seek to ensure the fidelity of future generations to the founders' intentions, with a tendency for such doctrinal prescriptions to become ever more detailed. The Trust Deed, so far as the church's property was concerned, represented a significant alternative authority to that of the church meeting, not least because of the history of those congregations which had lapsed into unitarianism and were the subject of litigation of national significance in the Lady Hewley Charity Case of 1842. Not surprisingly, by the mid-nineteenth century new churches often used the same form of deed as the churches that had parented them. Twenty years later certain lawyers active in the Associations began to devise deeds particularly suited to the needs of Baptist churches: in the East Midlands the special office of Custodian of the Deeds was created with [Sir] Joseph Bright, a solicitor from the Derby Road Church, holding the office.[25] In 1888 the Association promoted the first Model Deed which became the norm for newly established causes in the county until revised in 1907. Part of the motivation for this model deed was that the planting of a church was not simply a

24 *BM* September 1857, pp.533-4.

25 F. M. W. Harrison, *It All Began Here: The Story of the East Midland Baptist Association*, 1986, p.66.

'congregational' act but a result of 'associational' effort, both in terms of strategy and finance, and therefore the interest of the wider family needed safeguarding.[26] Balancing the interests of the local congregation and the wider Baptist community was clearly becoming more important.

Associations increasingly became partners with the local church in financing ministry by providing funds to support poorly paid pastors and by organizing provident and annuity funds to make some modest provision for their retirement and for the needs of their widows and orphans. Admittedly special in being a non-geographical association, the General Baptist Association [New Connexion] added to this from 1877 the establishment of a Board of Reference 'to facilitate the removal of ministers and the supply of churches'.[27]

Notwithstanding the development of Association life, a headstrong zeal for total autonomy constantly pulled in a contrary direction. In 1883 William Woods of Nottingham, later to become the first secretary of the East Midland Baptist Association which after 1892 united Particular and General Baptists in one body, calculated that approximately a quarter of Baptist churches were not in membership with any Association. A little earlier John Aldis confessed that 'Individualism, independence and liberty are the idols of the day', an attitude which he identified as an over-reaction against the 'priestism' engendered by the Catholic revival. He questioned whether Baptists in reacting against 'tyranny' had not run to the opposite extreme of 'anarchy'.[28]

At the close of the century Associations were seen as discharging their duties equally in evangelistic enterprise, both at home and in support of the missionary society overseas, and in pursuing issues of social responsibility, specifically identified as the control of the drink trade, the promotion of undenominational elementary education and

26 K. G. Jones, 'The Authority of the Trust Deed: a Yorkshire Perspective', *BQ* 33, 1987, pp.103-18.

27 Payne, *Baptist Union*, p.123.

28 Cited in Payne, *Baptist Union*, p.117.

the cessation of the trade in opium, subjects which appeared in the agenda of many associations. 'The sneer as to our being political Dissenters should not deter us from discharging one of the first duties of our citizenship. Our Christianity must be applied both to politics and to commerce'.[29]

A NATIONAL UNION[30]

Towards the end of the Napoleonic Wars some more general union of Baptists was thought desirable. In June 1811 Joseph Ivimey, historian of the denomination, wrote an article for the *Baptist Magazine* under the signature of *Iota*, entitled 'Unity Essential to Prosperity', in which he argued that the establishment of the missionary society 'has already done more towards uniting our denomination than any plan that was ever devised'. This led to the question, 'Does not the constitution of our churches which prevents all external interference, and therefore preserves them independent of each other require some general bond of union?'. He answered this with the proposal, *'That an Annual Assembly be held either in London or at some of the larger, and most central towns in the country, composed of Ministers and Messengers from the neighbouring Churches, and of two deputies from every Association in the united kingdom'.* The suggested agenda for such an assembly was immediately four-fold: viz. to hear reports and encourage support for the Indian mission, similarly to receive a report from the secretary of the Baptist Itinerant Society, that 'a spirit of emulation to visit our dark and benighted towns and villages may be excited', then perhaps to consider 'a fund for the support of our Seminaries', as also one for the relief of 'aged and necessitous ministers'. The list was not exhaustive, ending with several emphatic '&c &c's'. 'Why', asked Ivimey, 'should we be so far behind other denominations in plans to promote the union, the peace, and the prosperity of the Church of Christ?'

---

29 *BM* July 1893, p.368.

30 For a fuller account of the founding of the Union, see Payne, *Baptist Union,* chapter 1, pp.15ff.

The target date for the new assembly was the summer of 1812.[31] A response to this clarion call came from 'B.D.' (almost certainly Bourne Draper, then minister in Chipping Norton, and thus a representative of provincial Baptist life) in a published 'Address to the Baptist Denomination', also arguing 'In our present disjointed situation, we are unacquainted with our own strength, we are ignorant of the effect we could produce if united in a general system of endeavour'. The London Missionary Society derived great support from its London assemblies, and Methodism had become a national movement because local preaching had been systematically organized. Baptists should follow such encouraging examples, which would help them to fulfil Christ's prayer in John 17, v.21.[32] Further support was forthcoming from Wales, whence it was argued, 'This destructive spirit of *too much independency* has raged too long among us and has done as much more real injury than all the combined legions of earth and hell without its assistance can accomplish.' Disunity caused indifference: even as Baptist church membership calls upon individuals to sacrifice their independence for the greater gains of fellowship in the local church, so that church, as also the association to which it belongs, needs to be prompted by the same vision of the strength to be secured by joining with others. 'UNION, UNION, yes UNION of the most extensive, firm and durable nature' was the object of the most heartfelt and unanimous plea from the principality.[33]

The *Baptist Magazine* for 1812 offered repeated support for the union project,[34] including in particular a full account of the preliminary meeting towards the setting up of a General Union, held under the chairmanship of Dr Rippon, at which special emphasis was laid upon the need for prayer before business. The earlier proposed agenda for the new organization was agreed, together with an emphasis on reports from the associations, plus a concern for

---

31 *BM* June 1811, pp.234-7.

32 *BM* August 1811, pp.326-30.

33 *BM* January 1812, pp.13-17.

34 *BM* 1812, pp.44, 157-61, 274, 291, 356-9, 417-14.

developing the best methods for catechizing the young and establishing Sunday Schools, with a suggestion that church planting be more strategically planned. Resolutions were passed which were to bring the new body into being on 25 and 26 June 1813. They included an invitation 'to our churches and associations in the country to appoint messengers to meet their brethren in London'; 'that the objects of the Association be the promotion of the cause of Christ in general, and the interests of the denomination in particular, with a primary view to the encouragement and support of the Baptist mission'; and finally, that the associated ministers in London should act as the committee for the first year. Forty-eight country pastors and eleven from London gave in their names as supporting the proposed union. Lest any erroneous impression be given, a resolution was passed at the final meeting that the society disclaimed all manner of superiority and superintendence over the churches and any authority or power to impose anything on those churches' faith and practice. They had, however, adopted a doctrinal basis for their unity which was deliberately Trinitarian and Calvinistic, with an emphasis on election, original sin, particular redemption, efficacious grace, the perseverance of the saints, the consolation and terrors of future judgment, and the congregational church order.[35]

An article in the *Eclectic Review* for August 1822 referred to the Baptists as that denomination 'which has been esteemed, not without reason, the most sectarian of sects, the most intrenched, and fortified in the narrow circle of its communion'. Joseph Ivimey did not doubt the reputation but questioned its reasonableness, referring to the denomination's long campaign for tolerance and liberty of conscience. Not all Baptists were closed communionists, but the logic of baptism as a necessary preliminary to communion could not be denied. Moreover, he argued that Baptists had been to the fore in the

---

35 *BM* May 1813, p.222; June 1813, pp.264-6; July 1813, p.310; August 1813, pp.351-2; June 1814, pp.260-2. The doctrinal basis of Association life in the eighteenth century had been the 1689 Particular Baptist Confession of Faith, of which this was a clear echo.

promotion of joint Christian enterprises: 'When did they object to unite with other Christians in any plan of humanity or benevolence; whether for the education of the poor, or the circulation of the scriptures? or anything in religion which did not exact from them the sacrifice of principle conscientiously held, and as they think scripturally proved?'. Rather they had been amongst 'the first and most active promoters' of Sunday Schools, the Tract Society, the Bible Society, the British and Foreign School Society, and work amongst sailors.[36]

Not all took the jaundiced view expressed by the *Eclectic Review*: John Stoughton, Congregationalist minister in Kensington and for ten years editor of the *Evangelical Magazine*, writing of the first thirty years of the century in which he lived, argued:

> There is more unity in Baptist history than in the history of Independents during the early part of the century. Baptists had stronger sympathies with each other; for their denominational zeal rallied round one distinct institute, the name of which ever shone on their banners. They, for the most part, co-operated more intimately, and with less diversity of organization and action, perhaps with a greater amount of *esprit de corps*; moreover to any one writing their history at the period, they supply links of connection in three controversies which they carried on without destroying denominational unity. The hyper-Calvinistic controversy, the communion controversy, and the Serampore controversy were so many family discussions.[37]

Such unity was preserved not least because people took different sides on different issues but still recognized that they belonged to one confessional family. Such unity had to be cultivated, and hence the importance of the work of the General Union. Two men amongst others stand out for their vision and patience in holding the Calvinistic Baptists together in unity: John Rippon supplied much of the initial

---

36 *BM* December 1822, pp.508-10.

37 J. Stoughton, *History of Religion in England*, VII, 2nd edition, 1884, pp.261-2.

vision and Joseph Ivimey, the denominational historian, much of the staying power, keeping - even amongst adverse circumstances - the churches together in common purpose.

THE REFORMING OF THE BAPTIST UNION

By 1832 it was deemed right to reformulate the General Union on a broader basis, which it was hoped might embrace members of the New Connexion. To effect this the Calvinistic articles of 1813 were replaced by the looser phrase inviting support from 'Baptist ministers and churches who agree in sentiments usually denominated evangelical', while the objectives were re-written to embrace the promotion of unity, to secure statistical data and to prepare an annual report.[38] One of the first actions of the newly constituted Union was to despatch a two-man delegation to the United States of America to attend the American Triennial Convention of Baptist Churches in 1835, and to make 'friendly expostulation' against the churches holding slave-owners within their membership.[39] This issue was to trouble not only the infant Evangelical Alliance but the Baptist Union itself.

Baptist involvement in slave-holding was also responsible for difficulties for the infant Union six years later. At the annual meeting of 1841, the Baptist Union faced a double crisis. In the first place the Treasurer, Mr James Low, a paper-maker and a member of New Park Street, resigned because of a deficit in funds. He was, however, persuaded to continue for another six years. Not so the secretary, Joseph Belcher, who found himself with resolutions on slave-holding, with which he did not sympathize, to communicate to the North American churches. The resolutions concerned, proposed by Charles Stovel and seconded by Belcher's colleague, J. H. Hinton, gave thanks for changes in Jamaica and other British colonies and then went on further to give thanks for 'the advance of their brethren and coadjutors in the work of emancipation on the continent of America', and 'to

38 Payne, *Baptist Union*, p.61.

39 *ibid.*, p.63.

trust that the present crisis will lead to important results in that country.' The Union's resolutions sought God's blessing on the Convention meetings in Baltimore and expressed the hope that by the efforts of those gathered there 'the moral power of the church may be employed in establishing universal liberty'. They concluded, 'This Union affectionately commends to the prayers and assistance of all who love the Lord Jesus Christ such operations of benevolence as may lead to the final annihilation of slavery and the slave trade throughout the world.'[40]

These were relatively mild words when compared with the language of a letter addressed to the American churches by the Baptist Union committee the previous November and which had as its signatories, Murch, Belcher and Steane, in that order. This had been provoked by the actions of the London Convention on Slavery, which itself had passed rather stronger resolutions, making it quite clear that slavery was contrary to all Christian principles of justice and was accordingly a sin against God, 'which acquires additional enormity when committed by nations professedly Christian'. Secondly the resolutions deeply regretted that the institution was protected and perpetuated by the action of churches which had not only failed to condemn it but had 'retained in the communion, without censure, those by whom it is notoriously propagated'. Thirdly, while disclaiming authority to dictate to Christian churches terms of communion, they nevertheless asserted that it was 'their incumbent duty to separate from their communion all those persons . . . who continue in the sin of enslaving their fellow creatures or holding them in slavery'.

The Baptist Union letter went further - whilst admitting Britain's part in the origin of slavery, it challenged: 'We are concerned for *you* because we tremble for the sincerity of that faith which under any circumstances can be reconciled to American slavery as it is'. They also stressed their concern for those who suffered from being enslaved, as also for our Lord 'whose name is everywhere blasphemed

40 *BM* June 1841, p.285.

on your account'. The letter further alluded to 'the God-dishonouring apologies for continuing the crime of slave-holding sent forth under their own names by men engaged in the Christian ministry', too many of whom evidenced 'a taste for the gratification yielded by the exercise of oppressive power' over their fellow men. It further posed the question whether it was not for such things' sake that 'the wrath of God cometh upon the children of disobedience'. That such actions were sanctioned by the US Congress in no way justified them.[41]

Belcher had greater connections with the North American scene than many English Baptists. As editor of *The Revivalist*, he had sought to relay news of Finney and the other revivalists in North America as a way of stirring sluggish Calvinist churches into new life. His unique contribution to the infant Baptist Union was that he combined the enthusiasm of the revivalist with the statistical concerns of the administrator. Thus his hesitations about British attitudes to their American colleages may well have been deep-rooted, if only taking final shape between November 1840 and April 1841. By then the issue had become a matter of conscience and he communicated to the Assembly, 'his entire dissent from the views entertained by the majority of the body in reference to the members of Christian churches in America holding slaves'. On account of such 'conscientious difficulties' in implementing these resolutions, he chose to resign as secretary, which reinforces the judgement that until that time he had discharged the main burden of the secretarial task.

On the third day of the Assembly, two committees reported. The first recommended no new nomination for treasurer, but that James Low be prevailed upon to continue in office, which in fact he did for a further six years. The second committee, significantly chaired by Dr Murch, briefly recommended that Belcher's resignation be accepted and that William Groser, the editor of the *Baptist Magazine*, be approached to succeed him. The Assembly accepted these recommendations, recording 'their high sense of the value of the services rendered by [Belcher] during the ten years past, and their

41 *BM* March 1841, pp.131-3.

cordial desire for his future co-operation as a member of their body'.[42] In fact, shortly thereafter Belcher emigrated to America, where he became a leader of considerable stature amongst those American Baptists whose life he so much admired and whose politics he refused to censure. His eighteen years of life and ministry in the USA, however, were spent entirely in the northern states. Like Ivimey before him, Belcher had done well to consolidate the early life of the reformulated Union. Denominational leadership suffered further depletion that same year through the tragic suicide of an over-worked John Dyer, senior secretary of the BMS, in his twenty-third year of service.

When William Groser declined the invitation to succeed Belcher, the Union turned to John Howard Hinton, the minister of the Devonshire Square church and a keen anti-slavery campaigner, whose father, the minister in Oxford, had briefly served as a secretary of the BMS after the death of Fuller. The Baptist Union in 1841 still had to establish itself: E. A. Payne draws attention to the fact that the 182 Baptist ministers who attended the Anti-Corn Law League Conference in Manchester that year were far larger in number than those who at the time came to Baptist Union Assemblies, which up to the middle fifties only attracted very modest attendances.[43] Once more the devoted service of a secretary was crucial to the survival of the Union. John Howard Hinton's obituary records that the Union 'owed its preservation in times of comparative feebleness to his perseverance . . . Without the need of much popular sympathy, he toiled for its fuller organization and development and laid down the principles and methods which are now more widely appreciated'.[44] Hinton himself, perhaps over-influenced by the Norwich Chapel case over terms of communion, put the same point on record: 'Denominational union among Baptists has been slow in manifestation and difficult of

42 *BM* June 1841, pp.285-7.

43 Payne, *Baptist Union*, pp.70-5.

44 *Baptist Handbook* (hereafter *BH*), 1875, cited by Payne, *Baptist Union*, p.83.

cultivation. We have long been a divided body and we are so still.'[45] The financial support given to the Union was feeble: with a total income of only £90, it is not surprising that the accounts for 1863 showed a deficit of £49.

J. M. Cramp's *Baptist History* identifies the appointment of J. H. Millard, minister at Huntingdon, to serve alongside Hinton in 1863 as a turning point in the Union's development, arguing that it was to him 'that the Union was indebted for much of its new and more vigorous life'. Whitley confirms this judgement: 'With 1863, the Union began to be a real factor in denominational life'.[46] His fifteen years' secretaryship, conjoined with his Huntingdon pastorate, saw the Union become a much more practical and effective instrument of joint action. That he was not a London minister was significant in helping to bind together the metropolitan and the provincial interest: soon assemblies were of such a size that they had to move out from the Missionary Society headquarters, meeting first at Upton Chapel whose new building accommodated just under a thousand, subsequently at other London chapels, returning to the new Mission House in 1871, but from 1875 for more than half a century London assemblies usually found their home at Bloomsbury Chapel.

From 1864 autumn sessions were held at different provincial centres: Birmingham, Bradford, Liverpool, Cardiff, Bristol, Leicester, Cambridge, Northampton, Manchester, Nottingham, Newcastle-upon-Tyne, Plymouth, and Newport all hosted such occasions. The *Baptist Magazine* for 1868 testified, 'The isolation which has so long characterized our body is yielding fast to a general growth of Christian love. The annual meetings in London never fully accomplished this; but these autumnal meetings are diffusing through our churches a

---

45 1863 address, cited by Payne, *Baptist Union*, p.85.

46 J. M. Cramp, *Baptist History*, 1875, pp.478-9; Whitley, *HBB*, p.318. Cramp, a Stepney student, and Secretary to the College 1823-6, held pastorates in London, Kent and Sussex, and was President of the Union in 1838. A church historian, he went to Montreal as president of the seminary there under the sponsorship of the BMS, and then to Acadia (1851-69).

spirit of brotherly affection.'[47] In the 1860s separate Unions were established for Wales (1866) and Scotland (1869), both of which in 1872 became affiliates of a Union now entitled, 'The Baptist Union of Great Britain and Ireland'. In the following year the Union revised its constitution. Essentially the Union was to remain a union of churches, but the colleges and associations also had representation. Its supreme governing body was the Assembly.

The Assembly embraced all ministers of member churches *ex officio*, as also the heads and tutors of affiliated colleges. In addition churches, associations, and recognized societies were allowed to appoint representatives proportionate to their size. Rather more contentious was the addition of personal members, though assurances were given that these already existed *de facto* and would in future be carefully vetted. A minimum subscription was set for membership of all classes, except of course those elected to honorary membership. The election of the Union's committee (later Council) was now to be by ballot of the Assembly which was to be provided with a record of members' attendance during the past year. Most significantly, the 1832 reference to 'evangelical sentiments' was dropped in favour of a statement recognizing the liberty of each church 'to interpret and administer the laws of Christ', declaring that 'the immersion of believers is the only Christian baptism'. No confessional basis was offered, only a prohibition against any potential development of centralizing interference in the life of the local congregation.[48]

The wisdom of such changes, given the changing theological climate, must be questioned, particularly from the vantage point of the testing of the validity and viability of the work of the Baptist Union that occurred fifteen years later in the Down Grade Controversy. That the changes made in 1873 were uncontentious is itself evidence of the unquestioned Evangelicalism of the Union at that point in time: the language of 'evangelical sentiment' was dispensed with not because it was under challenge but because it was so widely and

47 *BM* November 1868, p.689.

48 Payne, *Baptist Union*, pp.110-11.

comprehensively accepted by the body that its statement seemed unnecessary.

As the century progressed and the complexities of urban and industrial life increasingly impinged upon daily life, there was an increasing tendency in every walk of life to develop programmes of national rather than just local significance. Population movements, for example, called for strategic thinking about church planting and the material support of local ministries by the Baptist Union. County lists in the *Baptist Handbook* began to identify significant centres of population without Baptist churches as an agenda for action. The uneven distribution of wealth in the nation, as also among Baptists, argued for a national scheme to augment the income of poorer ministers, developing services previously provided by the Associations and the Particular Baptist Funds.[49] Founded as an independent society in 1870, under the leadership of Charles Williams and H. C. Leonard, the Augmentation of Pastors' Incomes Fund was incorporated by the Baptist Union in 1877, when some 188 grants of £20 per annum were being made to supplement ministers' salaries.[50] There was an argument, too, for a better building fund, because considerable denominational resources were being spent on interest charges to external bodies for chapel buildings, more in fact than was being contributed per year to the work of the BMS. A strengthened building fund to finance church extensions and church buildings was esssential:[51] in 1877 the annual income was still less than £6,000.[52]

In the 1870s it became increasingly obvious that ministerial careers that spread across Association boundaries made it desirable for retirement annuities to be provided by the Union rather than by more local bodies. Accordingly, a fund in excess of £50,000 was raised to guarantee a denominational scheme. C. M. Birrell started the fund

---

49 There were two Particular Baptist Funds, one based in London, the other in Bristol, both formed in 1717.

50 *BH* 1878, pp.79-80, 399.

51 Payne, *Baptist Union*, p.109.

52 *BH* 1878, p.405.

well with a gift of £500 as an act of sympathy for ministers who had been less well provided for than himself. A lot of the existing local funds soon agreed to amalgamate their funds with the provision now made by the Union.[53] Such financial provision might not seem visionary but it made the Baptist Union 'the centre of a real brotherhood', and for that two men were largely responsible. Charles Williams of Accrington and William Landels of Regent's Park Chapel, of whom it was said that he 'brought the Baptist Union out of obscurity and placed it in a position from which to make its voice heard'.[54]

J. T. Brown, from the presidential chair, saw these developments as part of a three-fold strategy. First, the Annuity Fund had to be put on a sound basis. Second, the Augmentation Fund was to be strengthened. The third prong was 'by joined hearts and hands to seek a more extensive usefulness'. For this he believed a greater intelligence based upon more careful investigation was necessary: 'the days require a closer drawing together. Not that we should be less independent, but more united - that there should be more real co-operation and a more equal distribution of forces . . . without killing life by too much nursing or by doing harm by the imperial overbearing of central power'. Rather the search was for 'a more perfect brotherhood among our churches' for it was a necessity that the richer and the poorer, towns and villages, the strong with the weak, should be joined together in affectionate helpfulness'.[55] With an income for the year of only £385, leaving a deficit of £37, it was boldly resolved that the income for the following year should be £1,000.[56] The income of the Baptist Union of Great Britain and Ireland was in fact less than that of the Scottish Union. It should also be noted, however, that the British and Irish Baptist Home Mission

---

53 *BH* 1878, pp.70-79, 392-8.

54 Charles Williams on Landels, in T. D. Landels, *William Landels DD*, 1900, p.336.

55 *BH* 1878, pp.62-3.

56 *BH* 1878, pp.81, 117, 386-7.

was separately funded with an income of £5,140 for the year ending March 1877 (to support some eighty evangelists, twenty of whom worked in Ireland), as was the Augmentation Fund with an income of £3,805 for that year.

A further consolidation of work was effected in 1877 when it was agreed that the work of the British and Irish Home Mission should be more closely integrated with that of the Baptist Union. This was effected by Millard taking on the secretaryship of the Mission jointly with that of the Union for a few months, but continuing with the secretaryship of the Mission after he had resigned from that of the Union in 1877. At the 1877 Assembly he presented his personal vision of Home Mission in a paper entitled, 'The Evangelization of Cities and Villages'. After paying tribute to the achievements of the Home Missionary Society over the past eighty years, he compared the Baptist presence in five rural counties with that in a similar number of predominantly industrial counties,[57] showing that in the agricultural counties there was four times as much provision per head of population for Baptist worship as in the four manufacturing counties, whilst Baptist church members were three times as strong within the rural communities.

Millard further compared the weakness of Baptist churches in an industrial county like Staffordshire with the strength of the Methodist presence there, noting particularly the rapid expansion of Primitive Methodists in the county with only a small number of full-time ministers: the secret of their success, he believed, was that their mission was spearheaded by an army of lay preachers. Thus the strategy proposed by Millard was to reinforce the missionary purpose of the Associations, as also the Union itself, with every Baptist church encouraged to take up membership; to engage in the widespread development of colporteurs and evangelists, using hired rooms initially, though the Union could wisely invest in securing permanent buildings which had strategic importance; thirdly, to link village

---

57 Bedfordshire, Berkshire, Buckinghamshire, Cambridgeshire, and Dorset, as over against Derbyshire, Durham, Lancashire, Warwickshire and Yorkshire.

churches together as a condition of national support; and finally, to motivate all church members to undertake the task of lay preaching, as 'without a very large extension of this agency no considerable or rapid denominational progress can be reasonably expected'. For this plan to be implemented the plea was for new funds of £5,000 per annum, and the whole work was to be superintended by a committee of the Assembly with direct Association representation upon it.[58]

Much of Millard's proposal must have lain dormant, for the Revd W. Woods of Nottingham gave an address on 'The Union and the Associations' to the Assembly in August 1883, laying out the same programme, including the motion that the Union should 'practically become a federation of the Associations for Christian work', arguing that the work would be 'largely evangelistic'.[59] The Baptist Union was to have a more purposeful existence, a judgement confirmed by Colonel Griffin during his presidency some fourteen years later: 'If this Union could more steadily pursue this second object for which it was formed, "To spread the gospel of Christ", the results that would follow would alone justify its existence.'[60]

ANTI-CATHOLICISM - THE TRACTARIAN THREAT

Baptists were not generally to the fore in anti-Catholic protests in England, though Wolffe records the vocalism of a group of Bradford Baptist ministers against Catholicism.[61] But Baptists, as conscientious voluntarists no less than doughty protestants, opposed a spreading Catholicism, especially when the government sought to increase public funds for the Roman Catholic seminary at Maynooth. William Brock published a speech he gave at a public meeting in Yarmouth in 1845, in which he questioned the seemingly incredible paradox that 'whilst the Constitution shudders from its extremities to its heart at the damnable doctrines which are inculcated at Maynooth,

58 *BH* 1878, pp.83-92.

59 *BH* 1884, pp.17-29.

60 Cited by Whitley, *HBB*, p.318.

61 J. Wolffe, *The Protestant Crusade in Great Britain, 1829-1860*, 1991, p.48.

Maynooth itself should be sanctioned with its patronage and provided with a princely income from its funds.'[62] At the Anti-Maynooth Conference held at Exeter Hall in 1845 Samuel Green of Walworth, J. P. Mursell of Leicester and Charles Stovel of East London were seen as rocking the protestant boat by insisting on hostility to all state endowments of religious causes, not just Roman Catholic institutions. Hugh McNeile pointed up the difference very clearly when he wrote in the evangelical Anglican journal, *The Record*, 'The honest Churchman in opposing Popery is opposing false doctrine but the honest Dissenter, the conscientious voluntary, in opposing Popery, is opposing Church Establishments and endowments also. There can, therefore, be no real *bona fide* co-operation.'[63]

The *Baptist Magazine*, argues Wolffe, was generally more interested in Tractarians than Roman Catholics, 'directing occasional Protestant darts more against Oxford than against Rome'. The Union itself unanimously agreed with a resolution proposed by its secretaries in 1839:

> That the recent systematic and vigorous efforts, under the highest ecclesiastical auspices, to establish a system of education based upon the soul-destroying heresy of baptismal regeneration, and inculcating other errors contained in the Church Catechism; together with the revival and wide circulation of the essentially papistical doctrines of the Oxford Tracts, countenanced by many of the more influential and reputedly evangelical Clergy, are circumstances which should awaken to diligent counteraction every lover of sound scriptural truth; and this Union, believing that the principles they hold, both in relation to Christian doctrine and to the constitution, the subjects, and the ordinances of Christ's spiritual kingdom, are eminently adapted, under the Divine blessing, to neutralize and successfully oppose the mischief, would earnestly incite all the Pastors and Churches composing it, to renewed and

62 Cited by E. R. Norman, *Anti-Catholicism in Victorian England*, 1968, p.27.
63 Wolffe, *Protestant Crusade*, p.141, citing *The Record*, 18 December 1845.

> persevering zeal in promoting their extension by means of the pulpit, the press, the Sunday-school, and all other legitimate methods.[64]

An article in the *Baptist Magazine* for May 1841 clearly articulates a Baptist view of the development of the Oxford Movement within the Church of England:

> Puseyism does not profess to adopt the religion of the New Testament exclusively, but that religion as interpreted, and developed, and brought out in its full beauty by councils, and fathers, and apostolical traditions. It recognizes the episcopally ordained clergy as a chartered corporation claiming, in virtue of official descent from the apostles, a monopoly of spiritual gifts and the sole guidance of the consciences of the laity. It proclaims the efficacy of sacraments as the channels of grace, imparting regeneration and justification when administered by official hands, whatever be the mental or moral qualifications of the authorized administrator. It is a mode of religion which glories in the observance of forms, and in the pomp of ceremonies; which views holiness as consisting not only in the love of God and man, but as especially exemplified in fasts, and penances, and veneration rendered to holy times and places, to sacred relics, and departed saints. It is, in fine, a system which would place the reason and the conscience, the nation and the government, the spiritual guidance of all adults, and the education of all children, under the authority and power of priestly rule.

From this development the author argued that dissent was a more honourable path than ingenious sophistry in attempting to secure a meaning to the thirty-nine articles that could not legitimately be placed upon them. That this could be attempted demonstrated the 'utter inefficiency of articles and subscriptions . . . to secure either unity of heart or uniformity of opinion', for manifestly they did not secure this end.

---

64 *BM* June 1839, p.268.

> A large proportion of the clergy, it is well known, are Arminian, and yet they do not hesitate to subscribe their belief in articles which are quite as Calvinistic as they are Protestant. The evangelical clergy, in general, object to the doctrine of baptismal regeneration, and yet thank God for regenerating every infant which they baptize. The fact is, that almost every shade of sentiment, from Antinomianism to Pelagianism, from Athanasian orthodoxy to Unitarianism, from the wild enthusiasm of the Irvingites to the rationalism of Germany, has been, and probably still is, held in the church which demands subscription from all, and imposes on all the same forms.

Thus the Church of England failed to face the issue of differing views of grace and election that painfully divided Baptists. Already - twenty years before Spurgeon's 1864 sermon - the ambiguity of Evangelicals using the Prayer Book declaration on infant baptism is underlined, whilst the charismatic interruptions of Edward Irving found their place alongside the critical ideas coming out of Germany in unsettling the evangelical presence in the Church of England.[65]

Three years later J. M. Cramp returned to this issue, asserting that 'Puseyism is popery disguised. There is an avowed dislike to Rome with an adoption of her destructive principles . . . the clergy are now preaching a crusade in favour of priestcraft, magnifying their office beyond all that is apostolic and Christian, assuming acts of authority much more suited to her of Babylon than to a reformed church.' Accordingly, protestant Christians were called upon to new clarity of conviction on reformed principles: 'justification by faith, the sufficiency of the scriptures, the right of private judgment and of public profession and worship, and the supremacy of the Lord Jesus Christ'. The debate was not about trifles but fundamental principles.

> It may seem a light thing to fast on this day or feast on that; to call a table an altar, put candles upon it in broad day, and to mark a child with the sign of the cross . . . [but] the adoption of these rites is unwarranted by Scripture.

---

65 *BM* May 1841, pp.222-6.

To combat such seductive teaching, there needed to be well-defined programmes exposing popish error, renewed emphasis upon Christian education and the distribution of the scriptures, a revitalization of personal piety and prayerfulness, and a seeking of the presence of the Spirit. Such a situation also posed the need for Christians to overcome their divisions - the times called for 'more union among those who are agreed on fundamental truths and can sympathize with one another as joint partakers of grace'. To relate to one another on the basis of shared faith and conviction did not involve compromise or lack of respect for their particular understandings of Christian truth: 'The fellowship of the people of God of different persuasions, by gatherings for prayer and exhortation, by joint efforts for the spread of the gospel, by continued attacks on some common foe, and by other means, is imperatively called for in these times, and must have a beneficial tendency'. But that said, Cramp further argued 'The contest with popery must in the issue be chiefly carried on by protestant nonconformists; for the foundations of the Church of England are substantially popish'.[66]

THE EVANGELICAL ALLIANCE

Baptist Noel, in his Anglican days, had penned some lines on what he called 'Schism':

> For man-made discipline let bigots fight,
> Canons and rules our fathers have approved;
> By us may those whose faith and life are right
> Be owned as brothers and as brothers loved.
>
> All true believers are the ransomed church,
> Children of God by Jesus owned and loved;

---

66 *BM* September 1844, pp.449-54, adapted from J. M. Cramp, *Lectures for These Times*, p.308.

And in the day when God the heart shall search
Will they who part them be schismatic proved.[1844][67]

Noel perhaps best links the informal pan-evangelicalism of the earlier part of the century with the securing of institutional shape to common evangelical witness in the founding of the Evangelical Alliance in 1846. As early as 1828 Noel had published a sermon entitled *On Protestant Unity in Fundamental Doctrines*, a unity, of course, in opposition to Roman error. In 1834 George Radford, Independent minister in Worcester, wrote to the editor of the *Congregational Magazine*, suggesting the holding of a general convention of all the orthodox protestant churches of Great Britain, Europe and America, but nothing seems to have come of this.[68] Contrariwise, F. A. Cox complained that, at the conclusion of the meetings of the great Christian societies each year, Christian leaders 'separate, it is to be feared, generally with undiminished prejudices, jealousies and dislikes, with scarcely a shake of the hand, never to meet again till another anniversary'.[69]

In May 1842 John Angell James took up the issue once more in an address to the Congregational Union, in which he argued that that body should take an initiative, with other evangelical Christians, against 'Infidelity, Popery, Puseyism, and Plymouth Brethrenism'. Initially the idea was a union of voluntarists, but in a letter to the *Congregational Magazine* in July he extended his vision to embrace 'pious clergy of the Churches of England and Scotland'.[70] Angell James's initiative seemed to secure the interest of a number of

67 B. W. Noel, *Protestant Thoughts in Rhyme*, 1844, cited by J. Wolffe, 'The Evangelical Alliance in the 1840s: an attempt to institutionalize church unity', *Studies in Church History*, 23, 1986, p.333.

68 Radford to Blackburn, 16 April 1834, cited in Wolffe, 'Evangelical Alliance', p.334.

69 F. A. Cox, *On 'Christian Union': being a Brief Inquiry into the Causes of Disunion among Christians and the Reasons of Failure: the Efforts at Union hitherto made*, 1845, p.7, cited Wolffe, 'Evangelical Alliance', p.335.

70 *Congregational Magazine*, 1842, pp.458-62, cited Wolffe, 'Evangelical Alliance', p.335.

individuals but was rather less successful amongst church bodies. Nevertheless, a meeting to promote Christian union was held in London on 2 January 1843, at which Baptists were present. A further meeting in February embraced some Anglicans, such as Baptist Noel. For his part, Thomas Price, Baptist editor of the *Eclectic Review*, who had been active in the early stages of the process, thought the admission of churchmen 'degraded the initiative to the level of a farce'.[71]

The context was not favourable: at home the educational clauses of Graham's Factory Bill seemed to drive Church and Dissent apart, whilst in Scotland the Disruption divided Scottish Christendom with new seriousness. However, the furore over the government's proposal in 1845 to increase the grant to the Roman Catholic seminary at Maynooth restored a concern for protestant unity, though Wolffe argues that the intercourse between the Anti-Maynooth Committee's work and the various meetings called to secure the founding of the Evangelical Alliance must not be over-emphasized. The two strands were, however, linked together in the person of Sir Culling Eardley Smith, the prominent Congregational layman who became Chairman of the Anti-Maynooth Committee and also chaired a meeting called in Liverpool in October 1845 to prepare for the formation of a possible Evangelical Alliance. Some eighteen out of the 216 present at the Liverpool meeting were Baptists. T. R. Birks, son-in-law to Edward Bickersteth, Cambridge theologian and sometime secretary of the Alliance, saw its formation as responding to both a positive and a negative cause: positively it responded to 'the growing connection, in the minds of sincere Christians, belonging to different bodies, that their real union of heart and judgment was far greater than the outward appearance', and negatively to 'the progress of Popery'. Significantly, James Hamilton, minister of the Scottish Free Church in Regent Square, London, stressed the former, regretting that the impression should be given 'that this were, even chiefly or principally, an Anti-Papal movement, or even an Anti-infidel movement, or that

71 *Eclectic Review*, 1846, p.500, cited by Wolffe, 'Evangelical Alliance', p.343.

it took any mere *anti* form.' So mild was the new Evangelical Alliance's attitude to the Roman Church that a separate Protestant Alliance was formed in 1851, as Thomas Chalmers had originally proposed.[72]

Agreement on the desirability of establishing an alliance necessarily led into the difficult question of the basis for the work and the terms of membership in particular. Some thought communicant status within a mainstream church sufficient, Chalmers argued for an acknowledgement of Scripture as the sole repository of truth, but men of the calibre of Baptist Noel and John Angell James, who in his 1842 appeal had already outlined both protestant and theological principles for the proposed body,[73] argued that a specific doctrinal standard was required. This was attacked as excluding Quakers and possibly Brethren, now seen as protestant allies rather than a dark threat, from membership.

The *Baptist Magazine* of January 1846 linked together the general and theological concern with the particular motivation of the moment. The theology of unity was admirable: 'Christ is the centre of union, to him all true believers are united, and in virtue of their unity with him they are united to each other.' Not to acknowledge the unity already secured, and to make Christian unity only the object of Christian hope was to concede too much to Romanists and unbelievers. Incarnating theology in practice was more difficult. Many Baptist authors were happier with ideas of 'spiritual unity' than attempts to earth this in practical programmes and organizations: thus the *Baptist Magazine's* judgement, 'Nothing has been more productive of division and strife, in former days, than injudicious attempts to secure unity.'[74] The differences between Christians were real and the dangers of muzzling consciences were apparent. Sacramental practice (who should be baptized and who should come to the table), church government (congregational, presbyterian, episcopal), church-

72 Cited Wolffe, *ibid.*, p.340.

73 R. W. Dale, *Life of John Angell James*, 1861, p.401.

74 *BM* January 1846, pp.18-19.

state relations (establishment versus voluntaryism), grace and election (Calvinist or Wesleyan) all laid down lines of division.

The *Nonconformist* significantly attacked the new organization on account of its restricted doctrinal basis, whilst noting its liberality on the ministry and the sacraments, and also, significantly, on the future punishment of the wicked. There were also problems with patterns of inclusion and exclusion. 'Whether this should be the result of a creed or of a demand for the recognition of principles generally but not universally admitted by true believers, or by united celebration of the Lord's Supper', argued the editor, 'it would, in our view, be fatal to the innocence of the plan, being fatal to its catholicity'. This, in fact, got near to the heart of the theological problem, namely that the proposed Evangelical Alliance seemed to require a form of credalism at odds with many dissenting consciences for, in defining evangelical, a principle of exclusion was entertained which not only excluded the old Unitarian bogey but also 'some of the wisest and best men' of the Baptist denomination, who objected either to the basis of belief or to 'the united celebration of the Lord's Supper'.[75] Thus the instrument of unity served to sow discord, which was the more unfortunate since from the beginning the Christian standing of those who could not in conscience join the Alliance was fully recognized.[76]

To turn from theological to practical issues did not improve the prospects of concord. In the first place there was still some unhappiness at the way in which the Liverpool Conference of 1845, which first began to formulate the shape of the future Evangelical Alliance, arose out of the negativism of the Anti-Maynooth Conference of the same year. Leading Baptists had difficulties with the Anti-Maynooth platform, based as it was not only on the reformed faith but upon the sovereign's coronation oath to uphold the established church. Accordingly they opposed the Maynooth grant for different reasons and consistently declined to join in the work of the

75 *BM* January 1846, p.19.

76 See Resolutions of Meeting on 15 January 1846, recorded in *BM*, March 1846, pp.174-5.

Central Committee. Some unwise attacks in the press left the Baptists feeling isolated, until the Congregationalist, the Revd John Blackburn, spoke of the need for a 'moral crucifixion which we are to pass through in order to be conformed to Jesus Christ', after confessing his proneness to make unkind remarks with reference to Baptist usages. This was taken to indicate that Liverpool promised a better spirit between the churches.[77]

However, when the new organization was extended to include European evangelicals, such as J. G. Oncken of Hamburg, a founding member,[78] and North American Christians, yet another divisive issue arose in terms of the possibility of sharing fellowship with those who owned slaves. J. H. Hinton proposed an amendment specifically to exclude slave-holders from membership. Rather than vote on the amendment, the committee looked at a way out of the impasse and, in a presentation made by F. A. Cox, proposed that the matter be dealt with simply by listing slavery 'as a sin and a social evil'. This severely challenged the international character of the Alliance, which now became a federation of National Alliances. Hinton successfully pressed the case that slave-holders should be ineligible for membership of the British branch.[79]

The attitude of the *Baptist Magazine*, no doubt influenced by the hesitations of William Groser, the then editor, remained cautious, with a studied policy of giving equal weight to the arguments of those in favour of and those opposed to the new organization.[80] Groser argued that the Evangelical Alliance, far from being ecumenical, was 'essentially sectarian': 'You do not call on all who are confiding in [Christ's] grace and exerting themselves for his glory, to unite with you; but lay down a basis for union by which some of them are

77 *BM*, January 1846, p.23.

78 J. W. Ewing, *Goodly Fellowship*, 1946, p.85.

79 *Eclectic Review*, 1846, pp.747-80.

80 See particularly the two articles in May 1846 on 'Reasons for Joining' and 'Reasons for Not Joining the Proposed Evangelical Alliance', the second in fact from the pen of the editor, pp.274, 278.

formally and systematically excluded'. How could the new body, whilst indicating an 'avowed object of exhibiting the essential unity of the Christian church', exclude those whom it still believes to be 'the Saviour's friends - members of his mystical body'? Straight from the shoulder, Groser addressed the Baptist members of the provisional committee: 'You have assented to the adoption of a creed as the text of admission. The belief of that creed neither you nor I regard as justifying faith. The acknowledgment of that creed is not, in your own judgment, any proof of vital religion', and 'since there are genuine Christians whom that creed will exclude . . . Is it not just . . . to say that your union is not catholic, in the good sense of that term, but sectarian?'

Certainly the existence of the Alliance required people to make choices - either to continue in the Liberation Society (Anti-State Church Association) or join the Alliance because, it was argued, bonds of loyalty would not allow membership of both. Thus *The Record*, as the voice of evangelical churchmen, had attacked both Dr Cox and Dr Campbell, editor of *The Patriot*, for their stubborn and persistent hostility to all ecclesiastical establishments. Not only did *The Record* urge the Congregational Union to distance itself from *The Patriot*, but it secured the support of the Wesleyan *The Watchman* for this purpose.[81]

Evangelical Christendom was far from united, as was demonstrated by Spurgeon's attack upon evangelical churchmen and their seeming support of the doctrine of baptismal regeneration in 1864.[82] Notwithstanding such reservations and controversy, a number of leading Baptists took part in setting up the Evangelical Alliance, Dr E. J. Steane, J. H. Hinton, F. A. Cox and Baptist Noel in particular. The Alliance was not to be a federation of churches and did not therefore raise the issue of different forms of church government: 'What the Alliance proposes is, without interfering with those churches or bringing them into such an affinity with each other,

81 *BM*, May 1846, pp.279-283.

82 See chapter 3, pp.39-41.

so far to act on the principle of their organization as to unite in one grand company the members of which they are severally composed.' The Alliance was to be an alliance of clergymen and Christian leaders, not of denominational organizations and, therefore, played its own part in strengthening the individualism of a *laissez-faire* culture as it impacted upon church life. Though an important step in inter-church co-operation, it did not provide a true basis for abiding ecumenical relationships; that would have required churches to relate to one another as churches. It did, however, undertake important work in advocating the interests of persecuted evangelical and other religious minorities, including Swedish and German Baptists.[83]

Of Steane, at the time one of two secretaries of the Baptist Union, it has been said that he had 'the lion's share in shaping the constitution of the Alliance and a chief part in its early administration', serving as founding editor of its periodical, *Evangelical Christendom*.[84] He too was the moving force behind the evangelistic meetings organized in the Exeter Hall by the Alliance in London in 1855, which he commended to all members of the Alliance in the following year. Alongside Steane, Baptist Noel travelled widely for the Alliance in defence of evangelical minorities. When it met in Copenhagen, Dr Underhill took the opportunity of thanking the Danish crown for the protection offered to Carey at the beginning of the Indian mission. Joseph Angus was one of the founders who was noted as being present at the Jubilee service in 1896. Even though the Alliance had its own confessional standard, it was not in this period narrow in its fellowship, so that Joseph Parker, the Congregationalist, Dean Alford, and John Clifford were all involved in its work.[85]

TWO BRANCHES OF CONGREGATIONALISM

The Bunyanite tradition of not dividing over water baptism, reflected upon by such eighteenth-century Baptist leaders as Daniel Turner of

---

83 Ewing. *op.cit.*, pp.59-74.

84 Payne, *Baptist Union*, p.82.

85 Ewing, *op.cit.*, pp.28-32, 35, 41, 54.

Abingdon, Benjamin Beddome of Bourton-on-the-Water, and John Ryland of Northampton and Bristol, had found expression in the existence of a number of open-communion churches which were of significance in enabling Baptists and Paedobaptists to come together in common fellowship. Some saw this as a way forward to greater unity, either by way of pluralism of baptismal procedure within one denomination or by regional federation, as in Bunyan's own Bedfordshire, which was seen to provide a mechanism for common fellowship and Christian witness. It is not surprising, therefore, that for almost the length of the century there should be a succession of calls for the two parts of the congregational family to unite. In October 1830 a Scottish correspondent warned that denominational barriers were assuming too great an importance, and that more properly Christian energy should be devoted to secure more unity in communion and fellowship, citing in particular 'the difference between congregational churches on the subject of baptism' as not being a cause of division.

Noting that in the Great Commission the apostles were commanded to preach and not to baptize, he argued that a separation of the act of baptizing from the ministerial office would make it easier for churches to embrace both those of Baptist and Paedo-Baptist persuasions. The way in which those of such view had come to co-exist in counties like Huntingdonshire was commended. In such a way the mode and subject of baptism could be prevented from becoming a barrier to unity, and somebody convinced of the appropriateness of believer's baptism would not need to change denominations. This he believed would strengthen the Baptist position.[86]

The following year the *Baptist Magazine* carried a similar appeal under the heading, 'Union of Baptists and Independents', but its promoter eschewed the establishment of mixed-communion congregations as the way forward, rather suggesting a prayerful, reflective conference on the mode of baptism which, it seems, the

86 *NBM*, October 1830, pp.415ff.

writer saw as necessarily leading thinking paedobaptists to come to Baptist convictions.[87]

Four years later the *Baptist Magazine* contained a 'Candid Appeal to Congregational Christians', which started from the observation that

> Christians of all parties are now entertaining the hope that the day is drawing nigh when the spiritual vision of the members of Christ shall be so improved as to enable them to avail themselves of the full light of the gospel to subdue their respective prejudices and antipathies, and when love of Christ shall be so shed abroad in all hearts, as to lead them into that blessed state of union, into which it is predicted the church is to be brought'.[88]

The difference, the writer affirmed, between the two varieties of congregationalism was of such modest order that the movement for a wider Christian unity ought to start with them: they should take the initiative in seeking to unite together and thereby influence others in the same direction. The articulation of such sentiments did not inhibit the writer from concluding with a fourteen-point argument in favour of believer's baptism. In the same issue of the *Baptist Magazine*, 'Eta' provided a hymn entitled, 'Communion of Saints', which contained the stanzas:

> No more the party wall of pride
> Erected by one common foe
> The hearts of brethren shall divide
> While passing through the vale below.
>
> No more, secluded and unknown,
> In isolated paths they tread;
> Nor speed their devious way alone
> Till numbered with the silent dead.

---

87 *BM*, April 1831, pp.144-5.

88 *BM*, June 1835, pp.218-9.

One Lord redeemed them with his blood,
And rose triumphant from the tomb,
To lead them to one Father God,
Whose smiles their darkest hours illume.[89]

Of course, such pleas for wider Congregational unity ran parallel to the debate about the terms of communion, and the unwillingness of some Baptists to admit paedobaptists to the Lord's table, let alone enter into deeper relationships with them. In 1844 R. W. Overbury, the pastor of Eagle Street, Holborn, a member of the committee of the Baptist Union and the Baptist Board, and one of the leading strict-communionists in the capital, wrote a tract opposing the practical efforts then being taken to further Christian union. He claimed these favoured 'defective exhibitions of divine truth', proceeded on unscriptural principles, and set up 'false standards of brotherly love', and objected that without his consent his name had been a signatory to the invitation to others to explore practical steps towards greater unity.[90]

Nevertheless, the association between the two parts of the Congregational family remained close in mission, in polity, and in campaigning for full civil rights. For many years *Baptist Handbooks* included a list of London Congregational ministers, and the architectural Appendix included details of some new Congregational churches.

When in 1886 they united their annual assemblies, dignitaries from both Unions affirmed their essential unity, and arguments were made that church planting might be jointly undertaken, granted the interchange of members between Congregational and open-membership Baptist churches.

The significance of these joint meetings is difficult to judge. The two bodies held separate meetings at the beginning of the second week in May, the Congregationalists on 10th and 11th, the Baptists on 10th and 13th, a joint meeting was held on the morning of Friday, 14th,

89 *BM*, June 1835, p.224.
90 *BM*, March 1844, p.136.

with a public meeting in the evening in the City Temple. However, no record of this is given in the *Baptist Handbook* for 1887 or in the *Baptist Magazine*, whilst the information in the *Freeman* on 21 May was slender. Significantly, Charles Williams's presidential address on the Monday concerned 'A Plea for Union among Baptists', in which he made a passionate plea for union between the Calvinist and Evangelical Arminian branches of the Baptist family, in particular suggesting that in the East Midlands and Lancashire and Cheshire the example of working together in one geographical association, as in London, might be followed.[91] One other aspect of the 1886 Assembly needs to be noted: Edward White, the Chairman of the Congregational Union who was not altogether a stranger to Baptist Assemblies,[92] was present with the Baptists on the Monday morning and spoke in support of the appeal for Home Mission made by the president of the Baptist Union. Similarly Charles Williams was introduced to the Congregational Assembly on the Tuesday morning and addressed them on 'Free Church Foundations'. The *Congregational Year Book* of 1887 improves upon the Baptist record by declaring the agenda of the united meeting: Dr Conder[93] spoke on the common concept of the Church held by both bodies, Dale on the need for spiritual power to incarnate that ideal, Culross on the task of the Church in 'promoting Sound Theological Thought and conserving Essential Truth', and Angus on the relation of this to preparing and nurturing 'a Consecrated Christian Ministry'. Dr Clifford addressed the public meeting on 'The New Democracy and the New Testament Church', Guiness Rogers[94] on 'The Congregational System', Richard

---

91 *BH* 1887, Presidential address, p.21.

92 For Edward White, see chapter 6, p.166.

93 Eustace Conder, son of Josiah Conder, sometime editor of the *Eclectic Review* and hymn writer, was Congregational minister in Leeds and Chairman of the Congregational Union in 1873.

94 T. Guiness Rogers was Congregational minister at Grafton Square, Clapham, 1865-1900, Chairman of the Congregational Union 1874, confidant of Spurgeon and of Gladstone.

Glover on 'The Overseas Missions of the Church', and Dr Parker[95] on 'The Larger Congregationalism'.

In 1901 the two Unions again met together in joint assembly to think strategically about witness in the new century, which was to see the establishment of a number of Free Churches, particularly in new towns, which were dually aligned to both the Congregational and the Baptist Unions.[96] Unlike 1886, the joint nature of the 1901 Assembly was duly recognized.[97] McLaren, speaking as 'An Old Preacher on Preaching', began 'Fact and logic are both outraged by the names of the two Unions which join in this Assembly. The division into Congregationalists and Baptists is faulty . . . for all Baptists are Congregationalists. We are the closest of kin among the Free Churches and perhaps, therefore, have sometimes been furthest apart . . . But we do feel the influence of the uniting tendency which is so marked a feature of the present time'. Beyond that introduction the address made no further allusion to the peculiarity of the occasion. A patriotic resolution on the death of the Queen and the succession of Edward VII readily drew the two denominations together, as did an address by Principal Rainy, Moderator of the United Free Church of Scotland, on 'The Religious Outlook of the Times', because the uniting of dissenting presbyterianism in Scotland was seen as a symbol of what the denominations might achieve. In the evening there was a united Baptist/Congregational demonstration in the Queen's Hall, under the chairmanship of George White, MP, distinguished Baptist layman who became President of the Union in 1903, and addressed by

---

95 Joseph Parker was from 1869 pastor of the church which in 1874 became the City Temple; Chairman of the Congregational Union in 1884 and 1901, and President of the National Free Church Council in 1912. He crossed swords with Spurgeon on theatre-going.

96 See Letchworth (1905), Amersham (1908), Hampstead Garden Suburb (1910), Hutton and Shenfield (1913), in particular.

97 Even so the major addresses by Dr McLaren and Dr Parker only appeared in the handbooks of the sponsoring Unions - McLaren, *BH* 1902, pp.92-110; Parker, *Congregational Year Book*, 1902, pp.17-34.

Principal Fairbairn,[98] Mr Greenhough of Leicester,[99] and R. F. Horton,[100] with the benediction pronounced by John Clifford. The Joint Assembly significantly was suspended on the Wednesday for the laying of the foundation stone of the Baptist Church House. On the Thursday the second joint session passed resolutions on national education (proposed by Charles Williams) and on temperance (proposed by Professor G. S. Woodhead of Cambridge). Joseph Parker gave his address on 'The United Congregational Church', which only briefly alluded to the occasion on which it was delivered[101] and simply made a plea for a tighter church organization to replace the Congregational Union, a theme which he further elaborated in his October address, already an indication that some Congregationalists at least were becoming more hesitant about congregational polity than most Baptists. Neither of the principal addresses seem to have been alert to the possibilities of capitalizing on the occasion of a joint assembly.

---

98 Originally ordained into the Evangelical Union in Scotland, Fairbairn became Principal of the Congregational College in Bradford in 1877 and of Mansfield College, Oxford, from 1886-1909, where his evident scholarship considerably aided the acceptance of nonconformity within the university. He was Chairman of the Congregational Union in 1883.

99 See chapter 6, p.186.

100 R. F. Horton secured a double first at Oxford, was President of the Union and elected a Fellow of New College in 1879. His appointment to 'examine the rudiments of faith and doctrine' in the theological faculty was rejected as late as 1883 by Convocation apparently on confessional grounds. He was founder pastor of the Lyndhurst Road Chapel in Hampstead, Chairman of the Congregational Union in 1903, and President of the National Free Church Council in 1905. Because of controversy surrounding the publication of his *Inspiration and the Bible* in 1888, the officers of the Baptist Union, in the light of the Downgrade Controversy, agreed to accept his offer to withdraw from preaching the Home Missionary Sermon at the Baptist Union Assembly that year. M. D. Johnson, *The Dissolution of Dissent*, 1987, especially chapters IV and V.

101 *Congregational Year Book*, 1902, pp.20-21.

That eventually union was to be made by the Congregationalists and Presbyterians on the basis of a shared tradition in theology, rather than between Congregationalists and Baptists on the basis of shared polity, should not detract from the closeness of relationship between Baptists and Congregationalists in the last decades of the nineteenth century. But several issues worked against that consummation - first, an increasing interest in wider bonds of unity, secondly, an increasing divergence in theology and evangelical tone between the two bodies, and thirdly, the growth of world confessional consciousness with the foundation of the International Congregational Church in 1891 and the Baptist World Alliance in 1905.[102]

FREE CHURCH UNITY

Early co-operative activity amongst Free Churchmen in England had been defensive: it was against popery and state churchism and in defence of dissenting freedoms. In 1878 something different was proposed: the Congregational Union passed a resolution calling on the Free Churches to confer together on matters connected with the religious condition of England with a view to joint endeavours in evangelism. There was no immediate result. Twelve years later Guiness Rogers, prompted by the editor of the *Methodist Times*, Hugh Price Hughes, wrote an article for that journal about a possible 'Congress of the Free Churches', a proposal which received widespread support, including that of John Clifford and F. B. Meyer. Shortly thereafter a youthful Henry Lunn organized a remarkable meeting of the leaders of the Anglican and Free Churches in Britain at Grindelwald in Switzerland, at which Richard Glover of Bristol[103] and C. F. Aked of Liverpool[104] represented the Baptists. This meeting helped create an atmosphere in favour of closer relationships between at least the Free Churches in Britain.

---

102 See E. A. Payne, 'Baptist-Congregational Relations' in *Free Churchmen: Unrepentant and Repentant*, 1965, pp.93-104.

103 See chapter 2, pp.27ff.

104 See chapter 6, p.184.

In 1891 J. B. Paton, the Nottingham Congregationalist, persuaded a number of the Free Church leaders, including John Clifford, to sign a circular letter addressed to all Free Church ministers, suggesting further action. A meeting was convened in January 1892 in the Central Hall, Manchester. The tone of the meeting was very definitely not anti-Anglican but rather for the harnessing of Free Church energies for joint endeavour, demonstrating their essential evangelical unity. The old description of dissent and nonconformity was now to give way to the positive language of Free Churchmanship. Two resolutions were passed: the first was moved by Alexander McLaren in favour of convening a congress in Manchester in 1892. McLaren himself believed this to be one of his life's most significant actions. The second, moved by Percy Bunting, a Methodist layman, decided that invitations would be to individual Free Churchmen, not to church delegations which, *The Freeman* believed, explained a reduced Baptist participation in the forthcoming congress.

Some 370 people were present at this first Congress, of whom the denomination of 325 can be determined - just under one-tenth (30) were Baptists, in comparison with 145 Congregationalists and 134 Methodists of different groups. Alexander McLaren and John Clifford once more shared in the leadership, the former movingly conducting the concluding Communion Service.

The next Congress was held in Leeds in March 1894 when, notwithstanding pressures of official denominational delegations, it was decided that representation should be from local County or Urban Free Church Councils, very much under pressure from Hugh Price Hughes, who was anxious that delegates should meet as Free Churchmen rather than as members of their separate confessions. Two of those present were accordingly to become joint-secretaries for organizing Free Church Councils through the country: for urban areas Thomas Low, a Wesleyan minister from Bradford, and for rural areas J. M. Gwynne Owen, a Baptist minister from Southampton, shortly to move to Birmingham. Early in the movement, R. W. Dale had counselled against it becoming anything like a political caucus for urging particular party programmes. At Leeds, Richard Glover argued similarly, preferring that all the energies of the movement should be concentrated 'on the proclamation of the Gospel'.[105]

The following year, with Cadbury finance behind it, the Free Church movement was propelled into permanent animation with the appointment of its first full-time officers, though voluntary advocacy was crucial in making the movement strong throughout the country. Amongst Baptists active in that process were John Clifford (President 1898), Alexander McLaren, J. G. Greenhough (President 1901), and F. B. Meyer (President 1904 and joint editor of *The Freechurchman*). Some doubts remained: the *Baptist Times and Freeman*, early in 1900, carried a letter from James Jones of Griffithstown who expressed surprise at the number of Baptists who were in his judgement betraying their martyred fathers and deserting Baptist landmarks for a unity which was necessarily based upon a compromise. His intervention called forth firm rebuttal from the pen of John Clifford, especially since the work of the Council was based upon the 'unfettered autonomy' of each participating church and denomination.[106]

Evangelism was firmly at the centre of the new Council's concerns. In 1897 Gypsy Smith became the Council's full-time missioner, but with F. C. Spurr, the Baptist Union missioner, playing a significant part. The whole nation became the theatre for a Simultaneous Mission in 1901, when, according to Charles Williams, some 100,000 were won to the Christian faith in the capital alone, mainly drawn, in F. B. Meyer's judgement, from Sunday School scholars and those on the fringe of the churches' life.[107]

It was difficult for the infant Council to keep itself from criticizing the Church of England with what appeared to be the spread of ritualist practices. Similarly it was difficult to avoid politics: Clifford and

---

105 E. K. H. Jordan, *Free Church Unity: A History of the Free Church Council Movement 1896-1941*, 1956, pp.41.

106 *ibid.*, pp.64-5.

107 *ibid.*, pp.68-9. See chapter 9 of the present work, section on 'Evangelism at home and abroad'.

Meyer, with the support of J. H. Shakespeare, who since 1898 had been General Secretary of the Baptist Union, were foremost in drafting a Free Church Manifesto on the South African War. Shortly thereafter the Council was drawn into conflict with the government over education, and Dr Clifford became the recognized leader of the Passive Resistance Movement, which secured widespread Baptist support, including that of Shakespeare, T. R. Glover of Cambridge, and Charles Brown of Ferme Park. Soon a number of Baptist ministers and laymen, amongst other Free Churchmen, would be imprisoned for their conscientious refusal to pay the education rate.

Free Church unity was seen as at once reflecting congregational polity and offering a model to the whole church. Samuel Vincent, minister in Plymouth, chose to devote his presidential address to the Baptist Union in 1898 to the theme of Church Unity. Much of this expounded negative views of papal approaches to Christian unity, but he concluded by observing how Free Church unity sat easily with a Congregational willingness to unite with others in association. 'In recent years one further step of vast importance has been taken: the Evangelical churches, while preserving unimpaired their denominational integrity, have joined together in a federation of worship, conference and work in common . . . This is simply our Congregational polity carried one step further and applied to denominations . . . We engage together in work and worship, preach in one another's pulpits, meet at the Lord's table, and our very diversities are serviceable and emphasize the unity of a Christian brotherhood made visible to a careless world'.[108]

TOWARDS ECUMENISM

Broader issues of church relationships were raised by the Church of England adopting the so-called Lambeth Quadrilateral in 1888. This was an amendment of an earlier Chicago document drawn up by the Protestant Episcopal Church in the USA in 1886, which sought to identify the four basic issues thought to be 'essential to the restoration

---

108 *BH* 1899, p.118.

of unity among the divided branches of Christendom'. In 1889 Archbishop Benson enquired of the other churches in Great Britain whether they would be prepared, on the basis of the quadrilateral, to confer together to see 'what steps can be taken, either towards corporate reunion, or towards such relations as may prepare the way for fuller organic unity hereafter'.[109] The four points of the quadrilateral were:

(a) The Holy Scriptures of the Old and New Testaments as 'containing all things necessary to salvation', and as being the rule and ultimate standard of faith.

(b) The Apostles' Creed, as the Baptismal Symbol; and the Nicene Creed, as the sufficient statement of the Christian faith.

(c) The two Sacraments ordained by Christ Himself - Baptism and the Supper of the Lord - administered with unfailing use of Christ's words of Institution, and of the elements ordained by Him.

(d) The Historic Episcopate, locally adapted in the methods of its administration to the varying needs of the nations and peoples called of God into the Unity of His Church.

In responding, the Baptist Union Assembly[110] gave clear and sincere gratitude to God for 'the manifestation of a growing desire for union amongst the various bodies of professed believers in the Lord Jesus Christ in this land'. The primacy of scriptural authority was uncontentious but cautious Baptists believed that the other parts contained 'terms so obviously susceptible of two or more interpretations that they do not seem to us to promise a profitable issue to any deliberations founded upon them.' Four principal points were made in response: (1) Baptists 'hold that they have 'the Historic

---

109 Payne, *Baptist Union*, pp.122, 145.

110 The Baptist Union response is given as Appendix VII in Payne, *Baptist Union*, pp.272-4.

Episcopate as it is laid down in the New Testament', which they did not identify with the diocesan episcopate which they observed in the Anglican Church; (2) New Testament Christianity 'was essentially the introduction of a spiritual, personal and non-sacerdotal religion'; (3) New Testament Baptism presupposes a profession of faith by the candidate - and indeed that repentance that the Anglican catechisms, themselves, seemed to require ; (4) in submitting to the authority of God's Word, the internal government of each local church should be conducted by believing members 'and should be in no way controlled by the Sovereign powers of the State'. Saving their particular position on baptism, these views were shared by Baptists with the other Free Churches 'with whom we are not only united by the ties of brotherhood but also by a common concern for the salvation and well-being of all men'. At the same time, the response paid witness to 'the spirit of devotedness to the welfare of our fellow countrymen' seen in many members of the establishment, and whilst unable to respond positively to the Archbishop's invitation, the Baptist Union did acknowledge that invitation as of itself a helpful indication of improved relationships between the churches.[111]

Early in the new century a World Missionary Conference convened in Edinburgh in 1910 in part fulfilled Carey's ecumenical dream of just over a hundred years earlier. The BMS was duly represented at a conference which was overwhelmingly Anglo-American in its make-up. The question, however, was properly raised as to how far the divisions of the church were impeding her mission in the world, and in particular the credibility of her evangelism: to what extent were competing missionary societies, representing different locations and different confessions, a strategy that a church facing a non-Christian world just could not afford?[112]

---

111 Payne, *Baptist Union*, pp.145-6, and Appendix VII, pp.272-4.

112 R. Rouse and S. C. Neill, *History of the Ecumenical Movement 1517-1948*, 2nd edition 1967, pp.311-2, 315, 355. See also R. Rouse, 'William Carey's Pleasing Dream', *International Review of Missions*, 1949, pp.181-92. Fuller rejected the proposal. Rouse notes the original of Carey's letter as being

At the end of the nineteenth century Baptists were still struggling to secure a proper balance between the 'congregational' and 'associative' aspects of their churchmanship. By 1900, however, many more churches were in association. The demands of a nation-wide mission, and sustaining ministry in rural areas and downtown suburbs unable to fund this for themselves, put a premium upon fraternal co-operation and effective national organization. The strengthening of relationships both within the denomination and with others was in the first place a function of the Evangelical Revival which immediately made Baptists aware of the depth of Christian commitment of those of other traditions. It was experience of common mission that led William Carey and Robert Hall to embrace quite daring ecumenical sympathies, which were for Carey global and which for Hall were not confined to Protestantism but embraced devout Catholics as well. The scale and extent of all the human problems of a rapidly industrializing and urbanizing world called forth all the resources of the Christian churches, overriding all narrow and isolationist prejudices. The base for co-operation in the first place was a theological understanding, confining baptism to believers. This was soon extended to those sharing an inherited congregational church order, or a common commitment to non-established voluntary church institutions, or to a shared evangelical experience. The development of confidence in these relationships provided a solid basis for the cautious exploration of wider dimensions of bridging the divisions of Christendom in the new century.

---

preserved in the vestry of St Mary's Baptist Church, Norwich.

8

NUMBER, CLASS AND GENDER

COUNTING THE PEOPLE

One of the earliest calculations of Baptist strength was that essayed by John Ryland, Senior, in 1753 when he made the following estimation:

London: 9 churches of 50 members each	450
East and South of London: 24 churches of 40	960
The West: 18 churches of 40	720
S Wales: 20 churches of 40	800
North of England: 50 churches of 40	2000
	4930

Ivimey suggests an addition of one-third for deficient returns and then a further two-thirds of that total for excess of hearers over members and concludes that in the mid-eighteenth century Baptist churches were in touch with 19,720 or rather less than 20,000 people.[1] In other words, the Baptist constituency in the mid eighteenth century was small and inward-looking, before its destinies were set in a new direction by the warm fires of the Evangelical Revival.

It was the impact of this movement that Rippon began to record in his *Baptist Annual Registers* in the 1790s, and which was continued in early issues of the *Baptist Magazine*. Over four decades these various listings become increasingly more precise and professional. The earliest simply identify churches by counties, but by 1827 the data is tabulated, providing a list of churches by county, minister's name and date of settlement, together with the dates of each church's foundation. By 1831 the listing is not simply of Particular Baptist Churches but of 'Baptist Churches usually designated by the term evangelical without any regard to the varieties and shades of theological sentiment by which they are otherwise distinguished'. However, those 'susceptible of denominational distinctiveness as the General Baptists' are identified by a suffix 'G' attached to their names

1 Ivimey, *History of the English Baptists*, III, 1823, pp.278-9.

and thus shown in the abstracted tables. The New Connexion, the most denominationally minded of all Baptists, have in fact a better and more complete run of statistics from their foundation than any other Baptist grouping. 'Baptist churches usually designated by the term evangelical' comes very near to the language used in 1832-3 for the doctrinal basis of the reformed Baptist Union nine years later. Evangelical Baptists in search of unity they may have been, but ministers were presented in two separate lists of Particular and General. Churches were just shown by county and number in alphabetical order with membership figures, indicating that a full Baptist Directory was in the process of preparation. Those involved were conscious that the years of statistical study had produced a much more reliable data base.[2]

As Baptists became more consciously denominational, so they recognized the need for a rapidly increasing denomination to gather and publish reliable statistics as to their membership. There are pitfalls in this exercise. First, the geographical unit may be England, England and Wales, or the United Kingdom. The adjective 'British' is no guarantee of the inclusion of Scottish or Irish figures. Table 3, taken from the *Baptist Handbook* of 1869, bears the title 'British', but this can only mean English and Welsh. This can be deduced as the figure for 1851 equates to the English and Welsh analysis found in the *Baptist Manual* for 1852. Secondly, there are questions about the definition of 'Baptist'. Does it include those General Baptists who by the nineteenth century were *de facto* Unitarians? Does it include all or a proportion of those who were in membership of Union churches? Later figures tended to be those appearing in *Baptist Handbooks* which came to include not only churches in membership both with the Union and with the various associations, which included both the New Connexion and the better organized Strict and Particular Associations, but also many independent chapels, including both Strict and Particular churches and simply independent congregations which held aloof from most denominational agencies.

---

2 *BM* April, May and Supplement 1831, pp.160ff, 203ff, 590ff.

TABLE 2: BAPTIST ANNUAL REGISTER AND BAPTIST MAGAZINE LISTINGS OF BAPTIST CHURCHES 1789-1835

	1789	1790	1794	1798	1811	1823	1827	1831	1832	1835	growth factor
Bedfordshire	15	17	18	18	18	20	21	22	22	26	
Berkshire	5	6	7	8	9	9	11	14	14	17	3x
Buckingham-shire	11	9 [11]	10	10	14	26	28	30+3G	31	36	3x
Cambridgeshire	8	7 [9]	7	9	7	20	19	26+5G	26	32	4x
Cheshire	3	3	3	3	1	5	5	5+2G	6	7	2x
Cornwall	2	2	2	2	7	10	12	13	13	16	8x
Derbyshire	2	1	2	2	3	4	5	6+11G	6	21	10x
Devon	11	11	12	14	16	30	31	42+1G	42	44	4x
Dorset	2	3	3	3	4	5	5	6	6	7	3x
Durham	2	2	2	3	4	4	8	10	10	10	5x
Essex	9	10	11	12	16	21	24	31	31	34	3x
Gloucester-shire	16	17	16	16	19	24	27	32	32	38	2x
Hampshire	11	7	8	9	14	24	25	37+3G	36	37	3x
Herefordshire	3	2	2	2	4	6	9	11	11/12	14	4x
Hertfordshire	9	9	8	8	8	14	13	15+1G	15	16	
Huntingdon-shire	2	4 [9]	5	7	12	13	12	11+1G	11	13	6x
Kent	14	16	16	18	25	35	30	34+2G	38	39	2x
Lancashire	15	15	16	19	20	30	29	37+4G	34	40	2x
Leicestershire	6	7	6	8	7	9	13	17+22G	19	38	6x
Lincolnshire	4	4	3	4	8	11	14	17+19G	15/16	35	8x

	1789	1790	1794	1798	1811	1823	1827	1831	1832	1835	growth factor
London/ Southwark	24	23	21	21	28	32	32	41+2G	39	40	
Middlesex	3	3	3	8	12	17	23	25	24	25	8x
Monmouth	[7]	5	[8]	[8]	[12]	24	29	47	40	36	5x
Norfolk	10	11	11	14	19	31	32	37+4G	40	40	4x
Northampton-shire	17	19	20	19	26	28	40	41+2G	43	41	2x
Northumber-land [+ Cumb/ West...land]	5	4	3	4	6 incl 2xS	5	4	5	5	6	
Nottingham-shire	3	3	3	3	5	6	7	6+11G	6	17	5x
Oxfordshire	5	5	7	5	6	9	12	14	13/14	14	2x
Rutland	1	1	1	1	1	1	1	1+1G	1	2	2x
Shropshire	4	4	4	4	7	15	15	17	17	17	4x
Somerset	15	15	15	15	19	31	31	49	48	48	3x
Staffordshire	[2]	2	4	6	5	13	16	17 + 1G	17	19	9x
Suffolk	2	2	2	6	19	32	35	37	37	39	19x
Surrey	1	2	4	7	8	15	21	20	20	16	16x
Sussex	9	8	8	9	11	14	13	13	13	12	
Warwickshire	7	7	7	7	9	16	16	18+10G	18	29	4x
Wiltshire	13	13	15	16	20	27	31	43	40	37	2x
Worcestershire	10	9	11	12	13	18	22	22	22	21	2x
Yorkshire	28	27	30	29	35	48	51	55+8G	60	63	2x
Total (England and Monmouth)	316	315	334	369	477	702	778	924+ 113G	921-4	1042	3x
Wales (excluding Monmouth)	-	43	50	76	60	-	-	231 + 94?	-	-	
Scotland	-	-	-	-	-	-	-	28	-	-	

S = Scotch Baptist G = General Baptists

Table 2: Notes on Sources

1789 *BM*, 1823, pp.331-2. Monmouth figures here and later added from the Welsh list to provide continuity.

1790 J. Rippon, 'A List of the Particular Baptist Churches and Ministers in England and Wales', *BAR I*, 1790-93, pp.1-16. [ ] denotes variations on Rippon in Belcher's article in the *BM*, 1832, pp.303-8.

1794 J. Rippon, 'A List of the Particular Baptist Churches in England, 1794', in *BAR* II, 1794-7, pp.1-16.

1798 J. Rippon, 'A List of the Particular Baptist Churches in England, 1798', in *BAR* III, 1798-1801, pp.1-40.

1811 'Particular Baptist Churches and Ministers in England', correct to October 1811, *BM*, 1811, pp.458ff. Wales pp.496-7.

1823 'List of Particular and Calvinistic Baptist Churches' (excluding those with known Arminian, Antinomian, or Anti-Trinitarian ministry, and ministers not in pastorate or in the pastorate of Particular Churches), *BM*, 1823, pp.230ff, 331-2, 432. This list provoked correspondence: JBA identified an additional 28 churches not in the 1823 list, but JB offered convincing arguments against most of these. JB was probably Joseph Belcher, then minister of Oakham, Rutland, author of the influential 1832 statistical report provoking the reforming of the Baptist Union, with Belcher as the first secretary.

1827 'List of Particular and Calvinistic Baptist Churches', *BM*, 1827, pp.32ff, 80ff, 135ff.

1831 'List of Baptist Churches in England in 1831', *BM*, 1831, pp.160ff, 203ff. A list of Welsh and Scottish churches appear at pp.499ff. The 94? represents smaller chapels/preaching stations which appear in the Welsh list.

1832 J. Belcher's Report, *BM*, 1832, pp.303-8.

1835 'Statistical Account of Evangelical Baptist Churches in England', *BM*, 1835, pp.546-566.

TABLE 3: EXTRACT FROM TABULAR VIEW OF BRITISH [ENGLISH & WELSH] BAPTIST ASSOCIATIONS 1834-1868

Year	Number of churches associated	Members		Year	Number of churches associated	Members
1834	802	40,763		1852	1134	106,448
1835	892	66.431		1853	1158	102,815
1836	858	65,300		1854	1185	85,245
1837	891	71,183		1855	1154	88,130
1838	935	69.864		1856	1145	86,072
1839	950	70,702		1857	1109	86,217
1840	1022	86,233		1858	1140	87,789
1841	999	78,816		1859	1126	97,124
1842	1032	78,679		1860	1150	122,961
1843	1039	83.600		1861	1232	124,473
1844	1099	86.555		1862	1245	133,931
1845	1066	89,269		1863	1270	136,825
1846	1092	85.148		1864	1325	139,157
1847	997	84.262		1865	1327	140,164
1848	934	82.871		1866	1422	161,075
1849	1022	87,373		1867	1459	174,545
1850	1080	100,391		1868	1546	182,875
1851	1138	104,933				

Source: *Baptist Handbook* 1869, p.134.

TABLE 4: SUMMARY OF STATISTICS 1864-1915 BAPTIST CHURCHES, MEMBERSHIP, & SUNDAY SCHOLARS [ENGLAND AND WALES]

Year	Churches	Members	Sunday Scholars		Year	Churches	Members	Sunday Scholars
1864	2268	191,402	-		1883	2476	293,162	426,836
1865	2291	202,465	-		1884	2582	300,152	457,427
1866	2264	206,491	-		1885	2594	303,395	461,934
1867	2283	213,926	189,971		1886	2624	289,905 [303,303]	445,435 [467,477]
1868	2315	223,297	263,328		1887	2647	291,225 [300,792]	446,836 [465,904]
1869	2432	228,991	289,175		1888	2649	285,770 [309,624]	439,870 [469,054]
1870	2421	225,233	301,711		1889	2663	285,751 [314,409]	435,938 [469,935]
1871	2459	233,088	308,762		1890	2678	286,429 [315,056]	435,747 [469,798]
1872	2495	233,176	320,120		1891	2683	290,012 [318,616]	435,878 [469,861]
1873	2474	236,163	331,103		1892	2339	299,742 [321,669]	457,051 [473,554]
1874	2480	245,645	345,102		1893	2365	307,099	466,388
1875	2491	256,964	364,692		1894	2408	314,790	477,202
1876	2536	255,489	370,717		1895	2485	316,569	483,073
1877	2501	259,382	362,382		1896	2488	323,927	489,053
1878	2469	265,863	391,164		1897	2506	328,365	497,272
1879	2427	271,163	421,712		1898	2549	336,518	509,989
1880	2453	270,200	420,839		1899	2554	333,634	503,492
1881	2472	283,800	424,098		1900	2585	346,083	513,709
1882	2461	279,522	426,696		1901	2594	353,083	516,436

1902	2647	357,086	525,068		1909	2879	398,312	557,038
1903	2712	366,789	539,386		1910	2894	394,748	553,949
1904	2734	372,332	550,600		1911	2905	394,647	553,329
1905	2759	402,928	561,058		1912	2920	392,034	548,405
1906	2811	410,766	569,785		1913	2927	391,710	542,537
1907	2838	405,755	565,503		1914	2942	390,183	540,145
1908	2864	400,348	556,742		1915	2951	388,252	526,892

To secure a series which is compatible over the whole period, the figures cited are for churches in England and Wales together with the Isle of Man and the Channel Islands but excluding Scotland and Ireland.

In 1885 the Baptist Union Council resolved not to include any figures for churches which failed to make any return. The Editor of the *Baptist Handbook*, in producing comparative figures for the period 1886-1897, made an adjustment for these non-returns, generally reducing the last reported figure of such churches by 10% per annum, in later years offering more global additions. Bracketed figures give the guestimates for the years when they appeared in the *Handbook*, apportioning the additional figures pro rata between the different nations.

Clearly the pattern was one of growth - threefold between 1811 and 1832, argued Joseph Belcher, Baptist statistician and first secretary of the re-formed Baptist Union of 1832, especially if note was taken of new congregations not yet formalized as autonomous churches. But if he is also the 'JB' of 1823, he argued that there were limitations to growth equally evident in the data collected. The three colleges at Bristol, Bradford and Stepney, even if full to capacity, could only meet the need of about a half the expanded number of churches: more trained leadership, he argued, would have prompted greater growth, as indeed the Independents had experienced. Some churches were unable to support full-time ministry and this argued for the better funding of central agencies to assist with the support of pastoral services, especially in strategic locations. Similar provision needed to be made for the erection of chapels worthy of the denomination: the existing system of pastors travelling the country to canvass appeals was in urgent need of being phased out as soon as possible in favour of a central fund supported by the denomination's more substantial causes. On the other hand, proper caution needed to be exercised in establishing barely viable causes in sparsely populated areas.[3]

Nine years later Belcher was still arguing that the collecting of statistics was a 'perfectly new' task not understood by the churches who, of course, did not yet have the benefit of the penny post in sending in their returns. There was a more deep-seated problem in that 'not half of our churches are united in associations', underlining the difficulty of obtaining full information from 'those who are known only in their isolated capacity'. Nothing daunted, Belcher presented his comparison of generational difference between Baptist life in 1790 and 1832, but even by this date his figures for membership were too incomplete to allow of analysis. Not so the figures for churches: Belcher produced an analysis from which the following two series may be deduced:

<u>Absolute Increase of 25 or more churches</u>

Wiltshire	27	Devon	31
Monmouth	28	Yorkshire	32
Hampshire	29	Somerset	33
Norfolk	29	Suffolk	34

<u>Increase of 4x or more</u>

Hampshire	4x	Middlesex	7x
Durham	4x	Staffordshire	7.5x
Herefordshire	5x	Surrey	9x
Cornwall	5.5x	Suffolk	11x

Clearly there were considerable areas of Baptist strength. Portsea and Bath both had significantly more Particular Baptist churches than any other urban centre in this early period, whilst the New Connexion was already developing its strength east of the Pennines, in the industrial midlands and north into Yorkshire.

---

3 *BM* 1823, pp.159-162.

The bane of Baptist statisticians has been two-fold: first a failure of churches to associate, and secondly the failure of associated churches to make regular statistical returns. Here lies the explanation of the apparent discrepancy between the more conservative figures that appear in Table 3 and the rather more generous figures which appear in Table 4. Table 3, the 'Tabular View' which derives from figures appearing in the *Baptist Manual*, consists only of churches in association (whether or not these associations were themselves affiliated to the Baptist Union); those dually aligned associations like the Bedfordshire Union of Christians seem not to have counted for this purpose. Thus this table is compiled of annual figures, themselves the sum of association totals. By contrast the figures which appear in the later 'Summaries of Statistics and Comparative Tables' in the *Baptist Handbook* are compiled by counties and appear to include all Baptist churches that fell within those county boundaries, whether in association or not. Thus in the two listings of 1864, the 'Summary of Statistics', when compared with the 'Tabular View', yields an excess of 1108 churches and 52,245 members, narrowed in 1868 to 951 churches and 46,116 members. With extreme independency still a strong force, many churches, not all of them small and insignificant, were slow to associate. But arguably even the larger figures of the post-1864 summaries may not have told the full story of Baptist numbers because of the failure of many churches to make annual returns. In 1885 the Baptist Union Council decided to get tough and to exclude the statistics of such churches altogether, but the denting of Baptist pride by the reduction of aggregate membership which was a consequence of such rigour meant that as early as the following year a formula was devised to take account of the missing returns.

A further complication is the relationship between church membership and those who were regular and committed attenders. This was particularly a problem in closed-membership churches where baptism as a believer was a requirement for membership, and where others might associate out of appreciation of the church's gospel ministry. Even a man of the stature of Sir George Goodman, Lord Mayor of Leeds, delayed baptism and church membership until fairly late in his mature years, although very involved in chapel life earlier.[4] In the 1830s the evidence is of congregations being strikingly larger than membership, whilst the Religious Census of 1851 suggests a ratio of 4:1 between attenders and members, a ratio which seems to have continued well into the second half of the century. It has been argued that it was the churches' cultivation of a wide diversity of adherents and semi-adherents that protected its growth potential, for conversion from a totally non-churchgoing culture was relatively rare. More frequent was the conversion of those who were already adherents or associated with the church through its ministry amongst children and young people. Such a pattern of conversion and recruitment required that the pool of adherents had always to be replenished.[5]

In 1835 the *Baptist Magazine*, in the context of arguments in favour of the growth of effective Christian witness and of enhanced unity between the churches, defended the collection of statistics: 'the eye and ear of observation'. Such figures served well to dissipate absurd but commonly-held notions within human society generally. They were thus now appropriately to be compiled for the Christian churches, to show how much voluntary religion supplied at minimal cost when compared with the vast costs of state endowed religion.[6] In a changing world, dissent could be taken to foolish extremes of isolation. The attack, therefore, was on self-sufficient congregations: 'scattered like so many distinct atoms over the surface of society' or 'like a disbanded army, they are weak in their individuality, and are to be little regarded while concerned to preserve their individuality'. The needs of society by contrast demanded union in action in implementing effective Christian mission. Not only so, but the effectiveness of voluntary religion needed demonstrating: 'if it could be proved by figures which are a statesman's only arguments, that the moral and spiritual interests of the country can be better secured

4 D. W. Bebbington, 'Baptist MPs in the Nineteenth Century', *BQ* 29, 1981, p.12.

5 R. Currie, A. Gilbert and L. Horsley, *Churches and Churchgoers: Patterns of Church Growth in the British Isles since 1700*, 1977, pp.8-9.

6 *BM* 1835, pp.546-8.

without an ecclesiastical establishment than with one - is it to be supposed . . . that the public voice would not be raised against such a wasteful and inefficient system?' The statistics to give shape and form to the expansion in number and influence of dissent were, therefore, in vital need of collection: 'That the dissenters are on the increase; that by far the greater portion of religious instruction is disseminated through the kingdom by voluntary agency, and not by state endowments, and that every new species of Christian effort has been originated by dissenters',[7] were all known facts to dissenters themselves, but to prove such enterprise to others needed the objectivity of mathematical data. To the churches themselves a diagnostic tool was offered, suggesting phenomena of growth and decline that could be helpfully analysed.

Following this argument, 'all evangelical churches adopting the practice of believer's baptism' were listed.[8] The tables identify churches by counties, with the date of their foundation, together with the name of the pastor and date of his settlement, the association to which the church was affiliated and, most interestingly, the number of members plotted against average attendance and the population of the location. In addition, the number of subsidiary preaching stations and Sunday School scholars are provided. The ratio of hearers to members, and hearers to population, is most illuminating, and it is greatly to be regretted that such a comprehensive approach to collecting statistics achieved only such a partial response. Consider the following abstracted examples which illustrate generally those locations where Baptists were present in some substance, at least as far as hearers and scholars were concerned, if these returns approach an honest reflection of local support:

7 *ibid.*, p.547.

8 *ibid.*, pp.549ff.

TABLE 5: SELECT LIST OF BAPTIST CHURCHES AND THEIR ADHERENT STRENGTH AS SHOWN IN THE *BAPTIST MAGAZINE* FOR 1835

Church	Membership	Average Hearers	Scholars	Village stations	Population
Bedfordshire:					
Luton	250	800	560	6	4,000
Buckinghamshire:					
Amersham					2,800
1st church	205	800	300	3	
2nd church	104	250	80	2	
Chesham					4,000
1st church	256	550	130	4	
2nd church	53	240	-	2	
3rd church	277	600	150	2	
Haddenham	163	600	306	2	1,400
Fenny Stratford	198	500	150	6	635
Essex:					
Loughton	58	400	65	1	1,269
Gloucestershire:					
Chipping Camden	80	300	115		1,503
Chipping Sodbury	56	340	240		1,306
Hampshire:					
Lymington	200	600	200	1	3,361
Herefordshire:					
Ross on Wye	65	300	140		676
Kent:					
Eythorne	256	600	100		422
Lancashire:					
Bacup					6,000
1st church	147	750	350		
2nd church	52	300	200		
Middlesex:					
Staines	86	200	100		2,486
Northamptonshire:					
Long Buckley	62	400	110		2,078
Ravensthorpe	58	250	96		496
Walgrave	44	200	40		575
Somerset:					
Wells	30	200	50		11,000
Wiltshire:					
Salisbury	236	600	250		11,000
Worcestershire:					
Shipston-on-Stour	27	200	100		1,632

Yorkshire:				
Barnoldswick	77	200	215	4,000
Bingley	25	200	60	8,000
Farsley	95	230	250	2,637
Gildersome	32	350	120	1,652
Keighley	70	300	100	11,176
Meltham	42	170	140	2,746
Mirfield	44	350	150	6,496
Rishworth	36	150	300	1,536

The interpretation and use of such an incomplete and unverified series of figures is obviously problematical, but it does provide evidence for believing that attendance at Baptist churches in early Victorian England was significantly above membership. In the figures displayed no church admitted to having an average attendance of less than its membership, and only seventeen churches across the country provided figures where attendance was less than or around twice the membership. Average attendance of three to five times the membership was common and some small churches claimed a multiplier as large as eighteen. It clearly indicates that Baptist churches in particular were likely to have adherents who were reluctant to take on the full responsibility of membership, and that Baptist churches believed themselves to be in pastoral relationship with many more people than membership figures alone would suggest, even though some temptation might have been present to demonstrate the strength of voluntary religion. The claim for a number of towns is that a highly significant proportion of the total population was Baptist. These 1835 figures suggest a foretaste of the excess of attenders over membership revealed in the 1851 Census. Certainly the emphasis in 1835 was upon achievement, whereas when population figures returned to the tables later in the century it was to spell out the scale of the unfinished missionary task of the churches.

PATTERNS OF GROWTH AND DISTRIBUTION

Analysis of Baptist growth patterns over time, as shown in the 'Tabular View', suggest certain periods of greatest success. 1834-5 and 1839-40 were periods of growth, with a peak of over 86,000 achieved by 1840. By contrast it took a further ten years to push the denomination beyond a membership of 100,000, first achieved in 1850. A high of 106,500 in 1852 was not sustained and it took the 1859 Revival to take the denomination back through the 100,000 marker. This it did spectacularly with a growth of some 25,000 members in the year 1859-60. Steady growth for five years led to a second spectacular leap of 20,000 in 1865-6 to a membership in excess of 161,000. The thirty-four years of the statistics shown in the 'Tabular View' saw the number of churches in association and making returns double, and membership increase about four and a half times. The average church size was increasing at the end of the period from just under 100 members to about 125.

The 'Summary of Statistics' suggests steady growth throughout the last three decades of the century: 1867-8 witnessed a growth of nearly 10,000 members, 1880-81 an expansion of more than 13,000, and the last decade of the century an increase of more than 12,000, with a membership in excess of 400,000 achieved by 1905. 1906 was to prove the peak year for England and Wales jointly: England on its own peaked a year later and held that growth till 1911, but by then the Welsh churches had lost some 17,800 members. Sunday School scholars also peaked in 1906, but here the pattern of decline diverged, support for Sunday Schools declining more slowly in Wales. But even the increases of late Victorian and early Edwardian England failed to keep pace with the growth of the population.

One other statistic is worth extracting: the last twenty-five years of the nineteenth century saw the number of churches fairly constant but membership growing by some 36%. By contrast, the twenty years prior to the First World War saw the number of churches increase by 18% but membership by only 24%. Great effort was apparently being put into establishing new congregations, but those congregations had not the capacity as in former years to convert and nurture an ever expanding membership; even after 1906 churches continued to increase in number, although membership was on the decline.

Such a judgement is supported by the findings of several oral history projects which suggest that 'the churchgoing minority in the later Victorian working class was larger than is generally recognized, that more account needs to be taken of the influence of Christianity on those who seldom went to church, and that the decline of the churches was a very long-drawn-out process'.[9]

Professor Tillyard's pioneering analysis[10] of the distribution of Baptist churches drew attention to several interesting patterns. First he noted that the historic churches of old dissent focused in two groups, one in London, the Home Counties and Eastern Counties, and the other in the South West. These were areas of reasonable Anglican strength. By contrast, new dissent thrived where Anglicanism was weak, especially in areas of industrial growth and development. The following were noted as counties of historic Baptist strength: Lincolnshire; Bedfordshire, Berkshire, Kent; Gloucestershire, Worcestershire, Somerset, Wiltshire and Devon. Secondly, Tillyard made an analysis of ministerial presence plotted against county populations. Given the need to support ministry locally in the nineteenth century, he believed that density of ministerial provision suggested a fair indication of areas of denominational strength. In this analysis London was omitted because of the complications it raised. Emerging from this early study was the complementary nature of old and new dissent. The ten counties[11] best provided with ministers of old dissent included no county which came in the top ten for the Methodists; the same was true of the least well-provided counties in

9 H. McLeod, *Religion and the Working Class in Nineteenth-Century Britain*, 1984, p.10.

10 F. Tillyard, 'The Free Churches in England', in *The Sociological Review*, 27, 1935, pp.1--18.

11 Tillyard argues for twelve counties but this is not accurate because Huntingdonshire/Cambridgeshire appear in both lists. The counties of old dissenting strength were Huntingdonshire/Cambridgeshire, Buckinghamshire, Northamptonshire, Suffolk, Bedfordshire, Hertfordshire in the centre and east, and Somerset, Herefordshire, Devon and Wiltshire in the centre and west. With the exception of Cornwall and Norfolk, all the Methodist counties were north of the Bristol to the Wash line: the North, West and East Ridings of Yorkshire, Lincolnshire, Westmorland, Shropshire, Cumberland and Derbyshire.

each series. Centres of significant Baptist strength were again noted, according to this methodology, namely Leicestershire, Bedfordshire, Buckinghamshire, Norfolk, Northamptonshire, Herefordshire and Nottinghamshire.

THE 1851 RELIGIOUS CENSUS

Analysis of the one and only census of Religious Attendance, undertaken in 1851, suggests that Baptist churches across England and Wales attracted well over half a million and possibly as many as 600,000 worshippers on Census Sunday.[12] With Sunday School scholars added, the community figure could rise to around three quarters of a million or possibly rather more, whereas membership probably stood at around 150,000.[13]

---

12 Horace Mann, *Census of Great Britain 1851: Religious Worship*, 1853. There are two complications in establishing Baptist figures. (1) What percentage of General Baptists should be excluded at this date as *de facto* Unitarians? (2) How many of those listed under Isolated Congregations were in fact Baptists? From Table 'A' which gives further analysis to this entry, it can be deduced that most union congregations are listed here, together with some congregations shared by Baptists with Methodists, Moravians and Presbyterians. If approximately 50% of those aggregated in their united congregations represented the Baptist element (some 8,500 attendances), they might be thought to balance the unorthodox element among the 21,376 attendances attributed to the General Baptists. The other difficulties are common to all the figures: (1) How many Sunday School scholars were included in the general totals and how many scholars separately listed need to be added to these figures? (2) How can the number of attenders be deduced from the number of attendances? Horace Mann, the Registrar General's Superintending Statistician, aggregated all the morning worshippers with half the afternoon worshippers and a third of the evening worshippers as not having worshipped previously. Applied to the Baptist statistics, the sum becomes 353,061 plus half of 219,407 plus one-third of 334,612 = 574,352. Harold Perkin uses the simpler formula of two-thirds of the total number of attendances to yield a figure for attenders: in the case of Baptists two-thirds of 907,080 is 604,720. Figures for Scotland are separately recorded. Harold Perkin, *The Origins of Modern English Society*, 1969, pp.34-5.

13 The figure for churches in association for 1851 given in the 1852 *Baptist Manual* number 104,933, but those returns also indicate 114 churches failing to make

Gay's geographical analysis of religious attendance for Census Sunday gives a not dissimilar distribution to that suggested by Tillyard. This is shown in the accompanying map. The following counties are identified as centres of Baptist strength: Leicestershire, Rutland, Northamptonshire, Bedfordshire, Huntingdonshire, Buckinghamshire, Cambridgeshire, Hertfordshire, Suffolk and Essex of the eastern counties, and Gloucestershire and Wiltshire in the west. Within this general picture Tillyard had further underlined the strength of Baptist churches in the old established towns of southern England, together with a rural strength in areas of traditional puritan allegiance. Baptists, however, found considerable difficulty in penetrating both the new industrial towns of the north and rural areas outside their areas of traditional strength. But the situation was changing: the distribution of New Connexion General Baptists was very much on the Methodist model, with the main strengths north of the line linking the Severn and the Wash, primarily in the four East Midland counties of Leicestershire, Derbyshire, Nottinghamshire and Lincolnshire, with extensions north into the West Riding and west into Warwickshire.[14]

The tendency to write all Nonconformist history in the light of a Congregational norm has led historians into over-emphasizing the middle-class dominance of the movement as a whole, whereas certain parts of it, most notably the Primitive Methodists and the Baptists, had

returns. Multiplying 114 by 102, the average size of church membership for that year, suggests a deficiency of 12,240. If the membership in associated churches was 117,173, then an addition of one-third for members in churches not in association begins to suggest a figure of 150,000 for Baptist church members in 1851. This shows surprising agreement with figures suggested by Dr Angus in 1884 where the following data are offered:

	English	Welsh	Total membership
1833	60,000	22,000	82,000
1863	150,000	50,000	200,000

which by interpolation would again suggest that a figure of around 150,000 for 1851 is likely. See also Payne, *Baptist Union*, p.116

14 Tillyard, *op.cit.*; J. D. Gay, *The Geography of Religion in England*, 1971, pp.118-22.

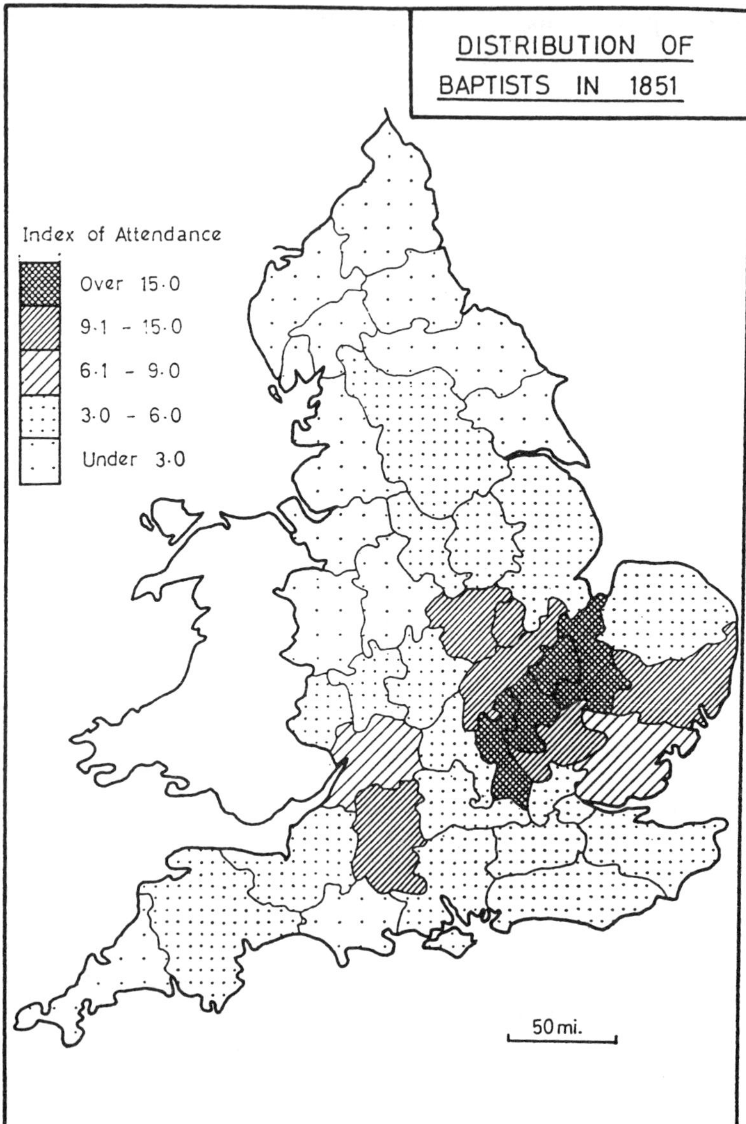

Index of attendance equals total attendances at all services on Census Sunday expressed as a percentage of population for the areas concerned. Gay's Map 27, reproduced with permission.

a more proletarian profile. Some warnings, however, have been sounded. W. L. Burn, questioning both the 'religiousness' of the upper-class and the 'irreligiousness' of the lower orders, thought it statistically 'unlikely that in a country where middle-class occupations were only gradually coming into existence the bulk of the five million attenders [at worship on Census Sunday] were of that or a higher class'.[15]

Harold Perkin argues the middle-order nature of dissent as the filling in his picture of England's religious sandwich with Anglicanism dominant both above and below; only those of some financial independency, he believes, could both afford to dissent and would wish so to find a group of like-minded peers among those 'who did not wish and would not hope for admission to the fringes of county society and its pleasures, political, cultural and frivolous'. He does qualify this, however: 'not all Dissenters were capitalists and not all capitalists were Dissenters: eighteenth-century Dissent embraced many yeomen farmers and ordinary textile workers on the one hand and excluded many great, especially London, merchants and bankers, West-country clothiers and Liverpool slave traders on the other. . . '. Under the iron forces of the Industrial Revolution the filling in the sandwich expanded very considerably, whilst the Anglican lower strata became eroded to an alarming degree.[16]

Kathleen Heasman points up the differential class appeal of different denominations, arguing, 'only the Baptists, whose tabernacles were to be found in the leading thoroughfares of the poorer districts, and the Methodists, who appealed largely to newcomers to the industrial areas, attracted large numbers of the working class'.[17] This is confirmed by C. Brown in his *Story of Baptist Home Missions* (1897), where he writes, 'Whatever be the fact in other denominations, it is not to be forgotten in relation to our own that in the majority of our churches and congregations the working classes,

15 W. L. Burn, *Age of Equipoise*, 1964, p.272.

16 Perkin, *op.cit.*, pp.196-7.

17 Kathleen Heasman, *Evangelicals in Action*, 1962, p.17.

as it is the fashion to call them, outnumber the middle class. In general, they are not more alienated from us than other sections of the community'.[18]

THE SOCIAL DISTRIBUTION OF ENGLISH BAPTISTS

Deryck Lovegrove[19] speaks of the 'wide popular support' secured by the itinerant movement of the 1790s and indicates the effectiveness of itinerancy amongst working-class respondents. Had the labours of the itinerants not been in some measure successful, they would not have provoked the hostility of local establishments that was all too apparent in some locations. Thomas Wastfield's journal, which Lovegrove transcribes,[20] shows quite clearly the modest status of some of the itinerants, their successful ministry amongst working men and women, and hostility from the socially superior and those of the lower orders that they could get to give a rowdy response to the preachers.

For a slightly later period, the *Autobiography of Joseph Mayett of Quainton, 1783-1839* bears testimony to one working-class Baptist's attitudes and behaviour.[21] Within the congregational order, the ministry of the church was highly vulnerable to economic depression:

> about this time I began to be in very narrow Circumstances in life the harvest before being very wet and the wheat much growed [i.e., sprouted] the bread was very dear so poor people Could not buy any or but very few of my goods that I had to Sell . . . I was hard put to it to pay my monthly subscription for the maintenance of the minister but I could not bear the thought of withholding it however I got three months behind and many others withheld their payments because they Could

---

18 C. Brown, *The Story of Baptist Home Missions*, 1897, p.37, cited by D. Tidball, PhD thesis (University of Keele, 1981) 'English Nonconformist Home Missions 1796-1901', p.141.

19 Deryck Lovegrove, *Established Church, Sectarian People: Itinerancy and the Transformation of English Dissent 1780-1830*, 1988, chapter 6.

20 *ibid.*, pp.166-181.

21 ed. Ann Kussmaul, *Autobiography of Joseph Mayett of Quainton, 1783-1839*, Buckinghamshire Record Society, 1986.

> not pay them so that the burthen lay very heavy on the gentleman who had enlarged the place [the chapel] for he had engaged to make up that which we Could not rise . . . '.[22]

A gospel of contentment that many preachers adopted at the time only made things worse:

> at this time there was a great many tracks [tracts] Came out and their Contents were Cheifly to perswade poor people to be satisfied in their situation and not to murmur at the dispensations of providence for we had not so much punishment as our sins deserved and in fact there was but little else to be heard from the pulpit or the press and those kinds of books were often put into my hands in a dictatorial way in order to Convince me of my errors for instance there was the Sheperd of Salsbury plain . . . the Farmers fireside and the discontented Pendulum and many others which drove me almost into despair for I Could see their design[23]

A. D. Gilbert analyses the occupational data in the non-parochial registers deposited with the Registrar General following the passage of the 1836 Act providing for national registration of births, deaths and marriages. This provides an interesting assessment of the class make-up of nonconformity in the first four decades of the nineteenth century. Unfortunately, however, Baptists and Congregationalists are aggregated.

---

22 *ibid.*,p.65.

23 *ibid.*, p.70.

TABLE 6: OCCUPATIONAL DATA OF BAPTISTS AND CONGREGATIONALISTS ABSTRACTED FROM THE NON-PAROCHIAL REGISTERS

Occupation or status	Distribution amongst all nonconformists	Distribution amongst Baptists and Congregationalists
1. Merchants and Manufacturers	2.2%	5.4%
2. Shopkeepers	7.1	8.2
3. Farmers	5.3	7.1
4. Artisans	59.4	63.0
5. Labourers	10.8	3.9
6. Colliers/Miners etc.	6.6	2.1
7. Other occupations	8.5	10.3
	100.0	100.0

It will be seen that just under 70% of Baptists and Congregationalists in that period came from categories 4-6: this compares with a distribution in society at large of only 41%, and shows that these groups, especially skilled craftsmen whether working independently or in factories, were heavily over-represented in the churches of evangelical dissent. Since Baptists were more inclined to lower-class backgrounds than the Congregationalists, it is likely that artisans, labourers and associated groups were twice as dense within Baptist communities at this time than in the nation at large.[24] P. T. Phillips's study of Lancashire cotton towns, using marriage and baptismal registers for the period 1830-70 also shows a continuing preponderance of working-class occupations amongst Baptist congregations.[25]

More local studies are required before we can be absolutely certain about the complexities of the social composition of nineteenth-century

24 A. D. Gilbert, *Religion and Society in Industrial England: Church, Chapel and Social Change, 1740-1914*, 1976, pp.62-7.

25 P. T. Phillips, *The Sectarian Spirit: Sectarianism, Society and Politics in Victorian Cotton Towns*, Toronto, 1982, as cited by McLeod, *Religion and the Working Class*, p.14.

Baptists. C. J. Radcliffe's careful analysis of the Prospect Place New Connexion Chapel (later Tetley Street), Bradford, 1837-52, is thus the more valuable. With information for some 46% of the membership over this fifteen-year period, he concludes that 'the membership was predominantly working class with a leaven of the lower middle classes', with some 60% of traceable members employed in the textile industry. The middle-class grouping was very small - eleven out of the fourteen being the clergy and their wives, some of whom came from a decidedly working-class background: Thomas Horsfield, for example, had been a woolcomber and his wife a former power-loom weaver. The only unequivocal middle-class member, apart from Richard Ingham, the first minister, was Charles Tetley, a worsted merchant who became a factory owner before moving on to become a mining engineer on the Isle of Man. The untraced members were predominantly female, for whom employment was often only a transitory phase of life. It is likely that their identification would in fact increase the density of the church's working-class membership.[26]

Radcliffe's figures by class are Middle Class (predominantly the clergy and their wives) 7.5%, Lower Middle Class 17%, Artisans 10%, Aristocracy of Textile Workers 10%, Textile Outworkers 13%, Textile Factory Workers 26%, Miscellaneous Working Class 7%, Females Without Husband or Occupation 6.5%, Under Age of Employment 3%. There was a substantial working-class presence amongst the deacons, and even more so amongst the lay preachers, 'exhorters' and those who conducted experience meetings, a group which might be seen as equivalent to Methodist class leaders. There is also evidence of women participating in the leadership of the church in conducting inquirers' classes and experience meetings, four each, with three recorded as lay preachers, one of whom was a worsted factory hand and another a power-loom worker. Perhaps more remarkable was the appointment of a woman, one Christiana Ellis, to

26 C. J. Radcliffe, 'A Textile Workers' Chapel: A Study of a General Baptist Church, 1837-1852', *The Journal of Regional and Local Studies*, 9, 1989, no.1, pp.35-53.

lead the Sunday afternoon meeting during a period of pastoral illness in 1850.[27]

That the church should take up a collection for the Woolcombers Emigration Society in 1858 is not surprising, given the nineteen members employed in the trade which was rapidly becoming extinct. The decline in male employment opportunities doubtless also explains the seven members who emigrated, three each to America and France, and one to Australia. Temptations in mid-nineteenth-century Bradford, especially to sexual licence and intemperance, were many, leading to losses from the church after discipline had been exercised, though where possible this was accompanied by forgiveness and restoration. For others, the nexus that the church provided offered opportunity for social improvement as the continued practice of 'thrift, sobriety, application and deferred gratification' brought their rewards, particularly amongst those whose membership was long standing.

Financing the work of the church with such a predominantly working-class congregation proved a problem. Missionary intention argued for the abolition of pew-rents, but balanced budgets required the reverse. Attempts were made to reduce rents but they were not totally eliminated, with only a quarter of the pews free at the 1851 Census. In the denomination at large they were being phased out in favour of free-will offerings from mid-century onwards.

Church books reveal how 'the Prospect Place members evangelised the factories' surrounding the chapel and 'the large number of factory workers attracted into the church bears testimony to the fruitfulness of this approach. Young people who became members found a democratic community in which they were valued for themselves. Women too were accepted with more respect than in society at large. Many working-class members were given responsibilities as deacons, lay preachers or conductors of meetings. The tensions thrown up by church discipline did not prove insupportable to the many who survived them . . . Prospect Place Chapel existed for the new urban working class who participated largely in its running . . . It

27 *ibid.*, p.39

represented an attempt by one section of the Old Dissent to meet the challenge of harsh, vague and volatile conditions. In this, for the first decade at least, Prospect Place had a great measure of success.'[28]

The question is how many Prospect Places there were within the denomination - and the answer to such a question can only be impressionistic. Certainly the large number of churches which were crippled by debt for many years would argue an absence of middle-class patronage, as also those many churches unable to afford pastoral oversight, where the pastor's salary was often seriously in arrears, or where pastoral oversight had to be curtailed for want of funds. F. M. W. Harrison, writing of the mid-nineteenth century, offers the statistic that only 25% of the churches in the denomination had over 200 members, and that together these made up 50% of the strength of the denomination. Small churches with precarious budgets seemed to account for a sizeable part of the Baptist presence. F. M. W. Harrison's analysis of Nottinghamshire Baptists, after surveying the membership of individual churches, concludes: 'all the Nottingham Baptist churches included a much greater proportion of working-class people among their members than all the other classes put together . . . In the agricultural villages members were farm workers or tradesmen, and in the industrial villages they were lace-makers, stockingers or miners'. General Baptist churches had fewer middle-class members than Particular Baptist, but even Particular Churches lost many members by emigration in periods of trade recession.[29]

Even Particular Baptist churches could be largely working class in constituency as, for example, Arthur O'Neill's Newhall Street congregation in Birmingham and the neighbouring People's Chapel in Great King Street, which had the support of Thomas Cooper, Chartist turned General Baptist preacher, who thought the church's designation 'a great title', which would require some living up to. To that end the members resolved to dispense with a separated ministry (the chapel

28 *ibid.*, p.49.

29 F. M. W. Harrison, 'The Nottinghamshire Baptists: Church relations, social composition, finance, theology', *BQ* 26, 1975, pp.174-6.

keeper was the only individual on the chapel's payroll), collections (though not the opportunity for the people to make discreet offerings) and pew rents, and to secure a democratic form of church government: an altogether attractive formula to its working-class constituency. Other city churches also attracted essentially working class congregations.

Hugh McLeod's analysis of *Class and Religion in the Late Victorian City* shows that Baptist churches recruited their members from all social classes except the aristocracy and the lowest order of the brute working-class. A church like that at Lee in South London was probably unique in its capacity to hold both Judge Willis and Sir Nathanael Barnaby in its membership, for judges and knights had a scant presence throughout the denomination.[30] More generally McLeod comments, 'the largest number of "converted working men" was probably to be found among the Baptists who had a large lower middle-class membership and a few distinctly wealthy chapels, but also a considerable working-class element in most of their chapels'.[31] Such a membership has been linked by a number of writers with the clarity with which Baptists expounded the traditional, even crude, Evangelical doctrines.

Charles Masterman in 1909 referred to 'the Baptist Chapel, where the minister maintains the old doctrines of hell and heaven and wrestles with the sinner for his immortal soul'.[32] Even more striking testimony comes from the pen of Bruce Wallace, the founder of the Brotherhood Church in South Hackney, a thorough-going nonconformist attempt at Christian socialism; he confessed that his creed had made little impression upon the local people but argued that the Baptists, the Salvation Army, and the Roman Catholics had each

---

30 Hugh McLeod, *Class and Religion in the Late Victorian City*, 1974, p.173.

31 *ibid.*, p.69.

32 C. F. Masterman, *The Condition of England*, 1909, p.75, cited by McLeod, *Class and Religion*, pp.69-70.

in some measure succeeded where he had failed.[33] A Poplar Baptist minister told Charles Booth's representative quite uncomplicatedly, 'If the people want pea soup they go to church; if they want the Gospel they come to chapel'.[34] McLeod usefully offers statistics (see Table 7) comparing the occupations of men married in Baptist chapels in Bethnal Green and Lewisham. Such figures reflect not simply on the employment of church members but upon the class of a wider group of adherents and associates. The Baptist constituency in East London was almost three times as large as that of the South London borough, where the Baptist presence was comparatively weak compared with other nonconformists. The Baptists clearly had a greater density of working-class support in less genteel Bethnal Green, largely because in Lewisham the skilled working-class membership was smaller and the clerical presence larger, but in both boroughs Baptist membership was heavily biased towards the working and lower middle classes.

TABLE 7: OCCUPATIONS OF MEN MARRIED IN BAPTIST CHAPELS IN BETHNAL GREEN AND LEWISHAM

	Bethnal Green		Lewisham	
Gentlemen	0		1 [1.3%]	
Professional	5 [2.4%]		1 [1.3]	
Employers and Managers	13 [6.3]		2 [2.6]	
'Junior' Professional	3 [1.4]		5 [6.6]	
Clerical	50 [24.0]		27 [35.5]	
Retail	22 [10.6]		8 [10.5]	
Working class				
Skilled	78 [37.5] }		15 [19.7] }	
Semi Skilled	22 [10.6] }	54.8	9 [11.8] }	42.0
Unskilled	10 [4.8] }		5 [6.6] }	
Service	4 [1.9] }		3 [3.9] }	
Forces	1 [0.5]		0 [0]	
	208		76	

[Note: The Bethnal Green figures are for 1880-1901, and Lewisham figures for 1899-1914]

33 Booth Collection B195, pp.24-6, B385, pp.161-7, cited by McLeod, *Class and Religion*, pp.68-9.

34 Booth Collection, B171, p.34, cited McLeod, *Class and Religion*, p.95.

Jeffrey Cox has demonstrated that Baptists had increasing difficulty, in common with other nonconformist denominations, in holding their more affluent members and certainly their offspring, citing the Tritton and Higgs families in particular: in both cases younger generation became Anglicans. One had provided a Treasurer of the Baptist Missionary Society and the other was a considerable patron of Spurgeonic ventures.[35] The same author is, however, over-dogmatic when he writes, 'The complete incorporation of Lambeth's Baptists into the middle class is particularly striking, although they partially protected themselves from the consequences by embracing a conservative theology which emphasized conversion and recruitment' in a way which other nonconformist groups in Lambeth seemed unable to do.[36]

Such a comment does, however, identify a major problem for late nineteenth-century Baptists. Simply stated, it is that a middle-class convert will probably remain and breed middle-class church members, but working-class converts will themselves be liable to upward class mobility and certainly are likely to breed middle-class offspring. The problem was well understood at the time. It was succinctly put by the minister of Upton Chapel: 'Our success contributes to our failure. As our people are brought in and become thrifty they move away toward Clapham'.[37] Even more precisely, W. S. Caine, of Baptist origins though in Lambeth ministering to the Congregationalists, noted of his working-class converts, 'When they are converted they give up drink. This adds 5/- to their wages and soon makes a difference in their appearance. Indeed it is a distinct hindrance now that our people look such decent folk'.[38]

Another Baptist minister compared life in inner Lambeth with the social ambience of Brixton suburbia where it was difficult to secure

35 J. Cox, *The English Churches in a Secular Society, Lambeth, 1870-1930*, 1982, pp.229-30.

36 *ibid.*, pp.251-2.

37 Booth Collection, B371, p.9, cited Cox, p.140.

38 Booth Collection, B270, pp.1,7, cited Cox, p.141.

support for mid-week events. By contrast, 'In [inner] Lambeth people almost made the chapel their home, but here the homes are comfortable and there is not the same necessity'.[39] Archibald Brown, in removing from East London Tabernacle to Chatsworth, West Norwood, nostalgically commented, 'What I miss is the working class - no artisans, nothing between villadom and dirty poverty'. Unimpressed by those who told him that East London methods were not for West Norwood, Brown, 'with typical Spurgeonic ingenuity', set about rectifying the situation, and 'conversion-orientated preaching and doctrinaire informality' worked, with five hundred new members added in three years.[40]

Brown had not wholly rejoiced in the working class during his East London incumbency. Their life-style had indeed received trenchant criticism from him - especially 'the noisy public-house scum' who made a nonsense of the concept of English liberty: 'This is English liberty - the liberty of the debauched to make life intolerable to the sober and quiet. All this serves to drive the respectable families away and with them goes the backbone of our churches'.

The outward migration of respectable chapel folk put at risk the viability of many downtown churches. A newspaper reporter, however, noted at the packed services at the East London Tabernacle, 'no shabby waterproofs or battered bonnets, not a black eye visible on all these intelligent faces' - but drew encouragement from the knowledge 'that there is such a nucleus of good, honest, respectable English life in the midst of this wilderness of seething poverty . . . Traders, managers, foremen, overlookers, and skilled mechanics, the very bone and sinew of the land'. Archibald Brown initiated special services for the very poor, believing that respectable and disreputable would not mix, noting of the latter, 'if these people were to come to the regular Sunday services, the respectable congregation would be frightened away'.[41] In St Giles George M'Cree saw the

39 Booth Collection, B303, p.147, cited Cox, p.141.

40 Booth Collection, B313, p.5, cited Cox, p.141.

41 As cited by McLeod, *Class and Religion*, p.150.

same problem from the opposite angle and was continually aware that converts rapidly became so much more respectable that new disreputable contacts might be uncomfortable at the Mission.

Not all were content to isolate classes in this way. The Revd Newton Vanstone of Catford Bridge Baptist Church was 'a political minister on strongly advanced, if not socialistic lines', who could not 'think of the administration of the Poor Law without his blood boiling'. Not all shared his righteous indignation and a split began to develop. He described his opponents as 'people who are glad to have the working man at their church, if they may condescend and patronise him, give him half a crown and pat him on the back & patronise him but who don't at all like being made equal with Tom, Dick and Harry'. In 1899, 154 out of 350 members left Catford Bridge to establish the new church at Perry Rise, Forest Hill.[42] A split in Catford and a church plant by schism in respectable Forest Hill still left Baptists ministering to essentially working-class congregations in the inner suburbs.

WOMEN[43]

From the very beginning of the century questions were raised as to what part women should play in the churches: the first issue of the *Baptist Magazine* raised the question of the appropriateness of their voting in church meeting.[44] The following year there was debate as to whether it was right for them to give testimony in the church prior to their being accepted as church members. Whilst some argued a Pauline prohibition, others maintained that this was a misapplication of Scripture - and that the Stennetts, Brine, Gill and Abraham Booth had not been in conflict with scripture in requiring female applicants

42 Booth Collection B315, p.167, cited McLeod, *Class and Religion*, pp.189-198.

43 For a wider consideration of the mission and ministry of Baptist women see *BQ* 31, July 1986, and in particular pp.337-52, J. H. Y. Briggs, 'She-preachers, widows and other women: the feminine dimension in Baptist life since 1600'.

44 *BM* January 1809, p.32.

for membership to give public testimony to their faith.[45] However, women's full participation in voting was clearly not general practice for a number of trust deeds from this period specifically confine voting on important issues to men.

An article on deaconesses in 1814 argued a more general use of female gifts, though the focus was on work amongst other women, questioning whether a neglect of women's gifts had not been to the impoverishment of the life of the churches. In July 1841 G. H. Davis of Weymouth made a plea for the restoration of the order of deaconess, after reference in March to their use by Bristol Baptists in the seventeenth century.[46] The main focus of their activity was envisaged as work amongst women - the instruction of candidates for baptism, the visiting of widows and the sick, and the needs of female servants were identified as areas of special concern. Each church, it was suggested, should appoint four or more who should be women eminent in piety and 'somewhat advanced in years'.[47]

Silent, or silenced, in church, women waxed eloquent with their pens. From the eighteenth into the nineteenth centuries hymn-writing became a major legitimate activity for Baptist women, whose names are to be found in some number in Julian's *Dictionary*: Marianne Hearn or Farningham (1834-1909), Mary Leslie (d.1834), Sarah Medley, Maria Saffery (1773-1858), Elizabeth Trestrail (b.1813), and her sister, Caroline Dent (b.1815).[48]

Next to the poetic women stand the educational women: some like Marianne Hearn, a staff member of the *Christian World* and editor of the *Sunday School Times*, operated in both spheres, but there were

---

45 *BM* 1810, pp.466, 559. For a similar debate for and against women speaking in church, see *BM* 1814, pp.150, 236-9.

46 *BM* March 1841, p.113.

47 *BM* July 1841, pp.334-5.

48 H. Wheeler Robinson, *The Life and Faith of the Baptists*, 1946, pp.50-6. W. T. Whitley, *History of British Baptists*, 1923, p.214. H. Martin, 'The Baptist Contribution to Early English Hymnody', *BQ* 19, 1962, pp.196f. J. Julian, *Dictionary of Hymnology*, revised 1907, entries. D. W. Music, 'Heroines of Baptist Hymnody', *Baptist History and Heritage*, 29, January 1994, pp.37-44.

others, like Henrietta Neale, the prolific late eighteenth-century Luton schoolmistress, and Martha Trinder (d.1794), Northampton school proprietor and author of school books, whose interests were more pedagogic. To them must be added the many women who opened proprietary schools and the thousands who flocked into devoted teaching in Sunday Schools which provided a wide sphere of female Christian usefulness. Others, like Esther Copley of Oxford (1786-1851), and Elizabeth Dawbarn of Wisbech made their name in educating their own number in matters of domesticity.[49]

Education could be a business undertaking or it could be a charitable enterprise. Philanthropy was practically liberating: 'the temperance and social purity movements took women to the brink of public affairs (and occasionally over it). Missionary support work, the YWCA, Christian Endeavour, and the Student Voluntary Missionary Union, all springing from evangelical soil, contributed to what one writer called 'the "Epiphany of Women" in the Victorian era'.[50] It was not only that such enterprises engaged the energies of prominent evangelical wives and daughters, but that they also began to employ paid female agents of a lower social order as Bible women, scripture readers, district visitors, and mission superintendents. Some who 'lived by faith' were not strictly speaking 'paid', though they were full-time in their charitable engagements. The denominational allegiance of many of these women, whose story is amply told in the biographical notices in *The Revival* and its successor *The Christian*, is difficult to determine, but undoubtedly Baptist women played their part within the great evangelical charities.

In South London two Baptists ran orphanages on similar lines. Mrs T. H. Montague was the founder and superintendent of the

---

49 W. T. Whitley, 'Index to Notable Baptists', *TBHS* 7, pp.182-239, 287.

50 Cited by D. Bebbington, 'Evangelicals and the Role of Women', *Christian Arena*, 37/4, 1984, pp.19-23. The writer cited is the American, A. T. Pierson, a Presbyterian who supplied the pulpit of the Metropolitan Tabernacle during Spurgeon's final illness and after his death from 1 October 1891 to September 1892. He was baptized as a believer by J. A. Spurgeon at West Croydon Tabernacle in 1894.

Brixton Girls' Orphanage, which provided for some three hundred 'fatherless children'. Miss Charlotte Sharman's Homes, supported by evangelicals generally, were strategically placed in West Square, half-way between the Metropolitan Tabernacle and Upton Chapel. To manage and promote an orphanage for three hundred girls, including their placement in service, and in the 'seventies the construction of purpose-built accommodation and the diversification of the work from South London to Kent and Sussex, was no mean achievement.[51]

Hymns, schools, charities, and fourthly missions overseas, perhaps the most important factor, all played their part in giving women new importance in both church and society, The way here was pioneered by the formidable Mrs Hannah Marshman, 'the only missionary wife who took a constantly active part in the [Serampore] Mission's work'. In the Serampore Form of Agreement was written a hope that work in female education might be undertaken, believing that 'a European sister may do much for the cause by promoting the tidiness and stirring up the zeal of the native female converts'.[52]

In mid-century came the initiatives of Marianne Lewis and Elizabeth Sale. Marianne Lewis, baptized in 1839, sister to George Gould of Norwich, married C. B. Lewis, a Bristol College student preparing for missionary service in Ceylon. In 1847 the couple transferred to Calcutta, and Mrs Lewis threw herself into the task of educating Indian women. Elizabeth Sale, born in the south of France

---

51 F. K. Prochaska, *Women and Philanthropy in Nineteenth-Century England*, 1980, p.147. *The Christian*, 22 July 1887, pp.641-2. Miss Sharman's biographer was Marguerite Williams, daughter of the minister of Upton Chapel. K. Heasman, *Evangelicals in Action*, 1962, p.92. *The Christian*, 17 March 1887, p.213.

52 E. Daniel Potts, *British Baptist Missionaries in India,* 1967, pp.17, 21, who also quotes Carey on the need for women missionaries as early as 1796: 'to communicate the gospel . . . in a situation where superstition secludes all women of respectability from hearing the word unless from their own sex.' The only response to this was the sending out with Dr William Johns in 1810-2 of a Miss Chaffin 'to whom apparently belongs the honour of being the first missionary nurse.' But Carey records of her that, 'although an excellent woman', she was not 'of any use to the Mission' (pp.38, 65).

in 1818, came to Baptist convictions after an Anglican education and had to leave home. Baptized at the church in Blandford Street, Marylebone, she secured some instruction in medicine and surgery under the patronage of Sir David Davis, personal physician to Queen Adelaide. In 1848 she married John Sale, bound for mission work in Barisal, India. Elizabeth Sale was soon engaged in young people's work and medical work. It was when the couple moved to Jessore in 1854 that Mrs Sale first secured an entry into a Hindu Zenana, the secluded quarters where Indian women lived. Hitherto the wives of the missionaries had confined their activities to children and to Christianized women, but Mrs Sale continued her work in the zenanas when she and her husband moved back to Calcutta.[53]

In 1866 Mrs Lewis popularized Mrs Sale's initiative in a tract entitled *A Plea for Zenanas*, in which she suggested that the gratuitous service of missionary wives and daughters was insufficient and that there was now a need for dedicated agents for this special work. In the following year what came to be known as the Baptist Zenana Mission (the title adopted thirty years later) was founded. Initially in 1868 two British agents, Miss Page and Miss Robinson, were recruited in India and half a dozen local Bible women appointed. Four years later there were six centres of operation, eight lady missionaries and fourteen Indian helpers. By the time that Mrs Sale died in 1898, the BZM employed sixty-seven lady missionaries, all but nine of whom were single women.[54]

By 1898 two of the BZM missionaries were qualified doctors, and work was being undertaken not only in India and China, the earliest fields, but also in Ceylon, Congo and Italy. During the Boxer Rising China produced its zenana martyrs in Miss Renaut and Miss Timmis, who died on her way home from China, leading to the withdrawal of

53 Anon, *Jubilee 1867-1917: Fifty years work amongst women in the Far East*, n.d. but 1917; E. A. Payne, *The Great Succession: Leaders of the BMS during the Nineteenth Century*, 1938, chapter VII.

54 B. Stanley, *History of the Baptist Missionary Society 1792-1992*, Edinburgh 1992, pp.227-32.

women from the China field until 1902. While the Zenana Mission provided a specialized agency to harness women's energies, the existence of the BZM in fact made it more difficult for single women to secure appointment with the BMS itself, though from 1879 several were appointed to the African field.

Essential changes in social relationships were being created by such activity, as the Revd T. Moscrop was quick to perceive: 'India's future is bound up with the regeneration of her women . . . not until woman everywhere has the status and opportunity which Christ would give her and which are her right in Him, will His purposes be accomplished. Without her perfecting and endeavour, His Kingdom cannot fully appear.'[55]

At home the enterprise called for administrative talents from Baptist women: first the labours of Mrs Angus, whilst later Miss Isobel and Miss Amelia Angus, Miss Jessie Taylor, Miss Rooke, Miss Ella Lockhart, Miss H. Bowser and Miss Marion Horsfall all contributed to the leadership. At the local level Baptist women played an essential part as fund-raisers: by 1849 the BMS was looking to its Sunday School supporters to raise some £3000 per year. Women teachers played the major part in enthusing the young to this task. Before the First World War there was talk of the BZM being fully integrated into the BMS, but all that happened was a change of name to the Society's Women's Missionary Association. Thus until 1927 women missionaries were listed under BZM/WMA, rather than with the men in the BMS lists. It was not until 1926, the year in which the WMA was finally integrated into the BMS, that women were first elected on to the BMS General Committee, with Lady Pearce Gould becoming its first female chairman in the same year.

Even though for sixty years men and women worked in separate organizations, the general argument holds that Baptists, like others, were readier to employ women overseas than at home, and in due time the inconsistency of employing one rule abroad and a different one at home began to be felt, especially as in the new century

---

55 *Jubilee 1867-1917*, pp.5-6.

ecumenical thinking also made its impact. The Edinburgh Conference of 1910 reflected on women's role in world mission: 'A vast proportion of any population would have to be left without the message if there were no women to present it . . . The Christian Church, the Christian nation, might indeed be organized but could not be built up apart from the education and training of the womanhood of each community into Christian ideals of wifehood, motherhood, leadership, and this only Christian women can supply.'[56]

Speaking of all the activity undertaken by women in the post-1859 world of care and witness, Olive Anderson affirms:

> Undoubtedly female participation in such religious activities played a significant part in bringing both lower and upper middle-class women out of their homes (the former to church and chapel gatherings, the latter to mission work of all kinds) and in winning such a state of affairs from their menfolk, just as the beginning of paid religious work by women made a small contribution to that expansion of their occupational opportunities which was so important in the late nineteenth century. Nevertheless such developments did not explicitly challenge either the social convention that respectable women played no public part in mixed society, or Christian teaching that women should be silent in the church.[57]

Both of these principles were, however, challenged by the decorous and intellectually well-founded preaching of the well-connected women of the Second Evangelical Revival who often used Baptist chapels for their expositions. They dealt with the Biblical record either by arguing that they possessed an exceptional call from God which overrode apostolic prohibitions or that those prohibitions were never intended to be universal but were limited to specific locations at a specific time, especially since the general trend of Pauline teaching

---

56 *ibid.*, p.31.

57 O. Anderson, 'Women Preachers in Mid-Victorian Britain: some reflexions on feminisim, popular religion and social change', *The Historical Journal*, 12/3, 1969, p.469.

was towards freedom and equality for women. They also argued that the prophesying in Acts 21.9 could easily have been translated as preaching, whilst Romans 16.1 referred to the office of deacon, rather than service in general.

One of the operating principles of William Booth's Christian Mission of 1870 was 'that women have an equal standing with men as publishers of salvation to the world', a rule that eight years later passed over into the so-called 'Women's Charter' of the Salvation Army.[58] The practice of the Salvation Army was critical in helping evangelical Christendom, Baptists included, to accept the ministry of women in practice: 'it was the Army's Major Barbaras and Hallelujah lasses who gave the most sensational stimulus to popular recognition in the late nineteenth century of women's capacity to teach, organize, and command, and they owed their existence not to any feminism on the part of Catherine Booth but to her ardent response to those religious influences of the 'sixties which together produced the crowd of female preachers . . . of whom she was one.'[59]

Following the Second Evangelical Awakening, Joseph Angus in 1862 turned once more to the Biblical texts in his exposition of the nature of *Christian Churches*. Noting the precedent of the place of Phoebe in the church of Cenchrea, Angus argued that deacons could be of either sex, underlining that Paul himself was indebted to Phoebe for the services she rendered to him, and that it was from such service that the word *deacon* derived. Although Paul suggested that for women to teach within the church was inconsistent with the divine order of nature (I Cor. 14.34; I Tim. 2.12), Angus argued that I Cor. 11.5 (cf. Acts 2.17, 21.9) legitimized women praying and prophesying in public.[60]

Anderson claims that in the writings of Angus's contemporary, William Landels, the Scottish pastor of the new Regent's Park Chapel from 1855, the changing social attitude to women's involvement in the

---

58 *ibid.*, p.482.

59 *ibid.*

60 J. Angus, *Christian Churches*, 1862, pp.54-5.

life of the church can be traced. In 1859 his *Women's Sphere and Work considered in the light of Scripture* argued that man was created for public life but woman was so created as to find her fulfilment in 'the sacred privacy of the home'. Five years later, *Lessons for Maidens, Wives and Mothers from some of the representative women of Scripture* fortified that position. In 1870 Landels published *Woman, her Position and Power* (republished in 1880 as *The True Glory of Women*); though many of the old reservations remain, Landels was now questioning whether the office of deaconess in the apostolic age did not argue for the admission of women to the ministry in Victorian times.[61] By that date, although the battle of the texts continued to rage, an essential pragmatism was at work in the evangelical mind which essentially argued that God's blessing of the fruits of women's labours in every disputed sphere gave a kind of *ex post facto* justification to those initiatives,

Women began to make an appearance as platform speakers at the Baptist Union Assembly, otherwise still an all-male preserve, in 1889, when two ministers' wives, Mrs Medley and Mrs Dawson Burns, addressed the spring and summer assemblies on Young Women's Guilds and Woman's Work in the Church. Two years later two single women, Dr Ellen Farrer and Miss Edith Angus, spoke of women's work among the sick poor and their concern for the social conditions of the neediest groups in society. This initiative, however, was not followed up: it was to be many years before another woman was to appear as an Assembly speaker. The first recorded female delegate to the Assembly was a Mrs Stockford, appointed to represent Moss Side Church in Manchester in 1894, an appointment which led the Council to pass a resolution specifically confirming that women were in fact eligible to serve in this way.

The suggestion that the first woman deacon of modern times was appointed at Pembroke Chapel, Liverpool, in 1912 is unlikely to be true. The first *Handbook* to list Church Secretaries is that for 1905,

---

61 Anderson, *op.cit.*, p.481; Bebbington, 'Evangelicals and the Role of Women', pp.19-21.

when more than thirty women were listed, all presumably members of local diaconates, suggesting that women deacons had already reappeared by the end of the nineteenth century. The size of the church fellowship and the availability of men to hold office was almost certainly a deciding factor here. At the other end of the scale, a large church like Bloomsbury had been in the practice of appointing both paid Bible women and volunteer church ladies of respectable social status to act as district visitors in the slums of St Giles in association with the mission there from the 1850s, but a proposal in 1875 to appoint Lady Church Visitors to visit absentees and sick members failed to find favour. In 1897 a forward-looking member, H. E. Jones, who at the previous meeting had suggested the introduction of electric light, proposed the church should 'consider the need of ladies being appointed to fill any vacancies that may occur in the eldership', but the deacons and elders would only agree to propose to the church that lady visitors be appointed for those women applying for church membership who expressly asked for this.[62]

The 1891 addresses by Dr Farrer and Miss Angus reflected initiatives taken the previous year by the London Baptist Association Extension Committee under the leadership of Dr F. B. Meyer. As part of the forward movement, they had opened the Baptist Deaconess Home and Mission at 59 Doughty Street, with four sisters and a lady superintendent. The initial work was essentially medical: in 1893 sisters living outside the home were granted a salary of £60 per annum, but out of this had to pay for their own nursing training. In 1919 the Baptist Union Council agreed to take over the responsibility for the training and settlement of deaconesses, and Havelock Hall, Hampstead, was purchased by the women of the denomination and opened as a centre for training women for work both at home and overseas. The programme of training lasted three years and included theology, social work and nursing. Of the first eleven students, three were preparing for service overseas. For the rest, their service to the

62 *Baptist Handbook*, 1892. E. A. Payne, *The Baptist Union: A short history*, 1959, p.150. Information *ex* Mrs Faith Bowers, Bloomsbury Church Books.

denomination witnessed not only a new opening for women's commitment, but a new engagement with the problems of the city.[63]

Early in the century the debate about the terms of communion found the closed table of disciplined church order in conflict with the open table that was the natural outcome of shared experience of mission. In similar fashion the participation of women within the ministry of the church at home and more especially abroad seemed to have received the imprimatur of the Spirit and thus called for a more sophisticated interpretation of those Pauline passages which had hitherto been seen to prohibit the active involvement of women in the leadership and teaching ministry of the church. Certainly there were many areas where their dedicated service could advance the church's mission, where otherwise it might have faltered for want of manpower. Some Baptists accordingly welcomed the evangelistic potential of women employed in the church's mission, whilst others were unable to persuade themselves that the Pauline prohibition did not still apply. In 1902-3 the *Daily News* took a census which revealed gender balances of church attenders in inner London. The percentage of females over fifteen at the census in the previous year was 53.88%. Anglican churches had the highest proportion of female attenders at 65.67%, the Primitive Methodists the lowest at 51.59%; the Baptist percentage was 59.80%[64]

By the end of the nineteenth century some local churches already had women's guilds. A national organization was only established in 1908. The first meeting took place in Mrs Russell James's drawing room, with women from Archway Road, Muswell Hill and Ferme Park. Mrs James confessed she was not as nervous as she might have been because the previous week she had chaired a large meeting of Liberal women. The vision was to capitalize on women's energies to raise funds for the support of mission work in Britain, to promote

---

63 Payne, *Baptist Union*, p.151. D. Rose, *Baptist Deaconesses*, 1954; *Order of Baptist Deaconesses, 1890-1975: Women in the Service of the Denomination*, 1967, pp.6-8. H. Martin, *Fifty Years of Carey Hall, 1912-62.*

64 Hugh McLeod, *Class and Religion*, Table 13, p.308.

evangelism and colportage, and to undertake such special tasks as welcoming church members moving from one area to another. Women were rapidly finding their identity within the denomination. In 1910 a cumbersome earlier title was changed to the Baptist Women's League, and in the following year ten women were co-opted to the Baptist Union Council. Eight years later the first woman pastor in England entered upon her ministerial duties.

9

MISSION AND EVANGELISM

Baptist life in the nineteenth century was a compound of three distinct but overlapping historical processes. The first ingredient was seventeenth-century Puritanism with its emphasis upon system and order. But the select religion of the Puritans had by the beginning of the nineteenth century been transformed by the ardour, vitality and enthusiasm of evangelicalism with its concern for experience rather than argument, life rather than system, the expansion of the church rather than the niceties of its polity. The critical interaction of these two forces is helpfully expounded by Geoffrey Nuttall when he writes, 'It was during the eighteenth century that historic dissent took the form in which it has been a recognizable part of the English scene; and the poles between which, by attraction and repulsion, it did so, were Calvinism and the Evangelical Revival.'[1] That is to say that the Puritan inheritance was already threatened by the wide response secured by the broadcast advocacy of the gospel seen in the history of the Evangelical Revival, long before liberation of thought made its impact.

However, Geoffrey Nuttall's dialectic has to be complicated by a third consideration, and that was the activism characteristic of nineteenth-century Baptists which was, in part, at least the consequence of the political, and to a degree the social, exclusion of the previous century and a half. This activism is partly to be seen in the politicization of Baptists along with other dissenters but is also to be observed in more aggressive programmatic emphases of local churches, associations and developing central denominational organizations, arising from a more acute sense of mission. All this required the development of practical societal models adequate to meet the needs of a rapidly changing world full of desperately urgent needs to be met by Christian action. Societies were to be the new instrument of such action. Societies for overseas missions, societies

---

1 G. F. Nuttall, 'Calvinism in Free Church History', *BQ* 22, 1968, p.420.

for itinerancy at home, societies for training pastors, societies for translating and disseminating the scriptures, societies for printing and distributing Christian literature, and so many more, all provided the vehicles for active Christians to pursue those aspects of Christian mission which claimed their energies.[2] The danger of this was a potential secularization of the church, were it to be seen as no more than a kind of collective of different societies, justified functionally, rather than as the covenant community of Christ, at once the gift and creation of the Spirit. Whilst the mission-orientated agenda of the early part of the century may have broadened by the end to embrace the wider aspects of human welfare, the societal methodology remained paramount. This process was aided by the disintegration of the high Calvinism of the previous century and its replacement by a too easy sanctification of voluntaryism - English dissenters used to like to think that they themselves had created the word - which seemed a sufficient justification for the brashest forms of activism. These now took the field as an extensive philanthropic machine designed to meet the needs of those who without its assistance would have remained destitute or unnurtured.

So far as Baptists are concerned, it would be totally unreal to write their history in terms of societies specifically Baptist. From the beginning of the century up to the present day, much Baptist energy has been invested in interdenominational activities, a form of evangelical ecumenism *avant la lettre*. Many Baptists, not least Joseph Hughes, the minister of Battersea Chapel, became heavily involved in the work of the Religious Tract Society, of which Hughes was Secretary 1799-1833, and the Bible Society, of which he has been called the father. Following Hughes, Samuel Green and Samuel Manning both served with distinction in the secretariat of the Religious Tract Society. A letter from a clergyman to the London City Mission

---

2 Ford K. Brown, *Fathers of the Victorians: the Age of Wilberforce*, 1961, especially chapter 9, 'Ten thousand compassions and charities'; W. H. Brackney, 'The BMS in proper context: some reflections on the larger voluntary tradition', *BQ* 34, 1992, pp.364-77.

in 1837 indicated his resignation from the mission because so many of its agents were Baptists.[3] Whereas many of the societies and periodicals of the pan-evangelicalism of the years 1790-1810 tended to fall to Congregational management in the years of denominational assertion, Baptists, as those who benefited most from the Second Evangelical Awakening in the years following 1859, were particularly active in the new kind of missionary society of the 1870s - the faith missions that modelled themselves on Hudson Taylor's China Inland Mission of 1865 - and within the holiness movement at home that found its focus in the Keswick Convention. Prior to 1900, however, F. B. Meyer was the only Baptist to gain prominence on the Keswick platform.[4]

Granted that some major societies, such as the Liberation Society and the Evangelical Alliance and the various education societies that found their focus in the growth of Baptist colleges, belong to other parts of this analysis, the societal activity of Baptists may be gathered into four principal groups, all, of course, inter-related. First, there were those societies primarily concerned with the promotion of evangelism at home and abroad. Secondly there were a group of societies concerned with children and youth. A third group of societies were broadly concerned with philanthropy, whilst a fourth area, worthy of separate consideration, was that concerned with temperance.

EVANGELISM AT HOME AND ABROAD

Both the Baptist Missionary Society (1792) and the Baptist Home Missionary Society (1797) antedated the effective establishment of the Baptist Union by a substantial number of years. The BMS was *the*

---

3 The preparation of several parts of this chapter benefited greatly from supervising Derek Tidball's PhD thesis (University of Keele, 1981), 'English Nonconformist Home Missions 1796-1901'.. Chapter 3 analyses the activities of Baptists, but the reference here is to pp.248-9.

4 D. W. Bebbington, *Evangelicalism in Modern Britain: a history from the 1730s to the 1980s*, 1989, p.178.

society in the life of Baptists, the Union itself existing 'to furnish a stimulus for a zealous co-operation in our own denomination, and especially to encourage and support our Missions'.[5] It is significant that, whilst other denominational societies have over the years become departments of the Union, which has accordingly expanded its function as it has acted as a kind of residual legatee of so many good causes, the BMS remains independent, partly because for much of the century it was much the stronger body. No history of Baptists in the nineteenth century can therefore be properly focused unless it underlines Baptist commitment to overseas missions and the energy spent in promoting and supporting such activity.[6]

In 1797 a cumbersomely titled 'Baptist Society in London for the encouragement and support of Itinerant and Village Preaching' was founded. In 1817 this became the Baptist Itinerant Home Missionary Society which five years later dropped the language of itinerancy. Debate took place as to whether such activity, desperately needed in an England challenged by the ferment of incipient industrialism, should be undertaken denominationally or interdenominationally. Behind the work of both lay the new evangelical academies, where itinerancy was wedded to scholarship, raising its practice above the common charge of unlearned ignorance. Theologically, the challenge was to the autonomy of local congregations and the supplementation of them by the creation of a number of itinerancies. These in turn called for new kinds of ministerial skills. The success of such ventures, it has been suggested, was measured in so far as they proved better at securing 'hearers' than making members, and this, 'by diluting the element of commitment . . . affected a fundamental change away from the serious character of eighteenth-century dissent with its strongly doctrinal emphasis', spawning in rural England a

---

5 E. A. Payne, *The Baptist Union: A Short History*, 1959, p.6.

6 See B. Stanley, 'Home Support for Overseas Missions in Early Victorian England, c.1838-73', PhD thesis, University of Cambridge, 1979.

particular form of church allegiance that often lacked clear denominational commitment.[7]

Concern for home mission came not only through the work of the Society - associations were rejuvenated and given a new purposefulness. Some indeed were created for the first time: their concern, as Geoffrey Nuttall makes clear in his comparison with older associations, was 'a missionary-design' for village preaching; they were 'out to convert, not conserve'.[8] But at the same time the Home Missionary Society increased the scope of its work. Full-time agents were first appointed in 1820, the initial four rising to forty by 1831. The ubiquitous F. A. Cox became joint secretary of the Society in 1824 and remained as such till 1835. Initially he encouraged the development of specialist missionaries who would be full-time in home mission work, but after his visit to the USA in 1835 he argued that settled ministers should also spend some time itinerating, pointing out the inconsistency in doing this to secure funds but not to promote religion *per se*.[9] Achievements in terms of churches planted (twenty between 1820 and 1827) and believers added to church rolls (300 in 1835) seemed only to be limited by the slenderness of the financial support forthcoming, which was less than a tithe of what the BMS, itself not among the richer societies, was able to command. In 1822 the *Baptist Magazine* reported the income of the Bible Society for 1821 as £104,000, of the BMS as £11,600 (well behind the Wesleyan Missionary Society, the LMS and the CMS, which ranged from £27,000 to £33,000), of the Baptist Irish Society as £2,000, and of the BHMS as only £930, clearly insufficient for effective working. The Society, for all its penury, which continued through many years, was

---

7 D. Lovegrove, *Established Church, Sectarian People: Itinerancy and the Transformation of English Dissent 1780-1830*, 1988, p.164.

8 G. F. Nuttall, 'Assemblies and Associations in Dissent', in *Studies in Church History*, 7, 1971, pp.304-5.

9 F. A. Cox, *Suggestions Designed to Promote the Renewal and Extension of Religion etc.*, Tidball, *op.cit.*, p.11.

careful not to employ men of 'slender abilities', lest 'they impair the cause they were employed to promote.'[10]

That was particularly important in view of the hostility that such activity provoked, especially from the Church of England and its allies, the landlords of rural England. The 'squarsons' and other members of the rural establishment were the more hostile because of the political context in the years that stretched from the revolution in France to the passing of the Reform Bill at home. From time to time there were outbreaks of popular opposition but these had not the consistency or durability of that offered by the Establishment. The Church opposed what it saw as a species of lay evangelism carried out by 'illiterate peasants' and 'mechanics'. The actual range of preachers was more varied: whilst some were laymen, others were settled ministers or specialist agents working well-defined itinerancies, which increasingly became institutionalised. Individual initiatives were now garnered up within the work of the Society which increasingly needed to show results to woo subscribers. As the years passed, preaching tended to move indoors from the open air, with the consequence that chapel building threatened to consume a disproportionate share of available resources. The spontaneity of the 1790s had become routine amongst the Baptists, as amongst others, because of the new pressures of denominationalism. The result was probably more systematic and efficient than the *ad hoc* local and individual action of the earlier period, but has not left evidence of being more effective.[11]

In the conflict between Church and Dissent, focused in the hostility to dissenting itinerancy, two views of English society stood opposed, the one static, closed and established, the other dynamic, open and pluralist. The second emphasis by implication challenged the very being of the former, quite apart from the Jacobin tendencies that conservative clergymen saw lurking behind a public front of evangelistic quietism. The political charges were hard to prove, but as itinerancy succeeded so an increasing number of thriving

---

10 *BM* 1822, pp.468; 1827, p.322.

11 Lovegrove, *op.cit.*, pp.157-61.

congregations across the English counties made the real pluralism of English religious life abundantly clear. All this was the background to Lord Sidmouth's attempts to restrict the Toleration Act by his proposals of 1811 to contain itinerancy. These had been mooted for over a decade and found some echoes in an increasing refusal by some justices to license both preachers and places of worship. Not only did Sidmouth's Bill fail in its objectives, but in the process it created a more aggressive dissent.

For its part Baptist dissent remained both conversionist and, to a degree, revivalist. Dr Cox offered *Suggestions designed to promote the revival and extension of religion* in 1836, whilst J. H. Hinton published *The Means of a Religious Revival* in 1829, and followed it in 1830 with *The Work of the Holy Spirit in Conversion*, and *Individual Effort for the Conversion of Sinners* a year later. Some of Hinton's thinking is distinctly curious and was seen to be so in his own day, but that was a day when these were matters of great concern hotly debated among the faithful. James Belcher combined the enthusiasm of the revivalist with the statistical concerns of the administrator. In an article published in the *Baptist Magazine* for 1832, he analysed the three-fold growth in numbers of Baptists from 1790 to 1832.[12] He himself edited *The Revivalist*, which purported to give news of developments in America as a means of stirring sluggish Calvinist churches in Great Britain into new life. Belcher thus became a publicist for Finney and other revivalists, commending their practice to an English constituency in a state of theological flux.

At the end of this pioneering period, in 1835, Dr Cox, accompanied by Dr James Hoby, both twice presidents of the Baptist Union, visited the States to make an assessment of the quality of American revivalism. Cox's report on that visit became a key document in formulating subsequent home mission policy. He stressed the commitment of church members to work for the conversion, not merely the moral reformation, of others. To secure conversions the enquiry meeting was recommended as an appropriate

---

12 *BM* 1832, pp.303-8. See above, p.255.

technique. Fundamental to the American experience was the need for the work to be supported by groups committed to persistent prayer and, in particular, American revivalists encouraged the formation of maternal associations, charged with interceding for their own families, for the youth of the Christian family, it was argued, should be looked to as a natural source of new disciples. There needed to be a strategic planting of new churches in needy areas, whilst churches should plan their own bifurcation when they reached an appropriate size. The seconding of settled ministers to periods of itinerancy found new support. Finally, local evangelistic campaigns - 'protracted meetings' was their language - were recommended as part of home mission activity.[13]

Encouraged by Cox's support, the Home Missionary Society, under the motto 'Unceasing Conquest', adopted a fairly well-structured revivalist strategy for home mission, which entered its most successful period (1836-41) during the secretaryship of the energetic Charles Roe, son-in-law to William Steadman, and called by Carwardine 'the personification of the revivalist wing of the Baptist denomination'.[14] Aided by the twin threats of 'Infidelity' and 'Popery', Roe increased the income of the Society to £5,000 per annum, with the establishment of many more regional auxiliaries. He directed funds more strategically, withdrawing them from unproductive situations if need be. Effective evangelists like Thomas Pulsford, who passed through the churches 'like a flame of pentecostal fire',[15] were successfully deployed. Though successful in the short term, financial problems in the early 'forties (the watershed, according to Ward, between revival and revivalism[16]), coupled with less encouraging growth statistics (down to only four new members per church in 1846), promoted a reassessment of Home Mission strategy. As a consequence the

---

13 Richard Carwardine, 'The Evangelist System: Charles Roe, Thomas Pulford and the Baptist Home Missionary Society', *BQ* 28, 1980, p.210.

14 *ibid.*, p.212.

15 ed. C. E. Shipley, *The Baptists of Yorkshire*, 1912, p.208.

16 W. R. Ward, *Religion and Society in England, 1790-1850*, 1972, p.287.

revivalist approach gave way to a return to the older pattern of village evangelism in neglected areas. Churches ought not, it was argued, to be allowed to develop a dependency upon a succession of revivalists; the local pastor ought to be the proper evangelist. The problem was that once the Society had come to that conclusion it found it difficult to secure support for its separate existence.[17]

Indeed this was near the heart of Baptist difficulties about Home Missions. It was not that Baptists were in any way reluctant to offer support or were unenergetic in promoting such aims; quite the reverse, it was because they saw evangelism as so much the *raison d'être* of the life of the local church, that they were repeatedly uneasy about assigning that task to specialised agencies. Certainly many ministers made their congregations into missionary bases whence to plant new causes in the surrounding districts. The practice was so universal that exemplification is almost invidious. It is clearly seen in Isaiah Birt's ministry in Devonport, or in Isaac Mann's labours at Maze Pond Chapel in London. It can as easily be traced in the evidence of the Religious Census of 1851, where both churches of recent date and cottage meetings give testimony to the urgency of the concern of many a local church. At the same time the local congregation, with its gospel services, baptismal celebrations, tract societies and open-air witness, clearly demonstrated the evangelistic commitment of the members, contrasting sharply with both the non-invitation philosophy of an older Calvinism and the evangelistic impotence of the old General Baptists.

There were, however, areas where the sovereignty or competence of the local church did not obtain; that is why the Home Mission Society was better able to justify its work in areas of sparse rural population. It also for a time turned its energies to work in the centre of cities, again an area where Baptists were willing to admit the difficulty of applying their theology of the local church. Because of this they were prepared to sponsor 'missions', either the proprietaries of particular individuals, or the creatures of some larger autonomous

---

17 Carwardine, *op.cit.*, pp.220-21.

church within the same city. Admitting the difficulty of evangelism amongst working men, the New Connexion of General Baptists sought to deploy the services of Thomas Cooper, the one-time Chartist leader after his second conversion, to work for some months each year as connexional evangelist amongst working men and women. Thus the secular historian records, perhaps in somewhat puzzled tone, that Cooper spent the last thirty years of his life 'preaching the Gospel to all of the earth that he could reach'.[18]

Part of the issue was also the ongoing distinction between revival and revivalism. The Home Missionary Society was born out of the eighteenth-century revival: of that there can be no question. In the relatively short period from 1835-1841 the Society pursued its work by a straightforward adoption of the principles of transatlantic revivalism, but these were already beginning to drag by the opening of the 'forties and were accordingly dropped. Though the routine work of the Home Missionary Society continued through the 'fifties, in the 'sixties, the awakening of 1859 notwithstanding, the Society was struggling, and in 1865 was amalgamated with the Irish Society. The Baptist Society for the Propagation of the Gospel in Ireland, later known as the Baptist Irish Society, had been founded in April 1814 with Joseph Ivimey, the historian, as its first secretary. It established itinerancies in Ireland, supported colporteurs, and set up schools which were pioneering in their use of Gaelic. It supported Baptist witness in Ireland in years of economic depression, though significant growth in that witness only really came after the society had curtailed its work and home mission had become domesticated within the Irish churches.[19] From 1878 the combined Society began to work in ever closer association with the Baptist Union, until in 1882 the society merged with the Union, an amalgamation, it was argued, which would

18 *Minutes of the Ninety-First Annual Association of the New Connexion of General Baptists*, 1860, p.31. *Baptist Union Magazine*, 1892, obituary. G. D. H. Cole, *Chartist Portraits*, 1965.

19 See Joshua Thompson 'Baptists in Ireland 1792-1922: a dimension of protestant dissent', University of Oxford DPhil thesis 1988.

give home mission a more central position in the Union, and the Union a more urgent purpose. Not all Associations accepted this, some showing a distinct local mistrust of central forces; one Association, for example, declared that it would pursue its own strategies 'without reference to any central committee'.

The Home Mission Society may have decided against revivalism as a strategy but that did not prevent Baptist congregations and agencies being greatly affected by the Evangelical Awakening of 1859. Edwin Orr, the historian of that movement, pays tribute to the openness and co-operation of the denomination and sees this as explaining why, in the decade following 1859, the denomination was able to reap the harvest of the movement in increasing membership rolls and new churches established. At the end of the revival decade in 1868 the Home Missionary Society reported that 'not a single church had been without additions'. Moreover Orr also sees revival as in part responsible for the increasing number of churches taking up membership with the Baptist Union in the 'sixties, for unity and mission were seen to belong closely together.[20] In due course Baptists were again to take a leading part in the Moody campaigns in the late 'seventies and in the Torrey-Alexander campaigns at the turn of the century, a reversion once more to revivalist techniques of transatlantic origin, for which Baptists harboured a continuing affection.

The problem for the Home Missionary Society, then, was that it found itself caught between spontaneous revival movements and the basic Baptist belief that the local church, and the churches in their Associations, were supremely the engines of evangelism and, therefore, special agencies and the special techniques of the revivalist were secondary. More than that, there was conflict between churches planted by the society, covetous of their autonomy, and the society's desire to control development from the centre. This point was well made by Spurgeon when he addressed the Annual Meeting of the

---

20 J. Edwin Orr, *The Second Evangelical Awakening in Britain*, 1949, pp.190-92, Appendix B, pp.270-71.

Baptist Home Missionary Society in 1865: 'Much is said about not allowing small churches to be formed where they would not be self-supporting, but the attempts to suppress such modes of action would be more injurious than their permission and if we attempt always to gather up our strength, to centralize it too much, we might perform an act of spiritual suicide in our attempt to make ourselves strong and healthy.'[21]

A second issue of strategy presented itself in the second half of the century when the focus of concern became the great concentrations of unchurched urban masses rather than scattered village labourers. By 1851 44% of the population lived in towns and cities, and by 1881 this was little short of 60%. The *Freeman* in 1856 in an article on 'Evangelization' called for a new radicalism to meet this need: the church needed to go to the people rather than expecting them to come to church.[22] Open-air evangelism was to be energetically undertaken, supplemented by lectures given by ministers in theatres or halls not associated with religion. Thus J. P. Chown lectured in the Temperance Hall in Bradford, whilst Arthur Mursell addressed 7,000 members of the working classes in the Free Trade Hall in Manchester on the subject of 'Fire'. William Brock, the minister of Bloomsbury Chapel, preached at London's first theatre service in 1859. This was held at the Britannia Theatre, Hoxton - in default of Drury Lane which could not be secured because the actors there had objected for fear of converts deserting theatre-going because of their new-found faith, dissenting Puritanism being seen as hostile to the frivolities of theatre-going.[23] Mrs Humphrey Ward, niece of Matthew Arnold who so readily apostrophized the philistinism of provincial dissent in *Culture and Anarchy*, wanting in her novel *Helbeck of Bannisdale* (1898) to describe the austerity of the hero's

---

21 Tidball, *op.cit.*, pp.146-146a.

22 *Freeman*, 21 May 1856, p,279, cited Tidball, *op.cit.*, p.141.

23 C. M. Birrell, *Life of William Brock DD*, 1878, pp.225-7, cited in Faith Bowers, 'Bloomsbury Chapel 1848-1905', University of London MPhil thesis, 1984, p.113.

Jesuit-like way of life, writes, 'on the subject of balls and theatres he spoke sometimes with a severity no member of the Metropolitan Tabernacle would have outdone'.[24]

Hugh Stowell Brown launched out in the Concert Hall in Liverpool, speaking of 'the great Teacher and what he taught', and continued his annual series through to 1863. The ostensible reason for giving up was overwork, but Brown confessed a deeper cause for concern - namely, that such series seemed to sanctify a separation of classes rather than a drawing together of 'rich and poor' in 'the House of the Lord', where if necessary the style of sermon should be adapted to making working people 'feel that they are really welcome to God's house . . . Churches and chapels filled with people of all classes, and wherein distinctions of social rank should be forgotten would be far better than churches and chapels half-filled with the wealthier sort and halls and theatres crowded with working people'.[25] That was a proper theological objection, which was undergirded by the fact that theatre services had not bridged the gap between church and community but were only successful in so far as they were allowed to be an end in themselves.

There was no shortage of continuing concern for home mission - nor of strategies or papers presenting solutions to such a problem.[26] But the resources to carry out the work beyond the boundaries of the local church remained for the most part inadequate - financing a second-best strategy proved difficult. Spurgeon's commitment, for example, like that of so many, was to evangelism through the local church, though he admitted that the Home Missionary Society was a

---

24 Nelson Library edition, p.284.

25 H. S. Brown, *Autobiography and Commonplace Book*, 1887, p.90, cited I. Sellers, 'Liverpool Nonconformity 1786-1914', University of Keele PhD thesis, 1969.

26 See for example: J. P. Chown, *Church Work in Large Towns*, 1864; J. T. Brown, *Difficulties of the Village Ministry*, 1865; C. Short, *The Means of Overtaking the Religious Destitution of our Large Towns*, 1869; H. M. Bompas, *The Best Means of Evangelizing the Masses*, 1871; and E. G. Gange's Presidential Address, *Evangelistic Work: or a Call to Action*, 1897.

good second best: 'It was a grand thing when Fuller felt that if the Church would not do its work, the work must be undertaken apart from the Church organization, and it is a noble thing that if the Churches will not do their home-mission work there should be a society to take it under its care', but ideally the churches should make the society redundant and by the excellence of their own work provoke its demise.[27] That remained the root of the problem.

Throughout the history of the Home Missionary Society much of the initiative for evangelism had remained with the Associations, though even their commitment was intermittent. For example, the London Baptist Association had to be reformed in 1865 when its predecessor became moribund. Interestingly the *Freeman* notes of this venture, in which Spurgeon took a leading part, that 'the Strict Communion brethren' were very evident but that the basis of the new Association was so broad, 'it does not rest in a creed but simply with wide basis of evangelical sentiment'[*sic*][28]. The new Association set itself deliberate targets, including the opening of 'at least one new chapel each year'[29]. Spurgeon's contribution was highly significant. From a mere 232 at New Park Street, membership at the Metropolitan Tabernacle rose to 5,311, whilst the years 1854 to 1891 witnessed 14,460 baptisms there. In addition to this Spurgeon was instrumental in establishing over two hundred churches in the London area alone.[30]

His influence was more than regional. Whitley in his *Baptists of North West England* says, 'The new life in the south stirred up by the advent of Spurgeon to London had flowered in the Pastors' College and the seed was now being scattered over the north'.[31] J. M. G. Owen, in *Records of An Old Association* pays similar tribute for the

---

27 Cited by Tidball, *op.cit.*, p.158.

28 Cited by W. Y. Fullerton, *C. H. Spurgeon*, 1920, p.309.

29 W. C. Johnson, *Encounter in London*, 1965, p.2.

30 *ibid.*, p.19.

31 W. T. Whitley, *Baptists of North West England*, 1913, p.213.

West Midlands,[32] as the graduands of the Pastors' College entered into pioneering ministries up and down the country.

The Metropolitan Tabernacle sponsored its own set of societal agencies,[33] of which there were so many that Spurgeon once joked that the anniversary of one of them could be celebrated every week in the year. Some had a charitable focus, such as the almshouses, the orphanages, the Ladies Maternal Society and the Ladies Benevolent Society; some were pastoral, such as the Spurgeon Memorial Sermon Society, the Poor Ministers Clothing Society and Mrs Spurgeon's Book Society for Poor Ministers; whilst others were overtly evangelistic such as the Evangelists Association, the County Mission, and the Loan Tract Society. None was more important than the Metropolitan Colportage Association, Spurgeon's own home mission agency founded in 1866, which in the last years of Spurgeon's life employed just under a hundred colporteurs to undertake 'a Protestant, Evangelical, Home Mission Service' by visiting homes, selling the scriptures and other gospel literature and undertaking direct evangelistic work. There was heavy emphasis in the tracts distributed upon combating the errors of Puseyism and hence the Protestant emphasis of the work, which was highly economical: even at the end of the century only £45 p.a. was required from a sponsoring body to support a colporteur, the rest of their support coming from book sales and central funds. Whilst some of these societies were locally confined, others became national in their influence. In addition, the Metropolitan Tabernacle supported some twenty-two satellite mission halls and twenty-seven Sunday and Ragged Schools with over 8,000 scholars enrolled.[34] The Metropolitan Tabernacle was undoubtedly exceptional but it was also an influential model and other central

---

32 J. M. G. Owen, *Records of an Old Association* [the West Midlands Association], 1905, p.62.

33 *C. H. Spurgeon's Autobiography compiled from his diary, letters and records, by his wife and his private secretary*, IV, 1900, chapter 103.

34 *ibid.*, p.321f.; E. W. Hayden, *A Centennial History of Spurgeon's Tabernacle*, 1962, especially chapters 5 to 8.

churches, especially other Tabernacles such as those at Shoreditch and East London, developed similar patterns of work and outreach.

Elsewhere the initiative remained with the Associations. The Northern Association was particularly diligent in its evangelistic work, setting aside men as full-time Association evangelists, who were to be more than colporteurs but were required to resist the affectation of revivalists: in fact they look rather like Association pastors. In 1870 the Association sought funds for the support of two men and was delighted to be able to appoint four. Soon evangelistic outreach was being aided by the activities of Moody and Sankey.[35] This encouraged the Baptist Union in 1880 to commission a number of its leading ministers - Archibald Brown, J. R. Wood, Dr Landels, E. G. Gange, and T. W. Medhurst - to visit up to seventy towns for special missions (which were to be popular, though with care once more to distinguish them from revivalist services).[36] Evangelism remained very much a Union priority with a number of Baptist Union missioners appointed, the most notable of whom was F. C. Spurr who served from 1895-1905. At the same time F. B. Meyer encouraged his fellow Baptists to take part in a Forward Movement, linking together all the Free Churches, which did not compartmentalize evangelism and social concern, making an honest attempt to overcome the individualism of traditional evangelicalism.

Notwithstanding the faltering history of the Home Missionary Society, it has been argued that Baptists showed greater coherence in their approach to evangelism than any other denomination, largely avoiding both the extremes of revivalism and that of losing a concern for the spiritual needs of the individual in a concern for a merely social gospel.[37] By the end of the century, the strategy for evangelism was once more seen to be interdenominational rather than denominational - or at least to be undertaken on a Free-Church-wide basis as a fruit of the newly established National Council of

35 Tidball, *op.cit.*, p.160-2.

36 *Baptist Times*, 12 April 1901, p.291; cited Tidball, *op.cit.*, p.291.

37 Tidball, *op.cit.*, p.171.

Evangelical Free Churches, which sought to celebrate the dawn of the new unity with a simultaneous mission. Of this the *Baptist Times* observed:

> Differences in doctrine, church government, worship, have been lost in the blessed impulse of a Christ-like love for the souls of men. No one has remembered whether he belonged to the right or the left of the army, to the van or the rear guard, but only that he with his brethren was fighting under 'the banner of Christ'.[38]

Meyer, Thomas Spurgeon, Cuff, Clifford, and C. F. Aked, a General Baptist who had been called to the pulpit of Pembroke, Liverpool, were amongst the Baptist missioners taking part. Some small controversy was provoked by the inclusion of Aked.[39] Rather a rarity as a Baptist radical and social gospeller, Aked's *Changing Creeds and Social Struggles*, published in 1893,[40] contained an essay on 'The Gospel for the Day', which *The Christian* found, not surprisingly, doctrinally suspect. Moving dangerously near to Unitarianism, in the second half of the 'nineties he abandoned polemical theology for 'the more profitable task of enthusing his hearers with a passion for the good life: the Cross, as Evangelical critics were quick to note, was conveniently forgotten.'[41] Under Aked's ministry, Pembroke Chapel, Liverpool, had an Indian summer of prosperity, priding itself on carrying the torch for progressive religion in Liverpool with evening congregations little short of two thousand. But it was all froth, for when, to the consternation of his fellow Christian socialists and Fabians, he accepted the pastorate of Fifth Avenue Baptist Church in New York in 1906, his large congregation soon evaporated.

---

38 Cited *ibid.*, p.293.

39 Instead of the Congregationalist, R. F. Horton, whose controversial *Inspiration of the Bible*, appearing in 1888, the second year of the Down Grade, had led to the cancellation of an invitation to address the Assembly of the Baptist Union.

40 See Bebbington, *Evangelicalism*, p.198; Tidball, *op.cit.*, p.292ff.

41 Sellers, *op.cit.*, p.17.

Six years earlier Aked, as a missioner in the Simultaneous Mission, not only called forth comment from *The Christian* but provoked the Evangelical Alliance to question the Free Church Council on the matter, eliciting this defence of their missionary strategy:

> Pre-eminently the mission must be preaching of the gospel. The doctrine of the deity of Jesus Christ, the Saviour of the World, involves both His divine authority to forgive sins and His divine grace in saving; and the faith of this will make the efforts of the Churches powerful and tender. The greatness of Christ's sacrifice, and the reality of His atonement for the sins of the whole world, will prove an appeal to which the hearts and consciences of quickened sinners will respond.[42]

The Christian was satisfied, the Evangelical Alliance welcomed the statement but regretted the absence of a specific disclaiming of Aked's views. This did not seriously impair the harmonic working of the mission, though Archibald Brown opposed his appointment as missioner to Swindon.

That was the exception, elsewhere the Particular Baptists of Cambridgeshire co-operated with other Free Churches for the first time, whilst John Clifford worked harmoniously with Gipsy Smith who also had remarkable success at the Metropolitan Tabernacle. Equally impressive were the great provincial rallies that followed the London campaign. William Angus of Westgate Road Church, Newcastle-upon-Tyne, thought that there had been nothing like it since the time of Moody and Sankey and that in some respects the Simultaneous Mission was more impressive. The effectiveness of the campaign both revealed the power of the Free Churches when acting together and denied the accusation that they only acted together as a political caucus. For all the success, the *Baptist Times*, perhaps unrealistically, lamented that public houses had not been emptied, nor theatres closed, and that the majority of England had been left

42 Tidball, *op.cit.*, pp.293-4.

undisturbed in their indifference.[43] For that, there had, in F. B. Meyer's judgement, to be not only a more effective preaching of the gospel but a more effective living of it by the whole Christian community: the gospel had to be 'incarnated again in our self-sacrificing efforts for the good of the communities in which we dwell.'[44]

At just this time Charles Booth undertook his analysis of the religious influence on London life. Baptists he saw as high in their emphasis upon doctrine, which possibly limited their popular usefulness, and in their understanding of the importance of the local church - 'a Baptist congregation is no fortuitous concourse of individuals'. However, he judged them weak in their ability to foster national organization to pursue home mission, leading to evangelistic strategies which were too local, too *ad hoc* and too individualistic. Booth's often cited comments on the difference between the three main dissenting traditions remains significant:

> . . . While the religious influence of the Congregationalists turns largely on social and educational matters and finds in full and healthy occupation the balance wheel of life; and while the Baptists, filled with conviction of sin, cling to the anchorage of faith; the Wesleyans trust to the heightening of emotion to lift them out of sin and raise their hearts to God.[45]

WORK WITH CHILDREN AND YOUNG PEOPLE

The name of Robert Raikes has always enjoyed pride of place in Sunday School history. Yorkshire Baptists, however, have long revered the initiative of Mr Hudson of Gildersome near Leeds, whom the *Evangelical Magazine* of 1833 credited with anticipating Raikes's

---

43 E. K. H. Jordan, *Free Church Unity: A History of the Free Church Council Movement 1896-1941*, 1956, p.70; Tidball, *op.cit.*, p.303.

44 Tidball, *op.cit.*, pp.309-10.

45 C. Booth, *Life and Labours of the People in London*, 3rd series *Religious Influences*, 7 *Summary*, 1903, pp.137-138.

initiative in Gloucester.[46] It was a Baptist merchant, a deacon of the Prescot Street Church and first Treasurer of the Baptist Home Missionary Society, William Fox, who first conceived of universalizing Raikes's experiment and backing it up with proper national administrative support. This he did through the establishment in 1785 of the Sunday School Society which, it is claimed, for the first time bridged the gap between Church and Dissent and therefore became the model for both the Bible and the Religious Tract Societies. The patronage that Fox secured for the new society clearly indicated his credibility amongst the leading London evangelicals of all denominations.[47] The Society, directed by a committee composed of equal numbers of churchmen and dissenters, worked with the Bible as the only school book, all denominational catechisms being most specifically excluded. The Sunday School Society's usefulness was limited by its initial willingness to pay teachers and provide Bibles, Testaments and other teaching materials for local schools. Funding such commitments inevitably limited expansion until the expedient of gratuitous voluntary teaching was alighted upon.

Sunday Schools were initially just that: schools which took place on Sundays. Whilst conversions may have been hoped for from the very beginning, the immediate concern was to educate children to read and write. Indeed, it is difficult to disentangle the history of early Sunday Schools from chapel-sponsored day schools: so, for example, at Hebden Bridge John Fawcett was engaged in both day school and Sunday School teaching. The social and educational needs of the working-class populations were such as to overcome any conscience as to whether the churches should be engaged in secular education. The conscience that questioned this was a much later development among Baptists.

Two other Baptists, Joseph Fox and William Brodie Gurney, both still young men who had worked together in the Walworth Sunday School founded in 1793, were influential in establishing in 1803 the

46 *Evangelical Magazine*, 1833.

47 J. Ivimey, *Memoir of William Fox Esquire*, 1831; *BM* June 1827, pp.250f.

more long-lived Sunday School Union. At a very early stage Gurney's sister produced teaching materials for use in these schools: the Sunday School was early to provide a locale for women's service to the church. though not without some initial hesitation. In fact, an early prohibition of female attendance at Sunday School Union meetings was successfully challenged by James Upton's grand-daughter.[48]

The Sunday School Union was successful where the Society had failed. Indeed, by the mid-century the Society had become fused with the Union. Initially the Sunday School Union had no written doctrinal basis, though from the beginning there had been a working understanding on fundamental truth, but in 1824 a note was accepted that membership was to be confined to 'such schools only, whose conductors are of orderly character, and who hold the doctrines of the Deity and Atonement of Jesus Christ, the Divine influence of the Holy Spirit, and that all Scripture is given by the inspiration of God'. But that said, the Union worked on the broadest possible basis as one of several agencies of the time by which it was hoped that 'the divisions, heart-burnings and jealousies which have too long prevailed among us, may be brought to a close.'[49]

The Sunday Schools were not without their own sectarianism: when the ministers in Birmingham decided that children should not be allowed to wear Sunday School Jubilee medals at the jubilee service in 1831, the protests of the teachers of the Baptist Sunday School in Bond Street - 'very radical, very democratic, and very lay'[50] - virtually brought the work of the Birmingham Sunday School Union to a halt for a decade or more. The wearing of medals points to the great importance of the material culture of Sunday Schools. The

---

48 W. H. Watson, *The History of the Sunday School Union*, 1853; W. H. Groser, *A Hundred Years Work for the Children: The Centenary Record of the Sunday School Union*, 1903.

49 Watson, *op.cit.*, p.50, 23.

50 P. B. Cliff, *The Rise and Development of the Sunday School Movement in England, 1790-1980*, 1985, pp.110-2.

whole aspect of chapel architecture was radically changed when it became necessary to add school to sanctuary. A school's possession of its own facilities was much to be preferred to, for example, the expediency of the Castle Donnington Baptists who started their Sunday School in the club room of a local public house, where they met until they had raised sufficient funds to erect their own premises.[51] Sunday Schools often commenced their histories in less than ideal premises and only slowly developed the funds to secure purpose-built accommodation, sometimes of considerable size and dignity as, for example, the schools at Ogden and Accrington illustrated in Whitley's *Baptists of North West England*.[52] In due course, the existence of such premises enabled the local congregation to develop a social ministry which ranged beyond the Sunday School. Here was the architectural basis for the growth of the institutional church.

As William Fox soon discovered, Sunday Schools were not without their costs. If labour costs were reduced by gratuitous teaching, premises soon put a premium upon local fund-raising. The Anniversary Sermon was one celebrated way of raising funds, another was the Whitsuntide Walks in the North West, which served a dual purpose of witness and collecting from sympathisers. Expenditure embraced not only buildings and their upkeep but treats, prizes and equipment, together with the stocking of Sunday School libraries: the Wigan Sunday School, for example, boasted a collection of 800 carefully selected volumes.[53] James Hopkinson was librarian of the school at Stoney Street, Nottingham, and used the opportunity personally to read and make notes upon a number of serious volumes.[54] On the income side, Whitley observed that in Lancashire 'the pence once collected from the pupils [for school funds] are being increasingly devoted to such splendid objects as foreign missions',

---

51 Cliff, *op.cit.*, p.98.

52 Whitley, *op.cit.*, pp.273-4.

53 Whitley, *op.cit.*, p.267.

54 J. Hopkinson [1819-94], *Memoirs of a Victorian Cabinet Maker*, (ed. J. B. Goodman), 1968, pp.42-3.

noting that at Haslingden, initially a joint school with the Congregationalists which continued the teaching of secular subjects up to 1870, the change took place in 1873.[55] By contrast, at Sabden they paid children to attend Sunday School.[56] Discipline varied: the children at Cloughfold, made drowsy by the hot stove around which they clustered, were given a pinch of snuff or a sniff at a bottle of smelling salts to revive their interest in the catechism.[57] Only when a scholar could read the Bible was he promoted to the much coveted writing class, where the initial teaching was aided by the use of a sand tray to save costs. At Haslingden the discipline was such as to require the investment of five shillings in straps.[58] At Stoney Street New Connexion Sunday School 'it was no unusual thing for the Superintendent to call a boy out of the class and give him a severe caning'. Hopkinson commented, 'I must say we got better order, but at the same time I must say I never like to see it done in the sunday school'.[59] The same writer tells how in pre-temperance days, the Stoney Street Sunday School celebrated Queen Victoria's coronation:

> A grand dinner was given to the scholars. Two teachers besides myself fixed the tables in the grave yard, by driving short posts into the ground over the graves over which we placed the boards. We had a liberal supply of beef and plumb [*sic*] pudding, and I am sorry to say a quantity of Ale was likewise supplied to the children. The consequence was they became very demonstrative and we could not keep them in order as part of them were intoxicated. It was a sad sight to see such scenes with children of tender years feasting and drinking over the bodies of the dead along with those who ought to have known better.[60]

55 Whitley, *op.cit.*, pp.170, 266.
56 *ibid.*, p.147.
57 *ibid.*, p.266.
58 *ibid.*, p.267.
59 J. Hopkinson, *op.cit.*, p.45.
60 *ibid.*, pp.70-1.

Nationally the Sunday School Union focused on three tasks, the most important of which was acting as a publishing house and distributor of textbooks, teaching aids and magazines, the profits on which largely financed the work. Secondly, the Union sought to provide a professional service to aid teachers better to discharge their functions, by supplying libraries, and by arranging occasions for teachers to discuss their work and the best ways of recruiting and nurturing pupils. Thirdly, the Union acted as a pressure group, opposing, for example, undesirable schemes for national education, seeking to prevent Post Office working on Sundays, and the opening of the Crystal Palace on the Lord's Day.

Care should be taken not to over-emphasize national societies, because essentially the movement was dependent upon local initiatives, and within their localities the effective action was very often taken by men and women of the lower orders for 'the Sunday school from its earliest days was to a large extent a product of the working-class community'.[61] Laqueur summarizes the scale of enrolments by 1851 as being in excess of two million, calculated as 56.5% of those aged 5-16 or 75.4% of the working-class aged 5-16, indicating quite clearly the unabated popularity of Sunday Schools amongst the working classes in the first half of the nineteenth century. Baptists were, however, less involved than other Free Church denominations in this work (Methodists - all varieties - claimed just under 35% of all enrolments; Congregationalists 13.33%, and Baptists only 7.4%).[62]

Denominational authorities easily persuaded themselves that Sunday Schools were efficient recruitment agencies for the church. The requirement that baptism should follow commitment, it was argued, placed a special premium upon Sunday School work amongst Baptists. Thus the history of the West Midlands Association affirms 'it will be admitted by the vast majority of our ministers that the most faithful and useful members of the churches are, as a rule, the men and

61 T. W. Laqueur, *Religion and Respectability: Sunday Schools and Working-Class Culture, 1780-1850*, 1976, pp.28-9, 42.

62 Laqueur, *op.cit.*, p.45-6.

women who have been brought up in the atmosphere and associations of the Sunday School, and whose zeal and loyalty are largely due to the influence and instruction of their teachers.'[63] Whitley interrupts his history of Baptists in the North West to become positively exhortatory: 'If a boy or girl has not decided for Christ before the age of 17, the teacher has missed his greatest opportunity . . . A school which cannot point to a steady annual band of candidates for baptism ought to betake itself to the most earnest examination and prayer'.[64] More recent historians have been highly sceptical of the efficiency of Sunday Schools as church recruitment agencies, suggesting that less than 5% of those enrolled in Sunday Schools ever graduated to church membership.[65] It has, however, also been suggested that relating the ages of Sunday scholars to the age at which church membership could be expected means that a calculation has to be made upon a certain time-lag before ex-Sunday scholars can expect to be found in membership rolls.[66] Negatively, it has been argued that post 1880 a declining demand for Sunday School education, with the provision of a national system of secular education, 'necessarily reduced the growth rate of those churches that had large schools which had provided a significant proportion of juvenile church members'.[67]

That Sunday Schools could be potentially schismatic, that is to say could become separate empires only loosely related to the church, was recognized from a very early juncture.[68] As early as 1832 the Lancashire and Yorkshire Baptist Association Circular Letter, which was prepared by James Lister of Liverpool, complained that Sunday Schools 'have hitherto been too far removed, in most cases, for their efficient control and too little aided by the experience and counsel of

---

63 J. M. G. Owen, *Records of an Old Association*, 1905, p.59.

64 Whitley, *op.cit.*, p.275.

65 Laqueur, *op.cit.*, p.80.

66 Cliff, *op.cit.*, p.124.

67 Currie, Gilbert and Horsley, *Churches and Churchgoers: Patterns of Church Growth in the British Isles since 1700*, 1977, p.88.

68 Laqueur, *op.cit.*, pp.78-9, and *BM* 1833, pp.324-6.

Ministers and Churches'.[69] This judgement was confirmed a generation later by Samuel Green when he testified that 'positive alienation and mistrust are by no means uncommon. The Church is jealous of the School and the School suspicious of the Church . . . Where Sunday Schools are largest the sanctuaries are neglected'. Accordingly Green pleaded with churches to bridge the divide by the cultivation of an evident spirituality and an urgency of concern for the young. The Yorkshire Baptist Association centenary volume paid tribute to a marvellous transformation in relationships, but the problem identified was not always successfully resolved.[70] In other cases, however, the founding of a branch Sunday School soon led to the establishing of a new church.

Publication work led the Sunday School Union to an early involvement in the production of periodical literature for young people, as well as literature for teachers.[71] Unlike the earlier Sunday School Society, the Union encouraged the use of catechisms and made available those of different denominations without underwriting any one in particular. From 1843, however, after a referendum amongst members, denominational catechisms were withdrawn from sale at a time when the growth of Tractarianism within the Church of England provoked greater denominational self-consciousness. Sunday Schools continued to exercise a primitive ecumenism, adding from an early date the international to the interdenominational dimension. This found focus in the first World Sunday School Convention held in 1862. By that time Baptist Sunday Schools were for the most part church-attached and run on denominational lines, rather than the free-standing interdenominational enterprises of the beginning of the century. The adoption of the programme of the International Lessons Committee in 1874 led to a scheme of disciplined home Bible study,

---

69 Whitley, *op.cit.*, p.277.

70 Dr J. Haslam, 'The Yorkshire Baptist Association', in ed. C. E. Shipley, *The Baptists of Yorkshire*, 1912, p.309.

71 *The Youth Magazine* 1805, *Sunday School Children's Repository* 1815, *Sunday School Repository and Teachers' Magazine* 1815 etc.

in 1882 formalized in the International Bible Reading Association.

Domestically, Sunday School work brought chapel folk into close contact with the conditions of working-class life. This is demonstrated by the comments made by the visitors of the Sunday School of the Cannon Street Church in Birmingham. In their Visitors Book reasons are given for scholars' absences:

> 'Bad clothes', 'No clothes', are frequent, as is 'Detained by parents', or 'Detained at the work by the Master'. Then, 'Played truant', 'Very bad, has promised amendment', 'Says he was there', 'Burned his hand', 'Went to his uncle's', 'A degraded character', 'Incorrigibly bad', 'Says he was unwell', 'Mother did not know if he was sent or not', 'Disappointed in his shoes', 'Went to have his hair cut', 'Says he went for a walk', 'Clothes stolen', 'Too much of a gentleman to come'.[72]

Difficult home circumstances virtually limited the visitors to male teachers but as the century went on women were increasingly involved.

Evidence of the consumer's point of view comes from the Children's Employment Commission Report of 1843, where two examples from the dominantly Methodist Staffordshire Potteries reflect on the lives of typical Baptist Sunday scholars. Charles Hopkins, aged twelve, worked at the factory of Thomas Dimmock, a Congregationalist, proprietor of a second-class factory in Hanley described as 'an irregularly developed pot-bank, with poor ill-ventilated, dirty workrooms'. Hopkins confesses, 'Can't read very well; can't write, I go to Sunday School at Baptist chapel and went about four months to British School; learnt nothing else there but reading. I've got a father; he's a collier; he gets work most days in the week, but has got rheumatism now; I come to work about half past five and work for Thomas Chadwick, as a mould carrier; that is, I carry the ware from the moulder to the hot-house, and dry moulds

---

72 Cited in Cliff, *op.cit.*, p.121.

back again and leave work at six o'clock. Thomas Chadwick pays me 2s 6d a week, always regular; he gives me ½d or 1d sometimes when I am a good lad; he gives me a licking sometimes; not very often; and then only when I deserve it.' The overlooker at the factory confirmed Hopkins's report - the boys came at 5.30 to light the fires for the men who came at six. The men rarely worked on Mondays - 'they liked to enjoy themselves', according to the tradition of St Monday, when Monday was treated as a permanent holiday sanctified by the folk Christianity of popular esteem. Because of St Monday sometimes work had to continue late into the evening for orders to be completed later in the week, but in 1843 the factory was only working a five-day week.[73]

Mary Nixon was aged eleven and worked for the Alcocks, who were Anglicans, in their elegant, modern, well-constructed factory in Burslem. She told the commissioners, 'I am a paper cutter for Mary Sergeant; she is employed by Samuel Sergeant, the printer, who is her husband. We have two press men, two girls and four women working with me in the same room. I have been to work three weeks next Tuesday. Can read but cannot write. Went to Day School at Mrs Williams's; go every Sunday to Baptist school. I come to work at half past six, get my dinner in the same room in which I work; never heard bad language there; never hear swearing. I go home at six or half-past six. Work Mondays when there is much to do. Did not work last Monday. Samuel Sergeant is a very good man. I get now 2s a week, shall have 3s soon. I always take it home for my mother. My father is a slip-maker; mother stops at home to look after the young ones. Have two sisters and one brother; one of my sisters is older than I am; she is a transferer'.[74] Such a constituency explains how Sunday Schools swiftly led local congregations into other aspects of care for children and young people.

For the church's own young people a range of societies developed.

---

73 Second Report, Commission on Child Employment, Appendix Part I (431), *House of Commons Papers* 1843 (XIV) Witness 109.

74 *ibid.*, Witness 193.

Early in the nineteenth century there were mutual improvement societies, followed by a series of temperance organizations, especially the Band of Hope, as well as branches of the YMCA and YWCA. Children's Choirs secured high standards of proficiency in singing. Bridging the gap between school and church, the Bible Class fulfilled a critical function. Later in the century came the arguably chauvinistic Boys' Brigade, the more humane Life Brigades for both boys and girls, and after the turn of the century the more informal Boy Scouts and Girl Guides, together with other juvenile and female auxiliaries, and locally organized mutual improvement societies and clubs. The Christian Endeavour movement, imported from the USA in 1888 and heavily influential amongst Baptist churches, put the emphasis upon training young people for active service in the life of the church. Organized in Junior and Senior Sections, members were encouraged to pledge their service to Christ and his Church, such pledges to be renewed at the monthly consecration meeting. In practical terms leadership was developed by setting the the members of the society to work through a series of committees whose tasks varied from helping the aged, through care of sailors to missionary support. With many individuals called upon to convene, to record and report, all were made to develop a sense of self-esteem. Worship too was to be participatory with every encouragement given to sharing in sentence prayers, contributing a solo, or delivering a brief address. In such a way generations of deacons and lay preachers received their training, with loyalty to 'CE' and its ideals finding a high profile in many Baptist churches.[75]

Linking the church to the most destitute youth in the neighbourhood were ragged schools, refuges and reformatories, homes and orphanages. William Quarrier's Homes (1864), Stockwell Orphanage (1866), Brixton Orphanage (1876), and Miss Sharman's Homes at Newington, were all Baptist-promoted ventures. For the most destitute, despairing about the resolution of the problems of the Victorian city, there were the emigration societies, which sought to

---

75 cf. Whitley, *op.cit.*, p.275.

provide a new start overseas in one of the white dominions for those who came from homes all but destroyed by drink. Only the largest churches sponsored such agencies on their own, but vast amounts of Baptist energy - meetings, correspondence, prayers, subscriptions - went into the support of undenominational agencies committed to such purposes.

So far as Sunday Schools themselves were concerned, there was both the contribution of leading Baptists to the leadership of the movement nationally and the omnipresence of the Sunday School as part of the witness of nearly every local congregation. Nationally, founding figures like William Fox and W. B. Gurney were followed by people like W. G. Lewis, minister in Bayswater, to whom is credited the seed of the idea of the Sunday School Examinations that so long flourished as an incentive to disciplined learning within the movement. Started in 1870 for teachers, they were soon extended to embrace scholars. Both Augustus Benham of Bloomsbury and J. G. Tresidder served as secretaries; after the latter, a generous benefactor of the movement, the seaside rest home for lady teachers was named. Serial publications for young people early became an important aspect of the work. W. B. Gurney, at the beginning of the century, was first editor of the Sunday School Union's *The Youth's Magazine*, whilst Samuel Manning, sometime minister at Frome, as Books Editor of the Religious Tract Society in the 1860s promoted the publication of *The Boy's Own Paper*.[76]

An understanding of youth culture was an important aspect of evangelistic strategy. From the prolific pen of Marianne Farningham (Mary Ann Hearn), who also wrote under the pseudonym of Eva Hope, came many books, articles and poems, including the popular children's hymn, 'Just as I am, Thine own to be'. Throughout her life she combined an interest in education with religious journalism, writing for *The Christian World* from its inception for half a century. For six years she was headmistress of the infants' department of the British School in Northampton, and from 1867-1901 ran the College

76 Watson and Groser, *op.cit.*

Street Chapel Girls' Bible Class. In fact it was this that kept her living in Northampton when editorship of *The Sunday School Times* from 1885 might have enticed her to London. In the same year she also became an early female member of the Northampton School Board. All this was achieved by a woman whose cultural background was a deprived rural home in North West Kent and whose only education was that afforded in the Eynsford Baptist Sunday School and the British School it sponsored.[77]

COMPASSION AND PHILANTHROPY

Philanthropy could not be confined to the young, however seriously their plight might be taken. The obligation of Christian conscience to aid the destitute and disadvantaged of every age weighed heavily on the consciousness of nineteenth-century Baptists, leading them to become active both locally and nationally in the causes of amelioration and redress. Since anonymity is desirably associated with charitable giving, the tracing of benevolence by the historian is particularly difficult. Nevertheless, the evidence is sufficient to suggest princely giving by those who prospered in business and commerce, as well as those who were municipally involved or represented their constituencies at Westminster.[78] Others of lesser means responded equally handsomely to distress: Joseph Harbottle of Accrington was not the only minister to hire a donkey to distribute goods and clothes to distressed mill hands during slumps in the Lancashire cotton industry.[79]

Others threw their lot in with specialized agencies of an interdenominational kind. In addition to his work for Sunday Schools and overseas missions, W. B. Gurney was one of the founders in 1807

77 M. Farningham, *A Kentish Childhood: Chapters from the Life of Marianne Farningham*, edited and introduced by S. B. Black, Sevenoaks 1988.

78 For some examples, see this author's entries on Sir George Goodman and John Candlish as MPs, and Eleanor Coade and Richard Harris along with many others in the forthcoming *Blackwell's Dictionary of Evangelical Biography*, ed. D. M. Lewis.

79 *BH* 1865, obituary.

of the London Female Penitentiary, frequently conducting worship there, and involving other Baptists in the venture. Joseph Fox, in addition to his concern for day schools, was also a founding secretary to the London Society for Promoting Christianity among the Jews, serving from 1807 until dissenters were excluded from its management in 1815. Joseph Kinghorn was also interested in this society and helped under its aegis with the publication of modern Jewish scriptures.

L. J. Abington, a deacon of the historic Little Wild Street Church in London, moved to Staffordshire to work in the pottery industry and swiftly became involved in the Anti-Truck movement, which sought legislative constraint against paying workers in useless chattels. He was also active in the Society for the Diffusion of Useful Knowledge, as serving the interests of British industry in creating well-informed cohorts of intelligent artisans. These he saw as all of a piece with his interest in the work of the Religious Tract Society, the Bible Society and the Evangelical Alliance.[80]

William Angas of Newcastle-upon-Tyne, who after service in the navy became a member of John Rippon's Carter Lane congregation in London, not only canvassed the interests of the Baptist Missionary Society among Dutch Mennonites but made a major contribution to establishing evangelistic and welfare agencies for work amongst sailors, securing Dr Rippon's support for such work.[81] In this work 'Boatswain Smith', who had also seen service in the Napoleonic Wars, combined mission work amongst sailors with his pastorates of Baptist churches at Devonport and Penzance, having served for the last two years of the Napoleonic Wars as a voluntary chaplain to British troops in Spain. He has been credited with achieving amongst British seamen 'one of the greatest reformations England ever saw'.[82]

80 *Personal recollections of L. J. Abington, with Memoir etc.*, Hanley 1868.

81 F. A. Cox, *Life of W. H. Angas*, 1834; *BM* 1832, obituary; and D. M. Lewis, *op.cit.*

82 *DNB*; K. Heasman, *Evangelicals in Action*, 1962, chapter 14; D. M. Lewis, *op.cit.*

Whilst his principal concern was evangelistic, he did not neglect the material welfare of seamen and their dependants, founding hostels, orphanages, Seamen's Bethels, and a system whereby men could remit nominated sums to their families.

The same conviction motivated a number of London pastors who reached out from their church centres to the needy districts surrounding them. Of Archibald Brown at East London Tabernacle, Carlile wrote, 'A Conservative by training and conviction, he was a Socialist by instinct and practice'.[83] In his congregation were to be found the leaders of Orsman's Golden Lane Mission and Mr Hampton's Missions to the Blind. Brock at Bloomsbury, John Clifford at Paddington, William Cuff at Shoreditch, all developed district work of significance. Of John Wilson at Woolwich it was widely said that he had more influence in the Woolwich constituency than any political party.[84]

Such a list, however, does violence to the many equally worthy programmes of compassion that it leaves out. George M'Cree was nicknamed the 'Bishop of St Giles'; 'a man of consecrated common sense', it was said of him that he was 'as popular in the thieves' kitchen as on the temperance platform'.[85] M'Cree may stand as an example of metropolitan philanthropy, pioneering slum work in the heart of London before 'slumming' became popular. Having already worked with William Brock in Norwich, he followed him to London, giving himself to twenty-six years of unstinted compassionate service to the poorest of the poor. He was an ardent teetotaller, concerned for the special needs of London cabmen, and worked with cholera victims. He organized holidays and day excursions for the destitute, befriended prisoners, and acted as almoner in chief of the prosperous Bloomsbury congregation. He worked with William Williams in establishing the National Refuges for Homeless and Destitute Children

---

83 J. C. Carlile, *My Life's Little Day*, 1935, p.33.

84 *ibid.*, p.81.

85 See C. W. McCree, *George Wilson McCree: His life and work, with extracts from his journals*, 1893.

and with E. W. Thomas in working amongst London prostitutes, becoming with Baptist Noel one of the prime movers in the Midnight Meeting Movement, which also secured the support of Brock. This undertook in the 1860s more deliberate rescue work amongst these fallen women, in so doing breaking the 'conspiracy of silence' on this sensitive topic.

Work amongst costermongers, which M'Cree had begun in his Bloomsbury days, was continued when in 1873 he moved south of the Thames to become pastor of Borough Road Chapel in Southwark. Here he opened a mission hall in St George's Market and founded the Southwark Christian Mission Donkey and Barrow Club to help costermongers buy their own cart and donkey. M'Cree was a member of the Mansion House Committee on the Dwellings of the Poor, involved in temperance work through the Band of Hope, the United Kingdom Alliance, the National Temperance League and the London Temperance Hospital, of which he was an Honorary Life Governor. He sat on the Council of the Baptist Union, the Liberation Society and the Peace Society, and all the time was absolutely devoted to pastoral work and mission outreach.

M'Cree was exceptional only in the extent of his commitments: their range demonstrates something of the breadth of Baptist concern in the second half of the nineteenth century. Denominational mission and compassion cannot properly be represented without highlighting such comprehensive involvement in Christian philanthropy and social action. Whilst all these examples come from the capital, similar compassionate concern characterized the working out of the priorities of Christian mission in the newly emerged industrial centres of the north and of midland England.

The turning-point in the early ministry of F. B. Meyer followed D. L. Moody's unexpected visit to York in 1872, when Meyer became the first minister to welcome his British mission. In the process Meyer's own ministry was revolutionised, which was confirmed six years later when he concluded his four-year ministry at Victoria Road, Leicester, in order to secure more liberty in mission and outreach than the deacons there were prepared to allow. From

1881 Melbourne Hall, with a Sunday School of some 2500 children, soon became the centre of a more aggressive missionary strategy, a Forward Movement in the making. Meyer, freed from the ordinary discipline of a traditional pastorate, soon became engaged in prison-gate ministry, seeking to help released prisoners make a new start, unshackled by the downward thrust of strong drink. Rescue work soon led to preventative action - the building of Providence House as a home for young men in danger of drifting into the criminal life. To provide them with employment Meyer himself set up in business as a timber merchant to help them chop wood and sell it in the market, to which he soon added a Window Cleaning Brigade, and Christmas Meals for the Needy.

Such social involvement lived alongside his involvement in the Keswick movement's search for a deeper spirituality from 1887 onwards, when Meyer gave his first Keswick address. Meyer found such satisfaction in his involvement that he wrote to *The Baptist* inviting other Baptist ministers to commit themselves to praying early each Sunday morning 'to seek a fuller enduement of the power of the Holy Spirit for themselves and their brethren', out of which was born the Baptist Ministers' Prayer Union.[86] He was also the genius behind the birth of the Baptist deaconess order, which equipped and trained women to give leadership to the churches to engage with the social problems, particularly the absence of medical care, in the inner city. He saw this as an essential part of the Forward Movement which he encouraged Baptists to enter into as the nineteenth-century drew to its close. He also played a large part in transforming the disparate energies of the old Pleasant Sunday Afternoons for working men into the more purposeful Brotherhood movement, and in like fashion the old Pleasant Tuesday Evenings into the Sisterhood organization.[87]

---

86 W. Y. Fullerton, *F. B. Meyer*, second edition, c.1930.

87 Fullerton, *F. B. Meyer*, p.67.

BEYOND PHILANTHROPY

A further exemplar of Baptist philanthropy was J. C. Carlile, who in the early 1880s was sent by Spurgeon, whilst completing his pastoral training at Pastors' College, to work with a poor congregation at Dockhead, between Bermondsey and Rotherhithe, where he was joined later by two deaconesses sent by F. B. Meyer to care for the sick and feed the hungry. When at the end of a meal a six-year-old girl replied to the information that the food was all gone, with the request 'Can't I lick the plates?', Carlile records, 'That made me a social rebel. "Can't I lick the plates?" A little child with under-nourished body and hungry eyes wanting food in what was then the richest city in the world. Socialism may be a reaction without any reference to economic theory.' Carlile testifies to the support he received from Spurgeon, though the latter was concerned about his 'social propaganda'.[88]

One of Spurgeon's friends, Samuel Barrow, a Baptist, was a local leather factor, heading the firm of Barrow Brothers. With little education but great determination, an archetypal self-help figure, there was in Carlile's judgement 'scarcely any good work which was not indebted to him'.[89] Carlile tells of Barrow's concern for the families of his men when they were on strike and how he got Carlile to set up a relief fund which actually enabled them to continue the strike but kept their families from distress, the sole donor to this fund being Barrow himself. Soon Carlile was to become involved in the much more significant Dockers' Strike of 1889. Having a number of dockers in his congregation, Carlile became one of the representatives of the men on the South Bank of the Thames. He shared in the leadership of the Relief Committee, which embraced representatives of the churches and of labour organizations, so vital both to the survival of the men's families and thus their ability to continue the strike. He also at this time became a Trustee of the Dockers' Union,

---

88 Carlile, *op.cit.*, p.74.

89 Carlile, *op.cit.*, p.83.

a branch of which was named after him. The achievements of the strike in Carlile's view were not so much the monetary reward as the abolition of the old system of sub-contracting. Later Carlile was to find in Baptist village manses a poverty comparable to that he came across in South London and which, he was convinced, argued the need for the denomination to take proper care of its own pastors and their families, by making provision for minimum stipends and family support when pastors died in service.

As Jeffrey Cox clearly indicates, for some a centre of philanthropy was not enough: 'The Nonconformist Conscience compelled some chapel people to go beyond "mere philanthropy" to what they called social reform, to insist upon a regeneration of British society through positive voluntary and legislative action which would guarantee fairness and justice for everyone in England, rich or poor.'[90] J. T. Wigner, as president of the Baptist Union in 1899, addressing the Assembly on 'Christian Citizenship', argued the interrelationship of personal salvation and social responsibility:

> God forbid that any of us should put the doctrine of the Cross into the background; but are we not under obligations to proclaim also the lessons of the 'Sermon on the Mount', carry them into daily practice, and to let these toilers know that we drink into the Spirit of Him who said 'as ye would that men should do to you, do ye even so to them'? It surely cannot be that our 'Father in Heaven' wills, that in a land enriched by His constant bounty, thousands of honest toilers and their dependants should be starving, whilst yet working . . . [91]

That meant extending philanthropy into political involvement. A

---

90 Jeffrey Cox, *The English Churches in a Secular Society: Lambeth 1870-1930*, 1982, p.154.

91 J. T. Wigner, 'Christian Citizenship', *BH* 1890, p.54, cited by Philip R. Hart, 'The Social Conscience of English Baptists in the later Nineteenth Century with special reference to the work of Dr John Clifford', Edinburgh PhD thesis, 1962, p.106. I am indebted to Professor Hart for a number of references which appear on the next three pages.

man as pietistic and unsectarian as F. B. Meyer defended political engagement in all causes making 'for the betterment of the people', and himself co-operated with the Congregationalist, J. B. Paton, in 1895 in the Christian Union for Social Service, which established a farm colony for the unemployed at Lingfield in Surrey.[92]

Others went much further. John Clifford, who had been proposed for membership of the Fabians by George Bernard Shaw and Percy Dearmer, was the author of several of their tracts. He was a founder of a series of Christian organizations for active social engagement. An interdenominational body called 'The Ministers' Union' was founded in March 1893 to bring together 'ministers who feel that the Gospel has a Social message today', with Clifford as first chairman. A year later this became the Christian Socialist League again with Clifford as its first president. Its stance was exhibited in the declaration:

> This country cannot accurately be called Christian so long as the people in their collective arrangements practically deny the fatherhood of God and the brotherhood of men. The members of the Christian Socialist League believe that the principles of Jesus Christ are directly applicable to all social and economic questions, and that such application to the conditions of the times demand the reconstruction of society upon a basis of association and fraternity.[93]

At the end of the century the League changed its name again and became the Christian Social Brotherhood with a more exclusively Free-Church orientation.[94]

Some clearly were hesitant about moving beyond the ambulance work of philanthropy into the political implications of preventing destitution and deprivation through seeking a structural change within

---

92 Hart, *op.cit.*, pp.109-10.

93 J. Clifford, *Socialism and Personal Character*, c.1894, p.2, cited Hart, *op.cit.*, p.106.

94 Carlile, op.cit., pp.48-54.

society.[95] This was, by the beginning of the twentieth century, the more difficult because of the spread of Baptist political support between all three political parties, making the particularisation of remedies in practical programmatic terms that could be enunciated in the pulpit much more difficult than in the heyday of the Nonconformist-Liberal alliance, when a simple equation of church and political affections made political involvement comparatively easy.

A further remedy for social inequality was found in schemes for co-operative manufacture, which were championed by John Clifford and found tangible expression in several schemes pioneered by Baptist employers. As early as 1872 the *Freeman* had endorsed the idea of profit-sharing and industrial partnership.[96] In 1888 T. W. Bushill, managing director of Thomas Bushill and Sons, Coventry, publishers and boxmakers, and a pillar of the Queen's Road Chapel, initiated a profit-sharing scheme within the company, which far from diminishing the company's profitability in fact increased it. In 1889 the Baptist Union invited him to address its assembly on 'The Relationship of Employer and Employed in the Light of the Social Gospel'. He also gave evidence to the Royal Commission on Labour in 1892 and the year following published his *Profit-Sharing and the Labour Question*, which was highly commended by John Clifford, especially since it was based upon a successful example. His motivation was clear - without such initiatives he failed to see 'how the average workman had a fair chance of a man's share in life'.[97] By Bushill's system a decent wage was secured, savings were encouraged and a provident scheme was funded. The employees' motivation was increased, and so supervision became less onerous with less time lost to production. Trade Union membership continued but Bushill always aimed at

95 C. T. Bateman, *John Clifford, Free Church Leader and Preacher*, 1904, pp.179-80.

96 *'Notes and Comments'*, Freeman, 1 January 1872; 'Masters and Men', *Freeman*, 12 July 1872.

97 C. Binfield, *Pastors and People: The Biography of a Baptist Church, Queen's Road, Coventry*, Coventry 1984, p.106.

securing for his 250 workers something better than the union-negotiated minima.[98]

Other experiments were made by other Baptist industrialists. Edward Robinson, benefactor of the Baptist Union, the Baptist Missionary Society and Bristol Baptist College, of which he was Treasurer for fifty years, 1885-1935, was Lord Mayor of Bristol in 1908. When in 1885 he became a partner in his father's paper business in Bristol, he instituted a week's paid holiday for the workforce and a pension fund for the old and disabled, adding a profit-sharing plan in 1912.[99] These early examples heralded the later action of Ernest Bader, described as 'the volatile chemical manufacturer and Baptist turned Quaker', who had attended Ferme Park chapel though never a member. Bader became one of the few entrepreneurs ever to give his company, Scott Bader Ltd, which manufactured plastic resin, to his workers.[100]

Other Baptists, however, were less altruistic. David Bebbington notes that Alfred Illingworth was censured in 1894 for provoking his mill girls into strike action by seeking extra work for no addition of pay, whilst even the benevolent Sir George White was criticized by 'the Labour leader' for leading the opposition to a minimum wage in the shoe trade (though he did ensure that strike pay reached the families of his workers).[101]

TEMPERANCE WORK

So active were later nineteenth-century nonconformists in general, and Baptists in particular, in the temperance cause that it is of critical importance to recognize that a widespread identification of Baptists with teetotalism was relatively late and more conspicuously an urban

98 T. W. Bushill, *Profit-Sharing and the Labour Question*, 1893.

99 H. L. Taylor, *Edward Robinson JP*, 1942, p.5.

100 D. J. Jeremy, *Capitalists and Christians: Business Leaders and the Churches in Britain, 1900-1960*, 1990, p.406.

101 D. W. Bebbington, 'The Baptist conscience in the nineteenth century', *BQ*, 34, 1991, p.20.

phenomenon, as the impact of drink in the lives of the industrial poor became more and more apparent. It was intrinsically a social conscience rather than a moralistic peccadillo that aroused nonconformist consciences, with the plight of the drunkard's family the critical motivation. The movement represented a genuine attempt in a drink-sodden society to help the poor, not a conspiratorial attempt to impose middle-class manners on a reluctant working class. To this end the earlier, more aristocratic, anti-spirits movement, with its toleration of fermented but not distilled drinks, was inadequate; only the radicalism of teetotalism could make significant inroads amongst those whose lives were spoiled and destroyed by alcohol. In due course a further development would move on from pressing the need for individual conversion to sobriety to the possibilities of legislative solutions to intemperance in society.[102]

Whilst the corporate conscience of Baptists on the temperance issue was slow to evolve, a number of individual Baptists were involved in pioneering these developments. George Smith of Penzance, Baptist pastor and sailors' friend, is reckoned to have written the first temperance tract, urging the setting up of local temperance societies.[103] When the first society was formed in England, namely the Anti-Spirits Society in Bradford in June 1830, Benjamin Godwin, Baptist pastor and diarist, was reckoned one of its principal supporters.[104] It early appointed James Jackson, Baptist minister in Hebden Bridge, who had previously worked for the British and Foreign Temperance Society, to be its agent. Jackson relentlessly travelled all over the north of England in the cause of moderation and in his first years helped to found twenty-three new societies and pledged over a thousand people to the anti-spirits cause. Two 'powerful lectures' he gave in Preston were instrumental in the founding of the Preston Temperance Society in March 1832, out of

---

102 B. Harrison, *Drink and the Victorians: The Temperance Question in England 1815-1872*, 1971.

103 B. Harrison, *op.cit.*, p.102.

104 Dawson Burns, *Temperance History*, 2 volumes, 1889, I, p.42.

which emerged the more radical teetotal pledge in August.[105] In these Joseph Livesey, 'one of the Seven Men of Preston', played a conspicuous part. A self-educated hand-loom weaver, he was an active campaigner against both the new Poor Law and the Corn Laws. He threw in his lot with the Baptists, although attracted by the Quakers and opposed to all sectarianism; he was anxious that the temperance movement should not become the prisoner of the churches but be established in society at large. Early orphaned, he wished to improve himself until he became both a successful cheese factor and a local journalist of shrewdness and ability. He soon turned these gifts to the good of the temperance cause, eventually editing the *Preston Guardian*, the leading North Lancashire weekly newspaper.[106]

Sometimes, however, Baptists were not involved. They seem, for example, not to have taken part in the first Exeter Hall Conference of the London Temperance Society, founded in June 1831, for Dawson Burns, Baptist pastor and temperance historian, would not have omitted them when he so clearly identified Anglicans, Congregationalists, Presbyterians and Quakers.[107] Outside London, the contribution of the Revd Owen Clarke, a Baptist minister from Bath, was, in Burns's judgement, less than helpful. In 1834 Clarke was appointed an agent of the anti-spirits British and Foreign Temperance Society, a year later becoming their energetic travelling secretary, but unfortunately 'he at length opposed the advocacy of Total Abstinence in a manner which excited angry controversy without aiding the object of his own society.' In 1840 he became its secretary, serving until 1848, two years before the demise of this increasingly obsolete body.[108]

Other early temperance pioneers included Francis Beardsall, the

---

105 Harrison, *op.cit.*, p.120.

106 Harrison, *op.cit.*, *passim*. A. C. Underwood, *A History of the English Baptists*, 1947. pp.238-9.

107 Dawson Burns, op.cit., *I, pp.53-4.*

108 Dawson Burns, *op.cit.*, pp.76, 87, 103, 126, 324, 433.

son of an inn-keeper who drank to excess. He became a New Connexion minister serving in the East Midlands and Manchester, where he early encountered the consequences of excessive drinking. Convinced that the wine of the New Testament was unfermented - the subject of many lectures - he campaigned against the use of alcohol in the communion service and himself manufactured non-fermented grape juice for this purpose. He also edited the *Temperance Star*, produced the first temperance hymn-book, and was a strong advocate of the identification of temperance work with Christian principles. Unfortunately he died at sea *en route* to start a new life in America, 'that land of liberty . . . where his mind would not be pained by a people's suffering the results of heartless oppression'. Beardsall's advocacy of non-fermented wine was to have considerable success.[109] By the beginning of the twentieth century 2,077 out of some 2,900 Baptist churches indicated that they had abandoned fermented wine in their celebration, which probably indicates a near universal change.[110]

Jabez Tunnicliff, another New Connexion minister, was one of the founders of the Band of Hope, the children's temperance organization, in Leeds in 1847. Tunnicliff himself served as first president of an organization that proved immediately successful. A national organization, the Band of Hope Union, was soon needed; George M'Cree became Honorary Secretary from 1862 and salaried secretary for ten years from 1865, the period of the movement's most rapid growth. By the end of the nineteenth century it had some three million members, with 2,037 branches in Baptist churches by 1904. A ubiquitous instrument for inculcating nonconformist culture amongst the young, it developed its own distinctive methodology of teetotal catechisms, periodical and pictorial literature, special music, parades, concerts and rallies, mixing together educational and recreational

109 *BH* 1843, p.20.

110 *Payne,* Baptist Union, p.165.

activities.[111] Both Spurgeon's sons, it was noted in 1862, had joined the Metropolitan Tabernacle Band.[112]

It was in the interests of the temperance movement that Thomas Cook organized his first railway excursion in 1841. This identifies another aspect of the temperance story, namely the early realization that temperance had to offer an alternative cultural experience to the drink-focused leisure world of the public house.

From this consciousness arose the distinctive nature of 'chapel', quite unlike its eighteenth-century predecessors with their confined religious agenda. 'Chapel' now came to be an organization offering a complete educational and leisure programme, especially for the adolescent, through the instrumentality of what came to be known as the institutional church.[113] Thomas Cook found his first employment with Joseph Winks, a New Connexion pastor-publisher in Leicester. At the age of twenty, Cook was appointed General Baptist missionary to the County of Rutland, where in a single year he travelled about 2,700 miles, mostly on foot. Converted to the temperance cause by Father Mathew (the Irish Catholic of whom he wrote a brief biography), he founded the *Children's Temperance Magazine* in 1840. He was greatly ahead of his time in being equally opposed to smoking, but his periodical, *The Anti-Smoker*, made little impact even amongst Baptists and their ministers in this period. When he gave up his wood-turning business for the potentially more lucrative business of travel-facilitator, his wife opened a temperance hotel in Leicester. In 1851 he was appointed the travel secretary to the committee arranging temperance events in connection with the Great Exhibition, and secured special arrangements for teetotallers visiting the Crystal Palace. He also made sure that temperance accommodation was available for visitors at the newly founded

---

111 H. Marles, *The Life and Labours of Jabez Tunnicliff*, 1865; L. L. Shihan, *Crusade against Drink in Victorian England*, 1988, pp.134-55.

112 Dawson Burns, op.cit., *II, p.51.*

113 K. Young, *Chapel: the joyful days and prayerful nights of the Nonconformists in their heyday, c.1850-1950*, 1972.

International House.[114]

Jabez Burns, minister of the New Connexion Church meeting in Church Street, Marylebone, claimed to be the first to advocate temperance principles from a London pulpit, himself signing the pledge as early as May 1836. Daniel Katterns, F. A. Cox's co-pastor and successor at Hackney, undertook temperance work amongst the brick workers of West Drayton in the early 1840s. Charles Stovel, strict-communionist minister of London's oldest Baptist church, confidant of William Knibb, and President of the Baptist Union in 1862, became a Vice-President of the newly formed British and Foreign Society for the Suppression of Intemperance ('The Suppression Society'), and spoke at the first meeting of the National Temperance Society two years later. Isaac Doxsey, minister in Thame and called by Carlile 'a strongly radical reformer', became its Secretary and edited its journal, the *National Temperance Chronicle*. He was one of those who soon realized that the anti-spirits position was inadequate.[115]

Jabez and Dawson Burns - father and son - were perhaps the most tireless Baptist ministers in devoting themselves to every aspect of advocacy. Jabez Burns, only the second New Connexion minister to be called to the chair of the Baptist Union in 1850, was a frequent temperance lecturer and preacher both in this country and overseas. A fluent editor and author, and the principal organizer of the World Temperance Convocation which met in London in 1846, in 1847 he was involved in ensuring that temperance appeared on the agenda of the Evangelical Alliance in orderly fashion. Dawson Burns published his first temperance article at the age of twelve; at the age of seventeen was Assistant Secretary of the National Temperance Society and a year later its Secretary, a task he combined with the editorship of the *Temperance Chronicle*. In 1853 he helped to found the United Kingdom Alliance and served for over a quarter of a century as its Metropolitan Superintendent, and subsequently as one of the first

---

114 Dawson Burns, *op.cit.*, I, p.337.

115 *BH* 1900, obituary; and this author's entry in D. M. Lewis, *op.cit.*

historians of the temperance movement. A master of statistics, he was a formidable organizer of petitions and pressure-group politics: he was frequently to be found addressing the Social Science Association. Mrs Dawson Burns was equally active in women's temperance organizations.[116]

Closely associated with the Burns in their work were J. H. Hinton, George M'Cree and Spurgeon (who with his officers frequently made the Metropolitan Tabernacle available for temperance events). Spurgeon signed the teetotal pledge on 13 March 1866 but later under medical advice resumed the consumption of alcohol.[117] Other Baptists exercising leadership in the temperance movement were F. W. Newman (the Cardinal's brother, sometime a member of Broadmead, Bristol), J. P. Chown of Bradford and Bloomsbury, Baptist Noel, and W. S. Caine MP, one of the foremost spokesmen on Alliance concerns in the House of Commons, President of both the British Temperance League and the National Temperance Federation, and a member of Myrtle Street Chapel, Liverpool.

The founding of the Alliance was of more than temperance significance to many nonconformists. It heralded the search for a new kind of liberalism - a liberalism of legislative intervention and control rather than one which depended upon the traditional reliance upon the individual decision-making of classic *laissez-faire*, which hitherto, paralleled the independency of classic dissent. Thus, comments Brian Harrison, 'Mid-Victorian nonconformist temperance reformers, like seventeenth-century Calvinists, displayed two largely contradictory tendencies: a militant individualism, which the Liberal party found acceptable; but also an authoritative collectivism which was for many Liberals impossible'.[118]

As late as 1844 Dawson Burns recorded 'progress was made, though but slowly, amongst Christian churches'. Five years earlier in

---

116 *DNB*; *BH* 1877, obituary Jabez Burns; 1910, obituary Dawson Burns; and this author's entry in D. M. Lewis, *op.cit.*

117 Dawson Burns, *op.cit.*, II, p.68.

118 Harrison, *op.cit.*, p.296.

Newcastle upon Tyne a society had been formed linking together Baptists who were committed to the cause. Burns noted this as 'the type of those Denominational Societies which have so greatly assisted the Temperance cause in later years'.[119] For Baptists it was in fact to be almost forty years before a denomination-wide organization was to be established. In 1848 Dawson Burns produced his first census of ministerial commitment: 583 ministers were noted as teetotallers, of whom 87 were Baptists.[120] A second census in 1860 produced 224 Baptist signatures or one-seventh of the ministerial body.[121] The temperance organizations, looking to future success, paid special attention to the nonconformist theological colleges, forming a United Temperance Society of students in all Free Church theological colleges, uniting all of these together in 1856 to ensure that the next generation of ministers were sound in their advocacy of temperance principles, a strategy that by the 1870s was yielding considerable success. In October 1866 a first meeting of some forty to fifty Baptist ministers committed to temperance principles took place during the Baptist Union meetings. Two years later some two hundred ministers at the Bristol Assembly accepted an invitation to breakfast under the chairmanship of E. S. Robinson of Bristol, with Spurgeon, Chown and Clifford all offering addresses. In 1869 Dawson Burns recorded that 'the leading Nonconformist Denominations were now being more avowedly favourable' to the temperance cause, but as yet he was unable to cite any resolution from a Baptist Assembly,[122] though the General Baptist Association had passed a resolution concerning temperance work and the activity of the United Kingdom Alliance to its churches in that year.

In 1870, however, the Baptist Union did pass, with only two dissentients, a resolution in favour of the Permissive Bill, which sought to allow each local council the right to prohibit the sale of

---

119 Dawson Burns, *op.cit.*, I, pp.247, 161.

120 Dawson Burns, *op.cit.*, I, p.302.

121 Dawson Burns, *op.cit.*, *I, pp.443-4.*

122 Dawson Burns, *op.cit.*, II, pp.113-4.

alcohol within its locality. The following year Dr Thomas, president of the Union, argued that strong drink 'was undermining the life of the Church'.[123] In 1873, in parallel to the Congregationalists and Wesleyans, a committee was appointed to prepare a scheme for establishing a Baptist Total Abstinence Association, which was inaugurated the following year. The President was J. S. Wright, the Birmingham button manufacturer, elected in 1880 as Liberal MP for Northampton but dying before taking up his seat, with John Clifford and W. J. Meyers of Bristol as Secretaries. This marks the acceptance of temperance advocacy as an accepted part of Baptist church life. The number of Baptists declaring themselves abstainers was increasing rapidly, with the leadership of the Union frequently addressing the Total Abstinence Association, whose concerns now began to appear on the agendas of regional associations and in denominational journals. Until 1874 the editor of the *Baptist Magazine* had deemed temperance too delicate an issue for discussion in his pages.[124] By the end of the century the membership of the Total Abstinence Association was in the thousands and the society had its own travelling secretary.

But could there be a danger in all this? Was there an element of salvation by works associated with the isolation of this issue and the advocacy of determined action upon it? Certainly some felt the need to stress the priority of basic Christian commitment rather than any commitment to a pattern of behaviour. During this period of growth in the 1870s, the 'Blue Ribbon' movement had become the agency of 'Gospel Temperance', which was a prominent feature of the Moody campaigns. The wearing of the ribbon in public, which was supported by both Spurgeon and F. B. Meyer, signified at once both Christian commitment and the pledge of total abstinence.[125] During the latter's ministry at Christ Church, Westminster Bridge Road, there

---

123 Dawson Burns, *op.cit.*, II, pp.154, 178.

124 Bebbington, *The Nonconformist Conscience: Chapel and Politics 1870-1914*, p.46, citing *BM* 1874, p.359.

125 Heasman, *op.cit.*, p.133.

were two corners in the church illustrating the Blue Ribbon principle: the Teetotal Corner for those who wished to sign pledges and the Consecration Corner for those who wanted to identify their Christian commitment.[126] The Blue Ribbon also points to the importance of the argument from example in temperance work. All behaviour was under constant inspection: the strong were accordingly exhorted to exhibit patterns of self-denial and abstinence for the sake of the weak and those who had not yet developed patterns of self-discipline.

Until the end of the century temperance could prove a divisive issue: John Clifford's early annual sermons in connection with the Praed Street Chapel Total Abstinence Society were openly denounced by other officers of the Christian churches in Paddington.[127] At the opposite extreme there was the danger, not often articulated but nevertheless determining individual behaviour, of making abstinence a condition of church membership. In an article in the *General Baptist Magazine* for 1877 the eminent physician, Dr Benjamin Richardson FRS (later Sir Benjamin Richardson, President of the Medical Society of London for 1868, who was deeply involved in the work of the sanitary section of the work of the Social Science Association, editor of the *Journal of Public Health and Sanitary Review*, and President of the National Temperance Congress, which convened in Chester in 1895), argued for 'A Total Abstinence Church'. Commenting on the inclusion of a temperance meeting as part of the opening ceremonies of the new Westbourne Park Chapel, he said he believed 'it was Dr Clifford's entire aim to bring all who came under his ministration into the ranks of total abstinence from alcohol.' He would, if he could, Dr Richardson was sure, have a total abstinence congregation - and 'if he could attain that wonderful success he would set an example which would be of the most remarkable kind in the midst of the other places of worship and other great congregations of that great metropolis'.[128] Doubtless

126 Fullerton, *F. B. Meyer*, p.111.

127 Marchant, *op.cit.*, p.50.

128 *GBM* December 1877, p.452.

Clifford's interests were in moral suasion rather than legal criteria for church membership, but some danger signs were beginning to show.

Certainly by the end of the century it was no longer a case of the abstaining minister belonging to an angular minority. Most congregations now expected their pastor to reject the use of alcohol, and certainly those who did not would be unwise to give too public an exhibition of the breadth of their conscience. By 1907, 211 out of 214 Baptist theological students were total abstainers.[129] An attempt to have total abstinence declared a qualification for office failed at the Baptist Union autumn assembly in 1897: that it should have been attempted was of itself significant.[130] Reformation concerns with the interaction between faith and works were under threat from the temperance agenda where behavioural requirements seemed to challenge biblical teaching on salvation dependent upon faith alone: the danger was to give hospitality to heretical tendencies to require 'faith and . . . '. Temperance, nearly always interpreted by the end of the century as teetotalism, may well have been a proper Christian response to a particular social problem, but it could not be made either an article of faith or a term of communion.

---

129 Bebbington, *Nonconformist Conscience*, p.46.

130 *ibid.*

10

BAPTISTS AND EDUCATION

Both elementary and secondary education in England was in a parlous state at the end of the eighteenth century. Many of the endowed schools had ceased to fulfil the functions for which they had been created, whilst dame schools often offered little more than child-minding facilities. By default a number of Baptist churches were involved in education, for it was a fairly obvious means of supplementing inadequate ministerial incomes, and continued to offer that opportunity up to the 1870s. Baptists were well aware of the need to take initiatives in this area, with men like John Collett Ryland, John Fawcett (both of whom ran academies), Robert Hall, John Foster, and James Mursell all writing treatises on this topic.[1]

If education was to be extended to the labouring poor, it had to be cheap: this was part of the attraction of Sunday Schools dependent very largely on voluntary labour and of the new day schools established by the non-sectarian British and Foreign School Society and the Anglican National Society, which depended upon the use of senior scholars as monitors to teach younger pupils. Rivalry between church and dissent was to delay the coming of a national system of education in England for at least half a century.

JOSEPH LANCASTER, JOSEPH FOX, AND THE BRITISH AND FOREIGN SCHOOL SOCIETY

Claims as to who first introduced the monitor-system into British education were bitterly contested in the early nineteenth century: was it the Quaker, Joseph Lancaster, or the Anglican, Andrew Bell, who

---

1 The following titles were referred to in G. W. Rusling's unpublished Whitley Lectures of 1974: John Collett Ryland, *An Address to the Ingenuous Youth of Great Britain . . . to which is subjoined a Plan of Education*, 1814 edition; John Fawcett, *The Attention and Compassion due to the Children of the Poor*, 1808; Robert Hall, *Advantages of Knowledge to the Lower Classes*, 1810; John Foster, *Essay on the Evils of Popular Ignorance*, 1820 edition; James P. Mursell, *Letters on Education, its Nature, its Mental Advantages*, 1831.

had previously taught in a military school in Madras?[2] It may well be that Bell first deployed the system in India but that Lancaster, totally ignorant of Bell's endeavours, first introduced the system to England.[3] Significantly, George III gave royal patronage to Lancaster's work and the unsectarian principles that governed it. In 1808 Lancaster's initiatives were formalized in the foundation of the 'Royal Lancastrian Institution for Promoting the Education of the Poor', which later became the British and Foreign School Society. Such a nonconformist initiative provoked alarm in the Church of England which found in Andrew Bell its confessional champion and in the National Society of 1811 its agency for educational development. Direct opposition, the *Edinburgh Review* believed, was initially confined to the hierarchy: as far as general Anglican sentiment was concerned, there was 'rather a want of diligence than good-will until the great exertions of the Dissenters stirred up a corresponding spirit in the Church'.[4] Meanwhile, Anglican opposition to a Society which had received the patronage of the Head of their Church caused some philosophical difficulties. Basically the belated conclusion of churchmen was, as the *Edinburgh Review* expressed it, 'If the poor *must* be educated, let them be educated by the clergy of the Establishment'.[5]

The *Baptist Magazine* marvelled that leading churchmen 'should wage an implacable and relentless war against us teaching poor children to read the Bible'.[6] Lancaster's initiative, it has to be admitted, was not well administered, particularly with regard to finances. A prominent champion and defender of his work against the vituperative attacks of conservative churchmen was Joseph Fox, Baptist surgeon and dentist from Guy's Hospital and a deacon of John

---

2 For a full discussion of the topic see H. S. Skeats and C. S. Miall, *History of the Free Churches of England*, 1891, pp.417-24.

3 *Edinburgh Review*, November 1810, p.67.

4 *Edinburgh Review*, March 1821, p.228.

5 *ibid.*

6 *BM*, 1811, p.117.

Rippon's Carter Lane congregation.[7] Fox came to the aid of the infant society both financially, with a benefaction in excess of £2000, and administratively, accepting office as one of its secretaries until his untimely death at the age of forty in April 1816.[8] Henry Brougham always assigned to Fox 'the first place among those who befriended Lancaster', speaking of him as 'a man in a million'.[9]

Until the 1870 Education Act, the Bible-focused, non-catechetical British and Foreign School Society was to be the major vehicle for Baptist input into secular education, for most Baptists came to eschew denominational day-school education of any kind. However, some conscientious voluntaryists, such as Bloomsbury's William Brock, disapproved of the Society because of its acceptance of government funds. Whilst content to use British Society materials, the Bloomsbury school never affiliated to the Society, and its officers were understandably annoyed when a British Society inspector visited the school uninvited, even though his report was very favourable.[10]

HENRY BROUGHAM'S ENQUIRY AND BILL

In 1816 Parliament established a Select Committee to look into the Education of the Poor in the Metropolis, on the initiative of the liberal-minded Henry Brougham, hitherto seen as a friend of dissent. In 1820 he introduced an Education Bill into the House, but to buy off establishment opposition he proposed that the education should be funded by a rate, with the teachers, appointed on the nomination of the local incumbent, confined to members of the Church of England. To qualify for office they were to take the sacrament prior to their appointment. The education offered, as originally proposed, was not to be credal but rather based upon the Bible, with evening catechisms and requirement for church attendance, except for dissenters

7 Not a Quaker, *pace* Ford K. Brown, *Fathers of the Victorians*, 1961,p.351.

8 *BM* 1816, pp.254-5.

9 C. W. New, *The Life of Henry Brougham to 1830*, 1961, p.203.

10 Faith Bowers, 'Opting out in Victorian London: A school for the respectable poor, 1849-1870', *BQ* 34, 1992, p.242.

conscientiously objecting. Dissenters were bitterly disappointed in the proposals of one they thought to be their friend, and vigorously opposed the Bill, petitioning against it through the Protestant Society and through the General Body of Protestant Dissenting Ministers of the Three Denominations, chaired at that time by Dr Rippon.[11]

Analysis of Baptist objections to the proposed measure makes it quite clear that they believed universal education a goal of great importance, their objection being to the extension of the establishment principle entailed in the mechanisms for creating new schools in Brougham's proposals. In the event it failed to reach the statute book; Baptist hostility was 'not because they disapprove of a National System of Education for the Poor, nor because they object to contribute towards such an object, but because they cannot consent to a *sectarian* and *exclusive mode of education*, though the mode should be the *creed* and *catechism* of the sect which happens to be *endowed* by law'.[12]

THE 1833 AND 1839 GRANTS

In 1833 a reformed parliament decided on a different tack: namely that of offering grants to the two principal voluntary societies providing education for the poor, the grants from a central provision of £20,000 to be available to match funds raised through voluntary agency by these societies. In fact, in the first year the freely-raised sums were twice the capital offered by government funding, yielding £60,000 in all. The difference between the two societies was not precisely church against dissent, but catechetical and credal Anglican education over against unsectarian Bible teaching: the literature of the British and Foreign School Society simply states: 'All they contend for

---

11 For Baptist views on a bill, 'pregnant with danger to Protestant Dissenters', 'the most oppressive measure' since the reign of Queen Anne, see *BM* 1820, pp.340-42; 1821, p.75, 89-94, 118-123, 165-7, 169-70, 245.

12 *BM* 1821, p.121. Creed and catechism were not to be part of day-time education but were to be taught on a Sunday evening only when so desired by the parents. J. Murphy, *Church, State and Schools in Britain, 1800-1870*, 1971, pp.10, 12, 18.

is the great principle of LIBERTY OF CONSCIENCE - the utter abolition of religious tests in connexion with common day school education'. The terms of the 1833 bill confined grants to newly-built day schools and were not available to deal with past debts or provide support for Sunday Schools.[13]

The committee of the British and Foreign School Society, whose views were fully and persuasively reported in the *Baptist Magazine*, pressed its constituency to develop proposals 'believing that there are few towns of any size, in which one or more schools for the instruction of the poor might not be sustained'. It offered down-to-earth practical advice on how to make such proposals, suggesting, for example, the copying of all applications to the Treasury to the Society itself. The strings attached to the grants were minimal - the submission of building accounts and the agreement to report on the work undertaken, especially with details of the numbers of children being educated. If principles had to be established, then the chief criterion laid down was to favour 'large cities and towns in which the necessity of assisting in the erection of schools is most pressing'.[14] Lord John Russell, presiding at the British and Foreign School Society that year, drew attention to the grant and to his own support of the Society, asserting:

> in this country, where religious freedom had so long prevailed, the benefit of education could not be extended generally, if the children sent to the schools were obliged to conform to the principles of the catechism of the Church of England, or the tenets of any particular class of Christians. He thought it unwise, improper, and inconsiderate, when entering upon the great duty of education, to call upon children - whose minds had not yet considered the question, and whose faculties were not able to comprehend it - to bind themselves down to certain creeds which were superinduced, and did not belong to the

13 For a discussion of Baptists and Sunday Schools see chapter 9, 'Mission and Evangelism', pp.308ff.

14 *BM* 1834, pp.298-9.

> teaching of the Holy Scriptures. It was upon that principle that the Society was originally founded, and he trusted that by it it would continue to be conducted, and that it would flourish more and more, until education was placed in that relation to the general population of the empire which it ought justly to sustain.[15]

Although the distribution of funds was initially equitable, it was not long before dissenters, with some justification, were complaining of an undue weight of grants to the established church. In 1839 the educational grant was increased from £20,000 to £30,000 to enable a teacher training institution to be established, the administration now to be through a Committee of the Privy Council. Kay Shuttleworth, himself so vitally involved in the development of British education, recorded of those changes:

> The existence of Lord Melbourne's administration was endangered in 1839 by the attempt to lay the foundations of the education of the people, on the recognition of the equality of their civil rights in matters of religion. The Church was probably less alarmed by the recognition of this civil equality, than by the absence from that scheme of any definition of the limits of civil power. Such definition was then impossible, but its absence aroused the most extravagant terror.[16]

The Church of England, still hankering after a more dominant position in education and alarmed by what it took to be the threats of 1839, petitioned parliament in support of a more deliberate Anglican programme of national education. This the *Baptist Magazine* saw as 'an attempt to revive a long obsolete brand of priestly power, betraying a spirit as arrogant as it is unjust'. The imposition of such principles, it believed, could hardly advance education either - it must

---

15 *ibid.*

16 Sir James Kay Shuttleworth, *Public Education as affected by the Minute of Consent*, 1853, pp.3-4, cited in R. W. Dale, *The History of English Congregationalism*, 1907, p.651.

perpetuate 'popular ignorance, discontent and irreligion'. Public funding should be for 'the advancement of that Secular Education concerning which all are agreed, and not for Education in Religion, on which we are so much divided'.[17] Four years later the denominational voice had changed its tune, for in the 1843 debate the idea of secular education was very deliberately rejected: 'education to be of real value must be religious'.[18]

1843 FACTORY BILL CRISIS[19]

Early in Sir Robert Peel's Tory administration of 1841-6, Lord Ashley (later Lord Shaftesbury) pleaded for government action to deal with the ignorance, immorality and infidelity present among the young in the manufacturing districts of the nation. This provided Sir James Graham, the Home Secretary, with the opportunity of announcing a scheme for the compulsory education of pauper and factory children. He vainly hoped this might secure national support beyond the division of party and creed. The scheme, embraced by the educational clauses of Graham's Factory Bill, involved the public funding of essentially Anglican education - just the kind of scheme that churchmen had proposed against the Whigs' more egalitarian proposals of 1839. New schools to be built were to be funded one third by government grant, one third from the Poor Rates, and one third by voluntary subscription. In addition, the Poor Rates were to be responsible for an element of the ongoing maintenance costs, hence basically denominational schools were to be publicly funded but controlled exclusively by church authorities. The legislation also seemed to debar children in Baptist, Independent and Methodist schools from securing factory employment, unless such schools were

---

17 Resolution of the London Dissenting Ministers meeting 6 March 1840, under the chairmanship of Dr F. A. Cox. *BM* 1840, pp.198-201.

18 See below, p.349.

19 The proposed legislation and dissenting opposition featured prominently throughout the year in the *Baptist Magazine* and can be traced on the following pages, 213-4, 259, 260, 266-7, 271-2, 307-8, 319-20, 374, 380, 520-26.

registered with the British and Foreign School Society.[20] Other objections were made quite clear in the resolution passed by the committee of the Baptist Union in March 1843. In particular, the committee identified the following objectionable features:

> 1. It comprises in one measure, enactments relating to the general regulation of factories, and enactments relating to the education of children, whether employed in factories, or only residing in factory districts; widely dissimilar matters, united in the present instance in a manner calculated to embarrass, and otherwise injuriously to affect the question of education.
>
> 2. It subjects the competency of masters to give religious instruction, in all cases, to the judgement of the bishop of the diocese.
>
> 3. It places the selection of works of religious instruction exclusively in the hands of the clerical trustee of each school - in every case a clergyman of the established church.
>
> 4. It appoints as trustees of each school one clergyman and two church-wardens, with four persons selected by the justice of the division.
>
> 5. It imposes a fresh burden on the poor-rates, and takes from that fund for the support of a system directed to an ecclesiastical purpose, thereby rendering the poor-rate liable to the same objections as the church-rate.
>
> 6. It enforces attendance on the schools inflicting penalties unjust in their principle and severe in their application.

The Baptist Union fiercely objected to the composite nature of the legislation, tacking on to industrial legislation the educational provision, which raised major issues of 'rights of conscience'. It believed that the attempts within the bill to provide for dissenting interests were practically inoperable and that the legislation, therefore, was highly partisan to the interests of the establishment, inculcating

20 Dale, *ibid.* pp.654ff.

'habits of servility and religious thraldom'. It was seen as threatening all private schools and Sunday Schools in particular. To entrust educational authority to the established church at just that moment, when so many of its clergy were capitulating to Catholic error, superstition, and ritual, was the more offensive: the secretaries of the Baptist Union termed the new schools 'high church nurseries', as over against Baptist churches which were themselves seen as 'nurseries of freedom'.[21]

Worse than that, they claimed 'the whole scheme, in fact, is one of church extension - a mode of crushing dissent and putting an end to schism . . . at the expense of the people!' A form of petition was circulated, inviting churches to petition parliament against the proposed legislation, carefully reminding friends that such a petition could be written on ordinary paper and sent through the post without postal charge. The heart of the petition was framed in these words:

> That the educational clauses of this bill appear to your petitioners to violate the principles of civil and religious liberty; gratuitously to injure existing schools supported by voluntary contributions; to place under the absolute and exclusive control of the clergy, the education of the operative classes; and to apply the poor-rates to a purpose essentially ecclesiastical and sectarian.

Amendments to the bill were not enough, even an amended bill with its provision for the appointment of 'literary police', remained offensive. Total rejection was the only solution to this piece of legislation which undid all that was achieved in the 1820s to secure the civil rights of dissenters.[22] Denominational leaders were not slow to follow up the resolutions of the Union itself: the Baptist Board, a number of Associations, and all the principal dissenting societies passed resolutions and sent in petitions. The denominational journals favourably reviewed pamphlets by John Howard Hinton,

21 *BM* 1843, p.271.
22 *BM* 1843, pp.319-20.

Edward Steane and William Brock. Sometimes the argument was allied to a general advocacy of *laissez-faire*. Writing from the West Riding District of the Yorkshire Association, Francis Clowes argued: 'Large classes of the Empire - Roman Catholics, non-intrusionists; chartists, free-traders - are all finding out the great truth, that government has no right to interfere with trade or education, and, least of all, with religion; in short that *protection of life and property* is its only duty'.[23] A review of one of the many pamphlets issued made the same point: 'Furnish the parents with employment and pay them for their labour and they will soon obtain better education for their children than can be communicated by any national or parochial establishments'.[24]

Great had been the threat and great accordingly was the rejoicing when the educational clauses of Graham's Bill were abandoned in the early summer of 1843. The Baptist Union believed some 13,600 petitions (embracing over two million signatures) had been tabled against the original bill, with a further 10,777 sent up against the amended bill. The reasons for the depth of feeling were two-fold. First, the proposals were seen as extending the principle of establishment at a time when the established church was cavorting with a revived catholicism. Secondly, education was construed as a preparation for adult life with a concern for character training, the development of private judgement, and moral and religious discernment. This was far too influential a process to be lightly surrendered to their opponents.

Continual vigilance for the interests of civil and religious liberty remained necessary - but for the moment there was much rejoicing in dissenting Britain with many churches arranging services of thanksgiving. The editor of the *Baptist Magazine*, in his postscript, concluded by agreeing with his church opponents that 'education, to be of real value, must be religious, and therefore Scriptural . . . A merely secular education is not a defective education only; it is an

23 *BM* 1843, pp.271-2.

24 *BM* 1843, p.308.

essentially infidel education'. 'Believing that state machinery is as incompetent for this purpose as it is for the maintenance and promulgation of the Christian faith among adults . . .', he further affirmed, 'we call upon our Christian friends to apply themselves with redoubled vigour to the scriptural education of the children and young people amongst them'.[25] Certainly the confidence of dissent in general, and of Baptists in particular, in voluntary provision was not at this time dented, which presumably explains why otherwise compassionate men and women could cheerfully set on one side the possibility of a national system for the education of the poor.

At the end of the year the Baptist Union Committee sent the following resolutions, which they unanimously agreed, to the churches:

> 1. That this committee, while grateful to an overruling providence for the frustration of the educational scheme developed in the late factories' bill, cannot hesitate to express their conviction that vast as the work of popular education may be, it can be effectually conducted by popular energies; and that it cannot be interfered with by government in any manner, without both injury and danger.
>
> 2. That appreciating the urgency with which the late crisis and its happy issue enforce voluntary efforts for the advancement of popular education, and earnestly desirous that the resources of baptist churches in the united kingdom should be universally and systematically applied to this end, this committee warmly recommend to them a cordial and zealous co-operation in such efforts as may tend to diffuse education on the principles of the British and Foreign School Society, as a course most consistent with catholic principles, and most inducive to the public good.[26]

It glosses the solution with the comment:

25 *BM* 1843, p.380.
26 *BM* 1844, p.30.

In seeking to promote the universal diffusion of education on the British system, it is obvious that a commencement should be made with our own neighbourhood. Accordingly, the first recommendation which the committee would place before the churches is, that each should examine whether the means of general education be deficient in its immediate vicinity. Should so large a deficiency be found to exist as to be incapable of remedy by any practicable enlargement of existing schools, and consequently to require the establishment of a new one, it would then be expedient to solicit a combination of the friends of education of all denominations on the spot, in an effort to institute an adequate British school. In such an attempt aid might be sought from the British and Foreign School Society, if local means were insufficient.

The immediate and surrounding neighbourhood being provided for, a lively sympathy should, of course, be cherished with those parts of the country (unhappily too numerous) for which education must be provided, to a great extent, if not almost wholly, from extrinsic sources; and the efforts which the British and Foreign School Society are making to meet this demand should be cordially aided, whether by individual subscriptions or by congregational collections.

In such a course of exertion as the committee have now briefly sketched, it is evident that the baptist churches would be - not, indeed, using scholastic instruction as a means of sectarian increase - but [*sic*] making an effective and proportionate contribution towards the general education of the people; and, upon mature consideration, the committee recommend it in preference to the plan of denominational action. For the great object in view our brethren everywhere can do something, and something more, perhaps, than has yet been done. Were all to do what they could, an invaluable impulse might be given to the educational machinery which is now at work, and an example might be set at once honourable to the denomination, and influential on the members of other communions.[27]

---

27 *BM* 1844,pp.30-1.

In deciding thus to rally behind the strategies of the British and Foreign School Society, the editor of the *Baptist Magazine* regretted that the Wesleyans who were 'so much accustomed to act apart from other denominations' had decided to promote their own denominational schools. More alarming was the decision of the Congregational Union to follow such an example: 'Had the congregationalists, as a body, rallied cordially with the baptists, the quakers and the friends of education around the British School Society, as the various classes of churchmen have rallied around the National School Society, incalculable good might have been expected . . . Denominational schools are not what the exigencies of the occasion require'.[28]

Baptists had never been much involved in the running of day schools: a census late in 1843 recorded only thirty-five schools, with a further thirty-eight opened thereafter. This was very much fewer than either the Congregationalists or the Methodists, on account of Baptist commitment to work through the British and Foreign School Society.[29] Baptists were not quick to enter private secondary education either, though they did share in a number of general nonconformist ventures such as those at Mill Hill and Taunton, and those functionally-necessary establishments that made special provision for missionaries' children, such as Eltham for boys and Walthamstow Hall for girls. By contrast the Congregationalists, the Quakers, and especially the Methodists set up a considerable number of denominational secondary boarding schools.

There was by 1843 new uncertainty about the receiving of government aid by churches for educational purposes. This was apparently becoming less frequent, now that applications were made direct and not through the British and Foreign School Society. A number of Baptists, however, voiced conscientious objection to the

---

28 *BM* 1844, p.36; and *ibid.*, p.199, for leading Independents challenging the British and Foreign School Society on its premise that denominational action was not the most appropriate response to the post-1843 situation.

29 *Baptist Reporter*, 1844, p.64.

process, which became more acute from the end of 1846 when financial support was extended to salaries and maintenance. Part of the problem was uncertainty amongst dissenters about how best to forward the interests of national education. Edward Baines, the Congregational editor of the *Leeds Mercury*, believed that since education was concerned with minds and morals, it was a religious task and was properly an ecclesiastical function. Accordingly, all state interference in its provision was to be rejected with true education promoted by voluntary effort alone. By contrast, Robert Vaughan, who had recently moved from the Chair of History at University College London to the presidency of Lancashire Independent College, Manchester, did not accept that religion and secular education were inseparable. Accordingly, he used his newly founded and increasingly influential *British Quarterly Review* to campaign for state-funded secular education which alone, he thought, met the scale of national need.

This policy division was to rumble on for almost half a century. The Baptist Union, for example, did not abandon the secular platform until 1888, though Spurgeon carried many Baptist ministers with him when he declared for simple Bible instruction in the middle of the debate upon the 1870 Act.[30]

FORSTER'S EDUCATION ACT, 1870

Education, argues David Bebbington, was the issue that brought nonconformity most prominently into the political arena in the late nineteenth century and early twentieth century.[31] In the ten years following 1843 dissenting voluntaryists built almost 400 schools, yet voluntaryism failed to deliver all that it promised. Whilst Baptists continued to invest in Sunday Schools and to support the British and Foreign School Society, Whitley offers the summary judgement that 'their doings were quite out of proportion to the need', noting that

30 M. Cruickshank, *Church and State in English Education, 1870 to the Present Day*, 1964, pp.26, 59.

31 D. W. Bebbington, *The Nonconformist Conscience*, 1982, p.127.

'within the educational debate at every stage Free Church statesmen were more alert to oppose Anglican domination than to evolve a constructive policy', even though men like Dr Angus played an honourable part in formulating the new syllabus of Bible-teaching.[32] The problem was compounded by the fact that by 1870 the misplaced belief that all but a small minority of parents were capable of paying school fees had been exploded by enquiries in larger cities: even Edward Baines admitted defeat and spoke of 'retreating before irresistible numbers'. Population growth, population movement, and the needs especially of the working-class districts all demanded more strategic action.[33]

In dissenting minds the immediate context for W. E. Forster's[34] Education Act of 1870 was the prior legislation abolishing Church Rates in 1868 and disestablishing the Anglican Church in Ireland in 1869, both welcomed as curtailments of the influence of the establishment. By contrast, church education on the rates was seen as an extension of the establishment principle: were church rates to be abolished only to see their return in another guise as educational rates in support of church schools? There was, however, much in the Act to welcome. The provision that the form of religious education in Board Schools, which were to be publicly funded, should be unsectarian was gained by the Cowper-Temple amendment. A 'conscience-clause' in aid of dissenting parents and their offspring was to operate especially in single-school areas (normally rural areas with only an Anglican school). School Boards were to provide democratic control by representatives, who could be female. Where, after a period of grace, gaps were still left by the inadequacies of voluntary provision, Board Schools were to fill them, thus setting up the dual system of church and board schools.

---

32 W. T. Whitley, *History of British Baptists*, 1923, pp.324-5.

33 E. Baines, *National Education: Address . . . at Manchester*, 1867, pp.3-8, cited Murphy, *op.cit.*, p.47.

34 W. E. Forster was of Quaker stock and buried as a Quaker. Skeats and Miall, *op.cit.*, p.723.

Exchequer grants by way of a capitation fee to denominational schools were maintained and in fact increased, though building grants came to an end. Nonconformists raised objections to the provision of clause twenty-five that children in poor-law institutions should be sent to school as a charge on the rates. The numbers involved were minimal but the principle was seen to be crucial, and led to estrangement between nonconformity and the Liberal Party: 'The school rate becomes the successor of the church rate', charged the *Baptist Magazine*.[35] Clause twenty-five was abolished in 1876 when a conservative government made education compulsory in many parts of the country. By then most dissenters had become firm supporters of the School Boards and the non-sectarian Bible education they provided, which seemed the natural legatee of the work of the British and Foreign School Society.

Spurgeon deserted an earlier voluntaryism in favour of the Board system which alone seemed to meet the scale of the need of urban England. This was symbolized by his campaigning for W. R. Selway, a tutor at Pastors' College, for election to the London School Board. As late as 1887 Charles Williams admitted that, whilst in theory Baptists might prefer a secular system, in practice they gave their support to the Board Schools and their unsectarian teaching.[36] Beyond that Dr Angus had laid down for London the principle on which such instruction should be developed: teachers were to read the Bible 'with such explanations and such instruction therefrom in the principles of Morality and Religion as are suited to the capacities of the children'.[37]

While most Baptists accommodated themselves relatively easily to the new situation that developed under the School Boards from 1874

---

35 *BM* 1873, p.591.

36 *Third Report of the Royal Commission appointed to inquire into the working of the Elementary Education Acts, England and Wales*, 1887, XXX.1.p.86, cited Bebbington, *Nonconformist Conscience*, p.132.

37 H. B. Philpott, *London at School: The Story of the School Board, 1870-1904*, 1904, p.100, cited Bebbington, *Nonconformist Conscience*, p.132.

onwards, some, like Arthur Illingworth, MP, Treasurer of the Liberation Society, maintained an absolute position of hostility to public support for denominational schools regardless of the educational cost in delaying the coming of free education for all. Practical grievances continued in single area schools, nonconformity responding protestantly to every indication of High Church influence within Anglican schools. An additional grievance was that, whilst the state paid 95% of the costs of teacher training, only 20% of places available were such as nonconformists would compete for without confessional difficulties.

This led to division in local communities with the Anglicans rallying around Moderate candidates in School Board elections and nonconformists around the Progressives. Naturally the Tories in power looked for mechanisms to aid increasingly impoverished denominational schools. Proposals along these lines led John Clifford to believe that the government was intent on pouring half a million pounds into priestly pockets: 'If the sons of Hampden and Cromwell are going to submit to this,' he asserted, 'then we may say farewell to Britain's supremacy in commerce, in love of justice and in religion'.[38] Clifford was insistent that 'State education is from first to last a question of citizenship and not of Churchmanship and creed'.[39] Because of such opposition, government proposals were for the moment abandoned.

In 1902 A. J. Balfour brought forward new proposals to charge the support of the voluntary schools to the rates, a policy which John Clifford characterized as one 'which threatens to kill democratic control of education, increase educational inefficiency, add to the State endowments of sectarianism and fix more securely than ever the tyrannies of the State Church over the life of the land'.[40] Notwithstanding Clifford's furious campaign - in the press, on the hustings, and in many a public meeting - the legislation was passed

---

38 J. Marchant, *Dr John Clifford*, 1924, p.120.

39 *ibid.*, p.120.

40 *ibid.*, p.122.

and implemented, thus giving birth to the Passive Resistance movement, which John Clifford championed with all the force of his personality and oratory, supported by others such as George White, President of the Baptist Union in 1903 and Liberal MP for Norwich, a keen advocate of the Passive Resistance principle and of defiance through the withholding of the payment of rates. The editor of the Passive Resistance monthly, the *Crusader*, was Edmonds Sears of Esher Baptist Church. He was the nephew of J. Edward Sears, also a Baptist, who served on the Hendon School Board from 1898-1901 and sat on the London County Council from 1901-7, winning Cheltenham for the Liberal Party in the 1906 election.[41]

By February 1907 a survey of 190 Passive Resisters sent to prison showed that the Primitive Methodists provided 60, Baptists 48, Congregationalists 40, and Wesleyans 15, with the remaining 27 coming from smaller denominations.[42] Munson, however, judges that in the Passive Resistance Movement, it was 'the Baptists, for whom at the turn of the century the outlook was "full of hope" and who were arguably the most active Nonconformist group, who were the most energetic, closely followed by the Primitive Methodists'.[43] In practice, however, the 1902 Act was less of a triumph for the established church than Clifford and his colleagues perceived: statistical evidence suggests that in fact voluntary schools, partisan legislation notwithstanding, were losing out to Council Schools. Between 1902 and 1911 just under 5,000 voluntary schools closed or transferred to local Education Authorities whose schools were teaching an increasing proportion of the nation's children.[44] Whilst Free Churchmen might have won the educational issue, the failure of a Liberal government, even one supported by more nonconformists MPs

---

41 D. W. Bebbington separates out the two Sears in his article on 'Baptist Members of Parliament in the Twentieth Century', *BQ* 1986, p.272, thus correcting J. Munson, *The Nonconformists*, 1991, pp.263-4, who conflates the two.

42 Bebbington, *Nonconformist Conscience*, p.147.

43 Munson, *op.cit.*, p.273.

44 *ibid.*, p.287.

than ever before - over 180, including some seventeen Baptists - yielded little to nonconformist demands. Even at its peak nonconformist ability to influence public policy through the agency of the Liberal Party was shown to be extremely limited.

BAPTISTS AND THE FOUNDING OF LONDON UNIVERSITY

Baptist concern for higher education also involved conflict with the established church. The ancient universities were closed to dissenters on the argument that they were private ecclesiastical rather than national institutions. For their part nonconformists argued to the contrary: 'these institutions being national in their character and so regarded by the legislature'. They argued against the medieval identification of education at all levels as a church function and, therefore, entered into alliance with the educational reformers of the period to break the Anglican monopoly.[45]

The first stage in this process was the movement to secure a non-denominational institution of higher education in London. Baptists, and particularly Dr F. A. Cox, minister of Mare Street, Hackney, alongside philosophical radicals like Lord Brougham, played a large part in this campaign. As early as May 1820, a sketch had appeared in the *Baptist Magazine* entitled 'Protestant Dissenting Academy'.[46] Noting that dissenting students were at that time forced to study in either Holland or Scotland, the purpose of the new institution, which was to provide 'no abode for idlers', was to furnish students with a liberal education on a non-confessional basis. This was to prepare them either for entry into one of the learned professions, or 'to adorn private life with literary pursuits in the hours of leisure from business'. The institution was not to impinge on the work of theological seminaries; rather its instruction and curriculum were to be comparable to 'any of the most celebrated Universities in Christendom', though the University of Glasgow was singled out as

---

45 Minute of 6 March 1854 of the Liberation Society, cited in W. H. Mackintosh, *Disestablishment and Liberation*, 1972, p.84.

46 *BM* May 1820, pp.205-7.

the model to follow. Northampton and Reading were suggested as appropriate locations. Special mention was made of the possibility of enrolling Jewish students. The proposal was almost certainly the work of Cox, 'who led the Baptists throughout in their discussion of a university for dissenters', and gives him equal status with the poet, Thomas Campbell, in fathering the university. Indeed, Professor Lardner, writing in 1830, said 'the first notion of a university is said to have been suggested by a dissenting clergyman named Rev. Mr Cox'.[47]

Cox was not slow to form a committee, initially of Baptists only but later expanded to include other dissenters and Scottish churchmen resident in England. The enlarged group met together in April 1825 at the King's Head Tavern in the Poultry, the hostelry where so many dissenting, and Baptist in particular, agencies had their birth. The upshot was the appointment of a delegation of dissenting laymen and clergy to meet with Brougham and Campbell.[48] Amongst these were Benjamin Shaw and Cox himself, both Baptists, as well as the charismatic luminary, Edward Irving, of Regent Square Scottish Presbyterian Church.

There immediately ensued a debate as to whether or not to include theology chairs in the new institution. Brougham and his friends apparently wrote to Campbell, 'We think with you that the introduction of Divinity will be mischievous; but we must yield to the Dissenters with Irving at their head. We must have a theological college'. The immediate reaction of Anglican subscribers was predictable: the theology was to be Church of England or there should be no theology at all. The dissenting interest was apparently flexible. Presented with the Anglican response, their reply was, 'Enough, enough. We are convinced and concede the point that the University

---

47 C. W. New, *op.cit.*, 1961, p.362.

48 H. H. Bellot, *University College London, 1826-1926*, 1929, p.21; New, *op.cit.*, p.362. Bellot offers the innocent but spurious judgement that the committee remained sectional because confined to 'Baptists and Pedo-Baptists'; Seymour Price, 'The Centenary of the Baptist Building Fund', *BQ*, 3, 1926, pp.81ff.

shall be without religious rivalship'. Irving, however, had his doubts and confided to Carlyle: 'It will be unreligious, secretly anti-religious, all the same', the origin of the popular designation of the new university as 'godless Gower Street' in reference to its location. The issue of the inclusion or exclusion of theology was to rumble on for several years.[49]

Meanwhile, Cox's counsel was particularly important as one of the few amongst the planners who had experience in teaching in higher education by virtue of his tutorship at Stepney. He became honorary secretary of the provisional committee of the new university and it was he who presented the plan at the first public meeting chaired by the Lord Mayor of London, calling for 'a palace for genius'. The support of the London dissenters was very important to the new venture: they offered the new project a well-developed connexion, not only in London but reaching out into the provinces, whose wealth was needed for the new institution to get off the ground, not to mention their experience of the academies, and their close ties with the Scottish universities who, for their part, together with some North American institutions, gave dignity to dissent by the recognition of nonconformist scholars and leaders by the award of honorary doctorates.[50]

Ironically, cautions as to the secular nature of the new institution led to the exclusion of all clergy from the Council of the College and therefore of Cox (though he continued to serve as clerk and secretary until September 1828). Baptist interests were instead represented on the Council by Olinthus Gregory, Professor of Mathematics at the Royal Military Academy at Woolwich, evidence theologian (that is one who followed Paley in delighting in the argument from design)

---

49 Bellot, *op.cit.*, pp.22-3.

50 New, *op.cit.*, p.367. New is too extreme in his judgement that 'Birkbeck alone (and Cox, the Secretary) had been associated with any educational institution except as a student'. Cox's prior experience was, of course, as a tutor at Stepney, but Gregory also, from the dissenting side, was by then well-experienced in his appointment at the Military Academy at Woolwich. Both were graduates of Scottish universities.

and Robert Hall's biographer, who sat on the education committee and whose name is to be found on the foundation stone of University College. He was supported by Benjamin Shaw, Treasurer of the Baptist Missionary Society 1821-6 and sometime MP for Westbury.[51] Westbury was a famous pocket borough purchased in 1810 by Sir Manasseh Masseh Lopez, a convert from Judaism to the Church of England, who established something of a reputation for bribery and corruption in parliamentary elections for which he was both fined and imprisoned. Shaw was active in debates in the House of Commons, 1813-18, speaking mainly on commercial topics. He was a city merchant, financier and Lloyd's underwriter and it was presumably his professional interests in the city that introduced him to Lopez whose wealth was largely in East Indian stock. Benjamin Shaw became an important patron of dissenting societies, becoming involved in the work of the Dissenting Deputies, the Particular Baptist Fund, the Baptist Building Fund and Stepney College. In a skit on the new university, printed in *John Bull* and entitled 'Cockney College: An Invitation to Stinkomalee', Gregory is portrayed as 'Dr Olympus Gregory' who 'will instruct the junior fishmongers in the science of throwing shells', whilst it is said of Benjamin Shaw that he 'will explain the Rights and Privileges of the Underwriters at Lloyd's Coffee House'.[52]

With John Smith and I. L. Goldsmid, Shaw underwrote the purchase of the site for the university college at his own risk until the new institution had accumulated sufficient funds to secure it. The combination is an interesting one: liberal Whig MP, Jewish emancipationist, and Baptist man-of-the-city. Indeed, the whole enterprise involved a remarkable interplay of interests, with Cox

---

51 Cited in Bellot, *op.cit.*. pp.70-71. Shaw does not appear in D. W. Bebbingtn's 'List of Baptist MPs in the Nineteenth Century' but will appear in the 'Corrigenda' to the same. He is particularly interesting as adding to the number of dissenters who sat at Westminster prior to the Repeal of the Test and Corporation Acts in 1828.

52 Cited in Bellot, *op.cit.*, pp.70-71.

increasingly intimate with Lord Brougham, during whose rectorship of Glasgow University in 1824 Cox was awarded an honorary LLD. At Gower Street, perhaps as a substitute for not being a member of Council, he was appointed Librarian in 1827, Brougham having suggested this possibility two years earlier. He received a salary of £200 p.a., out of which, it was supposed, he would fund an assistant. Financial exigencies led to this appointment being terminated in 1831. Other Baptists involved in the early promotion of London University were Henry Waymouth, sometime chairman of the Dissenting Deputies, and Joseph Gurney.

The funds for the new institution were to be secured by the sale of 1,500 shares of a nominal value of £100 each, with Cox as a foremost advocate. One of the principal purchasers was the Duke of Bedford, for many years President of the non-credal British and Foreign School Society, 'of which he regarded Brougham as the founder'.[53] The religious issue still obstructed the project. As Irving's comments earlier indicated, whilst conscientious dissenters could convince themselves without difficulty of the necessity of proceeding on a purely secular, non-credal basis, Evangelical Anglican opinion, represented on the Council by Zachary Macaulay, was less certain. Regretfully declining an invitation to Brougham Hall, Cox wrote with regard to the sale of shares, 'Some of our *Evangelicals* however are at work in another way, and I or you or some of us may expect an attack (besides the caricatures shop) of which I am by no means sorry!' He encouraged Brougham to support the idea of launching the sale of a further thousand shares when most of the first issue was secured and also supported Joseph Hume's recommendation that large shareholders be encouraged to split their holdings to increase the number of sympathisers for the new venture.[54]

---

53 New, *op.cit.*, pp.364-5.

54 New, *op.cit.*, p.364; Brougham Mss 2 August 1825, cited New, p.365. Not that Cox himself was other than an evangelical dissenter. In his memorial sermon, *Maturity in Death Exemplified*, pp.8, 23, Daniel Katterns, his successor at Hackney, said, 'He was always a preacher of the gospel, yet more richly

Religion remained a problem. C. W. New notes that, whereas Evangelicals were troubled by a university not teaching religion, High Churchmen were shocked at the thought of a university not teaching the religion of the Church of England. William Wilberforce suggested 'a separate endowment for lectures on the Evidences of Christianity', begging Brougham to 'reflect seriously on the consequences of imparting to so influential a body of men . . . all branches of philosophical knowledge, leaving them wholly ignorant of the grounds and basis of Christian truth'.[55]

Fundamental questions were being raised about the nature of the new world being ushered in by the industrial revolution and associated changes. On the one hand, the Church of England stood for a Christendom view of society with only one legally promoted exposition of Christian truth. Dissent could not agree to that, and was even at this early date moving to a pluralist position, occasioned by its co-operation with establishment men, a powerful Jewish financial interest, and those of no religious commitment at all, as well as both orthodox and heterodox dissenters. A long history of disabilities coupled with the insistence of the established church on total control of educational institutions made secularists of pious dissenters, making them support an educational institution which itself would be deliberately detached from the advocacy of religious values.

The coalitioning involved in this was not unknown to evangelicals. Of their project against slavery Halévy says, 'By a strange paradox men who were Protestant to the backbone, zealots of the dogma of justification by faith, were so devoted to philanthropy that on the common ground of good works they were reconciled with the most lukewarm Christians, even with declared enemies of Christianity'. Indeed, both Brougham and Goldsmid had been involved in the slavery campaign, and in the struggle had won the confidence of the Evangelicals. Education was, apparently, another matter, though a

evangelical as he proceeded', though, at the same time, he noted that he was a well-finished biblical critic.

55 New, *op.cit.*, p.366.

younger Macaulay, the historian, came to the defence of the new college in the pages of the *Edinburgh Review*, arguing, 'We entertain a firm conviction that the principles of liberty, as in government and trade, so also in education, are all important to the happiness of mankind. We do in our souls believe that they are strong with the strength and quick with the vitality of truth'.[56]

For his part Brougham went on record: 'It was not because they disregarded religious education that the Council had omitted theological lectureships, but because they deemed the subject too important to be approached lightly or inconsiderately. Their object was to leave the religious instruction of the students to their parents and clergymen'.[57]

That statement may have been the spur which led three Anglican clergymen who held chairs at the college to announce in *The Times* that, with the approbation of the Council, at a place near the university, 'a course of divinity lectures will be delivered during the academic session'. The dissenters could hardly stand by, so Cox and the Congregational Joseph Fletcher announced that they would run a similar course outside the university on the Evidences of Christianity, Biblical Literature and Church History. The Council disclaimed approval of either, whereupon church and dissent joined forces to try and secure the Council's blessing, with Cox nominated privately to secure Brougham's support. He argued that such an approach would disarm the opponents of the college of the frequently uttered charges of godless secularism. This was apparently right, for Lord Althorpe was soon writing that the additional lectures had quite satisfied his qualms about the venture, and asking if he could now become a shareholder.[58]

---

56 E. Halévy, *op.cit.*, p.383; *Edinburgh Review*, February 1820, cited New, *op.cit.*, pp.370-71.

57 *The Times*, 28 February 1828, cited by New, *op.cit.*, p.379.

58 University College Correspondence No.647 of 27 September 1828, cited New, *op.cit.*, p.382.

For the committed Anglican, however, an alternative was soon provided with the establishment of the credally-based King's College London in 1828. Brougham was quite sanguine about the competition which he likened to that betwixt British and Foreign and National Schools. Thereafter what had originally been called 'London University' adopted the title of 'University College London' and the two institutions became parts of the federal University of London on its incorporation in November 1836: its degrees were to be open 'to persons of all religious persuasions, without distinction and without the imposition of [credal] test or disqualification whatsoever'.

RELIGIOUS TESTS AND THE ANCIENT UNIVERSITIES

Although the establishment of London University opened up admission to higher education for dissenters, and particularly those training for their ministry, exclusion from the ancient universities still smarted. The first stage was to secure the admission of dissenters to first degrees following the proposals of the Royal Commission of 1850, and this was achieved for Oxford and Cambridge in 1854 and 1856 respectively. But a declaration as to bona fide membership of the Church of England remained necessary for all University and College offices, thus denying to dissenters the possibility of a scholarly livelihood within those institutions.

Whilst religious tests were abolished in the University of Durham in 1865, at Oxford and Cambridge exclusion still obtained. A series of cases of dissenting scholars whose future careers were denied to the universities began to accumulate, amongst them several Baptists who paraded their disabilities on the platform of the Liberation Society. Henry Bompas of St John's College, Cambridge, subsequently a QC, was Fifth Wrangler in 1858, William S. Aldis, Senior Wrangler in 1861 (following the Presbyterian W. Sterling in 1860, the first Trinity man so to distinguish himself for thirteen years), James Aldis, Sixth Wrangler in 1863, and Thomas S. Aldis, Second Wrangler in 1866. One author estimated that during the 1860s Cambridge had lost no fewer than fourteen first-rate scholars because of their refusal to subscribe to Anglican articles. The Bompas parents, described as 'strict though not narrow Baptists', were members of Baptist Noel's John Street congregation, which may explain why Henry, at St John's College, Cambridge, took communion in his college chapel, though at the same time becoming more convinced in his Baptist views. He, therefore, refused to sign the declaration approving all the rubrics of the Book of Common Prayer and was thus excluded from a Fellowship in favour of an inferior scholar. Turning to the law, he had a distinguished career, serving for more than twelve years as a county court judge. He was an energetic patron of dissenting and Baptist enterprises, including the work of the Liberation Society.[59] He married the eldest daughter of the Revd Edward White, of conditional immortality fame, who whilst rejecting not only traditional doctrine in this area but also the validity of infant baptism, proceeded to the chair of the Congregational Union in 1886. The three Aldis boys were the sons of the Revd John Aldis of Maze Pond, London, and King's Road, Reading, their mother being a daughter of Dr Steadman, first President of Horton Academy.[60]

In 1869 the Senior Wrangler was a Jew named Hartog who was unwilling even to take his degree under the trinitarian formula with which it was offered. Therein lay a problem, for another statute said that until the Senior Wrangler had taken his degree the other candidates could not proceed to take theirs. The Senate was, therefore, confronted with the problem of issuing a Jew with a degree by special grace, or excluding 114 good Christians from theirs. The grace was allowed. The situation was further heightened by a Classics Fellow at Trinity resigning his Fellowship because he believed he could no longer conscientiously hold to the declaration he had once formally signed. A special lectureship was created for him, but again the case of the nonconformists was powerfully underlined.

---

59 M. D. Johnson, *The Dissolution of Dissent 1815-1918*, 1987, p.172. Henry Bompas was the brother, not the son, *pace* Mackintosh, *op.cit.*, p.178. of the first bishop of the Yukon.

60 *DNB*; H. Aldis, 'Reminiscences of the Abolition of Religious Tests in the Universities of Oxford and Cambridge', *BQ*, 4, 1929, p.249.

In 1871 religious tests at Oxford and Cambridge, with only a few exceptions, were abolished by parliament. Vigilance was thought to be necessary to capitalize on this, hence the importance of the Cambridge University Society for the Promotion of Religious Equality. At Oxford lawyers got rich quickly when J. H. Tillyard, probably of Baptist origins, presented himself as a candidate for election to a Hertford Fellowship announced as restricted to those in orders in the Church of England, arguing this was contrary to both the 1871 Act and the legislation that converted Magdalen Hall into Hertford College. A second case, also involving Tillyard, saw the Liberation Society taking action against the College in Queen's Bench, which did indeed find that Tillyard had not been properly examined, in contravention of the 1871 Act, giving judgment that a new election should be held. The Court of Appeal overruled Queen's Bench, thereby provoking additional legislation in 1882, which opened all headships (save three) to competition, whilst clerical fellowships were confined to those exercising a chaplaincy function, conducting services, and giving religious instruction. Even so, R. F. Horton was still opposed as a theology examiner in 1883, though he had the support of the Vice Chancellor and the House of Congregation.[61]

That was not the end of the story. Leading nonconformist families, having secured access to the ancient universities for their offspring, soon found that those institutions, and Oxford in particular, severely corroded dissenting commitments, and consequently many were lost to dissent, and indeed in some cases to Christian faith altogether. As sympathetic a commentator as T. H. Green, who was to accept office as Vice President of the Oxford University Nonconformists' Union, spoke of access to Oxbridge as 'an injury rather than a help to nonconformity', pleading with dissenting leaders to make better provision for the defence and maintenance of the religious life and faith of those who came there from their churches. This was the situation that promoted the founding of the Oxford University Nonconformists' Union in 1881, whose life seemed to centre around

---

61 Johnson, *op.cit.*, pp.210-13.

the person of R. F. Horton. Though it was mainly Congregationalist in character, Baptist involvement seems to have included W. J. Ashley, who eventually became an Anglican, and Frank Tillyard, with external support from people like H. M. Bompas, now a QC.[62]

Against this background Colonel Griffin, as President of the Baptist Union in 1890, proposed that a Baptist University be founded at a cost of £250,000 - but the idea met with thunderous silence. More significant was the decision to relocate Spring Hall College, the Birmingham Congregational theological college, to Oxford as Mansfield College in 1886, amidst much talk of nonconformity returning to the universities after their ejection in 1662. Apart from the desirability of educating Congregational ministers, and a fair number of Baptists as well, with the benefits of Oxford theology, the strategy was to provide a cultural focus in Oxford for nonconformist students. Trevelyan appositely argued that hitherto exclusion had provided nonconformity with its leadership, distinctively trained in its own principles, their aggressive loyalty to dissent sharpened by that very experience. The opening up of Oxford and Cambridge, by contrast, meant that such men 'have been absorbed in the general stream of national life'. He concluded, 'This change has contributed with other causes to the diminution of the dissenting bodies both in self-consciousness and power'.[63]

62 *ibid.*, pp.187-92.

63 G. M. Trevelyan, *British History in the Nineteenth Century and After*, 1937, p.284.

SOCIETY AND POLITICS

Nineteenth-century British Baptists were heirs not only to the historic religious divisions of the seventeenth century but more immediately to the social and political polarities brought into being by the tensions and suspicions of the revolutionary years and beyond. Deryck Lovegrove spells out the consequences aptly when he writes: 'In the years following 1795 the legal position of Protestant dissenters appeared increasingly precarious as political tension threatened to spill over into the religious field with measures designed to curb the insidious effects of popular preaching.' Thus Mr Pilkington, newly appointed agent of the Essex Baptist Association, sent to preach at Rayleigh in June 1797, found established opinion so hostile that he confessed, 'I am aware that I am liable to be cast into prison; but if you will leave me alone, I will begin and leave myself in the hands of the Lord',[1] a witness honoured by the gathering of the nucleus of a permanent congregation.

THE CAMPAIGN FOR THE REPEAL OF THE TEST AND CORPORATION ACTS

It was this new polarity, fruit of revolutionary suspicions, that not only threatened evangelical co-operation but came to colour church-chapel relationships in the new century. At the same time, renewed consciousness of disabilities led to a renewal of the fight for dissenters' rights.[2] This campaign dated back to 1787, when the first resolution for the repeal of the Test and Corporation Acts was put to the Commons, but the conservatism of the revolutionary decades at the end of the eighteenth and beginning of the nineteenth century inhibited progress. Tory churchmen were not without justification for

---

1 Deryck Lovegrove, *Established Church, Sectarian People: Itinerancy and the Transformation of English Dissent 1780-1830*, 1988, p.121.

2 R. G. Cowherd, *The Politics of English Dissent: The Religious Aspect of Liberal and Humanitarian Reform Movements from 1815 to 1848*, 1956, p.24.

their fears. In January 1798 the Revd John Martin, minister of Keppel Street Chapel, indicated in a sermon at Broad Street Chapel what he later said he believed to be incontrovertible necessity, 'that should the French land, some, yea many of these different and differing people [the dissenters] would unite to encourage the French, and to distress the country, provided they had a fair opportunity', specifying the commitment of both paedobaptists and Baptists alike. In so speaking, Martin offended the caution of denominational leadership, which at that time was only informally gathered together on the margins of different funds and in membership of certain clubs. For his pains, he was removed from the list of Broad Street Lecturers and also from the Jamaica Coffee House Society of Baptist Ministers and censured by the *Protestant Dissenters' Magazine*.[3] Martin, who did not find it difficult to antagonize his fellow dissenters, continued as minister of Keppel Street Chapel until 1814 and died six years later. The chapel, hard by the rear entrance of the British Museum, was wholly provided in 1795 by the princely generosity of one of the deacons, William Ashlin.

There was a clear difference between dissenting hopes of the Revolution in earlier years and pro-French sentiment in the context of potential invasion after the turn of the century.[4] In contrast to Martin, his fellow Baptists in such a context professed 'their loyalty to the Princes of the Royal House of Brunswick and their ardent attachment to the principles of the British Constitution',[5] though ironically Martin was later suspected of being in the pay of the government.[6] But the word had been spoken and behind it a sentiment cherished which made a conservative establishment wary of dissent at home.

---

3 Joseph Ivimey, *History of the English Baptists*, IV, 1830, pp.77-82.

4 See Stennett's comment on the Revolution. Ivimey, IV, p.82. William Winterbotham, Baptist minister at Horsley, was imprisoned for preaching sermons allegedly sympathetic to the Revolution.

5 Ivimey, *op.cit.*, p.81.

6 Sellers, *Nineteenth-Century Nonconformity*, 1977, p.66.

Thus right at the beginning of the century Baptists had set up alternative strategies in relation to political developments, on the one hand a righteous radicalism and on the other a cautious stance from parts of the leadership, lest in pressing dissenting claims too hard more might be lost than gained. The interplay between radicalism and caution was to continue throughout the century. The more dissenting grievances were in view, the more radical both word and action; the more remedies seemed either to challenge the state or provide for it a more active role, at variance with a dissenting delight in voluntaryism, the more individual radicals became isolated from both leadership and rank and file, even though the constituency always seems to have cherished the speech-making of its more advanced consciences. The alternative conscience is not so often articulated but it is nevertheless perennial. A Lancashire Baptist minister, writing to the *Baptist Magazine* in 1849, confessed, 'I cannot reconcile this warm part in all political matters, which is taken and openly defended, with the spirit of Christ's Kingdom, which is not of this world, nor with the true position of Christians as strangers and pilgrims on earth.'[7]

Hostility towards and suspicion of government reached a high point with Sidmouth's attempt as Home Secretary in May 1811 to secure an amendment of the Toleration Act, which would have empowered magistrates to exercise discretion in granting licences to both dissenting meeting houses and itinerant preachers such as the Essex Baptist, Mr Pilkington. Hitherto the function had been simply to register. Sidmouth disingenuously claimed that his purpose was to enhance the respectability of dissent and save them from having as ministers, 'tailors, pig-drovers, chimney-sweeps, and persons who could neither write nor read'.[8] The proposed legislation was such as to prompt John Wilks, son of a notable Independent minister and later radical MP for Boston, to secure the establishment of the Protestant

7 *BM* 1849, p.7, cited Derek Fraser, *Urban Politics in Victorian England: The Structure of Politics in Victorian Cities*, 1979, pp.269-70.

8 Ivimey, *op.cit.*, IV, p.109.

Society for the Protection of Religious Liberty, which energetically secured the submission of a very large number of petitions against the proposed legislation from both London and the provinces. Drs Cox and Newman of East London both served on its committee in these early years.

Dan Taylor of the New Connexion chaired a meeting of the Ministers of the Three Denominations at the Dr Williams's Library, which adopted five resolutions against the Home Secretary's proposal, and the Dissenting Deputies took similar action. Again, within their counsels, Baptist support was given in the persons of Joseph Gutteridge, Treasurer 1805-16 and Vice Chairman 1816-23, Benjamin Shaw, Member of Parliament for Westbury and sometime Treasurer of the Baptist Missionary Society, W. Burls[9] of Edmonton, sometime Chairman of the BMS, and Henry Waymouth, Vice Chairman 1825-32 and Chairman 1832-44.[10] Ivimey tells us that he himself was present in the House of Lords for the debate and witnessed the failure of Sidmouth's initiative there, testifying that 'in this arduous struggle the Baptists took their part'.[11]

Contrary to High Tory hopes, dissenters, far from being curbed, were provoked by this action into securing a clutch of much needed reforms. In 1812 the Conventicle and Five Mile Acts were repealed and meeting houses given further protection against rioters by the so-called New Toleration Act, 'a monument of the kind and liberal feelings of His Majesty's ministers . . . and of our present patriotic monarch' (the Prince Regent!).[12] This was important for, notwithstanding the rejection of Sidmouth's proposal, a number of local magistrates continued to discriminate against dissenters.[13] In

---

9 E. A. Payne, *The Excellent Mr Burls*, 1943.

10 Ivimey, *op.cit.*, IV, p.142: also on the committee of the Society for the Mitigation and Gradual Abolition of Slavery throughout the British Dominions, Cowherd, *op.cit.*, p.54.

11 Ivimey, *op.cit.*, IV, p.117.

12 *BM* 1812, 405-6; Ivimey, *op.cit.*, IV, p.116.

13 Ivimey, *op.cit.*, IV, pp.115-6; Ward, *Religion and Society in England 1790-1850*, 1972, pp.60-61.

1813 toleration was extended to the Unitarians, whilst in 1814 the Chancellor promised to exempt chapels from local rates.

At that stage, the 'preservation of the Toleration Act', in the judgement of W. R. Ward, 'enabled the same weapons [dissenters' basic reliance on prayer and preaching] to be used for the spiritual, theological and administrative reconstruction of dissent.'[14] That is to say, these secular pressures provoked the dissenting denominations into an increasing awareness of their conscientiously upheld tradition, and of the strength to be secured by working together in principled and religious coalition. For the immediate future this encouraged the United Committee for Repeal to reactivate itself. It met for the first time in its new format in April 1827, and decided to canvass broadly amongst the dissenting constituency to secure the termination of the offending legislation, aided now by a calculation that dissenters formed about a quarter of the population. Instances of abuse, particularly in rural parishes, continued, keeping the issue alive. The *New Baptist Miscellany* lamented the translation of the high-church Van Mildert to succeed the liberal and conciliatory Barrington as Bishop of Durham, for Van Mildert was remembered as the persecutor of Amos Norroway at Ewelme in Oxfordshire, whom he expelled from his cottage for allowing a Baptist minister to preach in it.[15]

The activities of the Protestant Society and other dissenting caucuses were regularly reported to its constituency by the *Baptist Magazine* with such dutifulness that one modern author (R. G. Cowherd) uses it as a prime source for charting their campaigns. The secretary of the Protestant Society regretted that each year it had to deal with so many cases of 'riots and disturbances of worship, assessments to the poor's rate, claims of turnpike tolls, refusals of marriage and interment, illegal pecuniary demands and many acts of intolerance and oppression',[16] all indicating the limits

14 W. R. Ward, *Religion and Society in England, 1790-1850*, 1972, p.53.

15 *New Baptist Magazine*, 1826, p.193.

16 *BM* 1827, p.277.

of toleration. The situation was complicated by the fact that Catholic emancipation was also on the table. Some nonconformist leaders believed that all dissenters, both Protestant and Catholic, shared a common cause over against the privilege of the establishment, but this ran the danger of provoking anti-catholic sentiment. Other dissenters were, according to Ivimey, inclined to veer away from an earlier neutrality and to oppose further liberation for Catholics. Ivimey brings out this distinction, suggesting that William Smith, the Unitarian MP for Norwich, was in this respect unrepresentative, though his liberalism had Robert Hall's backing.[17]

In the event, skilfully directed by Lord John Russell in the Commons and Lord Holland in the Lords, the Act repealing the two penal laws received the Royal Assent on 9th May 1828. The achievement was celebrated by a magnificent dinner at the Freemasons' Tavern under the Presidency of HRH the Duke of Sussex, who declared that the occasion was to celebrate 'the triumph of Religious Freedom and Christian Charity in the abolition of the Sacramental Test'. Baptist participation was through the voice of the ubiquitous Dr F. A. Cox of Hackney, who proposed a toast to the monarchy and members of the established church and the dissenting ministry, 'worthy successors' of those excluded in 1662.[18]

Repeal had a wider significance in that it revealed the constitution's capacity for amendment and in this sense, accompanied by Catholic Emancipation the following year, led into the reform crisis of 1830-32. Robert Hall had already made it quite clear that in his judgement, 'the connection between civil and religious liberty' was 'too intimate to make it surprising that they who are attracted to the one should be friendly to the other'.[19] Hall, in fact, is unique in linking the post-1815 campaign for reform with the earlier articulation of reform principles prior to 1789. In 1821, for example, he reissued his

17 Ivimey, *op.cit.*, IV, pp.161-4.

18 B. L. Manning, *The Protestant Dissenting Deputies*, 1952, p.249. *BM* 1828, pp.79, 274-5, 622.

19 Hall, *Works*, IV, 1866, p.109.

Apology for the Freedom of the Press, first published in 1793. In this he argued for the sovereignty of the people, criticized the random distribution of constituencies and franchises, made a plea for annual parliaments and universal suffrage, and added, in his reply to critics, advocacy of voting by ballot. When charged by Anglicans with 'meddling in party politics', his riposte, noting both the structural and the practical involvement of the clergy of the established church in political affairs, was that doubtless his crime must be 'meddling on the wrong side'.[20]

BAPTISTS AND THE REFORM MOVEMENT

When the Reform Bill passed the House of Commons by a single vote in March 1831, the editors of the *Baptist Magazine* enquired, 'Who can regard the operation of a Divine Hand in these affairs and not exclaim in reference to the past, "What God hath wrought", and in reference to the present, "This is the finger of God". May its results be seen in the future prosperity of ENGLAND and its COLONIES and the WORLD'.[21]

Baptist support for reform was both theoretical and practical. Benjamin Godwin's autobiographical letter to his son of 11 March 1852 contains lively recollections of the reform agitation in Bradford, intervened with other concerns such as the welfare of the Poles, the future of the Serampore mission, and the passionate advocacy of the slaves in the Caribbean. Godwin himself was persuaded to be the principal speaker at the town's first reform meeting. When Tory hecklers sought to silence him, the working class part of the audience indignantly came to Godwin's aid. He subsequently drafted the petitions that the citizens of Bradford sent to the king and to Lord Grey in favour of the Reform Bill after the House of Lords had voted against it. Subsequently he laboured hard for Henry Brougham's

20 Hall's reply to reviews of the reissue of *An Apology for the Freedom of the Press*, 2 February 1822, *Works* IV, pp.26-88, 137-8, 143.

21 *BM* April 1831, p.55.

return for the West Riding.[22] For example, one of the most ardent labourers for reform in Birmingham was George Edmonds, button-burnisher and later schoolmaster, a son of the Revd Edward Edmonds, minister of Bond Street Chapel, 1784-1823. George Edmonds's name is to be found associated with nearly every radical movement of the early nineteenth century. A founder of the Birmingham Hampden Club for political reform, he chaired the meeting in Newhall Hill, where between 18,000 and 25,000 people gathered, demanding separate representation for Birmingham in January 1817.[23] Presiding two years later at a meeting which elected Sir Charles Wolseley as Birmingham's 'Legatorial Attorney and Representative', he was with four others imprisoned for conspiring to elect an MP. In the reform movement of the 1830s, he joined with Thomas Attwood in forming the Birmingham Political Union and was one of those whose tireless activity secured the incorporation of Birmingham in 1838. As a reward for services rendered, he was elected the first Clerk of the Peace of the new borough, an office which was also conferred on another Baptist who proved himself a Liberal stalwart, James Richardson of South Parade, first Clerk of the Peace in Leeds.

Associated with Edmonds was another Baptist, William Morgan, briefly town clerk of Birmingham, the founder of the Birmingham Baptist Union and later Secretary of the Church of the Redeemer. Said to have been the last man in England challenged to a duel (for his strong temperance advocacy), he worked with the Quaker, Joseph Sturge, and Edmonds in the reform movement. He had his goods seized for not paying church rates, and gave strong support to the emancipation of slaves, William Knibb being a frequent guest in his family home. Morgan was the champion of a number of dissenting causes: in 1866 he visited Jamaica for the Anti-Slavery Society; he was deeply committed to suppressing the opium trade; and used his

---

22 B. Godwin's Autobiographical Letter, 11 March 1852, copy in the Angus Library, Regent's Park College, Oxford.

23 Cowherd, *op.cit.*, p.71-2; A. S. Langley, *Birmingham Baptists Past and Present*, 1939, p.231-3.

legal skills to secure the abolition of the Bible-printing monopoly, thus helping to get cheap Bibles into the people's hands. William Morgan's other enthusiasms were adult school work, again alongside Joseph Sturge, the pioneering of reformatory schools, alongside Carpenter and Davenport Hill, as well as relief work in Ireland.[24]

More colourful was Arthur O'Neill, a Glasgow medical student turned ordinand, who in the late 1830s became an ardent Chartist. Sent by the Glasgow Chartists to welcome the first two prisoners to be liberated from Warwick Gaol, he remained in Birmingham, accepting an invitation to pastor a small church in Livery Street which, with him, became Baptist in 1846, later moving to Newhall Street. That was after he had spent a year in Stafford Gaol himself as a Chartist prisoner for his part in a great peaceful Chartist demonstration at Cradley. After release from prison he continued with his congregation for fifty-six years until his death in 1896. His exemplar was the Serving Christ: 'I see Jesus washing the disciples' feet; I desire to serve the poor, the sick, the mourning, the ignorant, the aged and the child', he wrote to his congregation from prison, asking that his release be celebrated not with procession but by a prayer meeting.[25] Such Baptists were no cloistered pietists but fully immersed in the new urban experience spreading across the Midlands and Northern England.[26]

BAPTIST POLITICIANS

It was to be fifteen years before any Baptist presence in a reformed House of Commons was to reflect the new franchise. This came with the election of [Sir] Morton Peto for Norwich in 1847,[27] Richard Harris for Leicester in 1848 and Sir George Goodman for Leeds in

---

24 F. W. Butt Thompson, 'The Morgans of Birmingham', *BQ* 2, 1925, pp.265-6.

25 Langley, *op.cit.*, pp.150-2.

26 *BQ*, 2, 1925, pp.263-9.

27 *DNB* and H. Peto, *Sir Morton Peto: A Memorial Sketch*, 1893. Brian and Faith Bowers, 'Bloomsbury Chapel and Mercantile Morality: The Case of Sir Morton Peto', *BQ* 30, 1984, pp.210-20.

1852.[28] Each of these MPs, as well as the constituencies they represented, spelt out something of the new world of the nineteenth century. Norwich, an ancient borough, had been the centre of the old Norfolk textile industry but was now feeling the competition coming from Yorkshire, whilst developing shoe-making as an additional industry. Norwich retained its two seats at Westminster after 1832 and it was to one of these that Morton Peto was elected, even though William Brock, whose ministry he sat under at St Mary's, sponsored another candidate to stand against him, because Peto would not give categoric assurance that he would work for the separation of church and state. Builder and railway contractor, and princely in his benefactions to Baptist causes, Peto nevertheless persuaded Brock to become first pastor of the new church he had built in Bloomsbury, whilst he himself later gave good, though not uncritical, service to the Liberation Society and other dissenting causes.

Leicester, too, was an ancient borough that retained its members in 1832: Richard Harris, one of Robert Hall's converts and a manufacturer of fancy hosiery, was a lay preacher and deacon, first at Harvey Lane and subsequently at Charles Street.[29] Leeds received its own representation for the first time in 1832. Sir George Goodman was deeply involved in municipal affairs, as also in Baptist life. The first mayor of the reformed Leeds corporation, he was a wool merchant by trade. Though born into a Baptist family, he did not make his confession of faith till he joined Great George Street (later Blenheim) at the age of 58. His earlier associations were at

---

28 D. W. Bebbington, 'Baptist MPs in the Nineteenth Century', *BQ* 29, 1981, p.12; E. P. Hennock, *Fit and Proper Persons: Ideal and Reality in Nineteenth-Century Urban Government*, 1973; Derek Fraser, *op.cit.*, *passim*.

29 S. Mitchell, *Not Disobedient: A History of United Baptist Church, Leicester, including Harvey Lane 1760-1848, Belvoir Street 1845-1940, and Charles Street, 1831-1940*, 1984, *passim*, esp. pp.110-112. A. Temple Patterson, *Radical Leicester*, 1954, see index.

South Parade, where the Revd John Eustace Giles exercised a remarkable ministry from 1836-45.[30]

With George Goodman, Giles entered into conflict with the formidable Dr Hook, Vicar of Leeds, over church rates, as also on the educational clauses of Graham's Factory Acts. An advocate of complete suffrage, Giles gave an address at the great Anti-Corn Law League Conference for Clergy, attended by some 182 Baptists, out of 645 members present.[31] According to Kitson Clark, this was the only conference for which the thrifty Leeds Baptists paid their delegates' travelling expenses.[32] He also attended the first meeting of the British Anti-State Church Association in 1844.

Giles also did battle with the Owenite Socialists, believing socialism to be a threat to the life of the state, as providing licence for all forms of behaviour. He was, on the other hand, named by the Chartists as one of the dissenting clergy who both showed them sympathy and gave them active support. One of the reporters of the *Northern Star*, P. B. Templeton, a member at South Parade, was, however, expelled from the church for impugning the character of the minister. To the Chartists, Giles offered a number of affirmations: 'the working man's interest is my interest. The working man's food is my food, and the working man's welfare I have sought and will seek; the working man's friendship I value and his friendship I have.'[33] In all this it should be understood that Giles showed himself an ardent evangelist, adding 488 people to the church roll at South Parade in a seven-year pastorate. Indeed, his missionary passion, as much as his political involvement, occasioned some of the stricter of Leeds Baptists to accuse him of being 'virtually a Wesleyan', that is

---

30 For Giles, see D. B. Milner's article in ed. D. M. Lewis, *Blackwell's Dictionary of Evangelical Biography*, forthcoming.

31 Second only to 276 Congregationalists: K. R. M. Short, 'English Baptists and the Corn Laws', *BQ*, 21, 1966, p.314.

32 G. S. R. Kitson Clark, 'The Electorate and the Repeal of the Corn Laws', *Transactions of the Royal Historical Society*, 1951.

33 R. W. Ram, 'Dissent in Urban Yorkshire, 1800-1850', *BQ* 22, 1967, p.15.

to say, to broadcast the gospel appeal so widely that he seemed hardly to uphold commitment to the teaching of particular redemption.

Men like Giles were not merely concerned with the situation within this country. Chairman of the Baptist Union in 1846, Giles was twice sent by the Yorkshire Association to the continent to seek mitigation of the persecution endured by Baptist brethren from Lutheran state churches, first to Hamburg and secondly to plead the case of Danish Baptists before the King of Denmark. Declining an invitation to become Secretary of the Baptist Missionary Society, he took a leading part in seeking the abolition of the iniquitous apprenticeship system in the West Indies.

IMPERIAL AFFAIRS AND THE POLITICAL AGENDA

The careers of such men illustrate how dissenting disabilities, coupled with a concern for justice in the political order, enticed nineteenth-century Baptists into an active engagement with the murky world of politics. Their co-operation with Baptists in other countries, as also their missionary endeavours, led in the same direction. The situations in both Jamaica and India required political action. In Jamaica the withholding of licences to preach provoked a memorial to the Privy Council in 1804, which virtually secured the annulment of the act of the Jamaican legislature setting up the licensing system. But that was not an end of the matter: repeated attempts by the settlers (in 1807, 1808, 1811, 1827, 1829), through the Jamaican Assembly, to legislate against dissenters, provoked the Baptist Missionary Society and the Dissenting Deputies in London to get the mother parliament to reassert dissenters' rights.[34]

All this, which has to be seen in the context of the domestic struggle for full toleration, was the prehistory to the Jamaican riots and outrages of 1832 in which both Baptist missionaries and meeting houses suffered from deliberately fomented civil strife. Cowherd

---

34 See Manning, *op.cit.*, pp.425-30; B. Stanley, *The History of the Baptist Missionary Society 1792-1992*, 1992, pp.68f; and H. O. Russell, *Foundations and Anticipations: The Jamaican Baptist Story 1783-1892*, 1993, Columbus, USA.

comments 'the Baptists who were in a rage against the Tory government because their missionaries were being persecuted in Jamaica sent circular letters to their congregations urging them to pledge all candidates against slavery'.[35] At the same time they petitioned Lord Goderich, Secretary to the Colonies, for the protection of both missionaries and missionary property. Goderich, finding no truth in the charge of Baptists inciting the slaves to riot, ordered that they should be indemnified against damage to their properties. The Dissenting Deputies decided, against this background of illegal acts, that the only solution to the problem was emancipation, and accordingly purchased £200 worth of the pamphlet *Facts and Documents connected with the late insurrection in Jamaica*, prepared by Baptist hands, with a view to securing a vote against slavery in the forthcoming elections. It was a fitting culmination to that great anti-slavery campaign that had occupied evangelicals in church and dissent for nearly half a century. The act abolishing slavery in the British Empire, to the gratification of the Baptist constituency, was passed very early in the life of the reformed parliament in July 1833.[36]

India provoked concern in 1813 when the East India Company's Charter became due for renewal and it looked as if government was about to use the occasion of revision to impose a religious establishment on India, whilst making no allowance for the entry of missionaries of other denominations. To secure their interests, petitions, signed by well over 51,000 male signatories over the age of sixteen, were sent to both Houses of Parliament, seeking for dissenting missionaries rights of entry, protection by the government, and the ability to travel on company vessels to India directly, instead of travelling via America as was necessary until then. In addition, Andrew Fuller and Joseph Ivimey, together with three leading laymen, all Dissenting Deputies and all involved with city finance, Benjamin Shaw, Joseph Gutteridge, and William Burls, waited upon the Prime Minister and pressed their case forcefully in an amicable exchange of

35 Cowherd, *op.cit.*, p.75; *BM* 1830, p.343; *BM* 1833, p.80.

36 Manning, *op.cit.*, p.425-30; Ivimey, *op.cit.*, IV, p.85-7.

views. Liverpool, although professing his sympathy with dissenting interests both at home and overseas, refused to yield on the necessity of the Board of Control licensing missionaries to India, in order, so he pleaded, to control their overall number, and to exclude ridiculous sectarians such as the Southcottians. He emphasised, however, that no intention existed to favour episcopalians over the representatives 'of the respectable and decent sects of dissenters', arguing that government control was an improvement on company control, since Parliament would act as a court of appeal. On a wider front, the Dissenting Deputies and a special *ad hoc* Committee for Promoting the Introduction of Christianity into India, backed up the Baptist supplications. A case putting the new regulations to the test soon emerged when it became necessary for the Board of Control to countermand the decision of the Directors of the East India Company not to supply a Mr Yates with a licence.[37]

Jamaica and India impinge upon the story of British Baptists in so far as colonial or company legislation was seen as limiting toleration in dependent territories, thereby reducing the protection afforded by the Toleration Act at just that time when the same campaigners were seeking to expand its meaning at home, ideally through the repeal of all penal legislation. Such imperial legislation was seen as extending the principle of establishment overseas with all the threats therein involved. Moreover, in the context of reform, such threats also fortified Baptist ministers in encouraging their members to seek pledges against abuses in the Empire, so that abolition and reform came to be part of a single agenda. Jamaica and India were, moreover, to continue to foster Baptist political engagement, for after emancipation in Jamaica the difficulties of the apprenticeship system had to be fought and in the 1860s the BMS, and more particularly Dr Underhill, its then secretary, in defence of the Baptist victims of the Morant Bay Affair and in relentlessly pursuing Governor Eyre, found

---

37 Manning, *op.cit.*, pp.431-4; E. D. Potts, *British Baptist Missionaries in India 1793-1837*, 1967; B. Stanley, *op.cit.*, chapter 2.

common cause with English radicals.[38] Similarly, Carey and his successors drew the missionary interest into opposing *sati* and other abuses in Indian life, against the quietist desires of the East India Company.[39]

These cases also reintroduced Baptist leaders, of whom those associated with the Baptist Missionary Society were by far the best organized, to political activity, both denominationally and through such co-operative bodies as the Dissenting Deputies and the Protestant Society. They discovered therein the strength of ecumenical combination, however limited its range, notwithstanding the sectarian overtones of anti-establishmentarianism exhibited by some but by no means all combatants. This was seen especially in the Apocrypha debate in the counsels of the British and Foreign Bible Society, which saw the withdrawal of the hard-line Haldanites, a group of Scottish Baptists, from co-operative Bible work, signalling, as some have thought, the birth of modern fundamentalism.

THE LIBERATION SOCIETY, THE DISSENTING DEPUTIES AND DISSENTING DISABILITIES

Notwithstanding the achievements of 1828 and 1832, many nonconformist grievances remained on the statute book. To secure their removal, and eventually, it was hoped, the disestablishment of the state church, was the task for which the Liberation Society, originally the Anti-State Church Association, came into being in 1844. However, it had roots going back a generation in several earlier societies, the Protestant Society for the Protection of Religious Liberty (1811), the Society for Promoting Ecclesiastical Knowledge (1820), which existed to publish dissenting works and those challenging the

38 E. B. Underhill, *The West Indies, Their Social and Religious Condition*, 1862; E. B. Underhill, *A Letter Addressed to the Rt Hon. E. Cardwell*, n.d. (1865); E. A. Payne, *Freedom in Jamaica*, n.d. (1933); G. A. Catherall, 'British Baptist Involvement in Jamaica 1783-1865', University of Keele PhD thesis 1971.

39 B. Stanley, *The History of the Baptist Missionary Society 1792-1992*, 1992, pp.43-4.

validity of ecclesiastical establishments, the Religious Freedom Society (1839) and the Evangelical Voluntary Association (1839), in all of which Baptists were active. Indeed, as early as 1839 the Baptist Union had resolved that state establishments of religion were 'a palpable departure from the laws of Christ, a gross reflection on his wisdom and power, and the most formidable obstacle in the land to the diffusion of true piety'.[40]

At this time Francis Cox seemed foremost among Baptists in seeking in his own person to make an impact on public life,[41] serving on the committees of all these early societies. He was not alone. Others heavily involved included Thomas Price, minister of the Devonshire Square Church and later editor of the *Eclectic Review*, John Howard Hinton,[42] and a youthful Joseph Angus. The Congregationalist, Edward Miall, in his plans for a convention to take steps to secure a vigorous movement against State religion, expressed his distrust of the 'aristocracy of dissent', then focused on London's pulpits, so the call to such a convention was issued by seventy ministers mainly from the Midland counties. The convention took place in Leicester in December 1843, when two London Baptists, Francis Cox and Thomas Price, were asked to act as a committee with Miall. When it was enlarged to six, Charles Stovel of Little Prescot Street joined the committee, which was thus still half Baptist in membership. By the time the first executive had been appointed, Baptist representation was reduced to two out of a body of seventeen, dominated by eleven Congregationalists. Of all the denominations, however, only the Baptist Union sent official delegates to the conference. In the new association Price was appointed Treasurer, Cox joint secretary with Miall and J. M. Hare, whilst John Howard

40 Baptist Union Minutes 1 May 1839 p.181.

41 For Cox's connections in these societies see W. H. Mackintosh, *Disestablishment and Liberation: The movement for the separation of the Anglican Church from state control'*, 1972, index.

42 J. H. Hinton also served as a missionary for Joseph Sturge's National Complete Suffrage Union: Cowherd, *op.cit.*, p.114.

Hinton has been described as the most distinguished among the society's lecturers and wrote *The Test of Experience: or the Voluntary Principle in the United States* to promote the work of the Anti-State Church Association (Liberation Society).[43]

The name that constantly appears in the records is that of Dr Cox. He took a strong line of opposition to the government's proposal to increase its grant to the Catholic College at Maynooth.[44] As a former distributor of the *Regium Donum*, the small annual provision made by Walpole and his successors at the Treasury to relieve poor dissenting ministers and their widows, he appealed to his fellow ministers to forgo this help rather than allow it to compromise the voluntaryist principle. In this he was supported by Daniel Katterns, his successor at Hackney.

It is difficult to exaggerate the way in which, from the 1840s onwards, a tremendous amount of Baptist energy, and sometimes Baptist Union energy in particular, was invested in campaigning against dissenting disabilities and ecclesiastical abuses. These included action to combat the manipulation of trusts against nonconformists, the search for equality of educational opportunities, the securing of the legal recognition of dissenting registration of births and marriages, and of access to public burial grounds with the right to use a form of service acceptable to dissenters. The most important aspect of the work, however, was the campaign for the abolition of Church Rates for the upkeep of the fabric of a Church whose doctrine, liturgy and establishment they rejected. This took over thirty years to secure from its first being mooted in 1834 to its final achievement in 1868. Together these campaigns had both the anti-ecumenical force of maintaining and deepening the cleavage between the established church and dissent,[45] whilst uniting the different parties of dissent in common grievance and campaign. In the process, however, there

43 Mackintosh, *op.cit.*, p.30, 51.

44 See pp.389-90.

45 Manning, *op.cit.*, p.197.

also emerged the danger of secularizing dissent as a political fighting force.

Edward Miall's strident campaign style in promoting the Liberation Society was not to everybody's taste and among other dissenters severing their ties with the society in the 1850s were Thomas Price and John Howard Hinton. By that time, however, Sir Morton Peto was representing a Baptist view within the counsels of the Liberationist movement, taking a special interest in the issue of nonconformist burial rites, and the protection of their trusts. In the '60s he fell out with the society when it was discovered that he was the patron of a Norfolk living. By this date Peto had already begun to be suspicious of 'radical associations' such as Miall's. The society was, however, able to secure the advocacy of major leaders of the denomination: Alexander McLaren of Manchester, Charles Williams of Accrington, John Clifford, Dr Underhill (with a special interest in colonial affairs), Dr Trestrail of Bristol, the layman H. M. Bompas, as well as C. H. Spurgeon, all lent their support. Indeed, the historian of the Society says of Spurgeon that of all the great nonconformist leaders, 'Spurgeon was the most open in his sympathy with the aims of the Liberationist'.[46] In 1866, speaking to the Society, he urged the friends of voluntaryism not to be frightened of being called 'political dissenters'.[47]

Like other Baptist leaders before him, Spurgeon eventually became disenchanted with the Liberation Society, ceasing his subscription in 1891 on the grounds of not wanting to unite with those from whom he now diverged on fundamental doctrine. That was essentially a theological disagreement: ironically, in view of Spurgeon's counsel just cited, the deacons of the Metropolitan Tabernacle forbade its use for the 'political' purposes of the Liberation Society, confirming the secular image that the Society had by that date secured, and revealing an emerging pietism amongst Baptists of very different kinds. Richard Glover of Bristol, for example, not usually thought of as an extreme

46 Mackintosh, *op.cit.*, p.218.

47 E. A. Payne, *The Baptist Union: A Short History*, 1959, p.100.

pietist, argued 'that the Free Churches should keep out of all disputes between employer and employed and should concentrate all energies on the proclamation of the Gospel'.[48] By contrast, Arthur Illingworth, Bradford worsted spinner and treasurer of the Liberation Society for a quarter of a century and then its Chairman, a sturdy Yorkshire Baptist consistent in his objection to state intervention alike in his mill and in the chapel of which he was a member, continued a loyal liberationist in the House of Commons and was most frequently seen as the public face of the Liberation Society in these later years.[49] Neither position can be regarded as typically Baptist: rather Baptists of the second half of the century increasingly sat uneasily between the poles of political engagement and pietistic abstention from the affairs of this world.

The achievements of political campaigning were not inconsiderable: the resolution of grievances with regard to burial grounds and nonconformist marriages, access to the ancient universities (both for dissenting students and those aspiring to be fellows), the establishment of the dual system in education, the abolition of Church Rates and the disestablishment of the Irish Church. But all these were the results of the quieter advocacy of the Dissenting Deputies as much as the noisier Liberation Society. Bernard Manning characterises the relationship between the two organisations by calling the Liberation Society, from the perspective of the Deputies, 'a useful safety valve' but sometimes 'an embarrassing ally', arguing that in the long run 'history was to justify the cautious attitude' taken by the Deputies. The victory secured by dissenters on practical abuses amounted to 'a partial Disestablishment' which, together with actual disestablishment in Ireland (and later in Wales), made the Liberation Society's goal of total disestablishment of the established churches in the British Isles the more elusive.[50]

48 S. Koss, *Nonconformity in Modern British Politics*, 1975, p.28.

49 D. W. Bebbington, *The Nonconformist Conscience: Chapel and Politics 1870-1914*, 1982, p.19-20.

50 Manning, *op.cit.*, pp.342-3, 403.

PROBLEMS OF SOCIETY

There was more to political dissent than simple self-advocacy. Although the leadership of the campaign to abolish the slave trade was taken by evangelical Anglicans with Quaker support, local Baptist congregations were not slow to send in their petitions against the trade. By the time of the anti-slavery campaign, Baptist leadership was clearer: between June 1832 and August 1834 William Knibb stumped all over England in the interest of the cause. In the following year James Hoby and F. A. Cox were despatched to the Triennial Convention of the American Baptists, charged with issuing a 'fraternal expostulation' to those Baptists in the United States who were themselves slaveholders.

Anti-slavery easily led into anti-Corn Law sympathies and action. Payne points out that the 182 Baptist ministers attending the 1841 Manchester Conference organised by the Anti-Corn Law League was a far larger number than had to that date attended meetings of the Baptist Union. A petition from the Yorkshire Baptist Association argued that 'all monopolies are injurious to the general interests of a commercial and manufacturing nation and that they are pre-eminently oppressive and unjust when they interfere with the food of the poor'.[51]

'Anti-politics' continued to engage Baptists throughout the 1840s. There were protests against various forms of female employment but the major action concerned opposition to the educational clauses of Sir James Graham's Factory Bill that would have introduced a national system of education. The assurances that Graham gave to churchmen not unnaturally raised the ire of dissenters. 'The Church', Graham assured Gladstone, 'has ample security that every master in the new schools will be a Churchman, and that the teaching of the Holy Scriptures, as far as the limited exposition may be carried, will

---

51 Dr Haslam, 'The Yorkshire Baptist Association', in ed. C. E. Shipley, *The Baptists of Yorkshire*, 1912, p.304.

necessarily be in conformity with his creed.'[52] Such language was ominous. The proposals, the Dissenting Deputies claimed, were 'a severer blow at religious liberty than had been aimed at it since the rejection of Lord Sidmouth's bill in 1811'.[53] Over two million signed petitions against the educational clauses which were eventually withdrawn so that national education had to wait for another quarter of a century.

Part of the fear of church control of schools arose out of dissenting alarm at Puseyite inroads within the national church. Such protestant fears surfaced again in 1845 when Peel proposed to increase the government grant to the Catholic College at Maynooth. In the anti-papal fury that followed, Baptists proved uneasy collaborators with Establishment men in the Protestant fight. Samuel Green, Charles Stovel and J. P. Mursell indicated that their opposition to the Maynooth Grant was not just anti-catholic but was a conscientious objection 'to all endowments of religion under any shape',[54] a principle upon which they were unprepared to compromise, as their separately organized Anti-Maynooth Conference demonstrated.

Speaking of the North West, Whitley suggests[55] that after the 1840s concern about civil questions became less obvious until the advent of Charles Williams of Accrington renewed the Lancashire and Cheshire Baptist Association's concern with three areas of civil action, namely questions of 'Religious Equality (principally the issues of Church Rates, Disestablishment and Education), Social evils, and Principles of international dealing'. The latter curious phrase Whitley related to the Association's resolutions in favour of the abolition of the Corn Laws and the promotion of Free Trade: 'The final chapter here', he affirmed, 'has been the frequent demand that the forcing of opium upon an unwilling nation [China] should cease, a demand met at last with an ample response which too tardily removes a reproach from the

52 Manning, *op.cit.*, p.341.

53 *ibid.*, p.343.

54 E. R. Norman, *Anti-Catholicism in Victorian England*, 1968, p.45.

55 Whitley, *Baptists of North West England*, 1913, pp.281-5.

name of Britain'. At the same time Baptists increasingly opposed all forms of war and argued for diplomacy and arbitration in its stead.

In the 1860s the American Civil War brought the issue of slavery back on to the agenda. Although involving a violent conflict between Christian people greatly to be deplored, the war was followed with interest, as prosecuting the interests of freedom from that greatest of sins, slavery. This was challenged by Arthur Mursell in his article on 'The Grievances of War' in *The Church*.[56] Arguing that slavery was not the cause of the American war, Mursell commented:

> I know our agitators here would have us almost smile upon this conflict as a blow to cleave the fetters of the slave. It is not so. When did we hear a breath about liberation from the North, where the black man is more contemptuously despised than in the South, until it could be used as the last shift of a murderous and oppressive policy? How can we connect liberty with the embruted ferocity of this unnatural style, when protocols are issued promising emancipation in one line and re-enthralment in the next? It is the profanation of the holy name of Freedom to whisper it amidst the charnel jargon of this war. . . Sympathy with the North! Away with it! Sympathy with the South! Away with it! Infatuate maniacs fighting for a phantasy - Is it not time these weltering blades were sheathed? Have we not feasted full enough of butchery?

Mursell's rhetoric did not go unchallenged. The Revd Alfred Thomas replied in subsequent issues of *The Church* in much more Americaphile tones.[57] 1865 was, therefore, greeted as a year of achievement. King Leopold's treatment of black labour in Congo twenty years later,[58] and more generally the issue of Chinese indented labour, were seen as continuations of the same theme: slavery was not yet dead.

---

56 *The Church*, February 1863, p.31.

57 *The Church*, March 1863, p.66f.

58 *BQ* 29, 1981, p.56.

In Lancashire itself, the American Civil War caused great distress in the years of the 'Cotton Famine': 'Lancashire is writhing', wrote Arthur Mursell, 'with the smart inflicted by the scourge and grievances of war'.[59] Many church members and adherents amongst the population at large were thrown out of work or put on short time. An appeal was made by the Baptist Union for help, underwriting an earlier appeal made by the Lancashire and Cheshire Association, for which Spurgeon himself acted as London collector. A measure of the response is seen in that the two appeals together raised over £7000 in just three months. Dorcas Societies in many a local church went into action, making clothes, which, with serviceable bedding, were also collected for the distressed. Most carriers and railway companies, the Great Northern only being noted as an exception, transported them to Lancashire free of charge. In the county itself classes were established so that the unemployed could help themselves and also 'be usefully occupied and kept from wandering in the streets and falling into temptation'.[60]

THE NONCONFORMIST CONSCIENCE

Perhaps rather quaintly, Whitley focused on 'a well known triad of evils, drinking, gambling and whoring'. 'Laws', he advised, 'cannot make a people good, but they can make the way of the transgressor hard.'[61] In the case of the Contagious Diseases Acts it was the male transgressor who seemed to be defended, for this legislation effectively secured the compulsory medical inspection of prostitutes living within the vicinity of garrison towns. Prostitutes were not a category of person naturally to secure nonconformist support but that was overridden in this case in so far as the rights of the individual were trespassed upon by legislation compelling inspection, whilst at the same time embracing within legislation the sexual aberrance of the

---

59 *The Church*, February 1863, p.33.

60 *BM* 1862 p.585, 702 etc. *The Church*, October 1862, p.265, December 1862, p.338, January 1863, p.26.

61 Whitley, *op.cit.*, p.284.

military male. Notwithstanding the delicacy of the subject matter and the difficulties therein entailed in public debate, Baptists through Association and Union meetings spoke out in favour of repeal.[62] Only after a lengthy campaign, which excited the energies of nonconformity generally, were the acts first suspended in 1883 and finally repealed in 1885.

'Anti-politics' were in one sense easy because they did not raise the vital issue of the validity of intervention by the state in the life of the individual, and therefore did not threaten nonconformity's cherished advocacy of the principles of voluntaryism in both church and state. The publication in 1883 of a pamphlet called *The Bitter Cry of Outcast London* by Andrew Mearns, the secretary of the London Congregational Union, signalled the beginnings of changed attitudes. *The Bitter Cry* was primarily a piece of advocacy for inner-city evangelism, but in depicting both the plight and the degradation of the slum dwellers, Mearns appealed to the social-purity conscience developed during the Contagious Diseases Acts campaign by referring to the sexual deviance common to the over-crowded life of the slums. The conscience of pulpit and people was stabbed into a concern in which many Baptists participated. In one sense this was still protest politics, but the remedy, housing reform, could hardly avoid being interventionist, though it was not living conditions but sexual depravity which first caught the headlines and secured the interest of many nonconformists. In this way concern for social purity was harnessed to the new politics of housing the poor.

Social purity produced another sensation in the shape of a series of articles entitled 'The Maiden Tribute of Modern Babylon', published in the summer of 1885 by W. T. Stead, the Congregationalist editor of The *Pall Mall Gazette*. The articles would today be called investigatory journalism. Stead, in disguise and accompanied by a female Salvation Army officer, sought to show how easy it was to procure under-age prostitutes in central London with all too little constraint provided by the Metropolitan police. Whilst Stead was

62 Bebbington, *Nonconformist Conscience*, p.39.

imprisoned for a technical infringement of the law, conscience was again awakened so that the government had to rush a Criminal Law Amendment Act through parliament, raising the age of consent from thirteen to sixteen. Reactions to all this were mixed: whilst Spurgeon wrote to Stead and Clifford visited him in prison, the Baptist Union Council declined to seek the Assembly's support for the new legislation.[63]

How far, then, might the Nonconformist Conscience, and the Baptist Conscience in particular, go in challenging the current ordering of society and in harnessing the state as the agent of reform? Writing in 1913, Whitley confessed that the Lancashire and Cheshire Association had 'not felt sure enough of its corporate wisdom to deliver any public utterance' on those areas of 'social legislation where the interests of labour are concerned'.[64] Across the Pennines in Yorkshire, it was rather dubiously argued that the reason why 'political and civil questions' were not so frequently discussed at Association meetings after 1884 was that, with a further extension of the franchise so that the House of Commons could properly be called 'the People's House', such issues did not need the attention of Association representatives but could more fittingly be left to public platforms and the daily press.[65]

If the radical conscience was beginning to turn from the radicalism of individualism and *laissez faire* to a more collective radicalism, then it was by no means certain that nonconformity would move with it, or at least with sufficient unanimity to be either persuasive or influential.

THE RIGHTS OF THE WORKING CLASSES

In the opening decades of the century Robert Hall made clear his sympathy for the plight of the framework knitters of Leicestershire whose remuneration was so depressed 'as to place the means of

63 Bebbington, *Nonconformist Conscience*, p.44.

64 Whitley, *Baptists of North West England*, p.284.

65 Dr Haslam, *op.cit.*, p.310.

sustenance totally out of the reach of the industrious poor'.[66] 'The vaunted maxim of leaving every kind of production and labour to find its own level', that cherished *laissez-faire*, ought not, he argued, to be invoked selectively against oppressed workers when it was not deployed against the agricultural interest on whose behalf the state all too readily intervened.[67]

Hall's defence of the Leicestershire Framework Knitters' Fund, and the activities of the Framework Knitters' Friendly Relief Society, as it was first called, became, in his reply to William Cobbett and other opponents, a defence of 'the Union' whose methods Hall defended as entirely legitimate. 'The skill and labour of the poor man constitute his whole possession, and he has a right to place it to the best advantage, for precisely the same reason that the rich capitalist is entitled to make the most advantageous disposal of his wealth. He has consequently, if he pleases, a right to set aside a portion of his earnings towards securing the means of a just and natural remuneration of his industry. . . [namely that] which enables him to procure the necessaries of life for himself and his family.'[68] Hall would not defend the existence of a Union to raise wages arbitrarily; that 'the labourer was worthy of his hire' was, however, a good scriptural principle which challenged the contemporary practice of using a surplus of labour to depress wages below subsistence level.[69] This justified the use of the Friendly Society Fund, based entirely upon voluntary contributions, to withdraw from the labour market a sufficiency of labour to abstract that surplus which caused the immediate depression of wages, such redundant labour being supported by the fund which was to be partly subscribed by members' dues of sixpence a week from men in work at the approved rates and

---

66 R. Hall, 'An Appeal to the Public on the Subject of the Frame-Work Knitters' Fund', 1819, in Hall, *Works*, IV, 1866, p.171.

67 *ibid.*

68 'A Reply to the Principal Objections Advanced by Cobbett and Others against the Frame-Work Knitters' Friendly Relief Society', *Works*, IV, pp.189-90.

69 *ibid.*, p.189.

partly by sympathizers who it was hoped would include both enlightened hosiers and merchants.[70]

The respect afforded to Hall by his fellow Baptists, both in his own day and for generations to come, cannot have always embraced the full radicalism of his social outlook. This could not, however, be said of his immediate successor at Leicester, J. P. Mursell (Chairman of the Baptist Union in 1864), and the radical dynasty that he sired. One of those who *de facto* 'governed the town for many years after the passing of the Municipal Reform Act in 1835',[71] Mursell was more ready to express his radicalism organizationally than Hall. Skeats and Miall do no less than justice in calling him 'a potent tribune of the people',[72] whilst in Temple Patterson's judgement Leicester Baptists now became 'the shock-troops of local Radicalism'.[73]

A keen liberationist, at one with Edward Miall in his great campaign, Mursell was also a founder of the Leicester and Leicestershire Political Union, fervently working for political reform. In 1838 he wrote a series of letters to the local press on 'The Rights of Labour', seeking at the same time to revive Hall's plan of twenty years earlier to deal with the depressed wages in the hosiery trade.[74] His idealism cherished the notion of a Union in which masters and men should be equally involved. He easily secured working-class affection, and an orderly meeting of the Leicester Working Men's Association that same year presented him with an address of grateful thanks.[75] In the event the support of the hosiers was not forthcoming, save that of the self-made manufacturer and Baptist deacon, Richard Harris, who was even prepared to support a workers' manufacturing co-operative. Baptist influence on working-class

---

70 *ibid.*, pp.191f.

71 A. Temple-Patterson, *Radical Leicester: A History of Leicester*, 1954, p.188.

72 H, S. Skeats and C. S. Miall, *History of the Free Churches in England 1688-1891*, 1891, p.700.

73 Temple-Patterson, *op.cit.*, p.231.

74 *ibid.*, p.298.

75 *ibid.*, p.299.

aspirations in Leicester can also be seen in the activities of a framework knitter named Finn, lay pastor to a working-class General Baptist congregation, a leading member of the Working Men's Association and a founder of Leicester Chartism. Right from the beginning, he repudiated physical force and later came to chair the Leicester Working Men's Anti-Corn Law Association, a group which in 1842 joined with the advanced middle-class radicals in forming a Complete Suffrage Association in the attempt to secure a broader class basis for reform.[76] It has been said[77] that Mursell was the only middle-class radical to give any support to Leicester Chartism. Even he, however, became estranged from the movement, declining to attend a banquet to fête Feargus O'Connor because of his advocacy of the use of violence in a speech to Leicester operatives. Mursell, however, made it clear that his dissent was confined to means; he remained solid with the Chartists as to goals.[78]

ON TRADE UNIONS AND STRIKES

J. P. Mursell's son Arthur, also a master of pulpit oratory, was more cautious.[79] Whilst defending the workers' right to organize and to strike, he attacked Union intimidation and the 'too ready assumption' that depression always sprang from the harsh exploitation of employers. Wage reductions sometimes arose from 'a stern inevitable necessity' which it was folly to resist. Accordingly it behoved Unions to be discriminating in their use of the strike weapon.[80] Agricultural labourers were arguably the most difficult to organize into Trade Unions. But as with other sectors of the working population nonconformist radicalism fortified their resolve in a number of areas. Spurgeon gave his support to their cause in the dispute of 1874 and

---

76 See *ibid.*, pp.300-319 for Finn.

77 *ibid.*, p.302.

78 A. Mursell, *James Phillippo Mursell: His Life and Work*, 1886, pp.59f.

79 T. H. Darlow, *William Robertson Nicoll, Life and Letters*, 1925, p.192.

80 Mursell - Edin Ph.D p.151.

travelled back to the counties of his boyhood to assure the labourers of his sympathy.[81]

The 1879 *Baptist Magazine*, in discussing the Midland Railway Strike over a reduction in pay, was less supportive: 'We can hardly think a strike justifiable at all at a time when labour is, alas, so abundant and cheap', though the caution related to advisability as much as legitimacy. Complaints about an extension of working hours received rather more sympathy, largely on safety grounds, though this was 'naturally withheld from those who strike at a pecuniary reduction already undergone by myriads of deserving men in other branches of labour'.[82] By contrast, the *Freeman* was more supportive of striking miners in 1872: 'There can be no question that the masters have been making profits so exorbitant as naturally to provoke new demands from the men'.[83] Similarly in the following year it argued against the legal restraints of the Criminal Law Amendment Act, under which the striking London gas stokers were judged:

> That a law should exist under which it may become a penal offence to organize a strike, is an utter anachronism which ought to be swept away in the next session of parliament. That honest and intelligent workmen should be liable to be sent to prison for a whole year for an attempt to raise the rate of wages, savours rather of Russia in her worst day than of England.[84]

Together with other nonconformists, Baptists believed that wherever possible the proper way to deal with industrial disputes was through arbitration and reconciliation, a significant word very much part of their own sacred language. The lock-out in the building trade

---

81 H. Browne, *The Rise of British Trade Unions*, 1825-1914, 1979, p.61.

82 *BM* February 1879, p.89.

83 *Freeman* 26 July 1872, p.363, cited *Philip R. Hart, 'The Social Conscience of English Baptists in the later Nineteenth Century with special reference to the work of Dr John Clifford', Edinburgh PhD thesis, 1962*, p.149.

84 'The Gas Stokers' Agitation', *Freeman* 10 January 1873, p.18, cited Hart, *op.cit.*, p.149.

in 1872 inclined the *Freeman* to advocate arbitration and in 1895, following the Royal Commission on Labour of the previous year, George White, liberal politician and Norwich shoe-manufacturer, sought to secure the support of the Baptist Union, whose President he became in 1903, for the idea of a National Board of Arbitration. Two years earlier in 1893, when a coal strike had rumbled on for more than three months, the *Baptist Magazine*, amending an older voluntaryism, argued:

> The continuance of the strike would be a disgrace both to our civilization and our Christianity. It has already assumed the proportion of a national calamity. We rejoice in the generous efforts which have been made to help the distressed families . . . But has not the point also been reached when the Government should take the matter in hand? . . . We have no faith in Government by commissions when commissions are a screen for legislative inactivity. But if they are a *bona fide* prelude to action, they are of the highest service. We ought to know the whole truth *e.g.* about royalties, and also about the relations of supply and demand - the alleged increase of the former and the decrease of the latter. No theories as to Free or Fair Trade can justify the neglect of this governmental duty.[85]

In the event, after the failure of a voluntary conference, Gladstone wrote to both sides inviting them to a fresh conference under the chairmanship of Lord Rosebery, an action which 'even the most determined opponents of State intervention in industrial disputes approved'. The paper expressed great hopes of the Board of Conciliation established for an experimental period of a year, hoping that by proving its usefulness it would be made permanent.[86]

August 1889 witnessed the great London Dock Strike, in J. C. Carlile's words, 'one of the greatest upheavals of the industrial

85 *BM* November 1893, p.583.

86 *BM* December 1893, p.629.

life of England'.[87] Carlile, who very early in his career penned a pamphlet on *The Curse of Sweating*,[88] had been placed by Spurgeon in a struggling cause at Dockhead, Bermondsey, which immediately brought him into involvement with that same class of people that Andrew Mearns had publicised in *The Bitter Cry of Outcast London* and in particular with a socialist evaluation of their employment conditions. He soon developed confidences on both sides, developing contacts with fellow Baptists who were active both as employers and as trade unionists.[89] One of the employers was Samuel Barrow, tanner and leather factor, who through Carlile provided a relief fund to support his own employees when striking against him to ensure that their families did not suffer. Carlile argued that in the Great Dock Strike of 1889 at one time more than 100,000 men were on strike, with a quarter of a million of the 'submerged tenth' dependent upon the activities of the various Relief Committees. He paid tribute to the discipline of the dockers and their families under conditions of the most extreme deprivation. Carlile, later to become a trustee of the Dockers Union, at the time scandalized pietistic dissenters by his involvement in their protests to the extent that, though he had Spurgeon's support ('I don't see', he said, 'how you could have done anything else.'),[90] Dr Booth, then Secretary to the Baptist Union, asked him to withdraw from the strike committee. This produced Carlile's resignation from the Union, a resignation that was never cashed: instead Carlile, who was well aware that other ministers who had become absorbed by political issues had 'lost their passion for the Evangel', was invited once the strike was over to address the Annual Assembly on 'Labour Problems and Religion'.[91]

In 1911 Clifford, in the context of a national rail strike, argued for a legally enforced minimum wage, but F. B. Meyer, probably more

87 J. C. Carlile, *My Life's Little Day*, 1935, p.88.

88 *ibid.*, pp.47-8.

89 *ibid.*, pp.79-85.

90 *ibid.*, p.95.

91 *ibid.*, pp.92-3.

accurately reflecting the mood of the denomination, called for prayer for a pacific spirit, agreement to arbitration and assistance for the strikers' dependants.

NONCONFORMITY AND THE LIBERAL PARTY

Whereas an older dissent had been happy to see its interests in parliament represented by the Whigs, by the late 1830s younger men, Baptists well to the fore, were championing a rather more radical stance. In Leicester, for example, the progress of radicalism and Baptist life were seen as parallel functions. In the year of the French Revolution (1789), Temple Patterson says the Baptists 'were as yet more notable for their strong, narrow evangelicalism than for any political or cultural leadership'.[92] By the 1840s, and arguably five years earlier, he writes, 'The progress which the radical left wing was making, in fact, reflected the increasing influence of the Baptists, relatively to the Unitarians, in the political nonconformity of the town.'[93]

The first issue of the *Baptist Examiner* in 1844 argued, 'religion is the foundation of morals, morals of politics and therefore in an enlightened mind religion and politics are essentially connected. Accordingly politics must be made part of practical duty; religious principles must be carried into the concerns of the borough and the county'.[94] In 1868 the *Baptist Magazine* affirmed, 'If politics are proper for sovereigns, statesmen and senators, it necessarily follows that they are not improper for the *mass of the people*'.[95] The mandate was thus clearly enough stated: such an understanding became the determinant of that close alliance between nonconformity

---

92 Temple-Patterson, *op.cit.*, p.17.

93 *ibid.*, p.333.

94 *Baptist Examiner 1844, cited by F.* R. Salter, *Dissenters and Public Affairs in Mid Victorian England* (21st Lecture, Friends of the Dr Williams's Library), 1967, p.1.

95 *BM* May 1868, p.299, cited by D. W. Bebbington, 'The Baptist Conscience in the Nineteenth Century', *BQ* 34, 1991, p.18.

and the Liberal Party that came to dominate the second half of the century. Indeed, political dissent only made electoral sense whilst that equation held firm, even if an American author goes too far in suggesting that 'by 1880 Nonconformity was substantially absorbed into the Liberal Party'.[96] A better judgement is that of David Bebbington who argues that after 1875 Baptists were becoming more liberal than liberationist.[97] Until challenged by both the rise of labour and a wider questioning of the individualism of liberalism, not to mention an increasing social prosperity achieved by many dissenters, the identification of interests was so complete as to make popular preachers into powerful electoral advocates. At the 1880 election Spurgeon urged the electors of Southwark to support the liberal candidates by his own underwriting of its programme of peace, retrenchment and reform: 'Are we to go on slaughtering and invading in order to obtain a scientific frontier and feeble neighbours? . . . Shall all great questions of reform and progress be utterly neglected for years? Shall the struggle for religious equality be protracted and embittered? . . . Shall our National Debt be increased?'[98] The politics of George Wilson M'Cree, the Bloomsbury missioner, could, on the testimony of his son, be summed up in three words: 'William Ewart Gladstone'; whilst in 1885 the Shropshire Baptist Association approved Gladstone's electoral address and urged the members to exercise their votes 'in support of measures of progress, reform and peace'.[99]

But the Liberal-Nonconformist alliance was not without its difficulties. The 1870 Education Act provoked an 'abiding anger'

---

96 J. F. Glaser, 'English Nonconformity and the Decline of Liberation', *American Historical Review*, January 1958, p.356.

97 *ibid.*, p.90.

98 Cited in Bebbington, *Nonconformist Conscience*, pp.9-10. For Baptists and the peace issue, see P. R. Dekar, 'Baptist Peacemakers and Nineteenth-Century Peace Societies', *BQ* 34, 1991, pp.3-12.

99 Bebbington, *Nonconformist Conscience*, pp.7-10, citing C. W. McCree, *George Wilson McCree: his life and work*, 1893, p.167.

amongst Liberalism's dissenting partners,[100] whilst in 1886 Spurgeon, along with other dissenting leaders, forsook the Liberal Party and an 'Infallible' Gladstone for Liberal Unionism over Irish Home Rule: 'The whole scheme', wrote Spurgeon, 'is as full of danger and absurdities as if it came from a madman', the expression of which sentiment he later rather regretted.[101] Liberalism in the 1890s was becoming less and less capable of holding together all the tensions of a changing political scene. Nonconformity, and Baptists in particular, shared in that process of threatened disintegration. For example, whilst John Clifford wrote Fabian pamphlets, his fellow Baptist, Alfred Illingworth, Liberationist, worsted spinner and Gladstonian, was challenged by Ben Tillett, once a Shoreditch Tabernacle Sunday School teacher, as an Independent Labour Party candidate in the 1892 election in West Bradford. Tillett attacked Illingworth both as a capitalist and an employer, for defending an old-fashioned Liberal individualism. Both liberalism and nonconformity were losing the coherence that had formally given them strength. More than that, as J. F. Glaser writes, 'Liberalism in the 1890s appeared to many working-class voters as a Crotchet Castle, from which dreary teetotalling dissenters launched raids on pubs, music halls and politicians cited in divorce cases'.[102] This might seem a strange judgement in relation to Nonconformity's success in the 1905 election when enthusiasts claimed the election of some two hundred Free Church MPs. A Baptist MP writing in 1910 believed the figure vastly inflated: 'the denominational papers bragged of 200 but of these, I am told, not more than seventy or eighty at most could be relied upon'.[103] That marks the high point of nonconformist political strength, but split those MPs among the different parties and

---

100 Salter, *op.cit.*, p.19; D. W. Bebbington, 'Gladstone and the Baptists', *BQ* 26, 1976, pp.224f.

101 Cited D. P. Kingdon, 'Spurgeon and Gladstone', BQ 20, 1963, p.64 fn.3; Bebbington, *BQ* 26, 1976, pp.224-239.

102 Glaser, *op.cit.*, p.359.

103 Koss, *op.cit.*, p.78, citing a correspondent to the *Baptist Times*, 25 February 1910.

the weakness of political dissent in later years becomes readily apparent.

SECULARIZATION AND THE CHURCHES

Bernard Manning's concept of 'partial disestablishment' may be related to fundamental changes taking place in the relationship between nonconformity, the Church of England and the British state. A number of authors, following H. R. Niebuhr, have commented on the way in which history tends to modify the exclusiveness of sectarian religion, as crusading zeal accommodates to social change by the development of institutional patterns of organization. More recently it has been shown that the universal claims of a church-type organization such as the Church of England have also veered towards 'denominationalism' as it has been compelled to come to terms with the corrosion of a once unitary culture and the emergence of a pluralistic state. Even the Church of England has had *de facto* to abandon its claims to universality and unique legitimacy, instead recognizing that it is but one religious institution among many which together represent a minority Christian interest in an increasingly secular society. That is why A. D. Gilbert argues that by the end of the nineteenth century, in place of the old exclusive claims of the Church of England, in modern England the mainstream churches *together* came to claim a kind of 'pluralistic legitimacy'.[104]

It is in this context that the claim of the Baptist minister in Aldershot in 1894 to be granted official recognition as chaplain to Baptist members of the armed forces in the area needs to be measured. He vigorously contested the argument that he was seeking Caesar's aid in doing Christ's work, arguing that any payment he received would be just in so far as it related to the number of Baptists enrolled in the army which he believed mirrored the ratio in society as a whole, thus refuting any idea, such as often worried Baptists, of the population at large subsidising particular denominational work. At the same time

---

104 A. D. Gilbert, *Religion and Society in Industrial England: Church, Chapel and Social Change 1840-1914*, 1976, p.206.

it was argued that there should be Free Church as well as Anglican chaplains in workhouses. The argument was not so much for disestablishment as maximising the opportunities for Christian service.

Again, at Queen Victoria's Diamond Jubilee in 1897 the complaint was not against state religion but 'at the grudging allocation to Free Church leaders of places merely on the steps outside rather than inside St Paul's Cathedral'. However, J. H. Shakespeare, two years before his appointment as Secretary of the Baptist Union, told a group of Anglican Evangelicals that he did not believe the connection between Church and State was essentially wrong,[105] thus demonstrating a sharp divergence of opinion from Clifford and the main body of Baptist opinion which still held to belief in a sharp separation of Church and State.

The contemplation of a secular century did not any longer allow for interdenominational conflict within the public realm though in the turmoil of the education furore the new century witnessed renewed and intense battle between church and chapel. Described as 'the last flicker of the fight between Cavaliers and Roundheads', the early twentieth-century battle over education witnessed the last great confessional conflict in England, as also the last occasion when religious commitment and party allegiance aligned with one another. It was the last occasion on which religion divided the nation at large: 'Church-versus-chapel', argues Colin Cross of the first decade of the twentieth century, 'was a more potent public issue than capital-versus-labour'.[106] But it was not to last. Very soon it was said that 'the Nonconformist Conscience ceased to count in politics', and that, where creeds had once divided, now 'class stood out the more sharply'.[107] Christian leaders, whatever their particular confessional persuasion, when wise realized the need to work together for the defence of Christian values and virtues in a society where religion

---

105 Bebbington, *Nonconformist Conscience*, pp.29-30.

106 C. Cross, *The Liberals in Power*, 1963, p.5.

107 A. J. P. Taylor, *English History 1914-1945* (Volume 15 of the *Oxford History of England*) 1965, pp.169-70.

could all too easily be marginalized. A secular world at home as much as an unconverted world overseas called for Christians to emphasize their common life and faith rather than their differences of heritage and emphasis.

12

POSTSCRIPT

It is tempting to see the traumatic experiences of the brutality of trench warfare in the 1914-18 War as the great watershed between Victorian religiousness and twentieth-century apathy, a change bound to impact more upon nonconformity with its search for high levels of commitment than on the Church of England with its toleration of a more nominal relationship amongst its adherents. Long ago George Dangerfield, in his brilliant analysis of *The Strange Death of Liberal England*, argued that 'The War hastened everything - in politics, in economics, in behaviour, but it started nothing'.[1]

That is just as true of the history of the churches as for other aspects of early twentieth-century life. The most important pointers to the development of Baptist life in the twentieth century were already well in place before 1914. The two streams in denominational life - the Evangelical Arminianism of the New Connexion and the Missionary Calvinism of the Particulars - were finally and fully integrated amicably in the last decade of the nineteenth century. By contrast, the two strands of Congregationalism - the Baptists and the Congregationalists - failed to unite, but the Free Churches as a group were discovering how to work co-operatively together. 1888 saw the issuing of the Lambeth Quadrilateral. Aiming at 'the restoration of unity among the divided branches of Christendom',[2] it marks the beginning of the modern phase of the ecumenical movement, seeking a theological basis for improved institutional relationships between the churches in Great Britain. An even greater imperative came with the Edinburgh World Mission Conference of 1910 which focused concern on the worldwide scandal of a divided church.

Within the denomination the man for the new century was John Howard Shakespeare, installed as Secretary of the Baptist Union at its autumn assembly at Nottingham in 1898. He secured for the Union

---

1 G. Dangerfield, *The Strange Death of Liberal England, 1910-1914*, 1935, p.viii.

2 E. A. Payne, *The Baptist Union: A Short History*, 1959, p.122.

new financial stability (enabling it to care better for its village preachers and retired ministers), a worthy denominational headquarters in a prime London site, a new constitution, a new departmental structure, and a new denominational hymn book.

Baptist membership peaked in 1906 with a figure for England and Wales of 410,766, but it had long since failed to keep pace with the expansion of population. A. D. Gilbert argues that nonconformity suffered 'from the kind of institutional irrelevance which was the price, not of failure, but of success', for by the last decades of the century it had actually achieved that religious equality which it sought; the process of 'gradual disestablishment' was arguably almost complete. Gilbert relates the sectarian violence of 1902-6 over education to a temporary revival of the divisions of the pre-1885 era.[3] By contrast, he speaks of Church and Nonconformity together enjoying a 'pluralistic legitimacy' already before the end of the nineteenth century.[4]

In politics the old Liberal-Nonconformist alliance, which in truth always gave to nonconformity less than it promised, was at its zenith beginning to break up. Nonconformity could only hope for any political significance if it spoke with one voice through one agency. But with Baptists now supporting candidates from all three parties that influence, such as it had been, was crippled, with the pulpit more inclined to speak in pietistic tones. This was particularly dangerous at a time when upward mobility was making many nonconformist young increasingly dissatisfied with the religion of their fathers: a Baptist chaplain in Oxford reckoned that over forty dons were of nonconformist origin but no longer associating with the Free Churches.[5] Jeffrey Cox puts this in the context of wider trends:

---

3 A. D. Gilbert, *Religion and Society in Industrial England: Church, Chapel and Social Change, 1740-1914*, 1976, p.206.

4 *ibid.*, p.141.

5 J. Cox, *The English Churches in a Secular Society, Lambeth, 1870-1930*, 1982, p.239.

> Explanations of the decline of England's churches usually dwell upon 'secularization' or 'urbanization' or 'industrialization' or something of the sort. But it is possible to be much more specific about what happened to Nonconformity in the late nineteenth century and the early twentieth century. The chapels were hit at once by the emergence of new philanthropic, administrative and educational bureaucracies which destroyed their claims to social utility, by a changing age structure, and by a generalized revolt which struck Nonconformity with particular intensity . . . [6]

The denomination under Shakespeare was better organized and more coherent than that of earlier generations but it was already facing formidable sociological, intellectual and cultural problems before the carnage of the Western Front burst the bubble of liberal optimism with which modern dissent had too readily identified itself. Those who held to a more traditional theology, less coy about the consequence of human sinfulness, had perhaps a better explanation of *realpolitik* gone wrong, but that did not of itself incline those scarred in the process to respond to their ministrations. For them the possibility of a loving God and a benign providential order seemed remote. The world of 1918 offered as great a challenge to the churches as the turbulent world at the end of the Napoleonic Wars had done a century earlier.

6 *ibid.*, p.253.

PUBLICATIONS CITED IN TEXT

(not including those cited in footnotes only)

Bannisdale, 1898 301
Watchman, The 233
Watts, Isaac, *Psalms and Hymns* 35, 39, 42
Whately, Richard, *Rhetoric* 1828 189
White, Edward, *Life in Christ*, 1846 166
Whitley, W. T., *Baptists of North West England*, 1913 303, 311
Youth's Magazine [Sunday School Union] 319

INDEX